FUNDAMENTALISM IN AMERICAN RELIGION AND LAW

Why, from Ronald Reagan to George Bush, have fundamentalists in religion and in law (originalists) exercised such political power and influence in the United States? Why has the Republican Party forged an ideology of judicial appointments (originalism) hostile to abortion and gay rights? Why and how did Barack Obama distinguish himself among Democratic candidates not only by his opposition to the Iraq war but also by his opposition to originalism?

This book argues that fundamentalism in both religion and law threatens democratic values and draws its appeal from a patriarchal psychology still alive in our personal and political lives and at threat from constitutional developments since the 1960s. The argument analyzes this psychology (based on traumatic loss in intimate life) and resistance to it (based on the love of equals). Obama's resistance to originalism arises from his developmental history as a democratic, as opposed to patriarchal, man who resists the patriarchal demands on men and women that originalism enforces – in particular, the patriarchal love laws that tell people who and how and how much they may love.

David A. J. Richards is Edwin D. Webb Professor of Law at New York University School of Law, where he teaches constitutional law, criminal law, and (with Carol Gilligan) a seminar on resisting injustice. He is the author of sixteen books, most recently *Tragic Manhood and Democracy: Verdi's Voice and the Powers of Musical Art* (2004); *Disarming Manhood: Roots of Ethical Resistance* (2005); *The Case for Gay Rights: From* Bowers *to* Lawrence *and Beyond* (2005); *Patriarchal Religion, Sexuality, and Gender: A Critique of New Natural Law* (with Nicholas Bamforth, 2008); *The Deepening Darkness: Patriarchy, Resistance, and Democracy's Future* (with Carol Gilligan, 2009); and *The Sodomy Cases:* Bowers v. Hardwick *and* Lawrence v. Texas (2009). He has served as vice president of the American Society for Political and Legal Philosophy and was the Shikes Lecturer in Civil Liberties at the Harvard Law School in 1998.

FUNDAMENTALISM IN AMERICAN RELIGION AND LAW

Obama's Challenge to Patriarchy's Threat to Democracy

David A. J. Richards

New York University, School of Law

CAMBRIDGE
UNIVERSITY PRESS

CAMBRIDGE UNIVERSITY PRESS
Cambridge, New York, Melbourne, Madrid, Cape Town, Singapore,
São Paulo, Delhi, Dubai, Tokyo

Cambridge University Press
32 Avenue of the Americas, New York, NY 10013-2473, USA

www.cambridge.org
Information on this title: www.cambridge.org/9780521191227

First published 2010

Printed in the United States of America

A catalog record for this publication is available from the British Library.

Library of Congress Cataloging in Publication data

Richards, David A. J.
Fundamentalism in American religion and law : Obama's challenge to patriarchy's threat to democracy / David A. J. Richards.
p. cm.
Includes bibliographical references and index.
ISBN 978-0-521-19122-7 (hardback)
1. Constitutional law – United States. 2. Constitutional law – Religious aspects – Christianity.
3. Religion and law – United States. 4. Religious fundamentalism – United States. I. Title.
KF4552.R53 2010
342.7308′52–dc22 2009028635

ISBN 978-0-521-19122-7 Hardback

For Carol Gilligan and Nicholas Bamforth

"[F]undamentalist religious doctrines and autocratic and dictatorial rulers will reject the ideas of public reason and deliberative democracy."

– John Rawls

CONTENTS

ACKNOWLEDGMENTS

This book arises from two previous coauthored books I have published, Nicholas Bamforth and David A. J. Richards, *Patriarchal Religion, Sexuality, and Gender: A Critique of New Natural Law* (Cambridge: Cambridge University Press, 2008), and Carol Gilligan and David A. J. Richards, *The Deepening Darkness: Patriarchy, Resistance, and Democracy's Future* (Cambridge: Cambridge University Press, 2009). For this reason, I am very much in debt to both of my coauthors of these earlier books, Nicholas Bamforth and Carol Gilligan, for the collaborative inspiration that gave rise to both these earlier books and for their indispensable advice and support in writing this book.

Carol Gilligan and I have been teaching a seminar for the past decade at the New York University School of Law, and the manuscript profited from close criticism of a draft manuscript not only from Carol but also from the students in our seminar during the 2008–9 academic year, namely, Kathiana Aurelien, India Autry, Travis Coleman, Courtney Cross, Timothy Dixon, Deborah Fashakin, Danijela Gazibara, Morgan Janssen, September Lau, Marie Mark, Colleen McCormack-Maitland, Kira Mineroff, Lemar Moore, Leah Morfin, Lauren Nichols, Monique Robinson, Sarah Samuels, and Janine Tien.

I am also very much in the debt of the two editors at university presses who showed immediate interest in publishing this book, namely, John Berger at Cambridge University Press and Deborah Gershenowitz at New York University Press, and secured reviews that very much helped me in revising the manuscript. I must, in this connection, especially thank one of these external readers, Andrew Koppelman, for his invaluable comments and criticisms.

This book was researched and written during sabbatical leaves and during summers, supported in part by generous research grants from the New York University School of Law Filomen D'Agostino and Max E. Greenberg Faculty Research Fund. I am grateful as well for the financial support of the School of Law for the professional indexing of this work, and for the help and support of my assistant, Lavinia Barbu, in preparing the bibliography.

Finally, as always, my work on this book was illuminated by conversations with the person closest to me, my life partner, Donald Levy, whose love makes everything possible.

David A. J. Richards
New York, N.Y.
June 2009

FUNDAMENTALISM IN AMERICAN RELIGION AND LAW

INTRODUCTION

DEFINING THE PROBLEM

It is an important development in recent American politics that religious fundamentalists from diverse denominations and theologies (e.g., Protestants, Catholics, Mormons) have found common ground and not only have aggressively moved into American politics but also have been increasingly influential, notably on the two administrations of President George W. Bush.[1] One of the ways in which this development has been expressed is in the role such fundamentalists have increasingly played in influencing judicial appointments, including those to the Supreme Court. Their preferred approach to constitutional interpretation is originalism, a view advocated by Justices Scalia and Thomas, appointed, respectively, by Presidents Reagan and George H. W. Bush to the Supreme Court. More recently, two justices were successfully appointed by President George W. Bush to our highest court, Chief Justice Roberts and Justice Alito, at least one of whom (Alito) may be an originalist and the other (Roberts) often allied with them.[2] During the presidential election campaign of 2008, the Republican candidate, John McCain, though critical of many of the policies of George Bush, followed Bush and Republican Party orthodoxy in advocating strict constructionism as the appropriate criterion for appointments to the federal judiciary, including the Supreme Court (citing, as models, Roberts and Alito, and the late chief justice Rehnquist).[3] His Democratic opponent, Barack Obama, clearly rejected this approach to constitutional interpretation; indeed, as a senator, he opposed and voted against the appointments of both Roberts and Alito.[4] It is already quite clear, in terms of the pending nomination by President Obama of Sonia Sotomayor to the Supreme

[1] See Damon Linker, *The Theocons: Secular America under Siege* (New York: Doubleday, 2006); Kevin Phillips, *American Theocracy: The Peril and Politics of Radical Religion, Oil, and Borrowed Money in the 21st Century* (New York: Viking, 2006).

[2] See, in general, Ronald Dworkin, *The Supreme Court Phalanx: The Court's New Right-Wing Bloc* (New York: New York Review of Books, 2008).

[3] See Jess Bravin, "John McCain: Looking to the Framers," *Wall Street Journal*, October 7, 2008, A22.

[4] See Barack Obama, *The Audacity of Hope* (New York: Three Rivers Press, 2006), at 89–97; Charlie Savage, "Scouring Obama's Past for Clues on Judiciary," *New York Times*, May 10, 2009, 19.

Court (replacing the retiring Justice Souter) and probable later appointments, that arguments over judicial appointments by President Obama, including opposition to his proposed appointees, will continue to be framed in terms of what has become Republican Party orthodoxy on constitutional interpretation.[5]

If there were ever a time for a closer normative and explanatory study of these developments, it is now. The stakes could not be higher, and it is crucial that we understand what those stakes are. This book undertakes an original critical and psychological study of both these developments, one that is both timely and important. It both supports President Obama's rejection of originalism and illuminates why his approach deserves the support of Americans in general concerned with preserving the integrity of our democratic constitutionalism. Properly understood, the issue should transcend party affiliation, as all Americans have an overriding interest in what distinctively unites us as a free people under law, our constitutionalism. On examination, originalism, which claims to honor our founders, dishonors and betrays them.

Obama distinguishes himself from all other American political leaders in the way he has opposed originalism. Why? It is not just because compelling normative arguments are available that support his position. Such arguments have been available for some time,[6] but no politician of Obama's stature has felt moved to embrace them as part of a larger program for reclaiming and extending American democracy itself. There is both a cultural and a psychological question here. Culturally, why do these arguments come to have an appeal for Obama and others at a certain point in American cultural and political history? And psychologically, what in Obama's background explains why he is so moved to resist originalism? The interest of this book for many may be the ways its critical perspectives on the merits and psychology of fundamentalism as well as the resistance to fundamentalism yield, at the end of my argument, illuminating answers to both questions. To anticipate, let me sketch these answers now, as a way of persuading you that my argument may help you understand both how and why Obama has had the appeal he has, and what he may mean for the future of our democracy and for democracy everywhere.

On the cultural point, this book views the appeal of originalism to be rooted in a patriarchal psychology very much threatened by the advances in the understanding and protection of human rights made possible by the human rights

[5] See Jonathan Weisman and Jess Bravin, "Obama to Seek a Justice Attuned to 'Daily Realities,'" *Wall Street Journal*, May 2–3, 2009, A3 (citing Justice Scalia as "capturing the public imagination with compelling visions of constitutional law").

[6] See Ronald Dworkin, *Freedom's Law: The Moral Reading of the American Constitution* (Cambridge, Mass.: Harvard University Press, 1996); David A. J. Richards, *Toleration and the Constitution* (New York: Oxford University Press, 1986); Richards, *Foundations of American Constitutionalism* (New York: Oxford University Press, 1989); Richards, *Conscience and the Constitution: History, Theory, and Law of the Reconstruction Amendments* (Princeton, N.J.. Princeton University Press, 1993).

movements of the 1960s and later. These advances were themselves made possible, I argue, by a personal and political psychology of resistance to injustices that Americans had come to regard as in the nature of things. Originalism has had the appeal it has had not on its normative merits, but as the expression of a reactionary psychology that sought to limit and even reverse the advances made in the 1960s and later. American politics had been dominated since Ronald Reagan's presidency by a conservative movement that drew its appeal from this psychology. Obama's appeal arose at a time when Americans began to confront how bad the consequences of the power this movement had uncritically enjoyed for much too long had been for American democracy. Obama spoke very much in a voice made possible by the human rights movements of the 1960s, in particular, the voice of Martin Luther King, who appealed to Americans across the chasm of race that had unjustly divided them for so long. Obama, a man of color, found a voice with a similar appeal, resisting the ways in which conservative politicians had divided Americans from one another, appealing to a deeper basis of common values rooted in our common constitutional values. At a moment when national crisis brought into doubt the long domination of our politics by reactionary conservatism, Americans were ready to respond to this moral voice. So much for the cultural question.

On the psychological point, my argument offers a personal and political psychology that explains both how resistance to injustice arises and how such resistance is quashed. Because the argument appeals at both points to a psychology rooted in both resistance to and enforcement of patriarchal values and practices, it makes possible a fresh rethinking of psychological questions not previously addressed. In particular, it offers a plausible explanation of what it is in Obama's psychological development that explains why he sees what he has seen about originalism as a threat to democracy. I take what Obama sees – patriarchy as a threat to democracy – as the subtitle of this book because it explains, as I hope to show, what a certain kind of antipatriarchal developmental psychology makes possible in the emotional intelligence, including the ethical and political intelligence, of humans. What I show this psychology enables is hearing, listening to, and giving appropriate ethical and political weight to the resisting voices of precisely those groups whom patriarchy ignores, indeed represses. What Obama accordingly demands from constitutional interpretation is an interpretive attitude democratically responsive to those voices, grounded, as they often are, in the more just protection of the basic human rights owed to all Americans under our constitutionalism.

There have been a number of important studies of fundamentalism both in American religion and in American politics and constitutional law.[7] But, aside

7 See, e.g., Ernest R. Sandeen, *The Roots of Fundamentalism: British and American Millenarianism, 1800–1930* (Chicago: University of Chicago Press, 1970); George M. Marsden, *Fundamentalism and American Culture*, 2nd ed. (New York: Oxford University Press, 2006) (first published as

from one important book by Vincent Crapanzano, there has been little interest in what they share in common. Even Crapanzano, while placing the anthropological study of religion and law side by side, confesses having "not . . . much faith in most sociological or psychological answers" to the appeal of fundamentalism in law,[8] and acknowledges as well his "inability to view the two literalist discourses [in religion and constitutional law] from the same vantage point."[9] My aim in this book is, building on Crapanzano's insights (in particular, into fundamentalist American religion), to study fundamentalism both in American religion and in constitutional law not as separate, though related, topics but as aspects of one problem.

The problem is the continuing power of patriarchy over our conceptions of authority both in religion and in law. By patriarchy, I understand "a hierarchy – a rule of priests – in which the priest, the *hieros*, is a father. It describes an order of living that elevates fathers, separating fathers from sons (the men from the boys) and men from women, and placing both children and women under a father's authority."[10] It is important to be clear that patriarchy, thus understood, identifies, as its central case, a hierarchy in a priesthood (operative in religion and in personal life), and that, in placing fathers in this role, it divides not just men from women, but men from men and boys and women from women and girls. Patriarchy, properly understood, is an unjust burden on men as well as on women. It divides both from their common humanity and proscribes a structure of authority that expresses their common humanity – an ethics of equal respect and a democracy of equal human rights, including rights to voice.

Carol Gilligan and I argued in *The Deepening Darkness*, on the basis of Roman history and Latin literature, that patriarchy, thus defined, took a particularly extreme and influential form in the religion and politics of ancient Rome, linking the power of the patriarchal family in Roman private and public life to Rome's extraordinary psychological capacity to bear the burdens of relentless imperialistic violence in war.[11] We trace its later influence in the religion, art, psychology, and politics of Western culture, including its distortion of democratic constitutionalism. Patriarchy, as we study it, is a hierarchical conception requiring that only the father has authority in religion, politics, or law – resting on the

George M. Marsden, *Fundamentalism and American Culture: The Shaping of Twentieth Century Evangelicalism, 1870–1925* (New York: Oxford University Press, 1980); Damon Linker, *The Theocons: Secular America Under Siege* (New York: Doubleday, 2006); Kevin Phillips, *American Theocracy: The Peril and Politics of Radical Religion, Oil, and Borrowed Monedy in the 21st Century* (New York: Viking, 2006); Cass R. Sunstein, *Radicals in Robes: Why Extreme Right-Wing Courts Are Wrong for America* (New York: Basic Books, 2005).

[8] Vincent Crapanzano, *Serving the Word: Literalism in America from the Pulpit to the Bench* (New York: New Press, 2000), 297.

[9] *Id.*, 326.

[10] Carol Gilligan, *The Birth of Pleasure: A New Map of Love* (New York: Vintage Books, 2003), 16.

[11] See Carol Gilligan and David A. J. Richards, *The Deepening Darkness: Patriarchy, Resistance, and Democracy's Future* (Cambridge: Cambridge University Press, 2009).

repression of the free, resisting voice of those unjustly subject to his authority, both women and men. We offer a developmental psychology that explains how such patriarchal authority arises and is sustained, namely by traumatic breaks in personal relationships (including of sons from mothers), leaving a devastating sense of loss and a disjuncture between relationship and identification. The patriarchal voice becomes internalized, along with its gender stereotypes, accepted as in the nature of things or as the price of civilization. Such identification expresses itself through a rigidly binary conception of manhood and womanhood that not only accepts loss in intimate life as in the nature of things (e.g., loveless arranged marriages that serve patriarchal ends) but also is prone to forms of unjust repressive violence, including scapegoating, against any imagined threat to its authority, including resistance to its unjust demands. I call this personal and political psychology the Gilligan-Richards thesis.

Patriarchy expresses its demands in two related ways. First, it rigidly imposes a gender binary (e.g., reason as masculine, emotion as feminine), which tracks not reality but the gender stereotypes that support patriarchy. And second, it always places one pole of the binary in hierarchical order over the other. Our psychology of patriarchy offers an explanation of how these two features of patriarchy come to be culturally entrenched, quashing a moral voice that challenges both the gender binary and its hierarchical ordering. The opposite of patriarchy is, we argue, democracy, in which authority accords everyone a free and equal voice, a voice that both breaks out of the gender binary and contests hierarchy. What patriarchy precludes is love between equals, and thus it also precludes democracy, founded on such love and the freedom of voice it encourages. Because patriarchy is inconsistent with the normative demands of democratic constitutionalism, its persistence is a continuing threat to democracy.

My project in this book is to deepen and extend this analysis by showing how it offers a compelling normative critique as well as an explanatory account of the appeal of fundamentalisms for Americans both historically and, in particular, in contemporary circumstances. How is it possible that in an advanced, well-educated nation like the United States, in which there is such a deep consensus about the enduring values of our democratic constitutionalism, fundamentalisms should flourish both in religion and in law? If such fundamentalisms are in contradiction to our democratic traditions, how is it that this is so little understood and seen? That such views should have gotten so far in American politics shows something troubling about American culture and psychology in a constitutional democracy as developed and enlightened as that of the United States. That so many Americans cannot even see the problem defines, I believe, the problem.

At the heart of the problem is the degree to which patriarchal conceptions and institutions have been uncritically assumed by many American religions in general and fundamentalist religions in particular. Americans live under one of the most robust constitutional traditions protecting religious liberty. Such protections include not only a guarantee of free exercise but also, more radically, a prohibition on the state's establishment of religion.[12] The consequence has been what leading advocates of these protections anticipated: because religious teachers must draw support directly from the people (not from the state), America would develop and sustain one of the most diverse and pluralistic ranges of religious and philosophical convictions in the world. Americans, for example, are much more religious than Europeans, where established churches still exist.[13] Precisely because the state in America may not establish religion, religion in America is democratically closely tied to the people and has flourished in independence from state power. Sometimes, its independence has empowered American religions to criticize on the ground of ethics such state-supported evils as slavery as well as racism and sexism, and it has supported movements that questioned and resisted these evils (e.g., the abolitionist movement). But, in other cases, such independence has led American religions and the people who supported them to defend, as God's word, such evils (at one time, only the Quakers among American religions questioned slavery; the others were proslavery). My interest in this book is in these latter religions. Precisely because of the separation of church and state in the United States, my argument is directed not at the state, though it has implications for the interpretation of the religion clauses, as I argue in Chapter 8. I accept, as normatively sound, the general constitutional structure for the protection of religious liberty in the United States.[14] But it is the very democratic freedom of religion in the United States that has rendered it so powerful, and my argument is thus an internal one with my fellow Americans, namely, that they ask themselves whether the interpretation of patriarchal religion in their lives is not, in fact, inconsistent with the democratic values that have supported religious freedom in the United States, values in which, as with Americans generally, they take just pride.

What I am at pains to show (in Part II) is that these religions assume and carry forward patriarchal ideas and practices, which they have uncritically absorbed from the role Roman patriarchy played in the formation of Christianity under the Roman Empire, in particular, after Christianity became the established church of the Roman Empire. Such religions have not only flourished here but have also become important institutions in sustaining and defending patriarchy, a practice that the historical Jesus conspicuously questioned (see Chapter 5). In particular, in the face of any religious or other movement that deeply questions patriarchy, these religions have gravitated to forms of fundamentalism that structure authority in a patriarchal male priesthood, expressing a personal and political psychology of

[12] For a synoptic study of both guarantees, see Kent Greenawalt, *Free Exercise and Fairness*, vol. 1, *Religion and the Constitution* (Princeton, N.J.: Princeton University Press, 2006); *Establishment and Fairness*, vol. 2, *Religion and the Constitution* (Princeton, N.J.: Princeton University Press, 2008).

[13] On this point, see Andrew J. Cherlin, *The Marriage-Go-Round: The State of Marriage and the Family in America Today* (New York: Alfred A. Knopf, 2009), 72, 103–15

[14] See David A. J. Richards, *Toleration and the Constitution* (New York: Oxford University Press, 1986).

traumatic loss in intimate life that Christianity absorbed from Roman patriarchal and related practices. It is this structure of authority and its underlying psychology that do not just make the religion insensitive to resisting voices but also silence and demonize the voices and experience of the women and men who would reasonably resist its demands. The consequence is a sense of ethics and politics that fails to take seriously the voices and experiences of more than half the human race and that flouts the central principle of a democratic ethics and politics, equal respect for all. Patriarchy feeds on an echo chamber of its own narcissistic voice, endlessly speaking and hearing only itself. A religious culture, in which patriarchy becomes deeply entrenched, loses the capacity for reasonable doubt about its views, which is shown by the way the polemic of gender scapegoating against dissenters flourishes instead of reasoning with democratic equals. Its views even of its founder, Jesus of Nazareth, ignore what is most distinctive and moving in his antipatriarchal teaching (Chapter 5). Patriarchy thus undermines religion and the role of religion in supporting a democratic ethics and politics.

It is for this reason that it is so important to show, as I try to do in this book, how unreasonable these religions are in terms of their own internal traditions (notably, the antipatriarchal teachings of the Jesus of the Gospels), let alone unreasonable in light of larger developments in American politics and law. It is because of the role of patriarchy in these religions and the culture they shape that they have uncritically and aggressively moved into American politics and have had the appeal and impact they have had on constitutional law. My argument explains precisely what is so puzzling to many abroad: the failure of so many Americans not only not to see the problem but indeed to aggravate the problem by accepting a fundamentalism in law (originalism) that is as unreasonable as fundamentalism in religion, and much more pernicious because, in the name of the founders, it betrays the secular constitutionalism that is perhaps the founders' greatest legacy to us. The contradiction between patriarchy and democracy is not seen – indeed, is so easily dismissed – because our religion has so uncritically structured its authority in terms of a patriarchal priesthood and a supporting patriarchal psychology that we have come to regard patriarchy as nature, indeed as God's law. Both these patriarchal structures and the supporting psychology darken our ethical intelligence in religion and in law. We need, as Americans, to question the psychology of patriarchal manhood and womanhood – its force in our religion and in our politics– that has held us captive for much too long. We cannot deal with the problem until we can see the problem.

Fundamentalism is, in its nature, reactionary and repressive. It arises in reaction to progressive, antipatriarchal developments in religion or in law, which it represses. These contemporary developments have been of two sorts: first, a normative conception of basic human rights, including rights to conscience and voice, owed to all persons – irrespective of religion, race (ethnicity), gender, or sexual orientation; and second, questioning, as illegitimate forms of what I call moral slavery, traditional grounds on which entire groups of persons have been excluded from the scope of protection of basic human rights. I argue that patriarchy is an important explanatory element of these traditional grounds and, for this reason, questionable as a ground for authority in religion or law in a constitutional democracy. The civil rights movements of the 1960s and later had the impact they had on American constitutional law because they brought an antipatriarchal voice to bear on understanding and criticizing Americans' extreme religious intolerance, racism, sexism, and homophobia (Chapter 1).

Nicholas Bamforth and I elaborated a form of this argument in our critical study of new natural law, which attempts to defend the current views of the papacy on gender and sexuality on ostensibly secular grounds.[15] We argue, both on internal grounds of consistency and on external grounds of moral plausibility, that new natural law is certainly not the secular view it claims to be but, in fact, a highly sectarian religious view. In the course of that critique, we develop a definition of fundamentalism, a view relying on an appeal to the certainty of a specific understanding of authority, rooted in the past, a certainty that is to guide thought and conduct today irrespective of reasonable contemporary argument and experience to the contrary.[16] At the heart of fundamentalism is a form of irrationalism, a sectarian conception of certainty – itself demonstrably unreasonable – that refuses to be open to contemporary argument and experience. It is that refusal to be open to reason or to reasonable arguments that places fundamentalisms, as I shall argue, in such tension with the role of deliberative reason in constitutional democracies.

What I am undertaking in this book, drawing on these earlier works, is an integrated study of fundamentalism in American religion and constitutional law. Patriarchy has been as stable and persistent as it has been in human societies because a developmental psychology of traumatic breaks in intimate life sustained its demands on both men and women. Why and how does this psychology continue to enjoy appeal today even among contemporary Americans? My diagnostic aim in this book is to use the appeal of fundamentalism in America as an illuminating case study of the continuing force of this psychology. What may make my diagnosis of interest is that it offers a not obvious and illuminating explanation of a range of otherwise puzzling symptoms of fundamentalism both in American religion and in law – the need for certainty as opposed to reasonable grounds for belief, its ahistorical appeal to history, the anger and even violence directed at dissent, and of course, its demonization of certain contemporary claims for justice in matters both of sexuality and gender.

My interest in fundamentalism is not only diagnostic but also critical. Indeed, my sense that *diagnosis* is the appropriate term for my project arises from my sense that the appeal of fundamentalism should concern us, both religiously and

[15] See Nicholas C. Bamforth and David A. J. Richards, *Patriarchal Religion, Sexuality, and Gender: A Critique of New Natural Law* (Cambridge: Cambridge University Press, 2008).

[16] See *id.*, 280.

politically, because its doctrines are so critically problematic for two reasons. First, fundamentalist views arise as interpretive claims within a tradition, whether a religious tradition like Christianity or a constitutional tradition like American constitutionalism, and their interpretive claims introduce incoherence and even inconsistency into how the tradition is understood or to be understood. And second, such interpretive claims not only are internally flawed but also so interpret the tradition that it fails any longer to offer an attractive and reasonable view of the world and human life that can or would appeal to someone not already committed to the fundamentalist view. In a secular constitutional democracy, like the United States, such fundamentalist views must, as a basis for political action, let alone constitutional interpretation, be constitutionally problematic. If such fundamentalist views, on critical examination, carry with them such a high price of internal inconsistency and external unreasonableness, we must naturally ask why they enjoy the appeal that they have.

I come to this question, the question of diagnosis, in the same way any student of an irrationalist view, like anti-Semitism or racism, inquires into its continuing appeal. What makes my inquiry into fundamentalism, both in religion and in law, interesting is that it is not obvious that fundamentalism is as flawed by irrationalism, both internally and externally, as the now more widely acknowledged and understood irrationalist evils of anti-Semitism and racism. It is a matter of argument, the argument of this book, that fundamentalism in religion and law is irrational in terms of both internal and external criteria, and thus the further question of diagnosis arises – what psychology sustains such a problematic (because it is irrationalist) interpretive attitude? It is at this point that I turn, by way of deeper explanation, to the psychology that I argue sustains patriarchy, a psychology that clarifies as well the appeal of irrationalist prejudices like anti-Semitism and racism.

I begin in Part 1 with the examination of fundamentalism in American constitutional law, showing its critical defects and then turning to its appeal. The argument examines critically, in terms of both internal and external criteria of reasonableness, the form such fundamentalism takes in the school of constitutional interpretation called originalism (Chapter 2). Originalism, I argue, is a form of source-based fundamentalism, one not only marred by internal incoherence and even contradiction but also deeply unreasonable in the way it walls constitutional interpretation off from the growth in both our moral and our scientific experience over time and in contemporary circumstances. In particular, originalism draws its appeal from the way it forbids constitutional interpretation to take account of reasonable contemporary views of sexuality and gender, in effect, attacking often rather intemperately a range of constitutional decisions that give effect to such views, as I show in Chapter 3 by examining both the tone and the substance of Justice Scalia's dissents in such cases. Why does such an unreasonable view enjoy the psychological support it does? Why the angry, dismissive, even contemptuous tone of such dissents? It is, as a way of answering this question, that I turn to the diagnosis and critique of fundamentalism in religion. It is the persistence of American fundamentalism in religion that explains, so I argue, not only the psychology that leads originalists in law to take the position they do but also, more generally, why many Americans find originalism the attractive position they suppose, wrongly, it to be.

My argument in Part II examines three forms of fundamentalism in religion: the new natural lawyers as defenders of the normative views on sexuality and gender of the papal hierarchy of the Catholic Church (Chapter 4); Evangelical fundamentalists in Protestant denominations (Chapter 5), and Mormonism (Chapter 6). Catholics and Protestants, as orthodox forms of Christianity, disagree on matters of both theology and religious conviction; and both regard Mormonism as, at best, a highly unorthodox form of Christian belief. Nonetheless, all these divergent religious views, as interpretations of the Christian tradition, adopt fundamentalist views on matters of sexuality and gender, views that condemn and repudiate central claims of the progressive developments discussed in Chapter 1.

Although fundamentalists in religion often define themselves in terms of the certainty of a set of religious beliefs (the inerrancy of the Bible, or the Virgin Birth), the form of fundamentalism that is of contemporary interest – both in religion and in law – is one that ascribes an unquestionable certainty to beliefs about gender (the subordination of women in matters of religious and moral authority) and about sexuality (the intrinsic wrongness, for example, of contraception, abortion, and gay and lesbian sex). These views are fundamentalist because they ascribe a foundational certainty to such beliefs, as beliefs that must be held and acted on irrespective of reasonable argument to the contrary.

I distinguish two grounds for such fundamentalism: norm based and source based. Source-based fundamentalisms rest on an interpretation of the authority of sacred scriptures – for Evangelical Protestants, the Bible; for Mormons, the Bible as well as the *Book of Mormon*, *Doctrine and Covenants*, and *Pearl of Great Price*. Fundamentalists read such texts as the exclusive historical source (*sola scriptura*) of ultimate religious authority and further suppose that they require belief in and action on the certainties of gender and sexuality just mentioned.

Roman Catholicism, in contrast, ascribes ultimate religious authority to interpretive traditions that include but are not limited to the Bible, and that regard Bible interpretation as not limited to the more literal interpretations favored by many Protestants. Such a tradition – historically open to the interpretive relevance of secular philosophical traditions like Aristotelianism and even lessons learned from historical experience – may come to question and repudiate, as Catholicism did in Vatican II, many of the positions once regarded as fundamental to Catholicism, for example, its rejection of religious toleration in particular and political liberalism in general.[17] When Catholic apologists, like the new natural

[17] See John T. Noonan Jr., *A Church That Can and Cannot Change* (Notre Dame, Ind.: University of Notre Dame Press, 2005).

lawyers, defend traditional Catholic teaching on matters of sexuality and gender, a teaching affirmed by the papal hierarchy, they do so on grounds of an ostensibly secular argument for certain norms that, they argue, establish as certainties views of gender and sexuality that repudiate the progressive tradition on these matters.

I argue, examining each of these variant grounds for fundamentalism, that they are both internally inconsistent and externally unreasonable. An important argument for internal inconsistency is how they ignore or fail reasonably to interpret the life and teachings of the founder of Christianity, Jesus of Nazareth, an argument that has force against both source-based and norm-based fundamentalisms, as interpretations of the Christian tradition. Other arguments will have more force against one ground for such fundamentalism as opposed to another, for example, questioning the allegedly secular arguments of the new natural lawyers.

What organizes and explains these otherwise diverse religious views – in particular, their fundamentalism on matters of sexuality and gender – is the role that patriarchy plays in supporting their common fundamentalist views. This is shown not only by the limitation of the priesthood or ministry in Catholicism or Evangelical fundamentalists or Mormonism to men, clearly excluding women and the authority of women's voices and experience, but also by the requirements placed on the authority of such a male priesthood, namely that of patriarchal fathers. Catholicism, for example, imposes on its exclusively male priesthood the requirement of celibacy with consequences that I explore. And both the forms of more orthodox fundamentalist Christianity I examine (i.e., Catholicism and Evangelical Protestantism) crucially accord the kind of interpretive authority they do to a male priesthood or ministry because of a conception of original sin based on, as I shall argue, a highly controversial interpretation of the Adam and Eve narrative in Genesis that has appeal because of patriarchal assumptions never questioned. The role of patriarchy in Mormonism is, I shall argue, rather more stark, as it both arose from and appealed to an anachronistic revival of ancient Jewish patriarchy, embodied in the prophet Joseph Smith, as a solution to what Smith and his followers found to be the intolerable openness of American Christian freedom to new experiments in living, including the religious authority of women.

I turned to the study of fundamentalism in religion as a way of answering the question, Why does fundamentalism in constitutional law enjoy the appeal it does? In Part III, I show how and why originalists like Justices Scalia and Thomas are psychologically drawn to their position on the basis of an uncritical religious fundamentalism (Chapter 7).

In light of the critique and diagnosis of fundamentalism in both American religion and law, I then turn to the implications of this study for advancing and deepening political democracy in the United States and elsewhere (Chapter 8). First, I explore how my view offers a deeper explanation and criticism of developments in religion and law, which are almost always discussed in isolation from each other, a failure of intelligence that bespeaks the spell of the underlying psychological problem of disassociation that this book attempts to break through. Second, and perhaps more important, I show something that surprised me and may surprise you, namely how the psychological and cultural perspectives of this book cast a flood of light on both how and why Barack Obama has seen more deeply into and resisted originalism than any other American politician, and why, as this point in our history, his moral voice has found such a resonance in the American people. And third I ask, If patriarchy, as I argue, is the root of a range of political evils, some of them now constitutionally recognized as such, should we reframe our understanding of religious liberty and/or antiestablishment to take account of such compelling secular state purposes? My answer calls, if anything, for a more muscular defense of the antiestablishment values of religious liberty that our founders took so seriously and, paradoxically under the influence of the corrupt form of originalism I criticize in this book, we, to our cost, do not. Nothing in our constitutional traditions of free exercise and antiestablishment justifies the degree of political support patriarchal religion enjoys today in the United States. It was, rather, precisely such entanglement of the ostensibly democratic power of the state with undemocratic religion that, for Madison and Jefferson, corrupted both democratic politics and religion as, in their view, it had historically corrupted Christianity (once Constantine established Christianity as the church of the Roman Empire) into its support of illegitimate regimes, for example, imperialistic monarchies. It is a symptom of the constitutional pathology that originalism is that, in the name of the founders, it so nesciently betrays them and us.

Finally, the conclusion draws together the threads of my analysis in terms of the theory of faction that the deepest thinker among our founders, James Madison, took so seriously. Madison regarded religious faction as among the deepest threats to democratic constitutionalism, and I show that the unholy alliance of religious and legal fundamentalism today has unleashed on us this threat. I then offer reasons for thinking that my account of fundamentalism in the United States can be reasonably generalized to illuminate fundamentalism abroad as well, for example, constitutional debates in India, the world's largest democracy, as well as the aggressive resurgence of violent forms of fundamentalism abroad. If patriarchy is in these ways such a threat to democracy everywhere, it is perhaps time for us responsibly to understand and face the American dilemma as the contradiction between patriarchy and democracy that all peoples now face. It is for this reason that I argue that the continuing power of patriarchy today, in an age of democracy, poses the twenty first-century democratic dilemma.

Carol Gilligan, on reading an earlier draft of this book, observed that its appeal to reason expresses deep emotion as well, in particular, moral indignation. She pressed me better to understand both the content and tone of my argument. It is perhaps a feature of my own recent work, which has come self-consciously to question gender binaries (reason as masculine, emotion as feminine), that I should have written this book in the way I have. Carol Gilligan, all of whose work in psychology arises out of close observation of voice resisting patriarchy, classically has put the point as speaking in a different voice, and what she observed about this book, in contrast to the many others I have written on constitutional law, was its different voice. What Carol and I traced in *The Deepening Darkness* was a psychological argument about evidence of resistance to patriarchy (reoccurring through time and across culture). This book is itself an act of resistance – hence the tone of moral outrage, the impassioned voice, the contempt for those who perpetuate injustice and prejudice, using their power to silence dissent and abrogate the rights of others. The best of American constitutional law rests, I have come to believe, on the role it accords resisting voice, and the worst on the repression of such voice. Since I have come to see, as I argue here and elsewhere, patriarchy as the root of the problem, I have responded to the patriarchal rage that underlies originalism with a defense of democracy, a sense of what Carol calls righteous fury versus patriarchal rage. I have come to see my own wedding of reason and emotion in this book as the way I have found my voice and, through breaking the gender binary, to see what I believe in this book I came to see, and as a citizen of a great and beloved democracy, to share what I see with you.

CHAPTER 1

THE PROGRESSIVE RECOGNITION OF HUMAN RIGHTS UNDER AMERICAN CONSTITUTIONAL LAW

Contemporary American fundamentalism draws its reactionary force from the successes of movements for civil rights in the 1960s and thereafter, including judicial acceptance of many of the arguments of these movements about the proper interpretation of American constitutional principles. It is these constitutional developments that fundamentalism repudiates.

To set the stage for the study of American fundamentalisms (in law and in religion), we must understand these judicial developments, including their normative justification in the judicial elaboration of basic constitutional principles. These judicial developments are of two related sorts: first, the recognition of a basic human right of intimate life owed all persons; and second, the recognition that certain grounds like religion, ethnicity, gender, and sexual orientation cannot be a just basis for the abridgment of such a basic right. I begin with the basic right and then examine the suspect grounds as resting on a rights-denying tradition of what I call moral slavery. Finally, I argue that both developments can be plausibly understood as giving expression to moral voices in the civil rights movements critical of the role patriarchy played in distorting the interpretation of American constitutional values.

1. THE RIGHT TO INTIMATE LIFE

In 1965, the Supreme Court, in *Griswold v. Connecticut*,[1] constitutionalized the argument for a basic human right to contraception that had been persistently and eloquently defended and advocated by Margaret Sanger for more than forty years, a decision that Sanger lived to see.[2] The Court extended the right to abortion services in 1973 in *Roe v. Wade*[3] (reaffirming its central principle in 1992[4]),

[1] See *Griswold v. Connecticut*, 381 U.S. 479 (1965).

[2] See Ellen Chesler, *Woman of Valor: Margaret Sanger and the Birth Control Movement* (New York: Anchor, 1992), at pp. 11, 230, 376, 467.

[3] See *Roe v. Wade*, 410 U.S. 113 (1973).

[4] See *Planned Parenthood of Southeastern Pennsylvania v. Casey*, 505 U.S. 833 (1992).

and – after denying its application in 1986 to consensual homosexual sex acts in *Bowers v. Hardwick*[5] – reversed itself in 2003 in *Lawrence v. Texas*, holding that gay and lesbian sex was fully protected by the right and that laws criminalizing such acts were unconstitutional.[6] A related form of analysis was used, albeit inconclusively, in cases involving the right to die.[7] Three of these cases (contraception, abortion, homosexuality) can be understood on the grounds of a basic right to intimate personal life, one of them (death) involving another basic right (an aspect of the right to life or meaningful life).[8] I focus here on the first three cases.

Margaret Sanger's and Emma Goldman's arguments for the right to contraception were rooted in rights-based feminism, a feminism that challenged the traditional grounds on which women had been denied respect for the basic human rights that long had been accorded to men. Sanger's and Goldman's arguments had two prongs, both of which were implicit in the Supreme Court's decisions in *Griswold* and later cases: first, a basic human right to intimate life and the right to contraception as an instance of that right; and second, the assessment of whether laws abridging such a fundamental right met the heavy burden of secular justification that was required.

The foundation of the fundamental human right to intimate life was as basic an inalienable right of moral personality as the right to conscience. Like the right to conscience, it protects intimately personal moral resources (thoughts and beliefs, intellect, emotions, self-image, and self-identity) and the way of life that expresses and sustains them in facing and meeting rationally and reasonably the challenge of a life worth living – one touched by enduring personal and ethical value.

The human right of intimate life was interpretively implicit in the historical traditions of American rights-based constitutionalism. In both of the two great revolutionary moments that framed the trajectory of American constitutionalism (the American Revolution and the Civil War), the right to intimate life was one of the central human rights, the abridgment of which rendered political power illegitimate and gave rise to the Lockean right to revolution.[9]

5 See *Bowers v. Hardwick*, 478 U.S. 186 (1986).

6 See *Lawrence v. Texas*, 539 U.S. 558 (2003).

7 See *Cruzan v. Missouri Department of Health*, 496 U.S. 261 (1990). Justice Rehnquist, writing for a 5–4 majority, accepts that a right to die exists and applies to a case involving passive euthanasia but denies that the state has imposed an unreasonable restriction on that right on the facts of the case. But see also *Washington v. Glucksberg*, 521 U.S. 702 (1997) (where the Court unanimously refused to extend right of constitutional privacy to state prohibition of physician-assisted suicide, or active euthanasia, though five justices allowed for as-applied challenges to such statutes).

8 For further discussion, see David A. J. Richards, *Sex, Drugs, Death, and the Law: An Essay on Human Rights and Overcriminalization* (Totowa, N.J.: Rowman and Littlefield, 1982), at pp. 215–70.

9 On American revolutionary constitutionalism as framed by these events, see David A. J. Richards, *Foundations of American Constitutionalism* (New York: Oxford University Press, 1989); Richards,

At the time of the American Revolution, the background literature on human rights, known to and assumed by the American revolutionaries and founding constitutionalists, included what the influential Scottish philosopher Francis Hutcheson called "the natural right [of] each one to enter into the matrimonial relation with any one who consents."[10] Indeed, John Witherspoon, whose lectures Madison heard at Princeton, followed Hutcheson in listing even more abstractly as a basic human and natural right a "right to associate, if he so incline, with any person or persons, whom he can persuade (not force) – under this is contained the right to marriage."[11] Accordingly, leading statesmen at the state conventions ratifying the Constitution, both those for and those against adoption, assumed that the Constitution could not interfere in the domestic sphere. Alexander Hamilton, of New York, denied that the federal Constitution did or could "penetrate the recesses of domestic life, and control, in all respects, the private conduct of individuals."[12] And Patrick Henry, of Virginia, spoke of the core of our rights to liberty as the sphere in which a person "enjoys the fruits of his labor, under his own fig-tree, with his wife and children around him, in peace and security."[13] The arguments of reserved rights both of leading proponents (Hamilton) and of leading opponents (Henry) of adoption of the Constitution thus converged on the private sphere of domestic married life.

At the time of the Civil War, the understanding of marriage as a basic human right took on a new depth and urgency because of the antebellum abolitionist rights-based attack on the peculiar nature of American slavery; such slavery failed to recognize the marriage or family rights of slaves,[14] and indeed inflicted on the black family the moral horror of breaking them up by selling family members separately.[15] One in six slave marriages thus were ended by force or sale.[16] No aspect of American slavery more dramatized its radical evil for abolitionists and Americans more generally than its brutal deprivation of intimate personal life, including undermining the moral authority of parents over children. Slaves, Weld argued, had "as little control over them [children], as have domestic animals over

Conscience and the Constitution: History, Theory, and Law of the Reconstruction Amendments (Princeton, N.J.: Princeton University Press, 1993).

10 See Francis Hutcheson, *A System of Moral Philosophy*, 2 vols. in 1 (1755; repr., New York: Augustus M. Kelley, 1968), at p. 299.

11 See John Witherspoon, in *Lectures of Moral Philosophy*, ed. Jack Scott (East Brunswick: N.J.: Associated University Presses, 1982), p. 123. For further development of this point, see Richards, *Toleration and the Constitution*, at pp. 232–3.

12 See Jonathan Elliot, *The Debates in the Several State Conventions on the Adoption of the Federal Constitution*, vol. 2 (Washington, D.C.: Printed for the Editor, 1836), p. 269.

13 See *id.*, vol. 3, p. 54.

14 See Kenneth M. Stampp, *The Peculiar Institution* (New York: Vintage, 1956), pp. 198, 340–9; Eugene D. Genovese, *Roll, Jordan, Roll: The World the Slaves Made* (New York: Vintage Books, 1974), pp. 32, 52–3, 125, 451–8.

15 See Stampp, *Peculiar Institution*, pp. 199–207, 204–6, 333, 348–9; Herbert G. Gutman, *The Black Family in Slavery and Freedom, 1750–1925* (New York: Vintage Books, 1976), pp. 146, 318, 349.

16 See Gutman, *Black Family in Slavery and Freedom*, p. 318.

the disposal of their young."[17] Slavery, thus understood as an attack on intimate personal life,[18] stripped persons of essential attributes of their humanity.

It is against this historical background that it is interpretively correct to regard the right to intimate life as one of the unenumerated rights protected both by the Ninth Amendment and by the privileges and immunities clause of the Fourteenth Amendment, as Justice Harlan may be regarded as arguing in his concurrence in *Griswold*.[19] The Supreme Court quite properly interpreted the Fourteenth Amendment in particular as protecting this basic human right against unjustified state abridgment and, as Sanger and Goldman had urged, regarding the right to use contraceptives as an instance of this right. The right to contraception was, for Sanger and Goldman, so fundamental a human right for women because it would enable women, perhaps for the first time in human history, reliably to decide whether and when their sexual lives would be reproductive. Respect for this right was an aspect of the more basic right of intimate life in two ways. First, it would enable women to exercise control over their intimate relations with men, deciding whether and when such relations would be reproductive. Second, it would secure to women the right to decide whether and when they would form the intimate relationship to a child. Both forms of choice threatened the traditional gender-defined role of women's sexuality as both exclusively and mandatorily procreational and maternally self-sacrificing, and they were rejected for that reason.

But second, this human right, like other such rights, can be regulated or limited only on terms of public reasons not themselves hostage to an entrenched political hierarchy (e.g., compulsorily arranged marriages[20]) resting on the abridgment of such rights. For example, from the perspective of the general abolitionist criticism of slavery and racism, the proslavery arguments in support of Southern slavery's treatment of family life were transparently inadequate, not remotely affording adequate public justification for the abridgment of such a fundamental right.

These arguments were in their nature essentially racist:

> His natural affection is not strong, and consequently he is cruel to his own offspring, and suffers little by separation from them.[21]

[17] See Theodore Dwight Weld, *American Slavery as It Is* (1839; repr., New York: Arno Press and the New York Times, 1968), p. 56.

[18] See Ronald G. Walters, *The Antislavery Appeal: American Abolitionism after 1830* (New York: W. W. Norton, 1978), pp. 95–6.

[19] Justice Harlan, in fact, grounds his argument on the due process clause of the Fourteenth Amendment, but the argument is more plausibly understood, as a matter of text, history, and political theory, as based on the privileges and immunities clause of the Fourteenth Amendment for reasons I give in Richards, *Conscience and the Constitution*, chap. 6. For further elaboration of this interpretation of *Griswold*, see Richards, *Toleration and the Constitution*, at pp. 256–61.

[20] See Werner Sollors, *Beyond Ethnicity: Consent and Descent in American Culture* (New York: Oxford University Press, 1986), p. 112.

[21] Thomas R. R. Cobb, *An Inquiry into the Law of Negro Slavery in the United States of America* (1858; repr., New York: Negro Universities Press, 1968), at p. 39.

> Another striking trait of negro character is lasciviousness. Lust is his strongest passion; and hence, rape is an offence of too frequent occurrence. Fidelity to the marriage relation they do not understand and do not expect, neither in their native country nor in a state of bondage.[22]

The blind moral callousness of Southern proslavery thought was nowhere more evident than its treatment of what were in fact agonizing, crushing, and demeaning family separations:[23]

> He is also liable to be separated from wife or child . . . but from native character and temperament, the separation is much less severely felt.[24]

> With regard to the separation of husbands and wives, parents and children . . . Negroes are themselves both perverse and comparatively indifferent about this matter.[25]

The irrationalist, racist sexualization of black slaves was evident in the frequent justification of slavery in terms of maintaining the higher standards of sexual purity of Southern white women.[26] Viewed through the polemically distorted prism of such thought, the relation of master and slave was itself justified as an intimate relationship like that of husband and wife that should similarly be immunized from outside interference.[27] In this Orwellian world of the distortion of truth by power, the defense of slavery became the defense of freedom.[28] Arguments of these sorts rested on interpretations of facts and values completely hostage to the polemical defense of entrenched political institutions, whose stability required the abridgment of basic rights of blacks and of any whites who ventured reasonable criticism of such institutions.

If the antebellum experience of state abridgments of basic rights must inform a reasonable interpretation of the privileges and immunities clause,[29] the protection of intimate personal life must be one among the basic human rights thus worthy of national protection. The remaining question is whether there is any adequate basis for the abridgment of so basic a right – namely in the case of contraception, the right to decide whether or when one's sexual life will lead to offspring, indeed, to explore one's sexual and emotional life in personal life as an end in itself.

[22] See *id.*, p. 40.

[23] See, in general, Gutman, *Black Family in Slavery and Freedom*.

[24] See William Harper, "Memoir on Slavery," in Drew Gilpin Faust, ed., *The Ideology of Slavery: Proslavery Thought in the Antebellum South, 1830–1860* (Baton Rouge: Louisiana State University Press, 1981), at p. 110.

[25] See James Henry Hammond, "Letter to an English Abolitionist," reprinted in *id.*, at pp. 191–2.

[26] See, e.g., Harper, "Memoir on Slavery," at pp. 107, 118–19; Hammond, "Letter to an English Abolitionist," in Faust, *Ideology of Slavery*, at pp. 182–4.

[27] See, e.g., Thomas Roderick Dew, "Abolition of Negro Slavery," in Faust, *Ideology of Slavery*, at p. 65; William Harper, "Memoir on Slavery," *id.*, at p. 100 (citing Dew).

[28] For a good general discussion of such inversions, see Kenneth S. Greenberg, *Masters and Statesman: The Political Culture of American Slavery* (Baltimore: Johns Hopkins University Press, 1985).

[29] For further defense of this position, see Richards, *Conscience and the Constitution*, chap. 6.

That right can be justified only by a compelling public reason, not on the grounds of reasons that are today sectarian (internal to a moral tradition not based on reasons available and accessible to all). In fact, the only argument that could sustain such laws (namely the Augustinian[30] and Thomistic[31] views that it is immoral to engage in nonprocreative sex) is not today a view of sexuality that can reasonably be enforced on people at large. Many people regard sexual love as an end in itself and the control of reproduction as a reasonable way to regulate when and whether they have children consistent with their own personal and larger ethical interests, those of their children, and those of an overpopulated society at large. Today even the question of having children at all is a highly personal matter, certainly no longer governed by the perhaps once-compelling secular need to have children for necessary work in a largely agrarian society with high rates of infant and adult mortality.[32] From the perspective of women in particular, as Sanger and Goldman made so clear, the enforcement of an anticontraceptive morality on society at large not only harms women's interests (as well as those of an overpopulated society more generally) but also impersonally demeans them to a purely reproductive function, depriving them of the rational dignity of deciding as moral agents and persons, perhaps for the first time in human history, whether, when, and on what terms they will have children consistent with their other legitimate aims and ambitions (including the free exercise of all their basic human rights). Enforcement of such a morality rests on a conspicuously sectarian conception of gender hierarchy in which women's sexuality is defined by mandatory procreative role and responsibility. That conception, the basis of the unjust construction of gender hierarchy, cannot reasonably be the measure of human rights today.[33]

Similar considerations explain the grounds for doubt about the putative public, nonsectarian justifications for laws criminalizing abortion and homosexual sexuality. Antiabortion laws, grounded in the alleged protection of a neutral good such as life, unreasonably equate the moral weight of a fetus in the early stages of pregnancy with that of a person and abortion with murder; such laws fail to take seriously the weight that should be accorded a woman's basic right to reproductive autonomy in making highly personal moral choices central to her most intimate

30 See Augustine, *The City of God*, trans. Henry Bettenson (Harmondsworth, U.K.: Penguin, 1972), at pp. 577–94.

31 Thomas Aquinas elaborates Augustine's conception of the exclusive legitimacy of procreative sex in a striking way. Of the emission of semen apart from procreation in marriage, he wrote: "[A]fter the sin of homicide whereby a human nature already in existence is destroyed, this type of sin appears to take next place, for by it the generation of human nature is precluded." *On the Truth of the Catholic Faith: Summa Contra Gentiles*, trans. Vernon Bourke (New York: Image, 1956), pt. 2, chap. 122(9), p. 146.

32 On how personal this decision now is, see, in general, Elaine Tyler May, *Barren in the Promised Land: Childless Americans and the Pursuit of Happiness* (New York: Basic Books, 1995).

33 For further discussion of the right to privacy and contraception, see Richards, *Toleration and the Constitution*, pp. 256–61.

bodily and personal life against the background of the lack of reasonable public consensus that fetal life, as such, can be equated with that of a moral person.[34] It is for this reason that, as I argue at greater length in Chapter 4, most people do not believe that abortion is murder. Religious fundamentalists argue that it is. If they really believed that, the woman seeking the abortion would be the most culpable person. But even fundamentalists who believe in the death penalty do not call for her execution or for the execution of her doctor; most call only for fines and imprisonments. Certainly, punishing the doctor but not the woman makes no sense. In addition, a fair number of Evangelical fundamentalists (10 percent) would allow abortion in the case of rape or incest, and 19 percent of conservative Christians would permit abortion if the women's health were threatened. Neither view makes moral sense if the fetus were a person.[35]

There are legitimate interests that society has in giving weight, at some point, to fetal life as part of making a symbolic statement about the importance of taking the lives of children seriously and caring for them analogous to the symbolic interest that society may have in preventing cruelty to animals or in securing humane treatment to the irretrievably comatose to advance humane treatment of persons properly understood. But such interests do not constitutionally justify forbidding abortion as such throughout all stages of pregnancy.[36] Rather, such interests can be accorded their legitimate weight after a reasonable period has been allowed for the proper scope of a woman's exercise of her decision of whether to have an abortion.

Contemporary moral arguments for the prohibition of abortion claim that the fetus is a person and that abortion is morally the same as murder. But, as I earlier suggested, there is doubt as to whether even those who claim to believe this in fact really believe it. Rather, under the impact of the move of sectarian fundamentalist religion into American politics, fundamentalist Americans have organized around what is largely a symbolic issue for them about the proper role of women. Their views cluster around certain traditionally patriarchal conceptions of the natural processes of sexuality and gender, in which real women barely exist as moral persons and agents. Such patriarchal conceptions divide women into good asexual women on the pedestal and bad sexual women who are denigrated. This virgin-whore dichotomy is a gender mythology now very much under threat from real women and men who resist its demands in a different, antipatriarchal voice.[37] Reactionary religious fundamentalists have focused on abortion as a way to polemically quash women's resistance – women who choose to have abortions are transformed from real women who responsibly cope with difficult

[34] For further discussion, see Richards, *Toleration and the Constitution*, at pp. 261–9; Ronald Dworkin, *Life's Dominion: An Argument about Abortion, Euthanasia, and Individual Freedom* (New York: Knopf, 1993), pp. 3–178.

[35] See, on these points, Gary Wills, *Head and Heart: American Christianities* (New York: Penguin Press, 2007), at p. 525.

[36] See Richards, *Toleration and the Constitution*, at pp. 266–7.

[37] See, on this point, Carol Gilligan, *In a Different Voice: Psychological Theory and Women's Development* (Cambridge, Mass.: Harvard University Press, 1982).

moral choices into an unreal stereotypical image of bad (because they are selfish) women, indeed, murderers.

Once, however, one takes seriously that fetal life is not a reasonable public value sufficient to outweigh the right of reproductive autonomy, as the Supreme Court did in *Roe v. Wade*, the argument for criminalizing abortion is not a constitutionally reasonable argument for regarding abortion as homicide but a proxy for complex background assumptions that are often no longer reasonably believed in society at large, namely a controversial, powerfully sectarian ideology about proper sexuality and gender roles. From this perspective, the prohibitions on abortion encumber what many now reasonably regard as a highly conscientious choice by women regarding their bodies; their sexuality and gender; and the nature and place of pregnancy, birth, and child rearing in their personal and ethical lives. The traditional condemnation of abortion fails, at a deep ethical level, to take seriously the moral independence of women as free and rational persons, lending the force of law, like comparable anticontraceptive laws, to theological ideas of biological naturalness and gender hierarchy that degrade the constructive moral powers of women themselves to establish the meaning of their sexual and reproductive life histories. The underlying patriarchal conception appears to be at one with the sexist idea that women's minds and bodies are not their own but the property of others, namely men or their masculine God, who may conscript them and their bodies, like cattle on the farm, for the greater good. The abortion choice is thus one of the choices essential to the just moral independence of women, centering their lives on a body image and aspirations expressive of their moral powers. The abortion choice is a just application of the right to intimate life, because the right to the abortion choice protects women from the traditional degradation of their moral powers, reflected in the assumptions underlying antiabortion laws.

Antihomosexuality laws have even less semblance of a public justification (like fetal life) that would be acceptably enforced on society at large and brutally abridge the sexual expression of the companionate loving relationships to which homosexuals, like heterosexuals, have an inalienable human right. Plato, in *The Laws*, gave influential expression to the traditional moral condemnation in terms of two arguments: its nonprocreative character and (in its male homosexual forms) its degradation of the passive male partner to the status of a woman.[38] Homosexuality was, on this view, an immoral and unnatural abuse of the proper

[38] See Plato, *Laws*, bk. 8, 835d–842a, in Edith Hamilton and Huntington Cairns, eds., *The Collected Dialogues of Plato* (New York: Pantheon, 1961), at pp. 1401–2. On the moral condemnation of the passive role in homosexuality in both Greek and early Christian moral thought, see Peter Brown, *The Body and Society: Men, Women, and Sexual Renunciation in Early Christianity* (New York: Columbia University Press, 1988), at pp. 30, 382–3. But for evidence of Greco-Roman toleration of long-term homosexual relations even between adults, see John Boswell, *Same-Sex Unions in Premodern Europe* (New York: Villard Books, 1994), at pp. 53–107; I am grateful to Stephen Morris for conversations on this point. Whether these relationships were regarded as marriages may be a very different matter. For criticism of Boswell's argument along this latter line, see Brent D. Shaw, "A Groom of One's Own?" *New Republic*, July 18 and 25, 1994, at pp. 33–41.

human function of sexuality, marking the homosexual as subhuman and therefore wholly outside the moral community of persons. The exile of homosexuals from any just claim on moral community was given expression by the striking moral idea of homosexuality as unspeakable. It was, in Blackstone's terms, "a crime not fit to be named: *peccatum illud horribile, inter christianos non nominandum*"[39] – not mentionable, let alone discussed or assessed. Such total silencing of any reasonable discussion rendered homosexuality a kind of cultural death, naturally thus understood, and indeed condemned, as a kind of ultimate heresy against essential moral values.[40]

Neither of the two traditional moral reasons for condemning homosexuality can any longer be legitimately or constitutionally imposed on society at large or on any other person or group of persons.

One such moral reason (the condemnation of nonprocreational sex) can, for example, no longer constitutionally justify laws against the sale to and use of contraceptives by married and unmarried heterosexual couples.[41] The mandatory enforcement at large of the procreational model of sexuality is, in circumstances of overpopulation and declining infant and adult mortality, a sectarian ideal lacking adequate secular basis in the general goods that can alone reasonably justify state power; accordingly, contraceptive-using heterosexuals have the constitutional right to decide when and whether they will pursue their sexual lives to procreate or as an independent expression of mutual love, affection, and companionship.[42]

And the other moral reason for condemning homosexual sex (the degradation of a man to the passive status of a woman) rests on the sexist premise of the degraded nature of women that has been properly rejected as a reasonable basis for laws or policies on grounds of suspect classification analysis.[43] If we constitutionally accept, as we increasingly do, the suspectness of gender on par with that of race, we must, in principle, condemn, as a basis for law, any use of stereotypes expressive of the unjust enforcement of gender roles through law. That condemnation extends, as authoritative case law makes clear, to gender stereotyping as such whether immediately harmful to women or to men.[44]

39 See William Blackstone, *Commentaries on the Laws of England*, vol. 4 (Chicago: University of Chicago Press, 1979), at p. 216.

40 For further discussion of this point, see Richards, *Toleration and the Constitution*, pp. 278–9. For a useful historical overview on the social construction of homosexuality, see David F. Greenberg, *The Construction of Homosexuality* (Chicago: University of Chicago Press, 1988).

41 See *Griswold v. Connecticut*, 381 U.S. 479 (1965); *Eisenstadt v. Baird*, 405 U.S. 438 (1972).

42 For further discussion, see Richards, *Toleration and the Constitution*, at pp. 256–61.

43 See, e.g., *Frontiero v. Richardson*, 411 U.S. 677 (1973); *Craig v. Boren*, 429 U.S. 190 (1976). On homophobia as rooted in sexism, see Elisabeth Young-Bruehl, *The Anatomy of Prejudices* (Cambridge, Mass.: Harvard University Press, 1996), pp. 143, 148–51.

44 For cases that protect women from such harm, see *Reed v. Reed*, 404 U.S. 71 (1971) (right to administer estates); *Frontiero v. Richardson*, 411 U.S. 677 (1973) (dependency allowances to servicewomen); *Stanton v. Stanton*, 421 U.S. 7 (1975) (child support for education). For cases that protect men, see *Wengler v. Druggists Mutual Insurance Co.*, 446 U.S. 142 (1980) (widower's right to death benefits); *Craig v. Boren*, 429 U.S. 190 (1976) (age of drinking for men).

The decision in *Bowers v. Hardwick* was, for this reason, an interpretively unprincipled failure to elaborate properly the principle of constitutional privacy in an area of populist prejudice where the protection of that right was exigently required; and the Supreme Court in *Lawrence v. Texas* acknowledged this mistake, overruling *Bowers* and protecting gays and lesbians as the principle of constitutional privacy required.

In the background of the laws at issue in all these cases lies a normative view of gender roles. That is quite clear, as I earlier suggested, in the case of *Griswold v. Connecticut*, and less obviously so in *Roe v. Wade* and *Lawrence v. Texas*. On analysis, however, the little weight accorded to women's interests and the decisive weight accorded to the fetus in antiabortion laws make sense only against the background of the still-powerful traditional conception of mandatory procreational, self-sacrificing, caring, and nurturant gender roles for women; it is its symbolic violation of that normative idea that imaginatively transforms abortion into murder. Similarly, the Supreme Court in *Lawrence* repudiated *Bowers* because it failed to accord any weight whatsoever to the rights to privacy of homosexuals and decisive weight to incoherently anachronistic traditional moralism that reflected a still-powerful ideology of unnatural gender roles that rendered homosexuals constitutionally invisible, voiceless, and marginal.

2. RACISM, SEXISM, AND HOMOPHOBIA AS CONSTITUTIONAL EVILS: MORAL SLAVERY

The judicial concern with recognition of the basic human rights of groups traditionally deprived of such rights has historically been paralleled by an emerging constitutional doctrine that condemns as unconstitutional the basis on which such rights (and other less fundamental rights and opportunities) had been traditionally abridged. For example, the judicial expansion of the protection of the basic human rights of people of color (including their rights to conscience, speech, intimate life, education, and work) was associated with growing judicial skepticism of the political grounds on which abridgment of such rights has been rationalized, to wit, the invidious use of racial or, more generally, ethnic criteria – explicitly or implicitly – as a ground for state action. The expansion of the protection of constitutional rights to women and, more recently, to gay men and lesbians, has led to a similar development. The pertinent analogy has been the race cases and the condemnation of racism as a ground for public action.

Judicial concern along these lines was first suggested in 1971 in *Reed v. Reed*,[45] representing a sharp turn from the very different approach taken in 1948 by Justice Frankfurter for the Court in *Goesaert v. Cleary*,[46] and in 1961 by Justice Harlan

45 See *Reed v. Reed*, 404 U.S. 71 (1971).

46 See *Goesaert v. Cleary*, 335 U.S. 464 (1948) (prohibition on women from working as bartenders, except when supervised by husband or father, held constitutional).

in *Hoyt v. Florida*.[47] In the two latter cases, the Court invoked the traditional conception of gender roles as the reasonable basis for its decision upholding, in the one case, the exclusion of women from bartending and, in the other, from jury duty. In *Reed v. Reed*, the Court unanimously struck down, as an unconstitutional violation of equal protection, a state's mandatory preference for men over women in the appointment of the administrator of a decedent's estate. The state had defended the statute as a way of eliminating an area of controversy (and the need for a hearing) between relatives otherwise equally qualified. Chief Justice Burger, writing for the Court, conceded that the state's purpose was "not without some legitimacy,"[48] but he struck the statute down nonetheless because it drew a distinction that was "the very kind of arbitrary legislative choice forbidden by the Equal Protection Clause of the Fourteenth Amendment."[49] In light of *Goesaert* and *Hoyt* and previous cases, such a choice, based on traditional, normative gender roles, would appear to have a rational basis, perhaps one that could be relevantly rationalized further in terms of statistically significant differences in the experience of men (in the public world of business and affairs) and women (in a largely domestic life) that the acculturation in traditional gender roles had produced. The doctrinal oddity of *Reed* was its claim that, without heightening the standard of review as it would for a suspect class like race[50] or a fundamental right like voting,[51] it could find such a statute irrational when almost all comparable cases, subjected to rational-basis review, had been upheld as valid.[52] The legislative classification in *Reed* was no less overinclusive or underinclusive than many other such statutes and was, on that basis, no less rational.[53] The result in *Reed*, however doctrinally anomalous, suggested growing judicial skepticism about the place that traditional gender roles had been permitted to enjoy in the interpretation of equal protection.

The extent and basis of such judicial skepticism were clarified in 1973 in *Frontiero v. Richardson*,[54] in which the Court struck down (8–1) a federal law permitting male members of the armed forces an automatic dependency allowance

47 See *Hoyt v. Florida*, 368 U.S. 57 (1961) (exclusion of women from state jury held constitutional).

48 See *Reed*, 404 U.S. at 76.

49 See *id.*

50 See *Loving v. Virginia*, 388 U.S. 1 (1967) (antimiscegenation laws, using a racial classification, are subject to strictest scrutiny and held unconstitutional); *Palmore v. Sidoti*, 466 U.S. 429 (1984) (use of race to determine custody held unconstitutional).

51 See *Harper v. Virginia Board of Elections*, 383 U.S. 663 (1966) (use of poll tax for voting, trenching on fundamental right, held unconstitutional); *Reynolds v. Sims*, 377 U.S. 533 (1964) (malapportionment of state legislature, burdening fundamental equal right to vote, held unconstitutional).

52 See, e.g., *Railway Express Agency v. New York*, 336 U.S. 106 (1949) (New York City prohibition of advertising on vehicles, except self-advertising, subject to rational-basis scrutiny and held constitutional); *Williamson v. Lee Optical Co.*, 348 U.S. 483 (1955) (opticians but not sellers of ready-to-wear glasses subject to a requirement that buyer have had eye examination, held constitutional as having a rational basis).

53 On this mode of analysis of equal protection questions, see Joseph Tussman and Jacobus tenBroek, "The Equal Protection of the Laws," 37 *Calif. L. Rev.* 341 (1949).

54 See *Frontiero v. Richardson*, 411 U.S. 677 (1973).

for their wives but requiring servicewomen to prove that their husbands were dependent. Justice Brennan, writing for himself and Justices Douglas, White, and Marshall, interpreted *Reed v. Reed* as calling for heightened scrutiny for gender classifications and defended applying to gender at least the level of scrutiny accorded race. In support of such scrutiny, Justice Brennan acknowledged the nation's "long and unfortunate history of sex discrimination"[55] that was "rationalized by an attitude of 'romantic paternalism' which, in practical effect, put women, not on a pedestal, but in a cage."[56] To evidence the degree to which "this paternalistic attitude became so firmly rooted in our national consciousness,"[57] Brennan cited Justice Bradley's concurring opinion in *Bradwell v. State*,[58] which had made Catharine Beecher's normative theory of gender roles the measure of women's shriveled human and civil rights (see Chapter 4 [3]). In defending the analogy between race and gender, Brennan observed:

> As a result of notions such as these, our statute books gradually became laden with gross, stereotyped distinctions between the sexes and, indeed, throughout much of the [nineteenth] century the position of women in our society was, in many respects, comparable to that of blacks under the pre–Civil War slave codes. Neither slaves nor women could hold office, serve on juries, or bring suit in their own names, and married women traditionally were denied the legal capacity to hold or convey property or to serve as legal guardians of their own children.... And although blacks were guaranteed the right to vote in 1870, women were denied even that right – which is itself 'preservative of other basic civil and political rights' – until adoption of the Nineteenth Amendment half a century later.[59]

To further support the analogy between gender and race, Justice Brennan also pointed to "the high visibility of the sex characteristic," which, "like race and national origin, is an immutable characteristic" frequently bearing "no relation to ability to perform or contribute to society."[60] In a footnote, Brennan conceded "that[,] when viewed in the abstract, women do not constitute a small and powerless minority" but emphasized:

> [I]n part because of past discrimination, women are vastly underrepresented in this Nation's decisionmaking councils. There has never been a female President, nor a female member of this Court. Not a single woman presently sits in the United States Senate, and only 14 women hold seats in the House of Representatives. And, as appellants point out, this underrepresentation is present throughout all levels of our State and Federal Government.[61]

55 See *id.* at 684.
56 See *id.*
57 See *id.*
58 Cited in *id.* at 684–5.
59 See *id.* at 685.
60 See *id.* at 686.
61 See *id.* at 686, n. 17.

Brennan concluded "that classifications based on sex, like classifications based upon race, alienage, or national origin, are inherently suspect, and must therefore be subject to strict judicial scrutiny."[62] Subjecting the statutory classification to this standard, Brennan found that its claimed purpose, administrative convenience (more spouses of men than of women are likely to be dependent), did not justify use of the gender distinction when a more individualized assessment of dependence was available at little cost and was likely to save the government money on balance (many wives of male service members would fail to qualify for benefits under an individualized test).[63]

Four other justices concurred in Brennan's judgment for the Court but on the rational-basis standard of *Reed v. Reed*. Justice Powell, writing for himself, Chief Justice Burger, and Justice Blackmun, argued that *Reed* "abundantly supports our decision today"[64] without adding "sex to the narrowly limited group of classifications which are inherently suspect."[65]

A majority of the Supreme Court finally agreed in 1976 in *Craig v. Boren*[66] that gender classifications were subject to heightened scrutiny, an intermediate level of scrutiny certainly stronger than rational basis but not as demanding as the strict scrutiny accorded to race. Justice Brennan, writing for the Court, characterized this heightened scrutiny as applying both to the purpose and to the means-end reasoning of the statute: "classifications by gender must serve important governmental objectives and must be substantially related to achievement of these objectives."[67] The statute in question in *Craig* drew a gender distinction between men and women in drinking age (men at twenty-one, women at eighteen) allegedly on the ground that statistical evidence suggested higher rates of drunk driving and traffic injuries for men. On its face, the statute, in contrast to *Frontiero* and related cases of blatantly unconstitutional sex discrimination against women,[68] advantaged women in contrast to men. Brennan's analysis framed the constitutional issue in terms of the role gender, as a cultural stereotype, played in the statute. Assessing the statute in terms of appropriately heightened intermediate scrutiny, the Court accepted the legitimacy of the state's ostensible purpose for the statute, traffic safety,[69] but found its means-end reasoning constitutionally defective, particularly the role statistical evidence played in rationalizing the use of a legislative classification in terms of gender.

[62] See *id.* at 688.
[63] See *id.* at 688–91.
[64] See *id.* at 692.
[65] See *id.*
[66] See *Craig v. Boren*, 429 U.S. 190 (1976).
[67] See *id.* at 197.
[68] See, e.g., *Stanton v. Stanton*, 421 U.S. 7 (1975) (establishing female adulthood at the age of eighteen and male adulthood at the age of twenty-one for purposes of child-support payments held unconstitutional).
[69] See *Craig v. Boren*, 429 U.S. at 199.

The problem was not merely doubts about the accuracy of the statistical evidence. Even taking the most reliable such evidence presented, the statistics on driving while under the influence established that 0.18 percent of women and 2 percent of men were arrested for this offense. Although conceding that "such a disparity is not trivial in a statistical sense, it hardly can form the basis for employment of a gender line as a classifying device."[70] The point was not only that a 2 percent correlation hardly makes gender a reliable proxy for drinking and driving, for the use of gender would be constitutionally problematic even if it were much more accurate. The basis for the gender distinctions used in *Reed v. Reed* and *Frontiero v. Richardson* may be much more statistically reliable measures of, in the one case, relevant business experience and, in the other, dependency, but they were nonetheless problematic.[71] The constitutional evil, rather, was giving expression through public law to the unjust political force that a gender stereotype has traditionally enjoyed, often, as a consequence, creating reality in its own unjust image. Brennan made this point about age-differential laws like that in *Craig* in terms of the degree to which unjust social stereotypes may themselves distort the statistics: "'reckless' young men who drink and drive are transformed into arrest statistics, where their female counterparts are chivalrously escorted home."[72]

The analogy to race and ethnicity was, Brennan argued, exact:

> [I]f statistics were to govern the permissibility of state alcohol regulation without regard to the Equal Protection Clause as a limiting principle, it might follow that States could freely favor Jews and Italian Catholics at the expense of all other Americans, since available studies regularly demonstrate that the former two groups exhibit the lowest rates of problem drinking. . . . Similarly, if a State were allowed simply to depend upon demographic characteristics of adolescents in identifying problem drinkers, statistics might support the conclusion that only black teenagers should be permitted to drink, followed by Asian-Americans and Spanish-Americans. 'Whites and American Indians have the lowest proportions of abstainers and the highest proportions of moderate/heavy and heavy drinkers.' [citing study].[73]

We would not permit the use of even accurate statistics to justify racial, ethnic, or religious classifications in such cases for the same reasons that gender classifications should not be permitted on such a basis. The classifications themselves reflect a long history of unjust and unconstitutional treatment that has shaped reality in its image. Laws can no more constitutionally give expression to such classifications than they can to the facts such classifications have shaped. Brennan thus took the argument he earlier made in *Frontiero* about the unjust force a rights-denying conception of gender roles had been allowed to enjoy in

[70] See *id*. at 201.
[71] See *id*. at 202, n. 13.
[72] See *id*. at 202, n. 14.
[73] See *id*. at 208–9, n. 22.

American public law and culture (including its stark endorsement by members of the Supreme Court) and applied it to the unjust gender stereotypes such a conception had sustained. Such unjust gender roles and stereotypes included the idealized image of women's greater morality on the pedestal, rationalizing, as it did, abridgment of basic rights and opportunities. To condemn the political imposition of such gender roles was to condemn as well the cultural stereotypes such roles enforced on reality. From this perspective, not only men but also women suffered from the political enforcement of such stereotypes, which have rested on a rights-denying, dehumanizing idealization from which women in particular have suffered.

The constitutional standard of heightened scrutiny of gender classifications has certainly moved the constitutional treatment of gender closer to that of race. Heightened scrutiny is not, however, strict scrutiny. Although many gender classifications, as we have seen, have been struck down, others have survived, albeit sometimes by narrow majorities. In *Michael M. v. Superior Court*,[74] for example, the Court, 5–4, accepted the constitutionality of a state's statutory rape law that subjected men, but not women, to criminal liability for intercourse with a female under the age of eighteen and not his wife largely on the ground that women, in contrast to men, bore the risks of pregnancy. And in *Rostker v. Goldberg*,[75] the Court ruled, 6–3, that Congress could limit registration for the draft to men on the ground that women, in contrast to men, were excluded from combat.

The more recent case, *United States v. Virginia*,[76] however, suggests that the Supreme Court may be raising the level of scrutiny accorded gender to a level much closer to that of race. In striking down the exclusion of women from the Virginia Military Institute, the Court invoked the standard of whether the justification for exclusion was "exceedingly persuasive"[77] and was quite skeptical of the weight accorded putative gender differences as a rationale for the exclusion;[78] the Court expressly invoked an important racial case, *Sweatt v. Painter*, as a relevant analogy for the unconstitutionality of separate but equal in the realm of gender.[79] If so, the result in cases like *Michael M.* and even *Rostker* may now be constitutionally problematic.

In *Romer v. Evans*,[80] decided in 1996, the Supreme Court, even before the overruling of *Bowers v. Hardwick* by *Lawrence v. Texas*, found that sexual orientation was also, at least to some degree, a suspect classification, like religion, race or ethnicity, and gender. In response to political arguments by gay groups in

74 See *Michael M. v. Superior Court*, 450 U.S. 464 (1981).
75 See *Rostker v. Goldberg*, 453 U.S. 57 (1981).
76 See *United States v. Virginia*, 518 U.S. 515 (1996)
77 See *id.* at 533.
78 See *id.* at 533–4.
79 See *id.* at 553.
80 *Romer v. Evans*, 517 U.S. 620 (1996).

Colorado, laws had been legislatively approved by various municipalities in the state that protected gays and lesbians from discrimination on the ground of sexual orientation (on the analogy of the state and federal laws that forbid discrimination on grounds of religion, race, ethnicity, and gender). Sodomy was no longer criminal in Colorado, but groups opposed to gay rights had secured passage of Colorado Amendment 2, an amendment to the state constitution that not only repealed such antidiscrimination ordinances but also forbade any such antidiscrimination laws or policies ever to be effective in Colorado.[81] *Bowers*, which allows the criminalization of gay or lesbian sex, was implicated in the arguments for Colorado Amendment 2 because, if the conduct central to a group's identity could be criminal, then it seems reasonable that a state, which could constitutionally wholly forbid such conduct, might take the less restrictive option of not criminalizing it but discouraging its public acceptability by forbidding any protections of gays and lesbian from people's desire not to associate with them.

Justice Kennedy's opinion for the Court was joined by five justices (including Justices O'Connor, Souter, Stevens, Ginsburg, and Breyer); Justice Scalia wrote in dissent for himself and for Chief Justice Rehnquist and Justice Thomas. Kennedy's opinion nowhere mentions *Bowers*, whereas the authority of *Bowers* is at the center of Justice Scalia's argument in *Romer*: "In holding that homosexuality cannot be singled out for disfavorable treatment, the Court contradicts a decision, unchallenged here, pronounced only 10 years ago, see *Bowers v. Hardwick*."[82]

What made *Romer* so important, in marking the Court's growing recognition of the constitutional rights of gays and lesbians, was its sense, from the very opening of Justice Kennedy's opinion for the Court, that what populist support for Colorado Amendment 2 reflected was a support analogous to that which supported state-endorsed racial segregation in *Plessy v. Ferguson*. Although Justice Kennedy's opinion in *Romer* did not mention *Bowers*, its opening appeal to Justice Harlan's dissent in *Plessy* a (the Constitution "neither knows nor tolerates classes among citizens"[83]) strikingly aligns Justice Harlan's dissent in *Plessy* with Justice Blackmun's dissent in *Bowers*. It was not only the style of Kennedy's opinion that questions the continuing authority of *Bowers*; it is its substance. Colorado Amendment 2 is unconstitutional, Kennedy argued, because it lacked any rational relationship to legitimate state interests, thus reflecting unconstitutional irrational prejudice. Kennedy did not recognize as legitimate what Justice Scalia, in his

[81] See Amendment 2 to Colo. Const. art. 2, sec. 2 (adopted Nov. 3, 1992). The full text of Amendment 2 is as follows: "Neither the State of Colorado, through any of its branches or departments, nor any of its agencies, political subdivisions, municipalities or school districts, shall enact, adopt or enforce any statute, regulation, ordinance or policy whereby homosexual, lesbian or bisexual orientation, conduct, practices, or relationships shall constitute or otherwise be the basis of, or entitle any person or class of persons to have or claim any minority status, quota preferences, protected status or claim of discrimination. This Section of the Constitution shall be self-executing."

[82] *Romer v. Evans*, 517 U.S. 620, 636 (1996).

[83] Quoted in *Romer v. Evans*, 517 U.S. 620, 623 (1996).

dissent, argued *Bowers* established as legitimate: an evil in gay and lesbian sex that justifies criminalization. If such an evil was a legitimate basis for outright banning, it must, Scalia argued, be a rational basis for drawing distinctions. Kennedy's denial of this point suggests that *Bowers* is not legitimate.

There is a rather brilliant argument in Justice Kennedy's opinion that clearly attempts to answer Justice Scalia's argument, again without mentioning or discussing *Bowers*. This is Kennedy's discussion of earlier cases dealing with the Mormons. These cases were of two sorts: those that constitutionally allowed laws that banned Mormon polygamy, though polygamy was then rooted in the right of religious liberty,[84] and those that allowed Mormons to be deprived of the right to vote.[85] Justice Kennedy does not question the authority of the case upholding a ban on polygamy (presumably, on the ground that banning a practice, rooted in a basic right like religious liberty, is justified if there is a compelling state interest – such as gender equality – that supports the ban); but the latter case, he argues, is no longer good law because it rests on the now constitutionally unacceptable view "that persons advocating a certain practice may be denied the right to vote."[86] Just because a religious practice may be constitutionally banned, it does not follow that advocacy of such a practice may be a ground for depriving the advocates of a basic right like voting. The analogy to gays and lesbian is evident: gays and lesbians now publicly claim their basic rights on fair terms with other Americans. It may be, if *Bowers v. Hardwick* is good law, that conduct rooted in their conscientious exercise of their right to intimate life may be banned because a compelling state purpose supports such a ban; but it does not follow that their public claims and lives as gays and lesbians may, for that reason, be the subject of discrimination.

What the analogy shows is how far, in the view of six justices of the Supreme Court, gays and lesbians had come in twenty years, bringing their ethical voices to bear on American politics and constitutional law. Although opposition to gay rights is often grounded in traditional religious views that condemn gay and lesbian sex as the unspeakable crime against nature not to be mentioned among Christians, the growing public presence of gays and lesbians in American intellectual and public life, including arguments by myself and others about the justice of their claims,[87] led the six justices of the Court to recognize the claims of gays and lesbians as being as much rooted in ethical conviction and

[84] *Reynolds v. United States*, 98 U.S. 145 (1878) (upholding application of a federal law making bigamy a crime in the territories to a Mormon claiming that polygamy was his religious duty).

[85] *Davis v. Beason*, 133 U.S. 333 (1890).

[86] *Romer v. Evans*, 517 U.S. 620, 634 (1996).

[87] See, e.g., David A. J. Richards., *Sex, Drugs, Death, and the Law: An Essay on Human Rights and Overcriminalization* (Totowa, N.J.: Rowman and Littlefield, 1982); David A. J. Richards, *Toleration and the Constitution* (New York: Oxford University Press, 1986); David A. J. Richards, *Women, Gays, and the Constitution: The Grounds for Feminism and Gay Rights in Culture and Law* (Chicago: University of Chicago Press, 1998). H. L. A. Hart, *Law, Liberty, and Morality* (Stanford, Calif.: Stanford University Press, 1963). On the background and character of the arguments I made, including their roots in my personal life, see David A. J. Richards, *The Case for Gay Rights: From Bowers to Lawrence and Beyond* (Lawrence: University Press of Kansas, 2005).

argument, at the core of the constitutional protection of religious liberty, as the arguments of their opponents. The analogy of the Mormons is thus striking in giving constitutional recognition to the voices of gays and lesbians as ethical voices, as much entitled to respect as any other voices in America. The argument also suggests that what may have moved the Court in *Romer* is the sense of religious discrimination against gays and lesbians: a sectarian cultural war on the personal and ethical convictions of gays and lesbians analogous to traditional Christian discrimination against Jews and no better justified on constitutional grounds of equal treatment of all forms of conscience, whether traditional religious claims or contemporary ethical voices challenging such claims.

3. RESISTANCE TO PATRIARCHAL VOICE AS THE KEY TO RESISTANCE TO ANTI-SEMITISM, RACISM, SEXISM, AND HOMOPHOBIA IN THE CIVIL RIGHTS MOVEMENTS OF THE 1960S AND LATER

How do political movements arise in resistance to long-standing cultural or political evils like anti-Semitism, racism, sexism, and homophobia, expressing themselves in the constitutional developments just discussed? These developments in the United States were energized by the various protest movements of the 1960s. These protest movements drew their psychological appeal from their resistance to the patriarchal psychology that supports such evils. We need first to understand the psychology that sustains such irrational prejudices and then, on that basis, clarify the psychology of resistance. I begin with these prejudices and what supports them, and then turn to the psychology of resistance that empowered the protest movements of the 1960s and later.

All these evils (anti-Semitism, racism, sexism, and homophobia) should be understood as instances of moral slavery: namely where a long-standing cultural tradition first abridges the basic human rights of whole classes of persons and then rationalizes that abridgment on the ground of cultural stereotypes that are not allowed to be reasonably contested either by those afflicted by them or by persons generally. Anti-Semitism is a clear example of this moral evil, as it clearly satisfies both features of moral slavery, and each of the other evils (racism, sexism, homophobia) exemplifies the two features as well.[88]

We can more deeply understanding these political evils in terms of the pivotally important role in each of them of patriarchy. The analysis of anti-Semitism supports this claim forthrightly: anti-Semitism, as a moral and political evil, arose (as we shall see in a later chapter) when Augustine, having renounced sexual love to be worthy of a celibate-male patriarchal priesthood, defended not only religious persecution in general but also anti-Semitism in particular on the ground of "carnal Israel," the centrality of sexuality to Jewish religious life and

[88] See, for a fuller statement and elaboration of this claim, David A. J. Richards, *Women, Gays, and the Constitution: The Grounds for Feminism and Gay Rights in Culture and Law* (Chicago: University of Chicago Press, 1998).

practice.[89] Augustine, himself acculturated within Roman patriarchy, adapted patriarchy to Christian religious institutions, in particular, the patriarchal priesthood in which he found, after much agonizing, his vocation. What, for Augustine, was central to the priesthood was, following Aeneas in *The Aeneid*, the renunciation of personal sexual love for the sake of the higher love of God, and it is this renunciation, the loss of real relationships, that explains the kind of identification with patriarchal voice that Augustine defends – the idealization of his own ascetic voice and the denigration of the sexual voice of the Jews (see Chapter 4 [4]).

The brilliance of the darkness made visible by Virgil in the *Aeneid* is the psychology of patriarchy he shows us: the traumatic disruption by the patriarchal voice of the gods of Aeneas's passionate love for Dido, a sexual love that was both egalitarian and cooperative (they were both good rulers who would have cooperated in constructing a new state, Carthage); Aeneas's identification with this patriarchal voice and loss of the personal voice of loving relationship; and Aeneas's violent savagery at the end of the poem.

What Carol Gilligan and I have argued elsewhere is that Roman patriarchy rested on this psychology of loss, which explains both its idealization of patriarchal men and women (including the often loveless arranged marriages that Roman patriarchy required) and its denigration of anyone who would challenge this arrangement, including its violence against its enemies and, in the civil wars, against one another.[90] And it is this form of Roman patriarchy that Augustine reads into the orthodox Christian tradition: having imposed such traumatic loss on himself, Augustine identifies with the imagined voice of a patriarchal father (the law of the father) and wars on any challenge to that voice. The psychology of such traumatic loss, arising from the breaking of real relationships of love and intimacy, replaces real relationship with identification, a form of what the psychoanalyst Sándor Ferenczi called identification with the aggressor (the Gilligan-Richards thesis).[91]

With Augustine, we quite clearly see the pivotal role played in patriarchy of the repression of sexual voice, which is the key to understanding how an evil like anti-Semitism could have become so prominent a feature of the Christian tradition. It is because anti-Semitism arises from the repression of sexual voice (Augustine's agonized argument with himself over his sexuality leading to the choice of celibacy) that Augustine must denigrate the role of sexuality in Jewish religion and life, rationalizing the form of religiously endorsed moral slavery of the Jews he, in fact, supported (the Jew as the slave of Christians, as he put it).

What this analysis brings out is how the very conception of manhood, Roman or Christian, resting on this psychology of traumatized loss, gives rise to a sense

[89] See, for discussion and citations, Gilligan and Richards, *The Deepening Darkness: Patriarchy, Resistance, and Democracy's Future* (Cambridge: Cambridge University Press, 2009), at pp. 133–34.

[90] See Carol Gilligan and David A. J. Richards, *The Deepening Darkness: Patriarchy, Resistance, and Democracy's Future* (Cambridge: Cambridge University Press, 2009).

[91] See, on this point, Gilligan and Richards, *Deepening Darkness*, at pp. 19, 25.

of honor that is acutely sensitive to real or imagined slights to its highly idealized sense of oneself and others (Romans or Christians), including, as in Christian anti-Semitism, the very existence of a people like the Jews, whose way of life it not only denigrated (because it challenges Christian asexuality) but also, as a standing challenge to orthodox Christianity, elicits among Christians a sense of dishonor, which expresses itself in violence. A psychology that, for the Romans, motivated their astonishing willingness to bear the burdens of endless imperialistic wars leads Augustinian Christianity aggressively to entrench the moral slavery of the Jews and to other forms of violent religious persecution, including not only of heretic Christians (the Donatists and Pelagians) but also of pagan religion (including the Isis religion).

Patriarchal voice plays the crucial role it does not only in Christian anti-Semitism but also in its later elaboration in the nineteenth and twentieth centuries into the genocidal violence of Adolf Hitler's fascism. There is the same pattern of patriarchal manhood, inherited from Roman and Christian patriarchy, resting on a psychology of traumatic national defeat and loss (Germany in World War I), which expresses itself in a national alignment with Hitler's idealized patriarchal voice and the propensity to scapegoat the very existence of the Jews (as long-standing outsiders to a religiously and ethnically based nationalism), who not only stood for its traditional values of sexual and family life, but also many of whom were drawn to and supported the political liberalism (including both sexual emancipation and feminism) that Hitler despised.

This analysis of the persistence of such irrational prejudices – starting with the patriarchal analysis of the roots of anti-Semitism – clarifies how important the lens of patriarchy is to understanding and coming to terms with such prejudices, including resisting them. It is through such a lens that the Gilligan-Richards thesis understands how it is that the supposed discrediting of one such prejudice has a way of leading to the expression of another such prejudice. Thus, the discrediting of the Catholic Church's role in Christian anti-Semitism has led to the displacement of this irrational prejudice to the church's prominent contemporary role in homophobia. Contemporary gays and lesbians, with their claim to the dignity of their love lives, are to the Augustinian orthodoxy currently maintained by papal Catholicism what the Jews were to Augustine: a reasonable form of conviction that challenges traditional teachings now very much in doubt and, for this reason, ferociously targeted for repression in a form of moral slavery (see Chapter 4). The underlying psychology is the highly patriarchal form of Christianity that the papal hierarchy of Catholicism continues triumphally to endorse, which leaves intact the underlying psychology that expresses itself in one or another form of irrational prejudice. Christian homophobia is, from this perspective, no better and no worse than the forms of Christian anti-Semitism that have disgraced Christianity uncritically for much too long; what was once the Augustinian dehumanizing sexuality of the Jews (carnal Israel) is today the dehumanizing sexualization of gays and lesbians. We cannot even understand, let alone deal with, such evils, the heart of darkness of contemporary religion, until we understand the continuing role of patriarchy in sustaining them.

The analysis explains as well a striking common feature of all these forms of irrational, dehumanizing prejudice, namely what the novelist Arundhati Roy calls

> the Love Laws. . . . The laws that lay down who should be loved, and how.
>
> And how much.[92]

Roy places the love laws at the center of her novel *The God of Small Things*, her exploration of the patriarchally tragic love story through the eyes of the next generation, who inadvertently have witnessed the tragedy. What is, for Roy, at the heart of patriarchy and its tragic impact on our lives and loves are the love laws, which crucially enforce the demands of patriarchy, which separate and divide us from one another and from our common humanity. The form of the love laws is historically familiar: prohibitions on sexual relations, including marriage, between Jews and non-Jews; between people of color and not of color (antimiscegenation laws); between married women and men who are not their husbands (Augustus's ferocious antiadultery legislation[93]); or nonprocreative sex between married couples (laws criminalizing heterosexual sodomy or use of contraceptives or access to abortion services), between gay men, or between lesbians. What is not so clear is why such laws play the important role they do in anti-Semitism, racism, sexism, and homophobia.

The Gilligan-Richards thesis powerfully explains the love laws, all of which rest on the role of patriarchal voice in personal and political psychology. That psychology – from Roman patriarchy to Augustine to Hitler – arises from the disruption of loving sexual relationships, indeed, from their repudiation as unmanly by the light of patriarchal manhood. Such disruption is pivotally important to patriarchal psychology because it is the traumatic breaking of such relationships that leads to loss of voice and memory, aligning one's own voice with the imagined patriarchal voice that required such disruption, as a condition of manhood (identification with the aggressor). It is identification with such an idealized patriarchal voice, made possible by the traumatic breaking of real relationships, which leads to the narcissistic idealisms that underlie prejudices like anti-Semitism, racism, sexism, and homophobia, and rationalize atrocity. What the account here adds to the study of these prejudices is a historically informed understanding of the pivotal role of patriarchy in sustaining them.[94]

92 Arundhati Roy, *The God of Small Things* (New York: HarperPerennial, 1998), at p. 33.

93 See, for fuller discussion, Gilligan and Richards, *Deepening Darkness*, chap. 2.

94 See, for an excellent study of these prejudices, Young-Bruehl, *Anatomy of Prejudices*. Our account is consistent with this study, offering a historical understanding of patriarchy as an explanation of their growth and persistence over time.

What patriarchy knows and depends on is the suppression of precisely the relational sensitivity and responsiveness of one person, as an individual, to another person, as an individual, precisely because such human connections are inconsistent with patriarchal demands (as Virgil tells us Aeneas's love for Dido was). Augustine carries this renunciation one step further into sexuality itself, thus suppressing or seeking to suppress one of the central ways humans experience love and connection in mutual pleasure and delight. But the suppression of intimate sexual voice and experience shuts down one of the important human ways that we, as individuals, come to relate and know one another, released, as Psyche was in Apuleius's *The Golden Ass*, from the taboo on knowing and speaking of our love and lover.[95] The Augustinian reimposition of this taboo, which he believed made true love possible, in fact destroyed our loving natures, rendering impossible one of the crucial ways we come to know one another as the individuals (not the stereotypes) we are and passionately value another person and their aims, precisely because they are the totally real, individual persons they are. If we can destroy loving connection in this way, we destroy as well the ethical sensitivities such connection makes possible, laying the psychological foundation for the dehumanization that rationalizes irrational prejudices (anti-Semitism, racism, sexism, and homophobia). If we can kill as powerful and connecting a human emotion as sexual love, we can, as patriarchy requires, kill all sympathy and its expression, as well as humane ethical imagination, thereby forging the enemies and scapegoats patriarchy requires and visiting on them illimitable atrocity as what manhood both permits and, indeed, in its heroes, requires (Heinrich Himmler on the heroism required to execute the Holocaust,[96] and Himmler's adjutant to recent recruits: "you are disciplined, but stand together hard as Krupp steel. Don't be soft, be merciless, and clear out everything that is not German and could hinder us in the world of construction"[97]). All forms of such prejudice war on loving connection across the barriers such prejudices artificially impose, precisely because such loving connection exposes the lies that such prejudices violently enforce. What supports the stability of the practices that patriarchy underwrites is the repression of a free and loving sexual voice and the relationships to which such a voice would otherwise lead. Nothing, on this analysis, more threatens patriarchy and the irrational prejudices patriarchy supports (anti-Semitism, racism, sexism, and homophobia) than loving across the artificial barriers patriarchy imposes to support its demands. The love laws express patriarchal violence directed against this very real threat to its authority.

The abolitionist feminists, the most radical antebellum critics of American slavery and racism, in these terms quite correctly analyzed the roots of the evils of American slavery and racism as the same roots of the evil of the American

95 See, for further discussion, Gilligan and Richards, *Deepening Darkness*, chap. 4.

96 See, e.g., Ian Kershaw, *Hitler: 1963–1945: Nemesis* (New York: W. W. Norton, 2000), at pp. 604–5.

97 See *id.*, pp. 242–3.

subjection of women and sexism, namely patriarchy.[98] Nathaniel Hawthorne's *The Scarlet Letter* – written under the influence of the abolitionist feminists – also critically examines his persecutory Puritan ancestors in terms of their "patriarchal" character,[99] and it carries the abolitionist feminist criticism of patriarchy a step further, portraying in Hester Prynne a prophetically antipatriarchal ethical voice rooted in her freer sexual voice and life that the New England patriarchy so condemned.

The criticism of patriarchy, as at the root of such constitutionally contradictory evils as slavery and racism, is thus hardly historically novel, as both the abolitionist feminists and Hawthorne's art make quite clear. But our patriarchal assumptions have been so powerful that the antipatriarchal core of the abolitionist feminist criticism of both slavery and racism was marginalized, as the Reconstruction Amendments emancipated both black men and women from slavery but emancipated black women into patriarchy. Elizabeth Stanton, who had been a crucial figure in securing ratification of the Thirteenth Amendment, opposed both the Fourteenth and Fifteenth amendments for this reason (the Fifteenth Amendment thus gave the vote to black men but not to women, including black women).[100] In effect, black women were no longer black but were only women. Thus, even the Reconstruction Amendments were compromised by patriarchal assumptions at war with their deeper ethical principles. And the continuing uncritical force of patriarchy explains as well the force, in the constitutional interpretation of the Reconstruction Amendments, of prejudices like racism, sexism, and homophobia that are, in fact, inconsistent with the deeper egalitarian democratic values of the Reconstruction Amendments.[101]

Consider, for example, the Supreme Court's decision in 1896[102] that held state-imposed racial segregation consistent with the equal protection clause of the Fourteenth Amendment (a decision unanimously reversed in 1954[103]). What rendered such segregation acceptable in 1896 was certainly, in part, as Charles Lofgren has shown,[104] the dominant racist social science of the late nineteenth century. The development of this alleged science of natural race differences in moral capacity (American ethnology) measured them in alleged physical

[98] See, for extended treatment of this argument, David A. J. Richards, *Women, Gays, and the Constitution*.

[99] See Nathaniel Hawthorne, *The Scarlet Letter* (New York: Penguin, 1983) (originally published in 1850), at p. 15, and see pp. 12–14, 18, 20, 132, 190.

[100] See, on this point, *Women, Gays, and the Constitution*, pp. 138–9.

[101] See, for a general critique of and commentary on constitutional interpretation of the Reconstruction Amendments along these lines, Richards, *Conscience and the Constitution*; Richards, *Women, Gays, and the Constitution*.

[102] See *Plessy v. Ferguson*, 163 U.S. 537 (1896).

[103] *Brown v. Board of Education*, 347 U.S. 483 (1954) (state-imposed racial segregation is a violation of equal protection).

[104] Charles A. Lofgren, *The Plessy Case: A Legal Historical Interpretation* (New York: Oxford University Press, 1987).

differences (physically measured by brain capacity or cephalic indices);[105] these measures afforded a putatively scientific basis for making the allegedly reasonable judgment that the separation of the races was justified. Segregation in transportation (the issue in *Plessy*) might thus discourage forms of social intercourse that would result in degenerative forms of miscegenation; and segregation in education would reflect race-linked differences in capacity best dealt with in separate schools and would discourage social intercourse.

However, the antebellum abolitionists had offered plausible objections to the scientific status of American ethnology, and similarly forceful objections were available at the time *Plessy* was decided in 1896. For example, Franz Boas, a German Jewish immigrant, had already published his 1894 paper debunking the weight to be accorded to race in the social sciences.[106] In effect, the putative reasonable scientific basis for *Plessy* was not, in fact, critically stated or discussed in the opinion but rather conclusorily assumed. Even given the state of the human sciences at the time of *Plessy*, the interpretive argument in the decision did not meet the standards of impartial reason surely due all Americans. Rather, our highest court registered uncritically the conclusory acceptance without argument of controversial scientific judgments hostage to a political ideology that protected the increasingly racist character of the American South. One justice (Justice Harlan, a Southerner) powerfully made precisely this point in his dissent in *Plessy*.

The South went to civil war out of a highly patriarchal sense of honor (self-consciously rooted in Roman patriarchy) acutely sensitive to any challenge to its institutions (slavery, in particular) as an insult that triggered violence. The South's defeat in the Civil War, like Germany's defeat in World War I, was also experienced as a bitter blow to its patriarchal honor, and it expressed its anger in terms of an ideological scapegoat, the black men and women freed from slavery by the Thirteenth Amendment, in the same way that political anti-Semitism in a defeated Germany turned on the Jews. "[T]he South was united [on racism] as it had not been on slavery."[107] The constitutional abolition of slavery and guarantee of equal rights of citizenship to black Americans were dead letters without some effective constitutional protection of the rights of black Americans against the

105 See, for good general treatments, Stephen Jay Gould, *The Mismeasure of Man* (New York: W. W. Norton, 1981); Thomas F. Gossett, *Race: The History of an Idea in America* (New York: Schocken Books, 1965); George M. Fredrickson, *The Black Image in the White Mind: The Debate on Afro-American Character and Destiny, 1817–1914* (Middleton, Conn.: Wesleyan University Press, 1981); John S. Haller Jr., *Outcasts from Evolution: Scientific Attitudes of Racial Inferiority, 1859–1900* (New York: McGraw-Hill, 1971); Reginald Horsman, *Race and Manifest Destiny: The Origins of American Racial Anglo-Saxonism* (Cambridge, Mass.: Harvard University Press, 1981).

106 See Franz Boas, "Human Faculty as Determined by Race" (1894), in George W. Stocking Jr., *A Franz Boas Reader: The Shaping of American Anthropology, 1833–1911* (Chicago: University of Chicago Press, 1974), pp. 221–42.

107 C. Wan Woodward, "Emancipations and Reconstructions: A Comparative Study," in C. Van Woodward, *The Future of the Past* (New York: Oxford University Press, 1989), at p. 166.

populist racism that flourished in the defeated South as the terms of Southern sectional unity. The Reconstruction Amendments stood for an ethical vision of national unity based on respect for the human rights of all persons. Southern attempts to perpetuate racist subjugation through law (the Black Codes) were inconsistent with such respect and could not legitimately be allowed expression through public law.

The equal protection clause of the Fourteenth Amendment afforded a nationally applicable constitutional guarantee and enforcement power aimed to protect American citizens against such subjugation.[108] The task was the novel one, not really anticipated by the abolitionists, of how such guarantees were to be understood, interpreted, and implemented against those who would unconstitutionally abridge the rights of Americans to equal standing before the law and were not open to reasonable persuasion on the question. If the abolitionists (with their historical mission of persuasion by conscience) were unprepared for the task before them, the nation at large had even less understanding of what was required to achieve its publicly avowed constitutional aims to rectify the American heritage of both slavery and the cultural construction of racism nationwide.

The principles of the Reconstruction Amendments could probably have been effectively realized only by a continuing national commitment to the ongoing federal enforcement of constitutional rights in the South; such federal programs would have included land distribution and integrated education for the freedmen (of the sort suggested by Thaddeus Stevens in the House[109] and Charles Sumner in the Senate[110]) and active and ongoing federal protection of black voting rights. However, mainstream antebellum abolitionist thought (besides radicals like Stevens and Sumner) was unprepared for the task that Reconstruction would pose,[111] and the rest of the nation was even less prepared. The dominant view in the Reconstruction Congress itself was that the guarantee of equal protection would not condemn state-sponsored racial segregation or antimiscegenation laws,[112] which were very clearly at odds with the antiracism of the antebellum radical abolitionist Lydia Maria Child.[113] The failure adequately to protect the freedmen exposed them to the hostile environment of the South committed with redoubled fury to the cultural construction of racism as the irrationalist symbol

108 See, for further discussion, Richards, *Conscience and the Constitution*, chap. 4.

109 On Stevens's abortive proposals for confiscation and distribution of Southern plantations to the freedmen, see Eric Foner, *Reconstruction: America's Unfinished Revolution 1863–1877* (New York: Harper & Row, 1988), 222, 235–7, 245–6, 308–10.

110 On Sumner's proposals for federally sponsored land distribution and integrated education for the freedmen, see Foner, *Reconstruction*, pp. 236, 308.

111 See, in general, James M. McPherson, *The Struggle for Equality: Abolitionists and the Negro in the Civil War and Reconstruction* (Princeton, N.J.: Princeton University Press, 1964); Michael Les Benedict, *A Compromise of Principle: Congressional Republicans and Reconstruction, 1863–1869* (New York: W. W. Norton, 1974).

112 See, on these points, William E. Nelson, *The Fourteenth Amendment: From Political Principle to Judicial Doctrine* (Cambridge, Mass.: Harvard University Press, 1988).

113 See, on this point, Richards, *Women, Gays, and the Constitution*, pp. 55–62.

of Southern sectional unity in defeat. Southern racism had evolved into a politically aggressive racism that the victory of the Union had, if anything worsened. By 1877, what inadequate congressional and presidential commitment to black rights there were (protecting voting rights and prosecuting the Ku Klux Klan) effectively ceased.[114]

We can see here the consequences of the patriarchal assumptions that, as we earlier observed, compromised the Reconstruction Amendments themselves and further explain the uncritical complicity of the Supreme Court itself in *Plessy* with the irrationalist racism it should have questioned rather than uncritically accepted. What led the Court unreasonably not to examine critically the scientific basis for its decision was its own patriarchally based view that, in light of the racist pedestal that idealized white women (as asexual) and denigrated blacks (as sexual), the state might separate whites from blacks to protect white women from sexual advances by black men. Such state-supported racism was invisible to the Supreme Court because of its own uncritical acceptance of patriarchal assumptions that corrupted its judgment about what should count as an irrational, dehumanizing prejudice condemned by the equal protection clause.

What makes such a judgment so shocking is that, in this period, a remarkable black woman, Ida Wells-Barnett, had exposed to reasonable public judgment the irrationalism underlying the racialized pedestal. Wells found that lynchings of black men rested not, as was claimed, on rapes of white women but on consensual sexual relations between white women and black men. Wells had stumbled across "facts of illicit [consensual] association between black men and white women,"[115] "that what the white man of the South practiced as all right for himself in sexual relationships with black women, he assumed to be unthinkable in white women."[116] She was convinced that the facts she had discovered put lynching in an entirely new light: it was an irrational expression of the Southern racist "resentment that the Negro was no longer his plaything, his servant, and his source of income."[117] Such racism expressed an unjustly enforced political epistemology of race and gender that dehumanized African Americans as sexually rapacious animals (nonbearers of human rights); it distorted reality to comply with its terms, in particular, repressing by "the cold-blooded savagery of white devils under lynch law"[118] the reasonable exercise by African Americans of the basic human rights that would challenge this orthodoxy. Lynching was the terroristic mechanism of this unjust dehumanization; it both polemically denied the exercise of intimate rights of association between black men and white women ("striking terror into

[114] See C. Vann Woodward, *Reunion and Reaction: The Compromise of 1877 and the End of Reconstruction* (New York: Oxford University Press, 1966).

[115] See Alfreda M. Duster, ed., *Crusade for Justice: The Autobiography of Ida B. Wells* (Chicago: University of Chicago Press, 1970), p. 69.

[116] *Id.*, p. 70.

[117] *Id.*

[118] *Id.*

the hearts of other Negroes who might be thinking of consorting with willing white women"[119]) and abridged the basic rights of conscience and speech by which such atrocities might be reasonably understood and protested by African Americans as atrocities (branding them "as moral monsters and despoilers of white womanhood and childhood," thus robbing African Americans of "the friends we had and silenc[ing] any protest"[120]). Like anti-Semitism, the irrationalist power of the ideology denied reality and imposed crude stereotypes of black sexuality as reality, remaking the consent of white women into rape and the consent of black men into rapist violence.

At the root of the racist ideology lay, as Wells came to see, Southern antimiscegenation laws, which

> only operate against the legitimate union of the races; they leave the white man free to seduce all the colored girls he can, but it is death to the colored man who yields to the force and advances of a similar attraction in white women. White men lynch the offending Afro-American, not because he is a despoiler of virtue, but because he succumbs to the smiles of white women.[121]

Wells's remarkable analysis probed, in a way never done before, the common roots of American racism and sexism. Many (including apologists for lynching) had observed before Wells "that the Southern people are now and always have been most sensitive concerning the honor of their women – their mothers, wives, sisters, and daughters."[122] But Wells gave this fact a new interpretation in terms of the place of an idealizing code of chivalry that dehumanized white women in a degrading idealization of their sexual virtue and black men and women in the mirror image degradation of their sexual vice. Wells insisted that her defense of the black victims of this code had no purpose "to say one word against the white women of the South."[123] "[I]t is their misfortune" to be treated not as persons but as tropes in a mythology of chivalry that in fact rationalized "barbarism."[124]

What makes Wells's analysis so important, for our purposes, is that it is directed against the patriarchal assumptions underlying not only the South's virulent racism but also the assumptions underlying the mainstream American racism (shared in the North and the South) implicit in the opinion of the Supreme Court in *Plessy* in 1896. Wells's analysis was directed at all Americans, black and white, women and men, who had accommodated themselves to the patriarchal terms of American racism, including suffrage feminists like Frances Willard

[119] *Id.*, p. 71.

[120] *Id.*

[121] See Wells-Barnett, *Southern Horrors: Lynch Law in All Its Phases*, pp. 14–45, at p. 19, in Trudier Harris, ed., *Selected Works of Ida B. Wells-Barnett* (New York: Oxford University Press, 1991).

[122] See Ida Wells-Barnett, *A Red Record: Tabulated Statistics and Alleged Causes of Lynchings in the United States, 1892-1893-1894* (1895), in Harris, *Selected Works of Ida B. Wells-Barnett*, 138–252, at pp. 146–7.

[123] *Id.*, p. 147.

[124] *Id.*

and others, whose struggle to secure the vote for women by ratification of the Nineteenth Amendment in 1920 led them to accommodate themselves to and sometimes endorse American racism. The victory of suffrage feminism in 1920 for this reason disappointed the political expectations of the suffrage feminists who had made such compromises of principle to secure it.[125] Only second-wave feminism, emerging in the 1960s, would expose for public discussion the issues that united black and white women.[126]

It is surely striking that the leading critics of American racism in the 1890s were a German Jewish immigrant (Franz Boas) and a black woman from the South who fled for safety to the North (Ida Wells-Barnett). Both these outsiders to American patriarchy find their moral voice in exposing to reasonable discussion and debate the racist assumptions, rooted in patriarchy, that Americans uncritically accepted and would not and could not question, as the Supreme Court's opinion in *Plessy* clearly shows. Both critics were ignored, and one of them (Ida Wells-Barnett), who found her voice in speaking from and about the sexual dehumanization of black women and men, was the target of patriarchal violence (her office in Mississippi was destroyed and her life threatened). In this period, the astonishing cultural astigmatism of Americans, who could not hear or listen to the most reasonable critics of our greatest evils, shows the power of American patriarchy in this period that, underlying both anti-Semitism and sexism as well as racism, could not hear or even attend to the voices of a Jewish man (not, for anti-Semites, a true man) or a black woman (for racists and sexists, a bad woman, all the worse for speaking in a sexual voice). Rather, the only voice that could be spoken with authority and heard was the patriarchally imagined voice that sustained the hierarchical authority of fathers over sons, daughters, and wives, speaking and hearing what sustained patriarchy in a hermetically sealed echo chamber.

Ida Wells-Barnett's work and life show, in particular, the importance of a free woman's sexual voice in resisting and destabilizing patriarchy, precisely because such a voice so bravely exposes the traumatic violence patriarchy imposes on intimate life. America could and would make no progress in coming to terms with its deeply entrenched racism and sexism until it would accord such antipatriarchal voices the authority they deserved. It was an important feature of the struggle of the National Association for the Advancement of Colored People (the NAACP) to secure the overruling of *Plessy* that the American conception of free speech be expanded to include protest of American racism,[127] and such protest undoubtedly had a profound impact on the overruling of *Plessy* by *Brown v. Board of Education* in 1954,[128] and on the Supreme Court's striking down of antimiscegenation laws in

[125] See, for fuller exploration of this point, Richards, *Women, Gays, and the Constitution*, at pp. 190–8.

[126] See, on this point, Richards, *Women, Gays, and the Constitution*, pp. 199–287.

[127] See Richards, *Women, Gays, and the Constitution*, pp. 208–24.

[128] See *Brown*, 347 U.S. 483 (1954).

1967.[129] Constitutional and legal developments after *Brown* were also facilitated by the further expansion of the American doctrine of free speech under the impact of the civil rights movement brilliantly led by Martin Luther King.[130] King certainly worked within the patriarchal assumptions dominant in the black churches, assumptions that the brilliant black, gay novelist, James Baldwin, exposed and criticized in his novel, *Go Tell It on the Mountain*.[131] But even Baldwin found something in King he never found in other black ministers,[132] a loving voice that spoke to Baldwin as it spoke to and empowered many black women, who played important roles in the civil rights movement. Later on, many of them would more deeply question the patriarchal assumptions in black culture and discover their voices, in relationship to white women and gay men, on the common antipatriarchal grounds that question racism, sexism, and homophobia.[133]

The impact of the resistance movements starting in the 1960s – the civil rights and antiwar movements, second-wave feminism, gay rights – was both to expand the constitutional conception of American free speech to include the voices of people of color, of women, and of gays and lesbians, and to move the contemporary constitutional interpretation of the Reconstruction Amendments, most notably, the Fourteenth Amendment, much closer to the views of the abolitionist feminists.[134] What is at the heart of this transformative development are the morally empowered voices of groups that reasonably challenged the repressive force of patriarchy, very much in the spirit of Ida Wells-Barnett. What made this challenge so fundamental and so compelling was that its voice included a free sexual voice that broke the repression and disassociation of sexual voice imposed by the love laws.

The civil rights movement began as a resistance movement against American racism, entrenched in American institutions through laws requiring racial segregation and condemning miscegenation that had been struck down only recently as unconstitutional by the Supreme Court of the United States.[135] Martin Luther King, the leader of this movement, spoke from a new voice in Christianity that challenged the role of Augustinian Christianity in the legitimation of religious persecution, including anti-Semitism, and soon directed his energies as well to an

[129] See *Loving*, 388 U.S. 1 (1967).

[130] See Harry Kalven Jr., *The Negro and the First Amendment* (Chicago: University of Chicago Press, 1965).

[131] See James Baldwin, *Go Tell It on the Mountain*, in *Early Novels and Stories*, ed. Toni Morrison (New York: Library of America, 1998), pp. 1–215. For commentary, see David A. J. Richards, *Disarming Manhood: Roots of Ethical Resistance* (Athens, Ohio: Swallow Press, 2005), pp. 138–42.

[132] See Richards, *Disarming Manhood*, p. 140.

[133] See Paula Giddings, *When and Where I Enter: The Impact of Black Women on Race and Sex in America* (New York: William Morrow, 1984).

[134] See, for defense of this view, Richards, *Women, Gays, and the Constitution*.

[135] See *Brown v. Board of Education*, 347 U.S. 483 (1954) (laws requiring racial segregation held unconstitutional); *Loving v. Virginia*, 386 U.S. 1 (1967) (antimiscegenation laws held unconstitutional).

antiwar movement, opposing the Vietnam War. King's insistence on nonviolent civil disobedience (a strategy he had learned from Gandhi) gave expression to free moral voice, rather than to violence, in resisting the violence of American racism, forging a conception of democratic manhood centered in voice, not violence, as a response to injustice. It is no accident that this antipatriarchal conception of manhood appealed to and empowered many women, black and white, who played important roles in the civil rights movement,[136] and their activism, on the grounds anticipated by the radical abolitionists, soon led to the emergence of rights-based feminist arguments (attacking laws criminalizing both contraception and abortion).[137]

Women in second-wave feminism challenged the traditional conception of patriarchal women as selfless, raising ethical questions about whether the imposition of the sacrifice of self on women deprived them of a responsible ethical voice, responsible for their relationships as a moral agent and as a free and democratic citizen with a voice.[138] Virginia Woolf, considering the psychological blocs she had encountered as a creative woman, wrote of

> the Angel in the House, I will describe her as shortly as I can. She was intensely sympathetic. She was immensely charming. She was utterly unselfish. She excelled in the difficult arts of family life. She sacrificed herself daily . . . in short she was so constituted that she never had a mind or a wish of her own, but preferred to sympathize always with the minds and wishes of others. Above all – I need not say it – she was pure. Her purity was supposed to be her chief beauty – her blushes, her great grace. . . . And when I came to write I encountered her with the very first words. The shadow of her wings fell on my page; I heard the rustling of her skirts in the room. Directly, that is to say, I took my pen in hand to review that novel by a famous man, she slipped behind me and whispered: "My dear, you are a young woman. You are writing about a book that has been written by a man. Be sympathetic; be tender; flatter; deceive; use all the arts of wiles of our sex. Never let anybody guess that you have a mind of your own. Above all, be pure." And she made as if to guide my pen. I now record the one act for which I take some credit to myself, though the credit rightly belongs to some excellent ancestors of mine who left me a certain sum of money . . . so that it was not necessary for me to depend solely on charm for my living. I turned upon her and caught her by the throat. I did my best to kill her. My excuse, if I were to be had up on a court of law, would be that I acted in self-defense. Had I not killed her she would have killed me.[139]

Woolf gives expression to the crippling effect on women's creative voices of patriarchally imposed images of self-sacrifice and sexual purity that effectively

[136] See, on all these points, Richards, *Disarming Manhood*, pp. 131–80.

[137] See, on this development, Sara Evans, *Personal Politics: The Roots of Women's Liberation in the Civil Rights Movement and the New Left* (New York: Vintage Books, 1980).

[138] See, on this point, Gilligan, *In a Different Voice*.

[139] Virginia Woolf, "Professions of Women," in *Women and Writing*, ed. Michele Barrett (Orlando, Fla.: Harvest Book, 1980), pp. 57–63, at p. 59.

cut women off, disassociated them, from their own minds and emotions. Women and men in the 1960s and later found their personal and ethical voices, as moral agents, similarly by individual and collective resistance to these images, finding and expressing their moral voices on issues of reproductive autonomy, among others.

Men in the antiwar movement, many of whom had served with distinction in Vietnam, refused continuing complicity with a violence that they had come to regard as unjust. Others found their voices in questioning a sense of manhood that had crushed their sense of conscience, leading them to serve in a war they had always regarded as unjust.[140] Still others, like James Carroll, found a voice in themselves not only to resist, as a priest, the Vietnam War but also to question the role their fathers had played in supporting that war, and, ultimately, to question their own vocation as priests.[141]

And men and women in the gay rights movement, which developed from the movement for women's liberation, questioned a conception of manhood and womanhood that warred on loving relationships between men and women of the same gender. Gay men, for example, in this situation found that resistance to the homophobic lies told about gay love was a necessary condition of experiencing love, of coming to trust themselves and others to live a life together in the truth of a loving relationship.[142] In so doing, such men come fundamentally to question patriarchy, which, imposing hierarchy not only between men and women but also between men and men, undermines the free and equal voice in relationship that breaks the taboo on seeing and speaking of one's love and lover, and thus makes love possible and sustaining.

These interconnected resistance movements – opposing, as they did, the injustice of racism, sexism, and homophobia – are grounded in a moral argument and psychology of resistance to the disassociation imposed by the patriarchal breaking of relationship. They arise from the protection of the loving relationships that the patriarchal love laws would disrupt. At the heart of it is speaking in a different voice,[143] one that, in resisting the traditional authority patriarchal voice has enjoyed in the politics, religion, and psychology of Western culture, speaks from the more embodied voice of our desires for sexual love and relationship. The increasingly important role of women's resistance in these movements is not surprising, nor is the role of men who find and strengthen their resisting voices through relationships to such women. It is what the Cupid and Psyche story would lead us to expect, as women's resistance to the patriarchal objectification and disassociation traditionally imposed on them makes possible new kinds of

[140] See, e.g., Tim O'Brien, *The Things They Carried* (New York: Broadway Books, 1990), pp. 39–61.

[141] See James Carroll, *An American Requiem: God, My Father, and the War That Came between Us* (Boston: Houghton Mifflin, 1996).

[142] See, on these points, David A. J. Richards, *The Case for Gay Rights: From Bowers to Lawrence and Beyond* (Lawrence: University Press of Kansas, 2005).

[143] See, on this point, Gilligan, *In a Different Voice*.

relationship, including new kinds of relationships between women and the men who love them.[144]

Such resistance to patriarchy – a resistance that has transformed American constitutional law – is historically quite remarkable on this scale and over such a broad front of interconnected movements (opposing anti-Semitism, racism, sexism, and homophobia). I believe it has not been fully honored or understood for what a democratic and democratizing movement it was or for its deeply ethical character. A fundamentalist reaction, to be discussed in Chapters 2 and 3, sought to denigrate its achievements, as patriarchal reaction always does, in terms of a libertine sexualization that ideologically transformed movements of genuine ethical struggle and achievement into sex, drugs, and rock 'n' roll.[145] These movements certainly called for liberalization of a range of criminal laws dealing with sexual and other matters, but they did so for ethical reasons critical of the injustice such laws patriarchally inflicted on women as well as men. Their ethical argument never was that women, for example, should have the same libertine sexual freedom men had under patriarchy, but that both men and women must be released from unjust constraints on sexual voice and life that destroyed loving relationship as a central sustaining value in a humane life.

Such resistance must always raise complex and sometimes difficult questions of identity and assimilation, classically raised by W. E. B. Du Bois. His historical studies challenged the dominant, often racist orthodoxy of the age.[146] And his 1903 *The Souls of Black Folk*[147] offered a pathbreaking interpretive study of African American culture and the struggle for self-consciousness under circumstances of racial oppression – "a world which yields him no true self-consciousness, but . . . this double-consciousness, this sense of always looking at one's self through the eyes of others, of measuring one's soul by the tape of a world that looks on in amused contempt and pity. One ever feels his two-ness, – an American, a Negro; two souls, two thoughts, two unreconciled strivings; two warring ideals in one dark body."[148] The struggle for justice was thus a struggle for self-respecting identity on terms of justice that would transform both:

> The history of the American Negro is the history of this strife, – this longing to attain self-conscious manhood, to merge his double self into a better and truer self. In this merging he wishes neither of the older selves to be lost. He would

144 See, on this point, Gilligan, *Birth of Pleasure*.

145 For a striking example of this ideological distortion, see the book review of David A. J. Richards's *Sex, Drugs, Death and the Law: An Essay on Human Rights and Overcriminalization* (Totowa, N.J.: Rowman & Littlefield, 1982) by Mark V. Tushnet, "Sex, Drugs and Rock 'n' Roll: Some Conservative Reflections on Liberal Jurisprudence," 82 *Columbia Law Review* 1531–43 (1982).

146 See W. E. B. DuBois, *The Suppression of the African Slave-Trade*, in *W. E. B. Du Bois*, ed. Nathan Higgins (1896; repr., New York: Library of America, 1986), pp. 3–356; DuBois, *Black Reconstruction in America, 1860–1880* (1935; repr., New York: Atheneum, 1969).

147 See W. E. B. DuBois, *The Souls of Black Folk*, in *W. E. B. DuBois*, ed. Nathan Higgins (1903; repr., New York: Library of America, 1986), pp. 359–546.

148 DuBois, *Souls of Black Folk*, pp. 364–5.

> not Africanize America, for America has too much to teach the world and Africa. He would not bleach his Negro soul in a flood of white Americanism, for he knows that Negro blood has a message for the world. He simply wishes to make it possible for a man to be both a Negro and an American, without being cursed and spit upon by his fellows, without having the door of Opportunity closed roughly in his face.[149]

I am struck by DuBois's statement of the problem as one of "self-conscious manhood," which raises an important question, namely whether resistance to injustice may not be compromised when it is grounded in assimilation to an ostensibly liberal political culture that is, in fact, compromised by its patriarchal institutions and assumptions. Whatever may have been the case with DuBois, Sigmund Freud's resistance to anti-Semitism, for example, may have been compromised by the way he assimilated to the dominant patriarchal assumptions of his place and period, leading him to the turn in his psychology that read patriarchy as nature, and thus compromised the psychology of resistance that was never more needed than in his place and period.[150]

The difficulties in resistance arise, I believe, from thinking that one can question one moral and political evil (e.g., anti-Semitism) without questioning any other, as Tolstoy, Gandhi, and King opposed the violence of racism without questioning the violence of their sexism.[151] The Gilligan-Richards thesis makes sense of these difficulties, which arise from the failure to see or appreciate the role that patriarchal voice plays in the stability of the various forms of irrational prejudice we have discussed. At the last, it is the problem of the uncritical persistence of patriarchal manhood even in men of the greatest goodwill.

4. THE REPRESSIVE PSYCHOLOGY OF PATRIARCHY UNDER THREAT

We can see this problem of uncritical persistence of patriarchal manhood quite clearly in the ways in which the psychology of patriarchy, particularly when under threat, responds repressively to such threat. The continuing power and appeal of patriarchy rests on its unjust repression of resisting voices, in particular, the voices of those groups (women and men) unjustly dehumanized by patriarchal values and practices. It is this repressive impulse that brings patriarchy into contradiction with democracy, whose legitimacy rests on equal respect for the free moral voices of all persons. The continuing power of patriarchy in American politics must, for this reason, be masked so that the contradiction is not seen, let alone resisted. My argument shows that patriarchy has existed alongside democracy for a very long time under American constitutionalism, and that the contradiction has been masked by the degree to which patriarchal values and practices naturalized

[149] *Id.*, p. 365.
[150] See, on this point, Gilligan and Richards, *Deepening Darkness*, chap. 7.
[151] See, on this point, Richards, *Disarming Manhood*.

injustices like anti-Semitism, racism, sexism, and homophobia as in the nature of things. It is the dynamic of this contradiction and its masking that explains how and why American constitutionalism has fallen so disastrously short of its democratic promises and demands, including those of the Constitution of 1787, the Bill of Rights of 1791, and the Reconstruction Amendments of 1865–70.

What makes the 1960s so important in this story is that the constitutional advances during this period and later – and they were advances – were made possible by the impact on our constitutional law and politics of a range of interconnected political movements for human rights that freed a moral voice that patriarchy had previously been allowed to repress, and thus exposed the contradiction for what it was. It was in this spirit that Martin Luther King led the civil rights movement to its stunning political successes (the Civil Rights Act of 1964 and the Voting Rights Act of 1965), and then played a prominent role as well in the resistance to the Vietnam War. What King saw was something President Lyndon Johnson tragically could not see, that the moral voice freed by the civil rights movement was the same voice that resisted the injustice of the Vietnam War. It was in this confused and confusing period that political liberals like Johnson, so important in the successes of the civil rights movement, were divided from allies like King. What King, the advocate of nonviolence, saw more deeply than Johnson did were the links between the patriarchal violence of both American racism and the unjust imperialistic violence of Vietnam, both rooted in a sense of patriarchal manhood under challenge. Both the civil rights and the antiwar movements, as well as the feminist and gay rights movements that grew out of them, certainly placed patriarchy under greater threat (by unmasking its contradiction with democracy) than it had ever been in American constitutional history.

Patriarchy was, however, so entrenched in American values and practices that, in a period of confusion and division among liberals, political conservatives both expressed and fomented the reactionary response of the patriarchal values and practices under real threat, which took the form of a resurgent political conservatism that sought to limit or reverse these developments. Confusion and division among liberals, of course, helped conservatives. The murder of King, followed by race riots, made possible a collective national amnesia of the brilliance and power of King's moral strategy of nonviolence. And President Johnson's tragic escalation and defense of the Vietnam War, leading to his withdrawal from politics, discredited his progressive economic politics (the War on Poverty).

What is politically and constitutionally of interest are the ways that politicians since the election of President Ronald Reagan have successfully harnessed these reactionary impulses to a conservative politics that has largely dominated American politics until quite recently. Reagan, with a background in film acting in Hollywood and a native good humor and geniality, put an attractive, smiling patriarchal face on American conservatism (in contrast to the more threatening and austere Barry Goldwater). Much of the support of this reactionary political conservatism initially came from the American South, which had borne the brunt of the successes of the civil rights movement and in which political racism remained a potent force in its politics, which was now increasingly dominated by the Republican Party. The great ethical achievements of the 1960s and later were ideologically distorted into sex, drugs, and rock 'n' roll.[152] Racial progress was marginalized as affirmative action was under attack, and the war on drugs largely targeted people of color. It was in this period that conservative politicians supported and used fundamentalism in both religion and law to achieve their reactionary ends, mobilizing around attacks on whatever advances the feminist and gay rights movements achieved. The Equal Rights Amendment was defeated, the AIDS health crisis was ignored for much too long, modest protections of gays from discrimination were reversed by referenda or by "don't ask, don't tell," and gay marriage was attacked at the state and federal levels (by "defense of marriage" acts) before it existed anywhere.[153] It was Reagan's 1980's brand of reactionary politics (reversing as well concern in the 1960s for poverty and economic inequality) that led to the rise in public debt and financial deregulation (leading to the rise in private debt) that prepared the way for the current economic crisis. The reactionary politics of this period rested on a disassociated psychology that warred not only on the rights of people of color, women, and gays and lesbians but on the poor as well, legitimating a second gilded age of nescient economic inequality and excess. We see now that its insular patriarchal psychology rested on economic improvidence as well, as conservative leaders "forgot the lessons of America's last great financial crisis, and condemned the rest of us to repeat it."[154]

My focus here is on the important role that fundamentalism in both religion and law have played in this reactionary politics, culminating in the presidency of George W. Bush, which aggressively defended patriarchal family values, led the nation into yet another unjust war (in Iraq), and prepared the way for our current economic crisis. I begin with the closer examination of originalism in constitutional law that aggressively entered American politics during the presidency of Ronald Reagan, whose attorney general, Ed Meese, defended this approach, leading to the appointment of Antonin Scalia to the Supreme Court and the abortive appointment of Robert Bork. I then turn to the pivotally important role that fundamentalist religion has played in aggressively supporting originalism in law, which is, I argue, as unreasonably fundamentalist in law as the fundamentalism in religion that drives and inspires it.

[152] See, on this point, Gilligan and Richards, *Deepening Darkness*, pp. 257–63.

[153] See, for fuller discussion, David A. J. Richards, *The Sodomy Cases: Bowers v. Hardwick and Lawrence v. Texas* (Lawrence: University Press of Kansas, 2009).

[154] Paul Krugman, "Reagan Did It," *New York Times*, June 1, 2009, at A21.

PART I

FUNDAMENTALISM IN LAW

CHAPTER 2

THE FUNDAMENTALISM OF CONSTITUTIONAL ORIGINALISM

John Rawls observed that "fundamentalist religious doctrines and autocratic and dictatorial rulers will reject the ideas of public reason and deliberative democracy."[1] Rawls was concerned specifically with religious fundamentalism. I understand such fundamentalism as relying on an appeal to the certainty of a specific understanding of authority, rooted in the past, a certainty that is to guide thought and conduct today irrespective of reasonable contemporary argument and experience to the contrary. It is the way fundamentalism ignores and even wars on such reasonable contemporary argument that gives rise to Rawls's objection to it as a basis for law under our secular constitutionalism. I earlier distinguished and later discuss further two kinds of such objectionable religious fundamentalism: those that are source based (Evangelical Protestantism and Mormonism) and those that are norm based (new natural law). We cannot, however, understand how and why such religious fundamentalisms have come to enjoy the illegitimate force they have had in recent American politics until we see them as the explanatory background of the ostensible appeal of yet another form of source-based fundamentalism in a different domain (law), namely originalism as an approach to American constitutional interpretation.

My argument in this chapter proceeds in two stages: first, an explication of what the objectionable form of originalism is; second, an internal and external criticism of its reasonableness. On this basis, I turn in the next chapter to a suggestion of its cultural and psychological roots, an argument that I develop more fully in the discussion of religious fundamentalism in Part II. Finally, Part III argues that religious fundamentalism is the basis of the appeal of legal fundamentalism and explains, on this ground, why legal originalism is an illegitimate approach to the interpretation of America's secular constitutionalism.

[1] John Rawls, *Collected Papers*, ed. Samuel Freeman (Cambridge, Mass.: Harvard University Press), at p. 613.

1. ORIGINALISM AS FUNDAMENTALISM

A source-based fundamentalism – the better-known variety of fundamentalism – is rooted in certain texts or in interpretations of such texts, ascribing to them an apodictic meaning and truth value that does not and cannot be squared with reasonable arguments available to and accessible to nonbelievers. Protestant fundamentalism is usually of this form, placing an interpretive weight on certain texts that is not open to other, often more reasonable interpretations, let alone to reasonable views of nonbelievers that do not regard such texts as authoritative.[2] Another form of source-based fundamentalism, not facially religious but still objectionable, is a specific form of historical originalism in American constitutional interpretation.

The U.S. Constitution, as amended, is the oldest continuous written constitution in the world, and plausible theories of how such an old text is and should be interpreted today must and do connect such contemporary interpretation to the history of the text broadly understood. There is a reasonable sense in which all such theories are originalist: they all claim to make the most reasonable interpretive sense of the relevant history of the text; and many of them do so in a way that plausibly connects the sense they make of history to contemporary reasonable argument and experience, showing, for example, how reasonable contemporary views of basic human rights advance a more coherent and principled understanding and elaboration of enduring constitutional values rooted in our history.[3] Nothing in my argument critically addresses these theories, one of which I have myself advocated and defended at length in light of relevant history.[4] My critical argument here does not engage such theories. To sharply define my own critical target, I hereinafter mark it by scare quotes as 'originalism' or 'originalist,' meaning the specific form of fundamentalist originalism that I discuss and criticize here.

'Originalism' in this sense calls for a specific form of semantic relationship between contemporary constitutional interpretation of a text and its history; namely contemporary interpretation must be governed by the specific things in the world that would, at the time of ratification of the constitutional text, have been pointed to or denoted by the text. Constitutional interpretation must, on this 'originalist' view, track founders' denotations: any interpretation outside these denotations is not acceptable. 'Originalist' argument in this sense repudiates any appeal to more abstract connotative meanings of the text that might, in light of

[2] See George M. Marsden, *Fundamentalism and American Culture: The Shaping of Twentieth Century Evangelicalism, 1870–1925* (New York: Oxford University Press, 1980).

[3] Thomas Colby and Peter Smith have shown that originalism means so many different things to so many different writers that it is not a single theory that one could be for or against. "Living Originalism," available at http://papers.ssrn.com/sol3/papers.cfm?abstract_id=1090282.

[4] See David A. J. Richards, *Toleration and the Constitution* (New York: Oxford University Press, 1986); Richards, *Foundations of American Constitutionalism* (New York: Oxford University Press, 1989).

relevant changed circumstances, reasonably be applied to different things in such changed circumstances. Only founders' denotations will do.

The only consistent 'originalist' in the United States has been Raoul Berger, who argued that no interpretation of a constitutional text can be correct that does not track the things in the world to which the text was or would have been applied by the founding generation that enacted the provision in question (whether the Constitutional Convention of 1787 and ratifying states, or the Congress and ratifying states for the Bill of Rights of 1791, or the Reconstruction Congress and ratifying states for the Reconstruction Amendments, including the Fourteenth Amendment of 1868).[5] Berger thus argued that most of the modern judiciary's interpretation of the Fourteenth Amendment, including striking down state-sponsored racial segregation as unconstitutional in *Brown v. Board of Education*,[6] was wrong, because the Reconstruction Congress, which enacted the Fourteenth Amendment, clearly regarded racial segregation as not violative of equal protection. A somewhat less consistent 'originalist' was Judge Robert Bork, abortively proposed by President Reagan for appointment to the U.S. Supreme Court, who accepted the current judicial understanding that racial classifications, including those underlying racial segregation, were forbidden but thought that it was wrong to extend constitutional interpretation any further; in particular, Judge Bork sharply objected to the principle of constitutional privacy in general, because, he argued, it did not correspond to any reasonably specific 'originalist' understanding.[7] Two current justices of the Supreme Court claim to be 'originalists,' Antonin Scalia[8] and Clarence Thomas.[9]

I regard 'originalism' as a source-based fundamentalism because it ascribes decisive normative weight not to the text of the Constitution (which could reasonably be interpreted connotatively) or to its interpretation over time but solely to a certain view of the authority of the founders, in particular, the ways in which the founders applied or would have applied the constitutional text in their enactment circumstances, what I have called founders' denotations. We can bring this objectionable source-based fundamentalism closer to the argument of this book by considering the form of it recently advocated by Hadley Arkes, who has supported many of the reactionary constitutional positions on matters of gender and

5 See Raoul Berger, *Government by Judiciary* (Cambridge, Mass.: Harvard University Press, 1977); Berger, *Death Penalties* (Cambridge, Mass.: Harvard University Press, 1982).

6 *Brown v. Board of Education*, 347 U.S. 483 (1954).

7 See Robert H. Bork, *Tradition and Morality in Constitutional Law* (Washington, D.C.: American Enterprise Institute, 1984); Bork, "Neutral Principles and Some First Amendment Problems," 47 *Ind. L.J.* 9 (1971).

8 See Antonin Scalia, *A Matter of Interpretation: Federal Courts and the Law* (Princeton, N.J.: Princeton University Press, 1997); Richard A. Brisbin Jr., *Justice Antonin Scalia and the Conservative Revival* (Baltimore: Johns Hopkins University Press, 1997).

9 See Scott Douglas Gerber, *First Principles: The Jurisprudence of Clarence Thomas* (New York: New York University Press, 1999).

sexuality of fundamentalist religious conservatives.[10] Arkes claims not to ground his position in religion at all but in an argument of historical 'originalism' that appeals to the place of natural rights in the constitutional thought of the founders, as well as in the constitutionally influential thought of Abraham Lincoln. Arkes is particularly exercised by what he argues is the illegitimacy of *Roe v. Wade*, because, in his view, the case appeals to a right to choose that is inconsistent with an 'originalist' understanding of natural rights.

The only plausible interpretation of Arkes's position is Bork's 'originalist' objection to the principle of constitutional privacy, namely that the founders of both the Bill of Rights and of the Reconstruction Amendments would not have accepted in their circumstances a right to constitutional privacy that encompassed contraception, abortion, and consensual gay or lesbian sex. But nor would they have accepted, we hasten to add, the Supreme Court's contemporary understanding of race and gender as highly suspect classifications (see Chapter 1). Arkes is, like Bork, not a consistent 'originalist'; his critical attention is, like Bork's, riveted not by the whole of contemporary constitutional interpretation but by selective bits of it, in particular, those parts that also absorb the other contemporary fundamentalists, particularly the cases that challenge patriarchal views of sexuality and gender.

2. THE UNREASONABLENESS OF 'ORIGINALISM': A CRITIQUE

There are a number of reasons for believing that 'originalism' is a deeply unreasonable theory of constitutional interpretation. I start with the reasons of internal incoherence and then turn to the substantive reasons it is unacceptable.

No approach to constitutional interpretation can be regarded as reasonable if its leading advocates never pursue its requirements consistently, and, with the exception of Raoul Berger, this is certainly the case with the leading proponents of 'originalism' who have come close to appointment to the Supreme Court (Bork) and in fact have been successfully appointed (Scalia and Thomas). There is a real question about whether the question of their 'originalism' was either clear or salient when Scalia and Thomas were appointed to the Court, but the issue was all too reasonably conspicuous at the time of Bork's abortive appointment and was one of the chief grounds on which the Senate rejected him.

One of the grounds for objecting to Bork's 'originalism' (as well as that of Scalia and Thomas) is, as we earlier saw, that Bork refused to follow his 'originalist' theory when it came to much of the jurisprudence of the Warren Court bearing on race, in particular, the decisions striking down the use of race by the state to segregate and to forbid the marriages of blacks and whites. The appeal of 'originalism' is supposedly that it fixes the meaning of constitutional language by reference to

[10] See Hadley Arkes, *Natural Rights and the Right to Choose* (Cambridge: Cambridge University Press, 2002).

historical inquiry into founders' denotations without reference to more vague criteria, like changed circumstances or changing moral consensus or political theory. But when it came to these important cases dealing with race, advocates of 'originalism' simply abandon their method. If their reason is simply the cynical one, that they know the 'originalist' condemnation of these cases would lead to their rejection by the Senate, then that raises questions of personal integrity, and their method – when publicly and deliberatively discussed for what it is – is rejected as deeply unreasonable, in part because it condemns pathbreaking decisions like those dealing with race that are regarded by Americans as among the most legitimate exercises of judicial review in American constitutional history. If 'originalism' cannot make sense of their legitimacy (and it clearly cannot), it must be rejected for the reasons that the Senate rejected Bork.

Once an advocate of 'originalism' departs from his theory, as Bork, Scalia, and Thomas do when it comes to race, the interpretive question that arises is why they depart from their theory here but not elsewhere. If, for example, they are willing to depart from founders' denotations when it comes to racism, why not also depart when it comes to sexism or homophobia? If there is no good reason to distinguish the cases (and there never is), we are left with a theory that rests on whim or prejudice or partisan politics, none of which is a reasonable basis for constitutional interpretation in any circumstances.

In fact, there is reason to doubt whether self-styled 'originalists' on the Court are actually making a conscientious effort to follow the denotations of the founders. Many scholars have pointed out that the 'originalists' are doing no such thing. Erwin Chemerinsky has thus noted the dubious 'originalist' credentials of Scalia's Second Amendment reasoning.[11] Ira C. Lupu argued, "Justice Scalia, the author of *Employment Division v. Smith*, 494 U.S. 872 (1990), claims to be an 'originalist.' *Smith* shows no signs, however, of any such orientation; the Court's opinion totally ignores both the text and history of the Free Exercise Clause."[12] Gene R. Nichol has argued that, in cases involving takings, free exercise, standing, and affirmative action, "Justice Scalia departs radically from his chosen theory when it suits his fancy."[13] And Eric J. Segall has noted that Justice Scalia's "votes to overturn flag burning laws, hate speech laws, and affirmative action programs cannot be reconciled with a strictly originalist approach to constitutional interpretation."[14] Examples of this sort show that judges like Scalia, much vaunted for his 'originalism,' are not honest 'originalists.'

[11] Erwin Chemerinsky, "It's Still the Kennedy Court," 11 *Green Bag* 2d 427, 429–31 (2008).

[12] Ira C. Lupu, "*Employment Division v. Smith* and the Decline of Supreme-Court Centrism," 1993 *B.Y.U. L. Rev.* 259, 260 (1993).

[13] Gene R. Nichol, "Justice Scalia and the *Printz* Case: The Trials of an Occasional Originalist," 70 *U. Colo. L. Rev.* 953, 969–71 (1999).

[14] Eric J. Segall, "A Century Lost: The End of the Originalism Debate," 15 *Const. Comment.* 411, 427–8 (1998).

Suppose I say that I'm going to enslave my will to that of Oprah Winfrey and do everything she says. Then I proceed to do exactly as I like, and cite Winfrey only where her dictates happen to coincide with what I feel like doing anyway. Now suppose that you find things in my actions to criticize. When you criticize me, you are not criticizing the procedure of obeying Winfrey, because I have not been following that procedure. Bringing up Winfrey in your criticism of my action only confuses matters.[15]

'Originalists' do not help themselves when, like Antonin Scalia, they appeal to precedent. When Scalia was confronted by the fact that the current scope of judicial protection of free speech in the United States (which Scalia defends) cannot be reasonably squared with founders' denotations,[16] he responded by appeal to "the doctrine of *stare decisis*," claiming that his expansive views of free speech protection were completely different from the Supreme Court's "novel" recognition of rights of homosexuals and women.[17] But Scalia's interpretation of the weight of precedent is neither 'originalist' nor reasonable. The Supreme Court cases extending stronger constitutional protection to women themselves are precedents, appealing to reasonable analogies between racism and sexism, and the Court's recognition of the evil of populist homophobia rests not only on compelling analogies to irrationalist prejudices like racism and sexism but also to sectarian religious prejudice, the longest condemned prejudice in American constitutional history. Scalia, when it comes to gender and sexual orientation, is always intemperate, which suggests not reason but prejudice (more on this later). This is what we get when judges claim to hold to a theory (i.e., 'originalism') that they do not in fact hold.

'Originalism' puts controlling weight in constitutional interpretation on a historical inquiry into founders' denotations, claiming that such denotations have a clarity that controls judicial interpretive discretion in a way no other approach does. But history must itself be interpreted, and the kind of certainty that 'originalism' ascribes to history bespeaks conservative ideology, not critical historiography, including interest in the normative history of ideas that enables us to make interpretive sense of a history as laden with political philosophy and political science as America's Madisonian constitutionalism. 'Originalists,' for all the weight they place on history, have little or no interest in critical history, as Scalia's views on free speech display rather conspicuously.

Certainly, nothing in the text of the American Constitution requires 'originalism' as its interpretive approach. The founders knew perfectly well how to bind constitutional interpretation to denotative exemplars, and clearly made a decision not to do so, preferring precisely the more abstract language that the

15 I am grateful to Andrew Koppelman for the example and putting it this way.

16 See, for arguments along these lines by Laurence Tribe and Ronald Dworkin, Antonin Scalia, *A Matter of Interpretation*, pp. 79–82 (Tribe), pp. 123–5 (Dworkin).

17 Scalia, *Matter of Interpretation*, p. 139.

U.S. Constitution displays. The choice of such language supports, if anything, a connotative approach to interpretation.

And, as Scalia's appeal to stare decisis shows, little or nothing in American constitutional interpretation over time – political or judicial – can be squared with 'originalism.' 'Originalism,' like the source-based roots of fundamentalist Protestantism, appeals to the founding (or, in Protestantism, the Gospels) as supreme authority over the interpretive traditions that may, as Protestantism believed of Roman Catholicism, have been corrupted by an irreligious union of church and state foreign to the Christian Gospels. 'Originalists,' like Bork, Scalia, and Thomas, modify their stance in light of stare decisis, which shows, unlike Protestant fundamentalism, that they believe that interpretive traditions matter. But which ones, and why? Nothing in 'originalism' can answer these questions, which suggest, once again, either conservative ideology or worse, prejudice. Neither can be a reasonable basis for legitimate constitutional interpretation in the United States.

What makes this approach so unreasonable, as I have argued elsewhere,[18] is not only that it fails to fit with the text and interpretive traditions over time of authoritative institutions like the Supreme Court and others but also that it corresponds to no defensible political theory of the values of constitutionalism and certainly not to the view taken of their authority to leading founders like James Madison.[19] Put simply, 'originalism' ascribes to leading founders, like Madison, an authority that they clearly believed they lacked. Madison, a political liberal in the tradition of the revolutionary constitutionalism of John Locke, clearly rejected any conception of his authority as a founder as having a patriarchal authority like that defended by Robert Filmer, against whom Locke wrote his *Two Treatises of Government*.[20] Locke had claimed "that *a Child is born a Subject of no Country or Government*...; nor is he bound up, by any Compact of his Ancestors."[21] Locke had made the argument against Filmer's patriarchal historicism, that is, the claim that political legitimacy had to be traced lineally to the authority of the original father of the human race. Locke, in contrast, argued that no such past figure could have a legitimate claim on his or her ancestors, because the normative basis of political legitimacy was not history but respect for the inalienable human rights that protected the spheres of reasonable self-government of free people. What made 'originalism' so unacceptable to Madison is that it would have ascribed to him a patriarchal authority that it was the aim of liberal

[18] See Richards, *Foundations of American Constitutionalism*.

[19] See, on this point, *id.*, pp. 102–5, 131–71.

[20] See *id.*, pp. 134–6.

[21] John Locke, "The Second Treatise of Government," in *Two Treatises of Government*, ed. Peter Laslett (Cambridge: Cambridge University Press, 1960), p. 365 (sec. 118). For illuminating commentary on Locke's opposition to Filmer's historicism, see Richard Ashcraft, *Locke's Two Treatises of Government* (London: Allen & Unwin, 1987), pp. 60–79.

constitutionalism forever to repudiate. The better way to square the authority of a written constitution with this view of the founders' authority is to allow later interpretive generations, including the Supreme Court, reasonably to recontextualize the abstract connotations of constitutional guarantees of human rights in contemporary circumstances.[22] The muscular contemporary American principle of free speech, which Scalia is anxious to defend, can be understood most reasonably in this way. But, the same perspective supports what Scalia, incoherently, does not, the constitutional right to privacy as a wholly legitimate principle of constitutional law in the United States, judged from the perspective of a contemporary constitutional culture now fairly responsive to the voices of women and of gays and lesbians, who reasonably find that constitutional principles of law (protecting the human right to intimate life as a basic right) apply to them in contemporary circumstances.[23]

There was certainly a time in the United States when judicial review was a highly controversial and controverted principle of our constitutional institutions, and one of the grounds of such skepticism was Thomas Jefferson's court-based skepticism that a preeminent role for the judiciary in the enforcement of human rights would compromise and even enervate the protection of human rights through democratic processes. Jefferson and Madison, for example, constitutionally opposed the Alien and Sedition Acts of 1798, because, in their view, the acts unconstitutionally abridged the right of free speech protected against Congress by the First Amendment of the Bill of Rights. It is doubtful that the judiciary of the period, then dominated by members of the Federalist Party of John Adams that had proposed and passed the acts, would have struck down the last as unconstitutional. Jefferson and Madison, in any event, took their case to the people in the presidential election of 1800, which Jefferson won in part on the ground that the American people shared his view that the acts were unconstitutional under the First Amendment. From Jefferson's point of view, this is the way to enforce human rights, namely by making one's case to the American people in democratic elections and winning, not by depending on the judiciary to do what should be the work of democratic politics under a republican form of government.

Jefferson's argument, like the form of it later made by James Thayer,[24] was not skeptical, as was Jeremy Bentham, about the existence of human rights. Jefferson had authored the Declaration of Independence that crucially appealed to egregious violations of inalienable human rights in the spirit of John Locke, as grounds for the right to revolution, and had argued in *Notes from Virginia* that slavery was politically illegitimate and must be abolished because it abridged

[22] See, on this point, Richards, *Foundations of American Constitutionalism*, pp. 131–71.

[23] See, on this point, *id.*, pp. 202–47.

[24] See James B. Thayer, "The Origin and Scope of the American Doctrine of Constitutional Law," 7 *Harv. L. Rev.* 129 (1893).

basic human rights. Jefferson clearly believed that respect for human rights was a necessary condition for the legitimacy of any government, and he believed democracy was to be preferred because human rights would be better protected through democratic elections than under other forms of government. Jefferson was skeptical about judicial review in part because the experience of the election of 1800 showed that democracy could protect basic rights better than the judiciary could. Accordingly, excessive dependence on the judiciary to protect human rights would compromise this function of democracy and might, in fact, result in less protection of human rights than otherwise.

Certainly, American constitutional experience before the Civil War might support Jefferson's court skepticism. The only two decisions of the Supreme Court during this period that held laws of Congress unconstitutional were *Marbury v. Madison* and *Dred Scott v. Sanford*, the latter of which constitutionally protected slavery in the territories and convinced abolitionists like Abraham Lincoln to return to democratic politics to rectify its violation of basic human rights through politics and, when politics failed, through the use of armed force that would end slavery forever in the United States through the Thirteenth Amendment of the Reconstruction Amendments.

But after the experience of judicial review in the twentieth century under the Reconstruction Amendments, Jefferson's court skepticism is much less plausible or appealing than it may have been earlier. It was not democracy that enabled America to confront and rectify its unconstitutional cultural racism, because democratic institutions failed to give just expression to the constitutional grievances of African Americans. African Americans were a political minority whose constitutionally guaranteed voting rights had been nullified through a populist racism in the American South, and even if democratic politics had been more fairly open and responsive to them (which it was not), American cultural racism was so pervasive that democratic majorities ignored African American grievances for a long period. What made some reasonable progress on these issues possible was the increasingly important role that the American judiciary played as a forum of principle that, precisely because it was not a democratic institution, was responsive not to voting blocs but to arguments of principle, demanding that constitutionally guaranteed basic human rights be extended to all Americans on terms of principle.

What such experience shows is that, properly understood, judicial review brought something to American politics that democratic politics could not and would not, namely an institution open to listening to and deciding on the basis of the deliberative arguments of small minorities that basic human rights, guaranteed to all Americans, be extended to them on grounds of principle. If the very legitimacy of democracy depended on the degree to which it protected human rights, the judiciary, properly understood, performed an invaluable role in better securing basic human rights than democracy alone could or would.

'Originalists' like Bork, Scalia, and Thomas clearly accept this conception of judicial review, as their support of the Supreme Court's work in the race cases shows. But their conception of the constitutional rights, worthy of protection by the judiciary, is limited to those that satisfy 'originalism.' But there is, of course, an alternative, much more plausible theory of interpretation, one that ascribes to the often quite abstract constitutional text not founders' denotations but a more abstract connotation that can be reasonably contextualized in terms of contemporary circumstances, including our cumulative experience as a free people about the meaning of basic human rights. At this point, the only justification for 'originalism' could be, in the spirit of Jefferson, an appeal to democracy as the best way to realize the protection of human rights outside the narrow confines of the 'originalist' understanding. But, of course, this argument from democracy would delegitimate the opinions of the Supreme Court in race cases that depart from the 'originalist' understanding, which are precisely the opinions the 'originalists' want, incoherently, to accept. And if they accept these, why do they not accept others that can be similarly justified in terms of ascribing to the constitutional context more abstract connotations?

There is no good justification – in history or text or precedent or political theory – for the refusal of the 'originalists' to protect rights beyond the 'originalist' understanding. There is, however, an explanation. 'Originalism' is an objectionable, source-based fundamentalism in a contemporary constitutional democracy because it appeals to a kind of patriarchal authority that is inconsistent with the political theory of Lockean liberalism, which is the key theory of the U.S. Constitution.[25] The 'originalism,' based on the founders' denotations, ascribes an authority to the founders that both they and political theory repudiate, precisely because it is insensitive to contemporary values of reason and deliberation. Hadley Arkes's claim that a constitutionally protected right to abortion is an abuse of the founders' conception of natural rights shows little understanding of the Lockean political theory of American constitutionalism and even less of the role of the judiciary in protecting basic constitutional principles of inalienable rights in light of the best reasonable contemporary understanding of what those rights are. What Arkes's argument comes to is ascribing to 'originalist' historical understanding a patriarchal weight that it cannot have, consistent with Lockean guarantees of basic human rights. This argument does justice neither to natural rights nor to American constitutionalism. Indeed, such a theory would be regarded, using Rawls's theory, as falling outside the remit of public reason.

I argue that all these forms of fundamentalism – whether in religion or in constitutional interpretation – are unreasonable, certainly unworthy of enforcement through public law in a constitutional democracy based on the separation of church and state (see Part III). What strikes me, however, is the focus of these

[25] For fuller defenses of this position, see Richards, *Toleration and the Constitution* (New York: Oxford University Press, 1986); Richards, *Foundations of American Constitutionalism*.

forms of fundamentalism in discrediting many of the constitutional advances in the United States that took place under the impact of the various resistance movements already discussed (Chapter 1), in particular, those advances dealing with matters of sexuality and gender (abortion and gay rights, including gay marriage). The analysis in the following chapter further examines this striking phenomenon.

CHAPTER 3

THE MOTIVATIONS OF CONSTITUTIONAL FUNDAMENTALISM

It is not good interpretive argument that leads to 'originalism,' for the 'originalists' offer no such argument. What moves both them and the audience attracted to their views is an imaginative transformation of America's Lockean Constitution, which justifies political power in terms of each generation's conception of respect for human rights, into what Locke regarded as the enemy of liberal thought and practice, namely Robert Filmer's patriarchalism. The entire project of liberal constitutionalism, as Locke argued for it, was set by his refutation of Filmer's patriarchal defense of absolute monarchy, as deriving from the patriarchal authority of Adam established by God and then passed down by legitimate succession. Locke's alternative conception is that all persons have inalienable human rights, the right to conscience prominent among them, and that the legitimacy of government is to be judged in terms of which constitutional institutions best protect human rights. His argument for the exercise of the right to revolution against the Stuart conception of absolute monarchy is that such absolutism resulted in the abridgment of basic human rights, including the right to conscience, and that the monarchy was therefore justifiably overthrown to establish alternative institutions, including a constitutionally limited monarch and a democratically elected House of Commons, which would better secure respect for human rights.

What moves the 'originalists' is a view of the authority of the founders that is a travesty of everything liberal constitutionalism was meant to establish. What moves them is the imagination that moves patriarchal men and women, the need to create the hierarchical authority of a patriarchal father over all others, as the model for authority. It is, as we shall see, a crucial feature of this culture and psychology that it repressively targets the voices of the women and men who would most reasonably raise doubts about its claims. We can see this feature clearly illustrated not only by the rejection by 'originalists' of the constitutional claims made by these groups but also by the overwrought, even violently contemptuous, ways that they rationalize their rejection. No 'originalist' better illustrates this point than Justice Scalia.

When Scalia is confronted by the historian Gordon Wood's worry that Scalia's 'originalist' appeal to the text might be "as permissive and as open to arbitrary judicial discretion as the use of legislative intent or other interpretative methods, if the text-minded judge is so inclined,"[1] he does not confront the way his own appeal to stare decisis manipulatively illustrates Wood's point. Rather, he evades self-criticism or the invitation to reasonable doubt about his views by going on the attack: "No textualist-originalist interpretation that passes the laugh test could, for example extract from the United States Constitution . . . the prohibition of abortion laws that a majority of the Court has found."[2] "The laugh test" is derisory. But if the precedents on this issue became stare decisis, Scalia would embrace the result, just as he has the current Court's expansive protection of free speech. Why so serious about speech but so derisory about abortion? It isn't usual for justices of the Supreme Court to deride claimants of constitutional rights, but Scalia too easily falls into this mode when it comes to arguments that express a woman's or man's free voice about pursuing sexual interests independent of patriarchy. Why?

Consider along these lines four such dissenting opinions of Justice Scalia: one dealing with the right to abortion, another with the unconstitutionality of state-supported all-male schools, a third with a claim of discrimination on grounds of sexual orientation, and a fourth with the expansion of the constitutional right to privacy to protect gay and lesbian sexuality.

In *Planned Parenthood of Southeastern Pennsylvania v. Casey*,[3] the Supreme Court faced the question of whether *Roe v. Wade*,[4] which extended the constitutional right to privacy to abortion services, should be overruled. Although three justices in the majority (Justices O'Connor, Kennedy, and Souter) had been appointed by presidents publicly hostile to *Roe*, the three refused, in an opinion joined by Justices Blackmun and Stevens, to overrule *Roe*. The crucial opinion on this point of the three justices defended the legitimacy of the inference of the constitutional right to privacy and indeed its application in *Griswold v. Connecticut*[5] to the purchase and use of contraceptives. Because the justices accepted constitutional privacy as a wholly legitimate principle of constitutional law, they also regarded the right to an abortion as resting on this right, an aspect of the right to form intimate relationships that was already protected in *Griswold*. The question for these justices about *Roe* is not whether it implicated a basic constitutional right (it clearly did) but whether the Court in *Roe* correctly identified the point (i.e., the viability of the fetus) after which the state had a compelling secular interest in forbidding abortions. On this point, the justices said that, if

[1] Quoted in Antonin Scalia, *A Matter of Interpretation: Federal Courts and the Law* (Princeton, N.J.: Princeton University Press, 1997), p. 132.

[2] *Id.*

[3] *Planned Parenthood of Southeastern Pennsylvania v. Casey*, 505 U.S. 833 (1992).

[4] *Roe v. Wade*, 410 U.S. 113 (1973).

[5] *Griswold v. Connecticut*, 381 U.S. 479 (1965).

they were deciding this issue as an original matter, they might have drawn the line differently, perhaps earlier. But because they believed some such line did constitutionally exist and that considerations of stare decisis supported deference to the line drawn in *Roe*, they reaffirmed the central principle of *Roe* (i.e., no criminalization until viability), although later in the opinion they allowed for more regulation of abortion than the *Roe* Court accepted or would have accepted.

Four justices dissented to upholding the essential principle of *Roe*, Chief Justice Rehnquist and Justices White, Scalia, and Thomas. In his dissent (joined by the other three dissenters), Scalia is characteristically certain: "I am sure it [a woman's right to an abortion] is not [constitutionally protected],"[6] as if the Constitution ordered this result "because of two simple facts: (1) the Constitution says absolutely nothing about it, and (2) the long-standing traditions of American society have permitted it to be legally proscribed."[7] What makes this all so simple and so certain, for Scalia, is that he reads the Constitution through the prism of his deeply patriarchal culture and psychology, which ignores not only the text that very much speaks to the existence and enforcement of such rights (the Ninth Amendment of the Bill of Rights and the privileges and immunities clause of the Fourteenth Amendment) but also the long American historical traditions that have identified the right to intimate life as among our most basic human and constitutional rights. Scalia, the textualist, is not, however, really interested in text; and Scalia, the 'originalist,' is even less interested in history or tradition, because his patriarchal psychology convinces him with certainty that nothing like the basic right protected by constitutional privacy could or should exist, precisely because it is a basic right that here expresses a free woman's sexual voice and conscience. As a patriarchal schoolmaster, Scalia "must . . . respond to a few of the more outrageous arguments in today's opinion, which it is beyond human nature to leave unanswered."[8] Reading human nature as patriarchy, Scalia's repressive anger pours out vitriolically, in particular, on the appeal of the plurality opinion of three justices to allegedly reasonable interpretive arguments of principle, with notable contempt directed at alleged shifts in the interpretive judgments of one of the women then on the Supreme Court, Sandra Day O'Connor.[9] The rhetorically overwrought features of the dissent rise to a crescendo as it nears its end. The plurality opinion's portrait of *Roe*, as "a jurisprudential Peace of Westphalia that is worth preserving, is nothing less than Orwellian,"[10] resting on "this Nietzschean vision of us unelected, life-tenured judges,"[11] an abuse of power comparable to Roger Taney's *Dred Scott*.[12]

[6] *Casey*, 505 U.S. at 980.
[7] *Id.*
[8] *Casey*, 505 U.S. at 981.
[9] See *id.* at 988–90.
[10] *Id.* at 995.
[11] *Id.* at 996.
[12] *Id.* at 1001–2.

This tangle of rhetoric shows how far removed Scalia is from a reasonable understanding of the case before the Court. The Peace of Westphalia was the political settlement of wars of sectarian religion, whereas the constitutional right to privacy reasonably protects a basic human right of intimate life from the unjust burdens of sectarian religion. Nietzsche warred not only on Christianity but also on the idea of basic human rights, in particular despising the idea of the rights of women; *Roe* and *Casey* rest on recognition and enforcement of the right of women to intimate life. *Dred Scott* entrenched slavery, a violation of human rights, in the territories; *Roe* and *Casey* extended basic rights to women on fair terms. The fact that Scalia cannot make elementary reasonable distinctions suggests a patriarchal rage that expresses patriarchal norms and values as moral certainties in a war on the voices of those who express reasonable doubts about such norms and values, seeing them as at odds with the norms and values of democracy.

The patriarchal character of this psychology is particularly well exemplified in Justice Scalia's long dissent in *United States v. Virginia*,[13] in which the Supreme Court, 7–1 (Justice Thomas did not participate in the case), struck down as an unconstitutional violation of the equal protection clause of the Fourteenth Amendment the exclusion of women from the Virginia Military Institute (VMI), the only single-sex school among Virginia's public institutions of higher learning. The school's exclusion of women was based on its purposes (the production of citizen-soldiers for leadership in civilian and military life) and its highly demanding, adversarial mode of education based on that of English public schools. Justice Ginsburg, writing for the Court, examined VMI's justifications for single-sex admissions and found them to rest not on acceptable compensatory purposes but on once-traditional views of women's proper place that, themselves reflecting patterns of discrimination, could not be a reasonable measure of opportunity today. In reaching this assessment, Justice Ginsburg noted the parallel historical uses of arguments, like those of VMI, to rationalize the exclusion of women from higher education and from the practice of law, from law and medical schools, and from policing. In all these cases, women's categorical exclusion, in total disregard of their individual merit, failed to do justice to women as "as citizens in our American democracy equal in stature to men."[14] The inclusion of women at VMI was called for on the same grounds that, in *Sweatt v. Painter*,[15] blacks were admitted to the University of Texas Law School: only integration into common public educational institutions can do justice to the equal rights of women as persons.[16]

What Justice Scalia offers, in dissent to Justice Ginsburg's nuanced, normative argument about how now discredited injustices should bear on VMI, is an appeal to "those constant and unbroken national traditions that embody the people's

[13] *United States v. Virginia*, 518 U.S. 515 (1996).
[14] *Id.* at 545.
[15] *Sweatt v. Painter*, 339 U.S. 629 (1950).
[16] 518 U.S. at 557–8.

understanding of ambiguous constitutional texts."[17] Of course, such traditions include American cultural racism and sexism, but Scalia, who abandons 'originalism' when it comes to race, holds to it tenaciously when it comes to gender, presumably because, read through the prism of his patriarchal psychology, patriarchy is not only traditional but also in the nature of things. Nothing better illustrates this psychology than the conclusion of Scalia's dissent, namely, his paean to "VMI's attachment to such old-fashioned concepts as manly 'honor,'"[18] which includes quotations to the "Code of a Gentleman," a booklet all first-year VMI students were required to keep in their possession at all times. What is striking about the code is how much its terms are gender defined:

> A Gentleman . . .
>
> Does not speak more than casually about his girl friend.
>
> Does not go to a lady's house if he is affected by alcohol. He is temperate in the use of alcohol.
>
> Does not hail a lady from a club window.
>
> A gentleman never discusses the merits or demerits of a lady.[19]

The conception of women on which such honor codes depend expresses and enforces rigid gender stereotypes, resting on the repression of women's voices, which cut men off from real relationships with women. Such loss expresses itself in idealization of the good women who comply with such stereotypes (including their temperance and asexuality) and the corresponding denigration of the bad women who transgress such stereotypes. Justice Scalia, himself a deeply patriarchal man, understandably idealizes what such an honor code idealizes and leaves unspoken and unrecognized, as patriarchal men do, the injustice it inflicts on women. It is revealing that a gentleman's relationship to women is largely defined by what he may not say, which shows how much patriarchy depends not only on the repression of women's voices but on the silencing in men of voice as well, in particular, a voice that might be in some equal relationship to the voice of a real woman. Scalia is certainly authentic in speaking so personally of his own investment in such honor codes and the way single-sex education perpetuates them. Both his dismissal of the opinions of the majority and his obliviousness to the dark side of patriarchal institutions bespeaks precisely the patriarchal psychology that, I believe, motivates so clearly Scalia's 'originalism.'

In the Supreme Court's two most important recent opinions recognizing the constitutional rights of gay and lesbian persons, Justice Scalia again authored dissents whose terms further clarify how the culture and psychology operates in

[17] *Virginia*, 518 U.S. at 568.
[18] *Virginia*, 518 U.S. at 601.
[19] Quoted in *Virginia*, 518 U.S. at 602.

the modern world, imaginatively transforming claims of basic rights into aggressive acts. These homophobic transformations are, I argue, analogous to the role anti-Semitism played under Augustinian Christianity, the orthodoxy underlying Catholic new natural law, and Protestant fundamentalism.

In *Romer v. Evans*,[20] the Supreme Court held, 6–3, that Colorado Amendment 2, which prohibited all laws designed to protect gays and lesbians from discrimination, was "so discontinuous with the reasons offered for it that the amendment seems inexplicable by anything but animus toward the class it affects; it lacks a rational basis to legitimate state interests."[21] In reaching this result, the Court emphasized that the protections, withheld by Colorado Amendment 2, "are protections taken for granted by most people because they already have them or do not need them; these are protections against exclusion from an almost limitless number of transactions and endeavors that constitute ordinary civic life in a free society."[22] Withholding such protections from a class of citizens cannot be constitutionally based on mere "animosity toward the class of persons affected."[23] Colorado Amendment 2 is, however, such "a status-based enactment divorced from any factual content from which we could discern a relationship to legitimate state interests."[24] The Court concluded "that Amendment 2 classifies homosexuals not to further a proper legislative end but to make them unequal to every else. This Colorado cannot do. A State cannot so deem a class of persons a stranger to its laws."[25] The ending of the opinion clarifies its opening citation to the words of the great dissent of the first Justice Harlan to the Supreme Court's legitimation of race-based segregation in *Plessy v. Ferguson*: the Constitution "neither knows nor tolerates classes among citizens."[26] The wrongness of racial segregation was forging the subhuman, inferior status of persons of color when there was no rational basis for such a distinction in the same way that Colorado Amendment 2 was marking off homosexuals as subhuman and inferior on no rational basis. The Court, Justice Kennedy argues, cannot constitutionally be complicitous in this way with forging and sustaining irrational prejudice.

The application of the rational-basis test in *Romer* is reminiscent of the first case in which the Supreme Court announced its skepticism about gender classifications, namely, *Reed v. Reed*.[27] The application of the rational-basis standard with the consequence of invalidating such laws was in doctrinal tension with the many cases in which comparable laws with equally overinclusive and underinclusive legislative classifications had been upheld. *Reed* suggested what later cases made clear, that the Court had interpretively come to the view that some heightened

[20] *Romer v. Evans*, 517 U.S. 620 (1996).
[21] *Id.* at 632.
[22] *Id.* at 631.
[23] *Id.* at 634.
[24] *Id.* at 635.
[25] *Id.*
[26] *Plessy v. Ferguson*, 163 U.S. 537, 559 (1896) (Harlan, J., dissenting).
[27] See *Reed v. Reed*, 404 U.S. 71 (1971).

level of constitutional scrutiny was owed gender classifications. The Supreme Court in *Romer* could have obviated this problem by adopting the standard that had been proposed by several law professors in a brief, as amici curiae, namely that any classifications (even a clearly nonsuspect one like renting one's home) would be per se invalid as the basis for a constitutional provision forbidding any local or state legislation that protects renters from any harm or loss.[28] The standard would have invalidated Colorado Amendment 2 but not a more narrowly drawn constitutional provision that forbade a single form of antidiscrimination statute – for example, local rent-control statutes or laws banning discrimination against homosexuals in hiring. Justice Kennedy wrote more broadly casting doubt on amendments of both sorts as long as they used the classification in question in the forbidden way. Accordingly, the same doctrinal criticism may be made of *Romer* that was earlier made of *Reed v. Reed*: why was heightened scrutiny owed this as opposed to other classifications?

If the decision is doctrinally problematic as a rational-basis decision, we need to ask how it might better be understood, particularly what the analogies might be that made this state law, in the words of Justice Scalia's bitter dissent, "as reprehensible as racial or religious bias."[29] Justice Scalia is correct on one point, namely the opinion suggests more such analogies than it expressly acknowledges. One such suggestion is implicit in a rather brilliant argument in Justice Kennedy's opinion, discussing earlier cases dealing with the Mormons. These cases were of two sorts: those that constitutionally allowed laws that banned Mormon polygamy, although polygamy was then rooted in the right of religious liberty,[30] and those that allowed Mormons to be deprived of the right to vote.[31] Justice Kennedy does not question the authority of the case upholding a ban on polygamy (presumably, on the ground that banning a practice, rooted in a basic right like religious liberty, is justified if a compelling state interest – such as gender equality – reasonably supports the ban; see, on this point, Chapter 6); but the latter case, he argues, is no longer good law because it rests on the now constitutionally unacceptable view "that persons advocating a certain practice may be denied the right to vote."[32] Just because a religious practice can be constitutionally banned, it does not follow that advocacy of such a practice can be a ground for depriving the advocates of a basic right like voting. The analogy to gays and lesbian is evident: gays and

[28] Professor Laurence Tribe of Harvard Law School was counsel of record, and he was joined by Professors John Hart Elly, Gerald Gunther, and Kathleen Sullivan of Stanford Law School, and by the late Philip B. Kurland of University of Chicago Law School. For illuminating discussion, see Ronald Dworkin, "Sex, Drugs, and the Court," *New York Review of Books*, Aug. 8, 1996, at 49–50.

[29] See *Romer*, 517 U.S. at 636.

[30] *Reynolds v. United States*, 98 U.S. 145 (1878) (upholding application of a federal law making bigamy a crime in the territories to a Mormon claiming that polygamy was his religious duty).

[31] *Davis v. Beason*, 133 U.S. 333 (1890).

[32] *Romer v. Evans*, 517 U.S. 620, 634 (1996).

lesbians now publicly claim their basic rights on fair terms with other Americans. It may be that conduct rooted in their conscientious exercise of their right to intimate life may be banned because a compelling state purpose supports such a ban (*Bowers v. Hardwick* was still ostensibly good law at the time *Romer* was decided, though later overruled by *Lawrence v. Texas*; see Chapter 1); but it does not follow that their public claims and lives as gays and lesbians may, for that reason, be the subject of discrimination.

What Kennedy's argument suggests is that the one ground for finding the use of sexual orientation in Colorado Amendment 2 suspect is that the initiatives in question express constitutionally forbidden sectarian religious intolerance through public law against fundamental rights of conscience, speech, and association of lesbian and gay persons protected by America's first and premier civil liberty, liberty of conscience.[33] As my argument in Chapter 1 shows, the grounds for discrimination against gay and lesbian conscience are themselves fundamentalist, sectarian religious convictions – sectarian in the sense that they rest on perceptions internal to religious convictions, not on public arguments reasonably available in contemporary terms to all persons. If discrimination against persons on grounds of sexual preference expresses constitutionally forbidden religious intolerance, the constitutional entrenchment of prohibitions on such discrimination (specifically naming a group in terms of the claims of justice it makes) is unashamedly in service of such discrimination and, as such, an unconstitutional expression of religious intolerance through public law. The character of the advocacy for such initiatives confirms the grounds for constitutional concern. Advocacy groups standardly distorted the true nature of their organizations, relied on discredited experts and facts, and concealed the true purpose of the proposed legislation.[34] Such irrationalist distortion of facts and values, in polemical service of a dominant orthodoxy now under reasonable examination, is at the core of the political irrationalism (the paradox of intolerance) condemned, as a basis for law, by the argument for toleration central to American constitutionalism.[35] In fact, advocacy of such initiatives rests not on reasonable arguments consistently pursued but on highly sectarian forms of controversial theological discourse that

33 See, in general, William Lee Miller, *The First Liberty: Religion and the American Republic* (New York: Knopf, 1987); Thomas J. Curry, *The First Freedoms: Church and State in America to the Passage of the First Amendment* (New York: Oxford University Press, 1986); Leonard W. Levy, *The Establishment Clause: Religion and the First Amendment* (New York: Macmillan, 1986).

34 See Note, "Constitutional Limits on Anti-Gay-Rights Initiatives," 106 *Harv. L. Rev.* 1905, 1909 (1993). See, for important recent explorations of this reactionary political movement and its power in contemporary American politics, Chris Bull and John Gallagher, *Perfect Enemies: The Religious Right, the Gay Movement, and the Politics of the 1990's* (New York: Crown Publishers, 1996); Didi Herman, *The Antigay Agenda: Orthodox Vision and the Christian Right* (Chicago: University of Chicago Press, 1997).

35 See Richards, *Conscience and the Constitution: History, Theory, and Law of the Reconstruction Amendments* (Princeton, N.J.: Princeton University Press, 1993), at pp. 63–73.

regard publicly identified gays and lesbians as devils unworthy of the most minimal standards of constitutional civility and respect.[36] If public law fails these standards (resting solely on a sectarian basis that uses public law in service of sectarian wars of religion), it violates basic principles of American constitutional law.

Although the issue has usually been discussed in terms of the cases forbidding constitutional entrenchment of laws forbidding racial discrimination, the more exact analogy would be constitutional entrenchment of prohibitions on claims of religious discrimination made precisely by groups most likely to be victimized in Christian America by such discrimination (i.e., Jews). To understand the force of this analogy between political anti-Semitism and homophobia (well supported in both historical and contemporary expressions of such sectarian intolerance[37]), we must remind ourselves of the nature of the constitutional evil of the expression of anti-Semitism through law, in particular, why such political anti-Semitism violates the argument for toleration central to the proper interpretation of American traditions of religious liberty.[38] Such political anti-Semitism unjustly abridged basic rights of Jews, in violation of the argument for toleration, precisely because their beliefs and ways of life raised reasonable doubts about the dominant religious orthodoxy. To not allow such reasonable doubts to be entertained, the dominant orthodoxy enforced its views as the measure of tolerable belief and practice, abridging the basic rights by which the Jews might reasonably have raised doubts on the grounds of irrationalist stereotypes that dehumanized them. This I have called the paradox of intolerance, the mechanism by which such an entrenched orthodoxy unjustly constructed the dehumanized status of dissidents from the dominant orthodoxy: in effect, precisely the views that the dominant orthodoxy most reasonably needs to hear are those, paradoxically, that are savagely repressed on whatever, sometimes quite irrationalist, grounds to sustain the embattled legitimacy of the dominant orthodoxy.[39] American constitutional principles, based on the argument for toleration, forbid laws based on such sectarian intolerance.

In light of these reasons, we would and should immediately condemn constitutional entrenchment of political anti-Semitism (in the form of an initiative that forbade all laws protecting Jews as such against discrimination) as an

36 For ample documentation, based on interviews with the Christian Right, about the roots of their claims in biblical inerrancy and premillennial theology, see, in general, Herman, *Antigay Agenda*.

37 For historical support of the idea of Satan to condemn Jewish unbelief and the analogy of such scapegoating to homophobia, see Elaine Pagels, *The Origin of Satan* (New York: Random House, 1996), at pp. 102–5; on the analogy between anti-Semitism and homophobia in the intolerance of the Christian Right, see Herman, *Antigay Agenda*, pp. 85–6, 125–8.

38 On the argument for toleration, see Richards, *Conscience and the Constitution*, pp. 63–73; see also, in general, Richards, *Toleration and the Constitution* (New York: Oxford University Press, 1986).

39 See, on these points, Richards, *Women, Gays, and the Constitution: The Grounds for Feminism and Gay Rights in Culture and Law* (Chicago: University of Chicago Press, 1998).

unconstitutional expression of religious intolerance, because such laws are in service of precisely the forms of majoritarian religious intolerance that constitutional guarantees of religious toleration condemn as a basis for law. A state that entrenched such initiatives would, in clear violation of free exercise principles, unconstitutionally burden specifically named conscientious convictions in a blatantly nonneutral way,[40] and in clear contradiction of the principles of our antiestablishment jurisprudence,[41] support a sectarian religious view as the one true church of Americanism to which all dissenters are encouraged to convert. A constitutional jurisprudence that questions the neutrality of unemployment compensation schemes that effectively impose financial burdens on the convictions of Seventh Day Adventists[42] must condemn, a fortiori, laws that specifically target for focused disadvantage the convictions of a religion or form of conscience, and it must regard as even worse the very naming of the group in question in the relevant law.[43] In effect, a state that entrenched such initiatives would itself be the unconstitutional agent of the political evil of intolerance, branding a religious group as heretics and blasphemers to American religious orthodoxy. American constitutionalism, which recognizes neither heresy nor blasphemy as legitimate expressions of state power,[44] must forbid exercises of state power, like the contemplated initiative, that illegitimately assert such a power, in this case, legitimating the dehumanizing evil of political anti-Semitism. The effect of such initiatives would be to enlist the state actively in the unconstitutional construction of a class of persons lacking the status of bearers of human rights, a status so subhuman that they are excluded from the minimal rights and responsibilities of the moral community of persons. Political atrocity thus becomes thinkable and practical.

The case of anti–gay and lesbian initiatives is, as a matter of principle, exactly parallel. A dissenting form of conscience, precisely on the grounds of its moral independence and dissenting claims for justice, is branded for that reason as heresy. The message is clear and clearly intended: persons should convert from this form of conscience that is wholly unworthy of respect to the only true religion

[40] Cf. *Church of the Lukumi Babalu Aye, Inc. v. City of Hialeah*, 509 U.S. 520 (1993) (law forbidding animal sacrifice by the Santeria religion held violative of neutrality required in state burdens on religious practices by free exercise clause).

[41] See, in general, Richards, *Toleration and the Constitution*, pp. 146–62.

[42] See *Sherbert v. Verner*, 374 U.S. 398 (1963), whose authority was reaffirmed in *Employment Division, Department of Human Resources of Oregon v. Smith*, 494 U.S. 872 (1990).

[43] The imagined case is thus even worse than *Church of the Lukumi Babalu Aye, Inc. v. City of Hialeah*, 509 U.S. (1993), in which the religion of Santeria was not specifically named in the statute, but the statute was found, on analysis, unconstitutionally to be directed against that religious group.

[44] *United States v. Ballard*, 322 U.S. 78, 86 (1944) ("Heresy trials are foreign to our Constitution," Douglas, J., writing for the Court). On the unconstitutionality of blasphemy prosecutions under current American laws of free speech and religious liberty, see Leonard W. Levy, *Blasphemy: Verbal Offense against the Sacred from Moses to Salman Rushdie* (New York: Knopf, 1993), pp. 522–33, commenting, inter alia, on *Burstyn v. Wilson*, 343 U.S. 495 (1952) (censorship of movie, as sacrilegious, held unconstitutional).

of Americanism. The initiative is as much motored by sectarian religion and directed against dissenting conscience as the intolerably anti-Semitic initiative just discussed. Homosexuals are to late-twentieth-century sectarians what the Jews have traditionally been to sectarians in the Christian West throughout its history: intolerable heretics to dominant fundamentalist religious orthodoxy.[45]

The conception that homosexuality is a form of heresy or treason is both an ancient and a modern ground for its condemnation.[46] In fact, there is no good reason to believe that the legitimacy of such forms of sexual expression destabilizes social cooperation. Homosexual relations are and will foreseeably remain the preference of small minorities of the population,[47] who are as committed to principles of social cooperation and contribution as any other group in society at large; the issue, as with all suspect classes, is not one of increasing or decreasing the minority but of deciding whether we should treat such a minority justly with respect as persons or unjustly with contempt as unspeakably heretical outcasts. Indeed, the very accusation of heresy or treason brings out an important feature of the traditional moral condemnation in its contemporary vestments. It no longer rests on generally acceptable arguments of necessary protections of the rights of persons to general goods; to the contrary, both the sexism and condemnation of nonprocreational sex of the traditional view are now inconsistent with the reasonable acceptability as general goods of both gender equality and nonprocreational sex (see Chapter 1). Today, such condemnation appeals to arguments internal

45 On the role that anti-Semitic ideology implicitly plays in the homophobia of the Christian Right, see Herman, *Antigay Agenda*, pp. 85–6, 116–28. On the historical background of such intolerance in ideas of Satan as the cause of Jewish unbelief and the analogy to contemporary homophobia, see Elaine Pagels, *Origin of Satan*, pp. 102–5. For further exploration of this analogy, see David A. J. Richards, *Identity and the Case for Gay Rights: Race, Gender, Religion as Analogies* (Chicago: University of Chicago Press, 1999).

46 Throughout the Middle Ages, homosexuals were prosecuted as heretics and often burned at the stake on that ground. See Derrick S. Bailey, *Homosexuality and the Western Christian Tradition* (New York: Longmans, Green, 1955), p. 135. *Buggery*, one of the names for homosexual acts, derives from a corruption of the name of one heretical group alleged to engage in homosexual practices. See *id.*, pp. 141, 148–9. For a modern use of the idea of treason in this context, see Patrick Devlin, *The Enforcement of Morals* (London: Oxford University Press, 1965), pp. 1–25. For rebuttal, see H. L. A. Hart, *Law, Liberty, and Morality* (Stanford, Calif.: Stanford University Press, 1963); Hart, "Social Solidarity and the Enforcement of Morals," 35 *U. Chi. L. Rev.* 1 (1967).

47 The original Kinsey estimate that about 4 percent of males are exclusively homosexual throughout their lives is confirmed by comparable European studies. See Gebhard, "Incidence of Overt Homosexuality in the United States and Western Europe," *National Institute of Mental Health Task Force on Homosexuality*, ed. J. M. Livingood (Washington, D.C.: U.S. Government Printing Office, 1972), pp. 22–9. The incidence figure remains stable, though many European countries do not apply the criminal penalty to consensual sex acts of the kind here under discussion. See Walter Barnett, *Sexual Freedom and the Constitution* (Albuquerque: University of New Mexico Press, 1973), p. 293. Recent surveys indicate that as little as 2.8 percent of the population identify themselves as gay and less than half of that number as lesbian. See Robert T. Michael, John H. Gagnon, Edward O. Laumann, and Gina Kolata, *Sex in America: A Definitive Survey* (Boston: Little, Brown, 1994), p. 176.

to highly personal, often sectarian religious decisions about acceptable ways of belief and lifestyle. When a moral tradition in this way abandons certain of its essential grounds in general goods, it may justly retain its legitimacy for those internal to the tradition, all the more so because it remains more exclusively constitutive of their tradition. But if those essential grounds are constitutionally necessary for the tradition coercively to enforce its mandates through the criminal law, the abandonment of those grounds must, pari passu, deprive the tradition of its constitutional legitimacy as a ground for enforcement though law. The tradition no longer expresses nonsectarian ethical arguments that may fairly be imposed on all persons but rather perspectives reasonably authoritative only for those who adhere to the tradition.

The English legal scholar Tony Honoré put the essential point well regarding the contemporary status of the homosexual: "It is not primarily a matter of breaking rules but of dissenting attitudes. It resembles political or religious dissent, being an atheist in Catholic Ireland or a dissident in Soviet Russia."[48] In effect, the enforcement of such sectarian perspectives through law, as through Colorado Amendment 2, is the functional equivalent of a heresy prosecution: persons of gay and lesbian identity, precisely in virtue of their conscientious claims to equal justice, are branded as subhuman heretics to true values and told unambiguously to convert or, at a minimum, to return ashamedly to the silence and invisibility of the closet. The grounds for prohibition are highly personal ideological or political views about which free persons reasonably disagree. The continuing force of the prohibitions rests not on protection of the rights of persons but on fears and misunderstandings directed at the alien way of life of a small and traditionally condemned minority, as if, at bottom, the legitimacy of one's own way of life requires the illegitimacy of all others. Constitutional toleration, which forbids heresy and blasphemy prosecutions and sharply circumscribes treason prosecutions,[49] must likewise be extended to condemnations through law that have the political force of heresy, blasphemy, and treason prosecutions.

As we have seen, such reasonable attack has included criticism of this tradition both for its mandatory procreational demands and for its sexism; and both criticisms have, under American public law, significantly been expressed through constitutional principles of privacy and antidiscrimination for the benefit of the dominant heterosexual majority of both men and women. The entrenched orthodoxy is much under reasonable critical attack certainly in almost every imaginable aspect of heterosexual sexuality.[50] The orthodoxy, in retreat in the domain of heterosexual sexuality, does not, however, extend such reasonable criticisms,

48 See Tony Honoré, *Sex Law* (London: Duckworth, 1978), p. 89.

49 See U.S. Constitution, art. III, sec. 3.

50 See, e.g., *Griswold v. Connecticut*, 381 U.S. 479 (1965); *Eisenstadt v. Baird*, 405 U.S. 438 (1972); *Roe v. Wade*, 410 U.S. 113 (1973); *Planned Parenthood of Southeastern Pennsylvania v. Casey*, 505 U.S. 833 (1992); *Frontiero v. Richardson*, 411 U.S. 677 (1973); *Craig v. Boren*, 429 U.S. 190 (1976).

as a matter of principle, to the examination of its traditional orthodoxy about homosexual sexuality. Rather, consistent with the paradox of intolerance as in the case of Christian reasonable doubts about transubstantiation, it displaces its doubts from the reasonable doctrinal criticism of which it is most in need to the irrationalist scapegoating of a traditionally despised and culturally subjugated minority. It thus acquiesces in a war on homosexuals on sectarian grounds it would never accept in the other areas to which sectarians extend their religious war (e.g., on feminism, on civil rights legislation in general).[51] To achieve such a constitutionally incoherent aim, its sectarian proponents suppress opposing views relevant to reasonable public argument; distort or misstate facts; disconnect values from ethical reasoning; and indeed denigrate deliberation in politics in favor of a conception of politics that allegedly requires the constitutional repression of dissent, a symbolic glorification of violence against claims of human rights.[52]

If I am right about these reasons for the suspectness of sexual orientation in *Romer v. Evans*, such reasons would explain and clarify both the substance and the rhetorical excesses of Justice Scalia's dissent, for Scalia's 'originalism,'on the view I have offered of it, may itself be rooted in highly sectarian religious views (see, on this point, Part III). What Scalia insists is that, because *Bowers v. Hardwick* is still good law, the moral purpose that sustained state laws, criminalizing sodomy, against constitutional attack must extend to the legitimacy of that moral purpose in sustaining the less intrusive demands of Colorado Amendment 2. Justice Kennedy's implicit analogy to religious discrimination, of course, addresses and answers that argument, and the very power of the argument is, I believe, exemplified by the terms of Scalia's dissent, namely that even were gay and lesbian sex to be decriminalized, there would be a legitimate state purpose in laws like Colorado Amendment 2 as democratically legitimate self-defense,[53] that gays and lesbians are not really politically unpopular because, despite small numbers, the "group... enjoys enormous influence in American media and politics,"[54] and, last, that the majority illegitimately depends on the elitist views of the law schools and legal profession.[55] When dealing with this topic, Scalia fails to observe the most elementary reasonable distinctions among grounds for criminalization, conflating gay and lesbian sex with murder or polygamy or cruelty to animals[56] in ways they bespeak not just the absence of reason but also a contempt for reason. Why?

51 On the antifeminism of the Religious Right, see Herman, *Antigay Agenda*, pp. 103–10; on their opposition to the civil rights agenda in general, see *id.*, pp. 111–36, 140.

52 See, for further development of these irrationalist themes, Herman, *Antigay Agenda*; for example, on manufacturing false or misleading data, see *id.*, pp. 76–80.

53 *Romer*, 517 U.S. at 645–6.

54 *Id.* at 652.

55 *Id.* at 652–3.

56 *Id.* at 644.

In fact, lesbians and gay men are a small minority of the American population. Although they are relatively affluent[57] and sometimes influential,[58] their political gains have been comparatively small,[59] and they remain radically underrepresented in key government positions.[60] In contrast, fundamentalist religions, in their reactionary war on gay rights, have mobilized, in contrast to gays and lesbians, much larger numbers and resources, including fund-raising advantages.[61] Against this factual background, making an argument of legitimate democratic

57 Marketing studies indicate that gay and lesbian incomes are far in excess of the national average. See Joya L. Wesley, "With $394 Billion in Buying Power, Gays' Money Talks; and Corporate America Increasingly Is Listening," *Atlanta J. & Const.*, Dec. 1, 1991, at F5. The 1990 census, measuring statistics for gay, unmarried couples for the first time, showed gay male couples to have higher incomes than any other group, including heterosexual married couples. See Margaret S. Usdansky, "Gay Couples, by the Numbers-Data Suggest They're Fewer Than Believed, but Affluent," *USA Today*, Apr. 12, 1993, at 8A.

58 For a popular media account of gay power and influence, see, e.g., Joni Balter, "Gay Power Brokers – Money, Stature and Savvy Give Leaders More Clout," *Seattle Times*, Aug. 1, 1993, at A1.

59 Only a handful of states and a comparatively tiny number of municipalities protect gays and lesbians from discrimination. Of the seventy-seven jurisdictions that have any sort of legislation or other government decree protecting lesbians and gay men, sixteen are merely resolutions, guidelines, or policy statements and are not fully binding. See affidavit of political science Professor Kenneth Sherrill, Defendant's Motion for Summary Judgment, *Steffan v. Cheney*, 780 F. Supp. 1 (Dist. D.C. 1991), *rev'd sub. nom.*, *Steffan v. Aspin*, 8 F.3d 57 (D.C. Cir. 1993), *reh'g en banc granted and judgment vacated* (Jan. 7, 1994), reprinted in Marc Wolinsky and Kenneth Sherrill, *Gays and the Military: Joseph Steffan versus the United States* (Princeton: Princeton University Press, 1993). Wolinsky and Sherrill, *Gays and the Military*, p. 114. Only four states – Wisconsin, Massachusetts, Connecticut, and Hawaii – have any statewide legislation protecting the rights of homosexuals, and seven others have executive orders issued by governors. These executive orders are limited by the range of gubernatorial power and are rescinded more easily than legislation. *Id.* In half of the states, no jurisdiction whatsoever has any legislation or other governmental decree or policy that protects the rights of lesbians and gay men. *Id.* The importance of this legislation should not be overstated; as a recent *Harvard Law Review* study observes, "[V]ery little legislation protects gay men and lesbians from discrimination in the private sector. No federal statute prohibits discrimination by private citizens or organizations based on sexual orientation. Nor do the states provide protection: Only Wisconsin has a comprehensive statute barring such discrimination in employment." "Developments in the Law—Sexual Orientation and the Law," 102 *Harv. L. Rev.* 1508, 1667 (1989).

60 The Supreme Court in *Frontiero v. Richardson*, 411 U.S. 677 (1973), found women as a class to be relatively politically powerless, despite that then, as now, they constituted a majority of the electorate, because they were "vastly underrepresented in this Nation's decisionmaking councils," *id.* at 686n17. The Court based its conclusions on the fact that no woman had ever been elected president; that there had not yet been a woman Supreme Court Justice; that there were then no women in the U.S. Senate (though women had served as senators in the past); and that there were then only fourteen women in the House of Representatives. *Id.* By this standard, lesbians and gay men are even more radically unrepresented. There has never been an openly gay president, Supreme Court justice, or even openly gay federal court judge; there are no openly gay U.S. senators today, and there have never been any. Until 1984, there were no openly gay members of the U.S. House of Representatives, and although there are currently two gay House members, Congressmen Gerry Studds and Barney Frank, neither revealed his sexual orientation until after being elected. See Sherrill, Defendant's Motion for Summary Judgment, *Steffan v. Cheney*, in Wolinsky and Sherrill, *Gays and the Military*, p. 20.

61 See, on this point, Tina Fetner, *How the Religious Right Shaped Lesbian and Gay Activism* (Minneapolis: University of Minnesota Press, 2008), pp. 21–2, 75, 81–3, 120.

self-defense to gay and lesbian advances bespeaks a use of facts and values all too familiar in the history of intolerance, most grotesquely so in the late twentieth century. Thus, the argument remarkably transforms the minority status of homosexuals, analogous to the similar irrationalist appeals central to political anti-Semitism, into a secret and powerful conspiracy against which politics must be protected.[62] In effect, the very attempt by homosexuals or Jews to make any basic claims of equal citizenship and any small gains thus secured (including relative affluence and occasional influence) are irrationally interpreted as a murderous attack on dominant majorities. Normative outrage at the very idea of an outcast's claim of rights remakes reality to rationalize the nullification of such rights. On this hallucinatory ground, aggression against basic rights of gay and lesbian persons is, as with Hitler's exactly comparable justification for his war on the Jews,[63] ideologically inverted into an argument of self-defense. No argument, offered in defense of Colorado Amendment 2, more starkly communicates the hermetically Manichaean sectarian world view of its proponents—its polemical power to act as a distorting prism to remake reality in its own ideological image of the wars of religion and to rationalize its conduct accordingly. The persecutor is imaginatively transformed into the victim, thus rendering persecution innocent and indeed honorable. It is in such terms that good Germans acquiesced in Hitler's war on the Jews; it is in such terms that good Americans acquiesced in Colorado's war on gay and lesbian persons.[64]

Justice Scalia is very much a player in this cultural war. His claims of gay and lesbian political power transform the victims of irrational fundamentalist rage into aggressors. His appeal to democracy is thus brigaded with an anti-intellectualism more familiar in Protestant fundamentalism than in a learned Catholic like Scalia, as he condemns the intellectual culture of academic and professional law because, as it seems, that culture questions the reasonableness of sectarian views Scalia is unable and unwilling to question.

Scalia's role in this reactionary cultural war is clear in his dissent in *Lawrence v. Texas*,[65] in which the Supreme Court extended the principle of constitutional privacy to protect from criminalization gay and lesbian sexuality (overruling *Bowers v. Hardwick*[66]). For Scalia, overruling *Bowers* works nothing less than "a massive disruption of the current social order,"[67] which, rather remarkably, he contrasts with the lack of disruption that *Casey* would have inflicted had it

62 See, for an illuminating study of this argument, Herman, *Antigay Agenda*, pp. 116–28; on the analogy to anti-Semitism, see *id.*, pp. 85–6, 125–8.

63 For a characteristic example of the inversion of victims into aggressors and the compelling need to defend against them, see Adolf Hitler, *Mein Kampf* (New York: Reynal & Hitchcock, 1940), pp. 824–7.

64 See, e.g., Stephen Bransford, *Gay Politics vs. Colorado and America: The Inside Story of Amendment 2* (Cascade, Colo.: Sardis Press, 1994).

65 *Lawrence v. Texas*, 539 U.S. 558 (2003).

66 *Bowers v. Hardwick*, 478 U.S. 186 (1986).

67 *Lawrence*, 539 U.S. at 591.

overruled *Roe*, which, of course, it did not. What Scalia does not see, what his patriarchal blinders disable him from seeing, is that the right to constitutional privacy itself, already elaborated in *Griswold* and reaffirmed and extended in *Roe* and *Casey*, has already disrupted what Scalia regards as social order. What *Lawrence* does is give the principle of constitutional privacy a wholly principled interpretation, overruling *Bowers* because it clearly was inconsistent with this principle (the same right to intimate life applies to abortion and to gay and lesbian sex, and, if anything, there was even less of a compelling secular state purpose to justify criminalizing the latter – nothing like the weight of fetal life). Why, then, this rather rhetorical overwrought, even hysterical accusation of "massive disruption" when it comes to gay and lesbian sex where, as Justice Kennedy points out in this opinion for the Court, there has been already a remarkable trend to decriminalization not only abroad but also in the United States. Scalia's quite homophobic response is simply to dismiss, as interpretively relevant, legal developments abroad,[68] not only because such developments are in line with the American decriminalization of gay and lesbian sex but undoubtedly because such developments also include the development of various legal partnership arrangements for gays and lesbians and, in some cases, marriage. Such empirical experience suggests not "massive disruption" but a conception of a range of legal arrangements for intimate life for both heterosexuals and homosexuals that are both more just and more sensible.[69] Where is the "massive disruption"? Such rhetoric bespeaks a specifically homophobic animus, not mentioning the reasonable changes in heterosexual relationships but rather calling such changes evils only when they arise from gay and lesbian relationships, an irrational animus that had been, as I argued, already rather starkly expressed in Scalia's dissent in *Romer v. Evans*.

In his *Lawrence* dissent, this animus finds its target in the concurring opinion of Justice O'Connor, which had struck down the Texas criminal statute (criminalizing only gay and lesbian forms of sodomy) on equal protection grounds (the statute in *Bowers* had been directed at all forms of sodomy, heterosexual and homosexual, which is evidently what led O'Connor to concur in *Bowers*). What provokes Scalia in O'Connor's analysis is her claim that, while criminalization of only homosexual sodomy irrationally violates equal protection, this would not apply to a similar discrimination in rights to marriage.[70] Indeed, Scalia ends his opinion by again taking up this theme, arguing that *Lawrence* throws into constitutional doubt the limitation of marriage rights to heterosexual couples.[71]

Many reasonable people, like Justice O'Connor, might have thought that there is a world of difference between criminalizing a sexual activity and extending

[68] *Id.* at 598.

[69] See, in general, William N. Eskridge Jr. and Darren R. Spediale, *Gay Marriage: For Better or for Worse?* (New York: Oxford University Press, 2006).

[70] *Lawrence*, 539 U.S. at 601–2.

[71] *Id.* at 604–5.

marriage rights to that activity. Certainly, the opinion for the Court of Justice Kennedy (which struck down as unconstitutional all forms of statute criminalizing sodomy not just those that criminalize homosexual sodomy) expressly distinguished its constitutional grounds for striking down criminalization from the question of "whether the government must give formal recognition to any relationship that homosexual persons seek to enter."[72] It is true that, when the Supreme Judicial Court of Massachusetts struck down such discrimination as unconstitutional under the Massachusetts state constitution, the opinion for the Court of Chief Justice Marshall argued that its view was consistent with its view of a reasonable analysis of the principles of *Lawrence v. Texas*[73] but that the grounding for its opinion was "[t]he Massachusetts Constitution[, which] is, if anything, more protective of individual liberty and equality than the Federal Constitution."[74] The federal constitutional issue remains very much open, which raises the question of why Justice Scalia is so certain that it is not open.

What seems specifically homophobic about Scalia's certainty is just that, its certainty and its rhetorical focus and, most important, its sense, once again, of the need to repel aggressively the homosexual threat. There is a patriarchal call to arms here, with a justice of the Supreme Court fomenting a repressive politics against such a patriarchally imagined threat. It is no accident that Scalia is a hero to religious fundamentalists, whose political mobilization – in response to his call to arms – explains the role that the issue of gay marriage has played in American politics and why, among the politicians who have most conspicuously used this issue (President Bush's endorsement of a constitutional amendment banning gay marriage[75]), Justice Scalia has been their exemplar of a good constitutional judge.[76] If a Supreme Court justice can so mindlessly denigrate the constitutional and human rights of a traditionally despised and silenced American minority, why can't a president or politicians generally? What we have had from our recent democratically elected leaders (Republican and Democrat) is not the moral leadership of a Lincoln or Truman or Johnson or Carter on human rights but a wedge-issue politics that supinely follows and foments a reactionary politics that demeans and denigrates people of goodwill as so subhuman that basic human rights cannot extend to them on equal terms.

If Scalia's 'originalism' is as unreasonable as I have argued it is, we must investigate further the psychological question not only of how and why Justices Scalia or Thomas may have espoused and defended it but also, more broadly, of how and why so many people have found it so appealing. It is for this reason that we must turn to the closer study of fundamentalist forms of American religion, for it is

72 *Id.* at 578.
73 See *Goodridge v. Department of Public Health*, 798 N.E.2d 941, 948, 953, 959 (Mass. 2003).
74 *Goodridge*, 798 N.E.2d at 948.
75 See Eskridge and Spediale, *Gay Marriage*, pp. 39–41.
76 See, on this point, "Did Bush Promise to Appoint a Justice Like Scalia," http://mediamatters.org/items/w00510130005.

these religions that display and legitimate the patriarchal psychology on which the appeal of 'originalism' depends. There is, at this point, a connection to be made between fundamentalism in constitutional law and in religion. To understand this connection, we must turn to the variant forms of American fundamentalism religion (Part II) and then investigate their impact on constitutional 'originalism' (Part III).

PART II

FUNDAMENTALISM IN RELIGION

CHAPTER 4

FUNDAMENTALISM IN ROMAN CATHOLICISM

It is against the background of the constitutional developments discussed in Chapter 1 that we can understand the nature and sources of the forms of religious (and later constitutional) fundamentalism that are the subject of this book. I focus here on forms of religious fundamentalism because I believe that it is through an understanding of their underlying culture and psychology that we can arrive at an understanding of the basis of the appeal today of fundamentalism generally, including fundamentalism in law.

How is it that religions, marked by such differences in theology and perspective, manage to agree and ally themselves politically around fundamentalism? Why, as in recent increasingly uncivil wars in a religion like the Anglican Church, do American conservatives find themselves more united by homophobia with African conservatives than with their own American church? We should be more puzzled than we are by how the deep differences among Christian religions and even within such religions ally themselves today on fundamentalist grounds in increasingly aggressive political ways. It is not theology and certainly not any close reading of the Gospels that leads to such alliances. What is it? The argument of Part II addresses this question.

My general thesis is that all these religious fundamentalisms are, whatever their other differences of theology or perspective, marked by, first, a common set of normative convictions held with certainty, and, second, a common underlying patriarchal psychology. Both the convictions and the psychology are, in contemporary circumstances, reactionary, in particular to the views on gender and sexuality that are at the heart of the constitutional developments discussed in Chapter 1, views that raise reasonable doubts precisely about the convictions fundamentalists hold with certainty. My argument in each case is in two stages: first, a discussion of the reasons for believing that the fundamentalism in question is in contemporary circumstances unreasonable both in its own internal terms and in external terms of facts and values now reasonably entertained at large; and second, exposure of the underlying patriarchal psychology that supports such irrationalist convictions in the domain of gender and sexuality.

My initial focus is on two forms of orthodox Christian fundamentalism – Catholic (in this chapter) and Evangelical Protestant (Chapter 5), and I then turn to an unorthodox form of Christianity, Mormonism, in Chapter 6. Of course, there are many other forms of religious fundamentalism, many of them not Christian, whether orthodox or unorthodox. But I am concerned here with the specific character of American religious fundamentalism, in which these forms of Christianity play a central role; to the extent non-Christian forms of religious fundamentalism play a role in America (e.g., orthodox Jewish), I believe that the explanatory features I identify in the course of my argument can be extended to them as well. At a later point, I show how the account, developed here, can be reasonably extended to other forms of religious fundamentalism, including, among others, Islamic and Hindu forms that flourish abroad.

In the American context, there can be few stranger bedfellows than the fundamentalism of the two forms of orthodox Christianity, shown in the quite different authority each accords to biblical texts. One of the matters that historically divided and continues to divide Catholics and Protestants is the greater reliance of Protestants on the interpretation of the Bible. Catholicism certainly regarded Bible interpretation as centrally important, but its style of Bible interpretation, reflected in the approach of Augustine of Hippo, was often much more open to nonliteral, more metaphorical modes of Bible interpretation and sensitive, as well, to relevant insights of classical philosophers, including, importantly, Plato (through Plotinus) and Aristotle. Authority in Catholicism thus rests on a complex interpretive tradition over time, resting on both the Bible and philosophical traditions, and one in which a celibate male priesthood is accorded sole authority in interpreting the tradition, itself hierarchically ordered to accord ultimate authority to the pope in Rome. Protestantism importantly challenged many of the terms of Catholic authority, calling, if anything, for a return to the Bible as religious authority, *sola scriptura*, challenging the role that a celibate male priesthood played in Catholicism and calling for an alternative conception of authority that rested on the conscience of all believers.

If Catholicism and Evangelical Protestants come to common ground in fundamentalism, it is through very different routes and in different ways. The form of Catholic fundamentalism that I discuss in this chapter is norm based, resting on the alleged self-evident rationality of certain norms of gender and sexuality. Protestant Evangelical fundamentalism is, in contrast, source based, resting on the authority of biblical texts. For this reason, our critical examination of the methods of argument of each form of fundamentalism must be different. My discussion of Catholic fundamentalism thus does not focus on biblical interpretation, for example, the internal incoherence of a Bible-based tradition, like Evangelical Protestantism, that fails to take seriously the life and teaching of Jesus of Nazareth, an important feature of the analysis of the subsequent chapter. Rather, I focus here on what Catholic fundamentalists argue is a basically philosophical argument, one, I argue, that is both internally incoherent and substantively unreasonable.

There is, however, a common theme in my examination of both these forms of orthodox Christian fundamentalism, namely the uncritical role that both a patriarchal conception of authority and an underlying patriarchal psychology play in supporting their common normative views of sexuality and gender. The patriarchal conceptions of authority are, as we will see, certainly different, but they converge on what both forms of fundamentalism take to be challenges to traditional forms of patriarchal authority. What underlies these conceptions is a common patriarchal psychology, reflected in a conception of original sin that both traditions share. The relationship between this psychology and this conception is a central topic of my diagnosis of what motivates Catholic fundamentalism, a discussion on which I will draw as well in the following chapter's discussion of the roots of Protestant fundamentalism.

The discussion of Catholic fundamentalism begins with the background and the substantive claims of the leading contemporary form of such fundamentalism (new natural law); I then discuss its defects, both its internal incoherence and its lack of substantive appeal. Finally, I turn to the diagnosis of the patriarchal psychology that supports it, one inherited from Augustine of Hippo.[1]

1. VATICAN II AND THE FUNDAMENTALISM OF NEW NATURAL LAW

The Catholic Church has had a decidedly mixed record in relation to religious toleration. On the one hand, historically speaking, we know that Catholicism developed one of the worst forms of institutionalized intolerance in the Christian West. The English historian and liberal Catholic Lord Acton commented in bitter terms on the roles of popes in the thirteenth and fourteenth centuries and their responsibility for the medieval Inquisition:

> These men instituted a system of Persecution, with a special tribunal, special functionaries, special laws. They carefully elaborated, and developed, and applied it. They protected it with every sanction, spiritual and temporal. They inflicted, as far as they could, the penalties of death and damnation on everybody who resisted it. They constructed quite a new system of procedure, with unheard of cruelties, for its maintenance. They devoted to it a whole code of legislation, pursued for several generations.[2]

On the other hand, undoubtedly motivated by the widespread sense of revulsion at the role Christian anti-Semitism had played as the cultural background for the

[1] The following account draws on Nicholas Bamforth and David A. J. Richards, *Patriarchal Religion, Sexuality, and Gender: A Critique of New Natural Law* (Cambridge: Cambridge University Press, 2008).

[2] Quoted in Perez Zagorin, *How the Idea of Religious Toleration Came to the West* (Princeton, N.J.: Princeton University Press, 2003), p. 14.

atrocities of the Holocaust, the Catholic Church fundamentally reconsidered and changed its position on intolerance, leading to the remarkable "Declaration on Religious Freedom" by the church's Second Vatican Council. In December 1965, the Second Vatican Council passed this declaration, also known from its opening words as "Dignitatis humanae personae," by an overwhelming majority. It stipulated that "the human person has a right to religious freedom." In defining this freedom, it stated that "all men are to be immune from coercion" by individuals, social groups, or "any human power," so that "in matters religious no one is forced to act in a manner contrary to his own beliefs. Nor is anyone to be restrained from acting in accordance with his own beliefs, whether privately or publicly, whether alone or in association with others, within due limits." The moral foundation of this right was "the very dignity of the human person," as known through "the revealed word of God and by reason itself." The only limit the declaration placed on the free exercise of religion was "the just requirements of public order." The declaration also acknowledged that, in "the vicissitudes of history," the church had acted at times in ways "which were less in accord with the gospel and even opposed to it." Finally, its conclusion stressed the imperative of universal religious freedom "in the present condition of the human family," in which different traditions were coming together in much closer relationships.[3]

It bespeaks the power and appeal of the idea of constitutional democracy in Europe after World War II that the Catholic Church, which had played little or no role in the historical development of the argument for religious toleration, should have embraced it in the form and on the grounds that it did. It was certainly not without internal controversy that the church made this remarkable decision. When first debated, it met with considerable resistance from some Vatican officials and a number of bishops. Its inspiration, however, was John XXIII's encyclical of 1963 on world peace and justice, *Pacem in Terris*, which appealed to "universal, inviolable, inalienable rights and duties" and used the phrase "the dignity of the human person" some thirty times.[4] Among its chief intellectual sponsors was the American Jesuit philosopher John Courtney Murray, who had been called to Rome as one of the papacy's theological advisers. In an essay circulated to the American bishops on the right to religious liberty, Murray criticized the opposing view in the Catholic Church as "intolerance wherever possible, tolerance wherever necessary."[5] Once the declaration had been approved, Murray observed that "in all honesty it must be admitted" that the church was "late in acknowledging the validity of the principle of religious freedom."[6] The historian Perez Zagorin observes, "Indeed, it was very late. Moreover, the document was far from confronting with complete candor the Catholic Church's long history of

[3] Quoted in *id.*, pp. 309–10.
[4] Quoted in *id.*, p. 309.
[5] Quoted in *id.*
[6] Quoted in *id.*, p. 310.

cruel intolerance and far from expressing any contrition or apology for its record of religious persecution."[7]

Vatican II represented a fundamental change in the political and moral views of official Roman Catholicism, and the question it opened was whether such a fundamental rethinking of its position on toleration would or should extend as well to its traditional views on gender and sexuality, including the authority accorded a hierarchically ordered celibate male priesthood. A school of thought, developed by the theologian Germain Grisez and later the legal philosopher John Finnis (the new natural lawyers), emerged that defended the view that reform must call a halt at toleration and extend no further. Grisez thus first came to prominence in the Catholic Church in the context of internal debates about contraception and abortion following Vatican II.[8] Historically, Grisez is credited with having played an important role in persuading Pope Paul VI not to relax the church's stance concerning the impermissibility of contraception; the church's traditional teachings on the issue were reiterated in the 1968 encyclical *Humanae Vitae*.[9] Grisez's arguments from the late 1970s concerning papal infallibility have been described as providing a "rallying point for theological conservatives"[10] and as having influenced the Vatican's pronouncements concerning the exclusion of women from the priesthood,[11] whereas Michael Northcott talks of "[p]apal reliance" on Grisez's and Finnis's work in the 1990s when formulating a human-centered account of basic goods in the context of the "non-human created order."[12] Richard McBrien, in turn, suggests in his comprehensive study guide to Catholicism that theorists such as Grisez and Finnis "strongly support the teaching of the hierarchical magisterium on sexual and medical issues."[13]

The new natural lawyers' concern to defend the authority of the church hierarchy – especially in the face of what they perceived as the crisis within the church provoked by post–Vatican II theological dissent – is evident in many of

[7] *Id.*

[8] For analysis of more recent developments in this debate, see Peter J. Boyer, "Annals of Religion: A Hard Faith – How the New Pope and His Predecessor Redefined Vatican II," *New Yorker*, May 16, 2005, p. 54.

[9] For analysis of the part played by Grisez, see Gary Wills, *Papal Sin* (New York: Doubleday, 2000), chap. 6; Grisez's role, though acknowledged, is given less prominence in John T. McGreevy's *Catholicism and American Freedom* (New York: W. W. Norton, 2003), chap. 8, pp. 243, 248; for Grisez's own account, see Russell Shaw, "Pioneering the Renewal in Moral Theology," in *Natural Law and Moral Inquiry: Ethics, Metaphysics, and Politics in the Work of German Grisez*, ed. Robert George (Washington, D.C.: Georgetown University Press, 1998), pp. 256–60; and for Grisez's critical analysis of the conduct of the Birth Control Commission, see his "How to Deal with Thoelogical Dissent," in *Dissent in Moral Theory*, ed. Charles Curran and Richard McCormick (New York: Paulist Press, 1988), pp. 461–7.

[10] Charles R. Morris, *American Catholic: The Saints and Sinners Who Built America's Most Powerful Church* (New York: Vintage, 1997), p. 346.

[11] *Id.*, pp. 347–8.

[12] Michael S. Northcott, *The Environment and Christian Ethics* (Cambridge: Cambridge University Press, 1996), pp. 136–7.

[13] Richard P. McBrien, *Catholicism: New Study Edition* (New York: Harper Collins, 1994), p. 963.

their writings.[14] Grisez's enthusiasm for the doctrinal conservatism of John Paul II and Benedict XVI is readily apparent:[15] John Paul II "has been a rock in the way of the dissenting theologians. His sophisticated conviction concerning traditional teaching has rendered hopeless his conversion to dissenting opinions."[16] Those Catholics who accept the views of dissenters are denying "any responsibility to assent" to papal teachings.[17] For Grisez, the correct alternative is to accept – as do the new natural lawyers – the authority of the pope and the bishops, "affirming all points of Catholic moral teaching which have been held and handed down by the universal magisterium . . . conforming one's conscience to the Church's teaching and . . . living according to one's Catholic conscience."[18]

It is against this background that the substantive views of the new natural lawyers must be understood. In *Natural Law and Natural Rights*, Finnis suggests that the morality of a decision or action depends not on its compatibility with an account of "human nature" as such.[19] Instead, two components – basic goods and requirements of practical reasonableness – enable one to formulate "a set of general moral standards."[20]

Turning first to the goods, Finnis suggests that there are "a set of basic practical principles which indicate the basic forms of human flourishing as goods to be pursued and realized, and which are in one way or another used by everyone who considers what to do, however unsound his conclusions."[21] The basic practical principles serve to orient one's practical reasoning, for example, by supplying a premise (explicit or implicit) for acting in a certain way: thus, the principle that knowledge is good can supply a reason for reading a book.[22] Finnis suggests

[14] For good summaries, see Germain Grisez, *The Way of the Lord Jesus*, vol. 1, *Christian Moral Principles* (1983; repr., Quincy, Ill.: Franciscan Press, 1997), chaps. 35–6 and "How to Deal with Theological Dissent," in Curran and McCormick, *Dissent in Moral Theory*, pp. 442–72; John Finnis, *Moral Absolutes: Tradition, Revision, and Truth* (Washington, D.C.: Catholic University of America Press, 1991), chap. 4.

[15] Note his endorsement of (then) Cardinal Ratzinger's 1985 investigation into theological dissent: "How to Deal with Theological Dissent," in Curran and McCormick, *Dissent in Moral Theory*, p. 445.

[16] Grisez, *Way of the Lord Jesus*, p. 907.

[17] *Id.*

[18] *Id.*

[19] John Finnis, *Natural Law and Natural Rights* (Oxford: Clarendon Press, 1980), pp. 23, 29, 33–4; see also Finnis, *Moral Absolutes*, p. 41; John Finnis and Germain Grisez, "The Basic Principles of Natural Law: A Reply to Ralph McInerny" (1981) 26 *Am. J. Juris.* 21, 22–5 (1981). For discussion of the role of human nature or "natural facts" in the new natural law theory, see Finnis, *Natural Law and Natural Rights*, pp. 17 ("there is no question of deriving one's basic judgments about human values and the requirements of practical reasonableness by some inference from the facts of the human situation"), 33–4, 36 (a denial that Aquinas relied on a conception of human nature), 85 (no inference from fact to value in relation to the forms of good), 91 (the frequent but not inevitable correlation between basic values and human inclinations).

[20] *Id.*, p. 23.

[21] Finnis, *Natural Law and Natural Rights*, p. 23; note also the formulations of *good* and *value* at p. 61.

[22] *Id.*, pp. 63–4.

that there are seven basic human goods in total:[23] life, knowledge, play, aesthetic experience, friendship, practical reasonableness, and religion (defined somewhat agnostically to mean speculation about the order of things). They are self-evident, obvious, intrinsic, and objective values that need no demonstration and are desirable for their own sake: they do not make or presuppose moral judgments.[24] Regardless of perspective, one can realize that they are good and desirable for human beings, and this understanding requires no further justification.[25] The practical principle that a particular good is worth pursuing is "underived. Neither its intelligibility nor its force rests on any further principle."[26] Expressed more fully, "if one attends carefully and honestly to the relevant human possibilities one can understand, without reasoning from any other judgment, that the realization of those possibilities is, as such, good and desirable for the human person; and . . . one's understanding needs no further justification."[27] It would thus seem that the goods are to be described as basic precisely because they are expressed in such terms that no one – whatever his or her personal circumstances or beliefs – could deny their value when making decisions concerning the way in which they should act. In relation to the good of truth, for example, Finnis suggests that, "[i]n explaining, to oneself and others, what one is up to, one finds oneself able and ready to refer to *finding out, knowledge, truth* as sufficient explanations of the point of one's activity, project, or commitment."[28]

The second component – "a set of basic methodological requirements of practical reasonableness" – serves to "distinguish sound from unsound practical thinking and . . . when all brought to bear, provide the criteria for distinguishing between acts that (always or in particular circumstances) are reasonable-all-things-considered (and not merely relative-to-a-particular-purpose) and acts that are unreasonable-all-things-considered, i.e. between ways of acting that are morally right or morally wrong."[29] The requirements thus provide reasons why things ought to be done or not done. A decision acquires its moral force by being reached in accordance with these requirements, which are to have a coherent plan of life, to have a degree of fidelity to one's commitments but also appropriate detachment, to have respect for the basic goods in one's every act (including not choosing to do anything that of itself does nothing but damage or impede the realization of any of the basic goods), to have a lack of arbitrary preferences between the basic goods or between people, to use methods that are efficient for their reasonable purpose or purposes, to follow one's conscience, and to have a

[23] *Id.*, pp. 90–2, where he suggests that this list is exhaustive; this position is maintained in Germain Grisez, Joseph Boyle, and John Finnis, "Practical Principles, Moral Truth, and Ultimate Ends" 32 *Am. J. Juris.* 99, 111–13 (1987).

[24] Finnis, *Natural Law and Natural Rights*, pp. 59, 61, 64–9, 85–97.

[25] *Id.*, pp. 64–73.

[26] *Id.*, p. 69; see also p. 87 (play).

[27] *Id.*, p. 73; see also p. 82 (on the distinction from urges).

[28] *Id.*, p. 61.

[29] *Id.*, p. 23.

commitment to the common good of the community. Finnis suggests that every moral judgment sums up the bearing of one or more of the requirements, which can be thought of as "mode[s] of moral obligation or responsibility."[30]

New natural law thus offers a set of self-evident basic goods and a set of constraints that forbid damaging any of these goods. The account preserves and explains Vatican II, because the right to conscience is an instantiation of these goods and cannot therefore be infringed. But the account also preserves traditional Catholic teaching about the intrinsic wrongness of contraception, abortion, and all forms of nonprocreative sex (including gay and lesbian sex) because, on the view taken by the new natural lawyers, all such actions threaten life, because they either end a life (abortion) or impede bringing a life into being through procreative sex. Its form of norm-based fundamentalism claims to find, in philosophical arguments rooted in an interpretation of the philosophy of Thomas Aquinas, support for a certainty about traditional views of sexuality and gender that condemn the constitutional developments discussed in Chapter 1.

2. THE INTERNAL INCOHERENCE OF NEW NATURAL LAW

a. Historical Thomism

Historical Thomism is, among attempts to defend religious beliefs, one of the most philosophical. Aside from the truth values of its claims, Thomism is of enormous interest in the history of thought for the way that it took the then-hegemonic form of religious belief in the West, Catholicism, and insisted that it could be appropriately defended and understood only in light of the best science and philosophy then available – which happened, in the view of Thomas Aquinas, to be the science and philosophy of Aristotle. Thomas certainly cited Christian scriptures (both the Hebrew Bible and the New Testament) and accepted all the then-orthodox doctrines of the Catholic faith (including the Incarnation, the Trinity, the Virgin Birth, the Catholic sacraments, celibacy as the religiously preferred state, and the like). But, what distinguished his defense of his religion in all its baroque doctrinal orthodoxy is the degree to which the authority of many of his contentions derived from closely reasoned philosophical arguments, starting with the arguments for the existence of God that are the cornerstone of the Thomistic architectonics. The language of God, for Thomas, was philosophical Aristotelianism, and the God of Thomas was very much a philosopher's God – accessible, if at all, only through mind-numbing exercises of dialectic that alone could reliably tell us what we might reasonably know and not know about the deity. Although Thomas certainly propounded both an ethical and a political system, his interests in ethics and politics were incidental to his metaphysical search for God. Celibacy was the religiously preferred state because it was felt

[30] *Id.*, p. 126.

to free men from a sensual life that would distract them from the kinds of demanding intellectual argument through which they might alone approach the reality of God. Ultimately, for Thomas, we can only know God after our deaths, an immortality for the saved expressed by the vision of God, *visio Dei*.[31]

There is a unity of theory and practice in Thomism, the theory being his metaphysical philosophy, the practice being his life as a celibate man and his teaching and writing while serving as a Dominican monk. Whatever may have been the biblical or other basis for a celibate priesthood in Catholicism before Thomas, he put the case in a very different way. Indeed, the whole of his philosophical enterprise might reasonably be regarded as placing celibacy on a new, sounder philosophical basis. What gave the celibate priesthood the religious authority it had over the noncelibate laity was, for Thomas, precisely the demanding and rigorous exercise of philosophical thought that celibacy alone made possible. What distinguished Christianity was, for Thomas, the religious authority of a celibate priesthood, in contrast – as he tartly put it – to "the case of Mohammed. He seduced the people by promises of carnal pleasure to which the concupiscence of the flesh goads us."[32] The philosophical rigor of Christianity was thus counterpointed to the "the fables of the Jews and the Saracens, who identified the rewards for just men with these pleasures"[33] (food and sex). What made Christianity, on this view, a philosophically preferred religion was that, unlike Judaism and Islam, it was much more skeptical about the role of food and sex in a religious life; in particular, it imposed on its clergy what neither Judaism nor Islam did, namely celibacy. We will be able to see how this follows from Thomas's philosophical argument after we have clarified the structure and some of the claims of that argument.[34]

The great appeal of Aristotle's science and philosophy for Thomas was the means it gave him for putting the philosophical case for thirteenth-century Catholic orthodoxy in a new and powerful way. Thomas certainly knew that both philosophy and science had flourished under Islam, whose scribes and philosophers preserved in Arabic the Aristotelian texts on which – in Latin translations – he depended (Thomas discussed the philosophical views of several of these philosophers at length[35]). What he aimed to show – in particular, in *On the*

[31] See, for illuminating general studies of the life and thought of Thomas Aquinas, Brian Davies, *The Thought of Thomas Aquinas* (Oxford: Clarendon Press, 1992); Anthony Kenny, *Aquinas* (Oxford: Oxford University Press, 1980); F. C. Copleston, *Aquinas* (London: Penguin, 1991). See also P. T. Geach, "Aquinas," in *Three Philosophers*, ed. G. E. M. Anscombe and P. T. Geach (Oxford: Basil Blackwell, 1961), pp. 69–125; Anthony Kenny, *Aquinas on Mind* (London: Routledge, 1993).

[32] Thomas Aquinas, *On the Truth of the Catholic Faith, Book 1: God*, trans. Anton C. Pegis (Garden City, N.Y.: Image, 1955), p. 73.

[33] See Thomas Aquinas, *On the Truth of the Catholic Faith, Book 3: Providence Part I*, trans. Vernon J. Bourke (Garden City, N.Y.: Image, 1956), p. 113.

[34] The best study of the structure of Aquinas's argument is that of Davies, *Thought of Thomas Aquinas*.

[35] See, on this point, Davies, *Thought of Thomas Aquinas*, pp. 23, 26.

Truth of the Catholic Faith[36] – was that this philosophy and science could reasonably be shown to support the claims of the Catholic faith in two ways. First, both Aristotelian science and philosophy could be used to make a reasonable case for the existence of God and, by a complex form of analogical argument, for God's nature as a creator by inference from the character of creation, including not only the physical world as it was understood by Aristotelian metaphysics and physics but also plant, animal, and human life according to Aristotle's biology, psychology, and ethics. Second, Aristotelian science and philosophy could be used to show that the other doctrines of the Catholic faith, those that were revealed in the Hebrew Bible and the New Testament, were not unreasonable. The case for these doctrines, as true, was made for Thomas by the role of miracles in showing that what they revealed was in fact true. The role of Aristotelian science and philosophy was not to make the case that these other doctrines were true but to show that they were not unreasonable – for example, not flawed by contradictions that would render them irrational and thus not worthy of rational assent.[37]

Aristotle's proofs for God's existence were expounded in various ways in *On the Truth of the Catholic Faith*[38] and *Summa Theologica*.[39] These proofs, while building on arguments in Aristotle's *Physics*[40] and *Metaphysics*,[41] were more intricate and complex; they are still closely studied by contemporary philosophers as offering a reasonable form of natural theology.[42] Such arguments offer reasons, at best, for supposing that there may be some very abstract, yet little-understood principle (an unmoved mover, if you will) in which we have some reason to believe, but that the principle might be some physical or other process, which is certainly not the personal God of Catholic theology.

How might the gap be bridged from such an abstract unmoved mover to a personal God of the sort Catholic theology contemplates? Thomas's way of bridging the gap was largely by a form of philosophical argument saying not what God's features are but what they are not. To make some reasonable sense of what God's positive features might be, Thomas drew on Aristotelian biology,

[36] See Aquinas, *On the Truth of the Catholic Faith, Book 1*; Aquinas, *Book 2: Creation*, trans. James F. Anderson (Garden City, N.Y.: Image, 1956); Aquinas, *Book 3: Providence Part I; Book Three: Providence Part II*, trans. Vernon J. Bourke (Garden City, N.Y.: Image, 1956); Aquinas, *Book Four: Salvation*, trans. Charles J. O'Neil (Garden City, N.Y.: Image, 1957).

[37] See, on these points, Davies, *Thought of Thomas Aquinas*.

[38] See Aquinas, *On the Truth of the Catholic Faith, Book 1*, pp. 85–96.

[39] See Thomas Aquinas, *Summa Theologica*, vol. 1, trans. Fathers of the English Dominican Province (Allen, Texas: Christian Classics, 1948), pp. 11–14.

[40] See Aristotle, "Physics," trans. R. P. Hardie and P. K. Gaye, in *The Complete Works of Aristotle, Volume 1*, ed. Jonathan Barnes (Princeton, N.J.: Princeton University Press, 1984), pp. 315–446, 407–46.

[41] See Aristotle, "Metaphysics," trans. W. D. Ross, in *The Complete Works of Aristotle, Volume 2*, ed. Jonathan Barnes (Princeton, N.J.: Princeton University Press, 1984), pp. 1552–728, 1688–700.

[42] See, e.g., Norman Kretzmann, *The Metaphysics of Theism: Aquinas's Natural Theory in Summa Contra Gentiles I* (Oxford: Clarendon Press, 2001). But see Anthony Kenny, *The Five Ways: St. Thomas Aquinas's Proofs of God's Existence* (New York: Schocken Books, 1969).

psychology, and ethics. On the assumption that the unmoved mover is creator and sustainer of all that exists, Thomas argued by analogy that we may reasonably ascribe to the unmoved mover, as cause, features revealed in that part of creation that most resembles him, namely humankind. It is at this point that Thomas crucially appealed to Aristotle's biology, psychology, and ethics to understand uniquely human faculties and what they may inferentially tell us about the unmoved mover. In short, the interest in human moral psychology and ethics arose incidentally to the larger inquiry into God, which was always at the center of Thomas Aquinas's essentially philosophical theology.[43]

What made Aristotle so compelling at this stage of the analysis was both his conception of our distinctive theoretical and practical rationality, and his ethical and political conception of the basic normative principles in terms of which our moral rationality orders and should order our lives. Aristotle's ethics and politics were a form of ethical naturalism, in which the concept of the right in ethics or politics was defined in terms of the fuller realization in the world of what Aristotle defined as our distinctive competences as human beings. For Aristotle, these competences were thought of as capacities for certain kinds of excellences displayed both in rational thought and in action. Aristotle certainly included among these excellences what we would call moral or political virtues, like courage, magnanimity, and a sense of justice, but these were, for him, largely instrumental virtues valued because they make possible a certain kind of way of life in which the most highly valued human excellences can be cultivated and displayed. Those most highly valued excellences were – for Aristotle – virtues of philosophical contemplation, in which persons are able, as in the cultivation and display of Aristotle's science and philosophy, to contemplate the metaphysical order of things, including the place of humans in that order. Aristotle argued at some length that what makes such contemplative competences the most valuable of our human endowments is that they are pursued for their own sake as an end in itself, not as the means to other ends. The practical moral virtues, in contrast, were for Aristotle instrumental, being required to sustain a way of life in which the highest human excellences could be cultivated and displayed.[44]

It is important to see that, for a perfectionist like Aristotle, the relevant excellences (the exercise and display of which must be maximized overall) are creative talents for intellectual and artistic work, which most people lack or possess only meagerly.[45] The implications of this ethical perfectionist conception for

[43] See, on these points, Davies, *Thought of Thomas Aquinas*, pp. 40–79.

[44] See Aristotle, *Nicomachean Ethics*, trans. Martin Ostwald (New York: Library of Liberal Arts, 1962). The whole of Aristotle's *Nicomachean Ethics* is an attempt to describe the human excellences that morality requires us to maximize; but see, especially, book 10 for a characterization of the special weight Aristotle gave to the human excellence of theoretical wisdom.

[45] Ethical perfectionism may, from this perspective, be usefully contrasted with another form of teleological theory, ethical utilitarianism, which maximizes pleasure over pain or desire satisfaction over frustration. Because all sentient beings, and certainly human beings, experience pleasure and pain, utilitarianism, as a teleological theory, gives a kind of weight to ordinary human life and

politics were certainly no more supportive of democracy than was Plato's conception. Human competences for excellence were, for Aristotle, distributed highly unequally among human beings. Even the moral virtues, like heroic courage in war, existed in some but hardly in all or most people. The intellectual virtues, displayed in activities like philosophy, science, and art, were even less common. Very few people, in Aristotle's view, had the competence to cultivate and display these excellences at anything like a high level of performance. But these were the only ultimate ends in themselves in terms of which other virtues could reasonably be understood and evaluated. Indeed, these practical virtues had value only instrumentally (i.e., to the extent that they made possible a way of life in which the ultimately valuable human ends – science, philosophy, art – were produced). Aristotle's ultimate ethical principle was thus a form of teleological perfectionism, in which acts and institutions were deemed right to the extent that they actualized a fuller realization of human excellences, giving appropriate priority to the supremely valuable excellences of our contemplative intellectual lives. Aristotle's interpretation of his ethics of teleological perfectionism as justifying both slavery and the subjection of women might well be consistent with his understanding of facts and circumstances (though substantively unattractive), as these forms of servility were – for Aristotle – when justified, supported by incapacities for more elevated intellectual lives in the servile and by the role their subjection played in allowing others the leisure and the wealth to pursue the intellectual competences that were the ultimate ends in themselves in terms of which his ethical perfectionism evaluated acts and institutions.[46] The closest modern analogy to Aristotle's normative view of ethics and politics is Nietzsche's comparable perfectionism, which resisted any democratic ethics in favor of forms of aristocracy and warred on liberal forms of egalitarianism such as feminism.[47] Certainly, there is in Aristotle no suggestion of the modern egalitarian conception of basic human rights, resting on equal respect for the dignity of each and every person.

Thomas Aquinas construed his search for the nature of God in terms of Aristotelian moral psychology and ethics. It is on the basis of such scientific and philosophical premises that Thomas came to a conception of what we are asked

experience that perfectionism usually does not. I have previously argued that utilitarianism may to this extent be preferable as an egalitarian view of ethics to perfectionism, though it may still not be egalitarian enough. On this point, see David A. J. Richards, *A Theory of Reasons for Action* (Oxford: Clarendon Press, 1971), pp. 110–20.

46 On slavery, see Aristotle, *Politics*, trans. Ernest Barker (New York: Oxford University Press, 1962), bk. I, chaps. 3–7; on the subjection of women, *id.*, bk. I, chap. 13.

47 For a clear statement by Nietzsche of the perfectionist principle, see Friedrich Nietzsche, "Twilight of the Idols," in *The Portable Nietzsche*, ed. Walter Kaufmann (New York: Viking Press, 1954), pp. 465–563, 534. For Nietzsche on slavery, see Nietzsche, *Beyond Good and Evil: Prelude to a Philosophy of the Future*, trans. Helen Zimmern (Edinburgh: T. N. Foulis, 1907), pp. 189, 196; Nietzsche, "The Antichrist," in Kaufmann, *Portable Nietzsche*, pp. 568–656, 639; on caste systems, see *id.*, pp. 644–6; and for Nietzsche's critique of feminist movements from the point of view of "the military and aristocratic spirit," see Nietzsche, *Beyond Good and Evil*, p. 188.

reasonably to suppose to be God's teleological aims in the human and nonhuman domains. God, construed as the supremely talented scientist, philosopher, and artist, can be understood in terms of the human beings made in his image. Aristotle's conception of the unmoved mover was an abstract philosophical and scientific conception, quite remote from anything like a personal God of the sort Catholic moral theology contemplates. Thomas, assuming the Catholic conception, interpreted the natural facts of human competences (in light of Aristotle) in terms of God's embodying of their supreme perfectionist values. God was seen, for this reason, as supremely intellectual[48] and – lacking a body – as lacking either appetites or the pleasures taken in human appetites (i.e., food and sex).[49]

It was as a corollary of this inquiry, having established the existence of God and ascribing to God the ultimate perfectionist virtues of Aristotelian ethics, that Thomas turned to his distinctive view of human ethics: namely his theory of natural law. What for Aristotle were distinctive human competences (valued by a perfectionist metric) become for Thomas the product of God's creative will for our good and were interpreted accordingly as natural laws. Human laws that failed to comply with the moral demands of such natural laws were, in turn, categorized as "more acts of violence than laws."[50] What is of particular interest, for our purposes, is the rather unsentimentally Benthamite, consequentialist way Thomas treated human sexuality and the moral issues arising therefrom.

Thomas's understanding of ethical perfectionism ascribed no intrinsic values to bodily pleasures as such (including both sex and food): "the aforementioned pleasures are not the ultimate end, nor are they concomitants of the ultimate end."[51] To the objection that consensual sexual relations outside marriage (fornication) harmed no one and therefore should not raise any moral questions, he responded that they harmed God's intended good for us, for "God exercises care over every person on the basis of what is good for him," and the only good in sexuality is that it is "necessary in regard to propagation of the species."[52] The pleasures in sexual love having, for Thomas, no value whatsoever, he ascribed to sexuality a purely instrumental good, consistent with God's larger purposes for humankind: namely procreation but procreation linked to the kinds of care and nurture of the young of the human species required for their proper development. Marriage was the only acceptable form of such procreative unions for completely consequentialist reasons: only an indivisible marital union reasonably secured the kind of long-standing relationship between a man and a woman consistent with appropriate kinds of care. Single-parent motherhood would not be justified, because, as Thomas read the facts of gender difference: "a woman alone is not

48 See, on this point, Aquinas, *On the Truth of the Catholic Faith, Book* 1, pp. 170–3.

49 See, on this point, *id.*, pp. 271–4.

50 Thomas Aquinas, "Summa theologica IaIIae 96," in *Aquinas: Political Writings*, ed. R.W. Dyson (Cambridge: Cambridge University Press, 2002), p. 144.

51 See Aquinas, *On the Truth of the Catholic Faith, Book* 3: . . . *Part* 1, p. 111.

52 See Aquinas, *On the Truth of the Catholic Faith: Book* 3: . . . *Part* 2, p. 143.

adequate to this task; rather this demands the work of a husband, in whom reason is more developed for giving instruction and strength is more available for giving punishment."[53] And monogamy between a man and a woman was also required for comparable consequentialist reasons. Men would have no incentive to commit themselves to a long-standing relationship to a woman "if there were several males for one female." And while several females with one man would satisfy this requirement, it would frustrate the desires of women, as of men, shared by animals and humans, to have an unimpeded liberty of access to a sexual partner.[54] Finally, such monogamous relationships were preferred for a further consequentialist reason: "friendship consists in an equality," and polygamy led, as Thomas argued experience demonstrated, to a situation in which "the friendship of wife for husband would not be free, but somewhat servile."[55] For Thomas, such consequentialist arguments are the most reasonable way, assuming Aristotelian science and ethics, to construe what the teleological aims of a just God are for us. It would violate the whole tenor and spirit of Thomas's rigorously scientific and philosophical argument to reverse the intellectual order of the argument, making a fixed sectarian conception of teleology the premise of the argument independent of good arguments of science and philosophy.

Thomas took moral objection on these grounds to all forms of sexual relationship that were not procreative in the required way, whether heterosexual or homosexual. It was for this reason that fornication was always deemed wrong, as was "any emission of semen apart from the natural union of male and female. For which reason, sins of this type are called contrary to nature."[56] Thomas took particularly serious objection to masturbation: "the inordinate emission of semen is incompatible with the natural good; namely the preservation of the species. Hence, after the sin of homicide whereby a human nature already in existence is destroyed, this type of sin appears to take next place, for by it the generation of human nature is precluded."[57] Thomas adopted such a bleakly consequentialist approach to sexuality because he evaluated it in terms of his own rather original interpretation of Aristotelian ethical perfectionism. Sexual pleasure, having no independent value whatsoever, had value only when it served an end, procreation, in a way likely to lead to real perfectionist ethical values. It was certainly not an activity that all men had any ethical reason to undertake. To the contrary, "Since procreation is not a matter of the need of the individual but of the need of the whole species, it is not necessary for all men to devote themselves to acts of generation; instead, certain men, refraining from these acts, undertake other functions, such as the military life or contemplation."[58] It is pivotally important

53 See *id.*, p. 145.
54 See *id.*, pp. 144–5.
55 See *id.*, p. 152.
56 See *id.*, p. 144.
57 *Id.*, p. 146.
58 *Id.*, pp. 192–3.

to historical Thomism to note that the choice between having a sexual life and having a life of contemplation were thought of as exclusive alternatives, in a way Aristotle certainly never thought of them.

Thomas certainly agreed with Aristotle that the only perfectionist end in itself was contemplation and indeed argued that only this end in itself afforded the guiding value in terms of which other ends were to be pursued:

> If sport were an end in itself, the proper thing to do would be to play all the time, but this is not appropriate. So, the practical arts are ordered to the speculative ones, and likewise every human operation to intellectual speculation, as an end. Now, among all the sciences and arts which are thus subordinated, the ultimate end seems to belong to the one that is preceptive and architectonic in relation to the others. . . . In fact, this is the way that first philosophy is related to the other speculative sciences, for all the others depend on it, in the sense that they take their principles from it. . . . And this first philosophy is wholly ordered to the knowing of God, as its ultimate end; that is why it is also called *divine science*. So, divine knowledge is the ultimate end of every act of human knowledge and every operation.[59]

In effect, Thomas took Aristotle's conception that only philosophy, science, and the arts were perfectionist ends in themselves and reinterpreted the conception in terms of his own highly metaphysical philosophical quest to know God, as the ultimate perfectionist value in living, to which all other ends were instrumental. Ultimately, that value was the vision of God (*visio Dei*), a vision we can have – if we are saved – only after our deaths in an immortality absorbed in contemplation of God, the final Thomistic end of our search and our quest: "only the occupation of the contemplative life will persist in the resurrection."[60] Those incapable of such excellence have, of course, a role to play, namely having and raising children in forms of life that will make possible an economy and society in which those capable of real excellence will be able to cultivate and display their talents.

What was wholly new in Thomas's interpretation of Aristotelian perfectionism was his argument that the pleasures of the body (food and especially sex) were distractions, indeed impediments, to the perfectionist end in itself.[61] Thomas took from Augustine's interpretation of the Fall a view of our sexuality that, to the extent that it was not rigidly in service of procreation, was a shameful loss of control, the mark on our flawed natures left by original sin (before the Fall, Augustine argued [for fuller discussion, see discussion of Augustine that follows], our sexuality was under the control of our rational procreational wills, men having erections and emissions at will when needed to procreate – as some men wiggle their ears at will, so before the Fall men had erections and emissions at will[62]).

59 Aquinas, *On the Truth of the Catholic Faith: Book 3: . . . Part 1*, pp. 100–1.
60 Aquinas, *On the Truth of the Catholic Faith: Book 4*, p. 319.
61 See *id.*, pp. 112–13.
62 See Augustine, *City of God*, trans. Henry Bettenson (Harmondsworth, U.K.: Penguin, 1972), pp. 568–77.

Thomas went beyond Augustine in offering a deeper philosophical rationale for why sex as such was problematic and why celibacy was the better way. On this Thomistic view, the great virtue of a celibate life was precisely that it was freed of the continuous "solicitude and occupation which encumbers those who are married, concerning their wives, children and the procuring of the necessities of life." But, what was most important was that its rigors freed the celibate from sexual desires themselves, making possible intellectual activity not otherwise available:

> The enjoyment of corporeal delights distracts the mind from its peak activity and hinders it in the contemplation of spiritual things much more than the disturbance that results from resisting the concupiscent desires for these pleasures, because the mind becomes very strongly attached to carnal things through the enjoyment of such pleasures, especially those of sex. For enjoyment makes the appetite become fixed on the things that is enjoyed. And so, for those people who devote their attention to the contemplation of divine things and every kind of truth, it is especially harmful to have been addicted to sexual pleasures and particularly beneficial to abstain from them.[63]

It was because some persons, like Thomas and other members of Catholic religious orders, had undertaken celibacy that they were capable of cultivating and displaying the ultimate perfectionist final end in terms of which all other ends were instrumental means. It was only through such celibacy that they were capable of the philosophical rigors of Thomistic argument, an intellectually demanding form of inquiry through which alone man might come to know God – which was, of course, the guiding aim of the entire enterprise.

It is not surprising in a philosophy so based on Aristotelian perfectionism in ethics and politics that Thomas, following Aristotle's preference for mixed government, should have recommended a kingship tempered or limited by elements of democracy and oligarchy.[64] But Thomas's views about the pivotal role played by a celibate clergy in achieving defensible ethical values introduced a dimension to his political theory that was not found in Aristotle – namely the level of authority accorded to a celibate clergy in a papal monarchy. In particular, Thomas accorded such authority to the clergy in his grisly arguments for intolerance, including of heretics and of Jews.

Heresy is apparently a concept that arose uniquely within Christianity. Gratians's *Decretum* (ca. 1140) authoritatively compiled and organized the Catholic view: according to Perez Zagorin, Gratian "explains that heresy is the Greek work for choice and refers to a bad choice of doctrine contrary to the meaning of Scripture given by the Holy Spirit."[65] Heresy thus arises in a person who once believed the true doctrine but then chose not to believe it. What was for Thomas

[63] Aquinas, *On the Truth of the Catholic Faith: Book 3: . . . Part 2*, p. 194.
[64] See Aquinas, "Summa theologica IaIIae 105:1," pp. 52–6.
[65] Perez Zagorin, *How the Idea of Religious Toleration Came to the West*, p. 37.

so intolerable about heresy was its corruption of true belief, an enormity that, if a person refused to repent, merited death:

> On their own side there is the sin by which they deserve not only to be separated from the Church by excommunication, but also cut off from the world by death. For it is a much more grievous thing to corrupt the faith which gives life to the soul than to forge money, which supports temporal life. Hence if forgers of money or other malefactors are at once justly condemned to death by secular princes, so much more should heretics be not only excommunicated but even justly put to death as soon as they are convicted of heresy.[66]

The subtext of this argument is that Thomas, himself a member of the Dominican order, was defending the role the Dominican order played in the Inquisition, as the judges deputed to make the authoritative judgments of heresy (judgments that were then enforced by the secular arm). This responsibility of Dominicans followed logically from the role Thomas's philosophy assigned to celibate monastics, like himself, as those competent to exercise, cultivate, and display the only form of argument – namely metaphysical philosophy – that produced knowledge of God. This was, in Thomas's own words, "divine science,"[67] the competence for which was the ultimate perfectionist end, the better pursuit of which gave a sense and place to the pursuit of all other ends, namely that they should consequentially make this ultimate end more likely to be realized. Heresy was, for Thomas, so profoundly evil because it corrupted the general belief among Christians that their lives had value only insofar as they supported and sustained the kind of role that orders of celibate monks needed to have to pursue divine science, the only ultimate perfectionist good worth pursuing. Undermining this belief was such a great evil because it deprived human life of the only ultimate perfectionist value it could have, namely advancing the pursuit of divine science. For Thomas, the death of an obstinate heretic, a life that in his terms not only lacked any value but also aggressively battled against such value, produced a net gain in perfectionist value by keeping others in line with the Christian beliefs and commitments that satisfied perfectionist ethical principles as Thomas understood and defended them.

Thomas's treatment of nonbelievers was similarly instrumental to his perfectionist ends. This was most conspicuous in his treatment of Jews. Thomas was quite clear that nonbelievers should not be coerced into Christian belief,[68] but he treated as a quite separate matter whether nonbelievers should be subject to the authority of believers,[69] and whether the public exercise of their rites might be tolerated.[70] With respect to the former, Thomas drew a distinction between Jews

66 Aquinas, "Summa theologica IIaIIae ll," pp. 274–5.
67 Aquinas, *On the Truth of the Catholic Faith: Book 3:... Part 1*, p. 101.
68 Aquinas, "Summa theologiae IiaIIae 10," pp. 267–9.
69 *Id.*, pp. 270–1.
70 *Id.*, pp. 272–3.

and other nonbelievers; the property rights of Jews (in slaves) in contrast to other nonbelievers could be subject to prohibition or regulation (e.g., freeing slaves of Jews who converted to Christianity), because "the Jews themselves are slaves of the Church."[71] Consistent with this conception, Thomas elsewhere endorsed Catholic canon law's treatment of the Jews, including requiring them to wear special clothes that marked them as Jews.[72] Thomas thus ratified Augustine's conception that, because the Jews, coreligionists of Jesus, refused to accept him as their savior, they might be kept in a servile status in a Christian society to make an appropriate public statement to believers about the negative consequences of their refusal.[73] In contrast, precisely because Jewish rites reminded Christians of how their religion was prefigured in the Hebrew Bible, the rites of Jews could be tolerated, whereas those of other nonbelievers were to be tolerated only when it was clearly shown that forbidding them did more harm than good.[74]

It is illustrative of the manipulative character of Thomas's consequentialism that, when he considered the question of prohibiting the rituals of nonbelievers who were not Jews, his analogy was to Augustine on prostitution:

> [Quoting Augustine:] "If you banish whores from human affairs, everything will be disrupted by lust." Hence, though unbelievers sin in performing their rites, they can be tolerated either because of some good which results from their doing so, or in order to avoid some evil.[75]

Why prostitution? The analogy is motivated by the general way in which Thomas treated two classes of nonbelievers, Muslims and Jews, both of whom he repeatedly distinguished from Christians because they did not adopt the attitude to human sexuality that Aquinas had argued was required by philosophical theology. As we noted previously, Aquinas argued that Muhammad "seduced the people by promises of carnal pleasure to which the concupiscence of the flesh goads us."[76] What marked the Jewish and Muslim "fables" of the afterlife was that they "identified the rewards for just men with these pleasures [food and sex]."[77] By contrast to "the error of the Jews and of the Saracens,"[78] Christians knew the truth: there would be no sexual love at the resurrection.[79]

Unjust sexualization of a group is one familiar way in which groups are demeaned as inferior, as the study of extreme religious prejudice (anti-Semitism),

[71] *Id.*, p. 271.

[72] See Thomas Aquinas, "The Letter to the Duchess of Brabant, 'On the Government of the Jews,'" in Dyson, *Aquinas*, pp. 233–8.

[73] Augustine observes: "The Jew is the slave of the Christian," cited in Gavin I. Langmuir, *History, Religion, and Anti-Semitism* (Berkeley: University of California Press, 1990), p. 294.

[74] Dyson, *Aquinas*, p. 273.

[75] *Id.*, p. 273.

[76] Aquinas, *On the Truth of the Catholic Faith: Book 1*, p. 73.

[77] Aquinas, *On the Truth of the Catholic Faith: Book 3: . . . Part 1*, p. 113.

[78] *Id.*, p. 316.

[79] Aquinas, On the Truth of the Catholic Faith: Book 4, pp. 311–20.

racism, sexism, and homophobia clearly show.[80] From this perspective, Thomas's way of connecting his own arguments for the superiority of celibacy to the errors of Muslims and Jews shows his own role in the unjust construction of religious prejudice in general and Christian anti-Semitism in particular. At the heart of such Christian anti-Semitism is Augustine's blatant sexualization of the Jews in his *Tractatus adversus Judaeos*: "*Behold Israel according to the flesh* ([1] Cor. 10:18). This we know to be the carnal Israel; but the Jews do not grasp this meaning and as a result they prove themselves indisputably carnal."[81] Thomas was an apologist for such Christian anti-Semitism, a fact starkly shown in the way in which he endorsed Augustine's view of Jews as slaves of Christians and the various unjust practices that this view rationalized (e.g., segregation, antimiscegenation laws, wearing markers of Jewishness). My point here is that his general treatment of sexuality rationalized such unjust stigmatization.

This problem seems particularly aggravated in Thomas's treatment of women. Women need men, Thomas argued, not just for propagation "but also for the sake of government, since the male is more perfect in reasoning and stronger in his powers."[82] Thomas unjustly denigrated the moral powers of women in this and other ways, because, following Aristotle's unsound understanding of human sexual biology and psychology, he reduced women's nature to an essentially passive role both in sex and in marriage, as a consequence of his general understanding of sexuality.[83] In this, Thomas follows not only Aristotle but also Augustine. As I argue later, we can make contextual sense of Augustine's view both of sexuality and of women in terms of a background culture of gender inequality and associated psychology of loss and disassociation that Augustine, like Thomas later, assumes to be in the nature of things. Today, we morally and constitutionally question this culture and psychology, in particular, criticizing the unjust force of the stereotypes on which they rest. It is a common feature of irrationalist prejudices against a group that they depend on stereotypes that draw their force from long-standing cultural traditions that deprive the group of any of the basic rights by which they might contest those stereotypes. Thomas's treatment of women certainly seems to rest on such unjust stereotypes, and prominent among them is the way his general view of sexuality unjustly sexualizes women, as if they lack any moral powers by which they might legitimately make reasonable choices about

80 See, for general treatments of this issue, David A. J. Richards, *Identity and the Case for Gay Rights: Race, Gender, Religion as Analogies* (Chicago: University of Chicago Press, 1999); Elisabeth Young-Bruehl, *The Anatomy of Prejudices* (Cambridge, Mass.: Harvard University Press, 1996).

81 Quoted in Daniel Boyarin, *Carnal Israel: Reading Sex in Talmudic Culture* (Berkeley: University of California Press, 1993), p. 1.

82 Aquinas, *On the Truth of the Catholic Faith: Book 3:... Part 2*, p. 147.

83 See, for good critical treatment of this issue, Uta Ranke-Heinemann, *Eunuchs for the Kingdom of Heaven: The Catholic Church and Sexuality*, trans. John Brownjohn (London: Andre Deutsch, 1990), esp. pp. 162–76; Kari Elisabeth Borresen, *Subordination and Equivalence: The Nature and Role of Woman in Augustine and Thomas Aquinas*, trans. Charles H. Talbot (Washington, D.C.: University Press of America, 1981), esp. pp. 141–341.

their public and private lives, including their sexual lives, that are not subordinate to male patriarchal authority.

We return again to the importance in Thomas of the philosophical quest for God, the only final end in itself that gives a sense to the pursuit of all other ends, of celibacy. Such a choice is, of course, available to both men and women, but, on Thomas's view of it, it was only men who could realize through it the greatest perfectionist good, namely philosophical reflection and contemplation. His conception of religious authority was thus completely patriarchal. Carol Gilligan has cogently defined patriarchy as "a hierarchy – a rule of priests – in which the priest, the *hieros*, is a father,"[84] a priest-father with exclusive access to religio-moral authority, placing him as an authority not only over all women but also over other men. The authority of the celibate clergy in Augustine and Thomas is clearly patriarchal in this sense. Celibacy played a pivotal role in this authority because, on the view Augustine and Thomas took of sexuality, only celibacy allowed men philosophically to achieve the highest perfectionist good of a human life. We have already suggested that it is this conception of sexuality that was responsible for Thomas's indefensible ways of rationalizing intolerance, including the judicial murder of heretics and the subjugation of Jews and Muslims in Christian societies. It was also responsible for Thomas's role in the unjust construction of sexism, which rests on a view of sexuality that fails to take seriously women as moral agents, including sexual agents with voices and interests of their own.

We have seen in this section, that although Thomas Aquinas was concerned with justifying his arguments by reference to the most reasonable science and philosophy available in his day (drawing a distinction between knowledge acquired through reason and through revelation), his views concerning the legitimate (and limited) role of sexual activity were directly tied to his belief in the importance of a contemplative life freed from bodily distraction. As we will see in the next section, this latter dimension is not apparent from the new natural lawyers' discussions of Aquinas – something that of course begs a broader question, namely how far the new natural lawyers' substantive theory can plausibly be categorized as rooted in Thomism.

b. New Natural Law as Pseudo-Thomism

The new natural lawyers openly admit that their arguments move beyond those of Thomas Aquinas. Thus, Finnis openly revises and develops Aquinas's account in a number of ways, and Grisez's arguments are presented as freestanding though informed by Thomas.[85] However, I aim in this section to go further and to suggest

[84] Carol Gilligan, *The Birth of Pleasure* (New York: Knopf, 2002), p. 4.

[85] For interesting discussion, see Denis J. M. Bradley, "John Finnis on Aquinas 'The Philosopher'" 41 *Heythrop J.* 1 (2000), A. S. McGrade, "What Aquinas Should Have Said? Finnis's Reconstruction of Social and Political Thomism," 44 *Am. J. Juris.* 125 (1999).

that there is a clear difference between the new natural lawyers and Thomas: namely that they argue in a non-Thomistic fashion and make selective use of Thomas's arguments.

The challenge for Catholic moral theology after Vatican II and in the wake of the Holocaust was to develop an approach that, in contrast to historical Thomism, could accord the right to free exercise of religious conscience and other basic rights of liberal constitutionalism a firm grounding in its tradition. A quite plausible approach might have been, inspired by the history of leading proponents of the argument for toleration, not to turn to a reinvention of Thomism, grounded, as it is, in a philosophy and science, like Aristotle's, not inspired by Christian sources. Rather, why not, like Sebastian Castellio or Roger Williams or John Locke (all leading figures in the development of the argument for toleration),[86] turn to the example of Jesus of Nazareth himself, contesting on the ground of a fresh reading of the Gospels the arguments for persecution that established churches had developed, often with little or no concern for the Gospels themselves? Of course, all these figures were Protestants, and radical Protestants at that. But the argument for toleration arose from their thought, and if the Catholic Church meant in 1965 to acknowledge the profound moral error of its traditionally intolerant views, why not, in an ecumenical spirit, turn to the specifically Christian sources that illuminate how unconnected to these sources these traditionally intolerant views were? If not follow them, why not at least follow their approach, one that could certainly be traced as well to Catholic skeptical, humanist thinkers like Montaigne and Erasmus?[87]

I mention these alternatives only to show that there are many reasonable ways that Catholic moral theology might responsibly address the moral insights of Vatican II. These alternatives include contemporary forms of Thomism, some of which have a rather different character than that proposed by new natural law.[88] But my concern here is with closely examining an approach, new natural law, which chose to so revise historical Thomism in a certain way that would accommodate Vatican II and nonetheless preserve much else in traditional Thomist and Catholic moral teaching about sexuality and other issues. I begin with the question of what it has kept and what it has changed.

(i) Basic Goods

For clarity on these points, we need to distinguish the two structural parts of Thomas's moral theory: first, the arguments for the existence of God; about the

86 On their importance and the nature of their arguments, see Perez Zagorin, *How the Idea of Religious Toleration Came to the West*.

87 See, on this point, David A. J. Richards, *Toleration and the Constitution* (New York: Oxford University Press, 1986), pp. 88–9.

88 See, for the range of contemporary views of Thomism (including new natural law), Charles E. Curran and Richard A. McCormick, S.J., *Readings in Moral Theology No. 7: Natural Law and Theology* (New York: Paulist Press, 1991).

nature of God; and as an analogy to understanding God's nature, about human nature and natural law (understanding God's nature by analogy to the creature, humankind, made in its image) – and second, the arguments about the content of Christian revelation (e.g., matters believed on the basis of miracles). Of these two parts of the theory, the first rests on arguments of reason that Thomas took to be open and accessible to all, arguments largely based on what he took to be the best science and philosophy available, namely Aristotle's physics, psychology, and ethics. The second, in contrast, examines beliefs based not on reason alone but on revelation; Thomas certainly believes that these latter beliefs are based on reasons (e.g., the miracles he supposed to certify their reliability as God's will), but his concern in this second, more specifically Catholic part of this theology is to show that none of these beliefs is irrational in terms of general arguments available to all persons. Although the first part of the moral theology is thus supported by positive arguments of reason that all (e.g., Christian, Jew, Muslim) could accept, the second part addresses the revealed content of Christian belief (which Jews and Muslims do not accept in the same way) and tries to show that none of it can be regarded as irrational. The aim of the moral theology, structured in these two ways, is to show that Christian belief is reasonable all the way down, though reasonable, as we have seen, in different ways.

The new natural lawyers claim to preserve essential features of historical Thomism, a claim that John Finnis defends at length in his monograph concerning Aquinas.[89] But there is a serious question, raised by important students of historical Thomism, as to whether their views are not more a contemporary invention than a serious interpretation of the aims of historical Thomism. There is, first, a rather startling repudiation both of Thomas's Aristotelian conception of natural ends and of his ethical perfectionism, topics I discuss at length shortly.[90] Further, an interpretation of a historical view like Thomism must also give a sense of its background world and thought, looking not only at texts but also at the background in terms of which those texts should be reasonably understood; otherwise, its alleged reconstruction is more a playing with words than a serious interpretation. From this perspective, Thomas is concerned not with political theory in the way both Plato and Aristotle were but with the powers of the medieval church "as a divinely established, unalterable monarchy,"[91] offering "a straightforward argument for the hierocratic view of cooperation between secular and ecclesiastical authorities in the maintenance (or crusading recovery or extension) of Christian society, a hallmark of the Latin High Middle Ages."[92] It is from

89 See John Finnis, *Aquinas: Moral, Political, and Legal Theory* (Oxford: Oxford University Press, 1998).

90 See, on this point, Ralph McInerny, "Grisez and Thomism," in *The Revival of Natural Law: Philosophical, Theological and Ethical Responses to the Finnis-Grisez School*, ed. Nigel Biggar and Rufus Black (Aldershot, U.K.: Ashgate, 2000), pp. 53–72; Ralph McInerny, "The Principles of Natural Law," in Curran and McCormick, *Readings in Moral Theology No. 7*, pp. 139–56.

91 McGrade, "What Aquinas Should Have Said?" pp. 125, 138.

92 *Id.*, pp. 136–7.

this perspective that one can make reasonable interpretive sense of the important place of intolerance, including the death penalty for heresy, in Thomas's thought. Thomas is not a political theorist and certainly not a serious theorist of constitutional democracy. The attempt of the new natural lawyers radically to unlink Thomism both from its concerns and from its rationale is, to say the least, interpretively unpersuasive.[93] They do not, unlike other contemporary Thomists, even plausibly attempt to show how Thomas's general moral theory might yield different results in different circumstances. Even Thomas's substantive moral views on abortion (he did not regard a fetus at conception as a moral person) cannot plausibly be aligned with the view taken by the new natural lawyers.[94] Finally, the attempt of Finnis to make Thomas into a pioneer of contemporary values of universal human rights is, to say the least, unpersuasive, as is shown by, among other things, Thomas's central preoccupation with the traditional authority of the Catholic Church, including its defense of intolerance. Finnis's arguments, at this point, come not from Thomas but from contemporary views and theories, including neo-Kantian values of equal dignity, to which Finnis is heavily indebted, though he never acknowledges the debt.

Finnis's views also come, particularly in the area of sexuality and gender, from the moral theology of Germain Grisez, whose underlying moral philosophy is, as we will see, decidedly not Thomist. Yet it is through the prism of Grisez's thought that Finnis makes sense of Thomas's thought, though he admits "Germain Grisez's 1993 treatise on sex, marriage, and family life clarifies large tracts of sexual morality which Aquinas's account left more or less obscure."[95] This makes Finnis's appeals to Thomas for authority, as in his critique of Andrew Koppelman's discussion of Thomas,[96] interpretively quite unreliable. Finnis's Thomas is not Thomas but whatever he can find in Thomas that agrees in conclusions with the freestanding moral theology of Grisez. This is shown by the inconsistent way Finnis interprets Thomas. He rejects everything in Thomas inconsistent with his alleged role as a pioneer of human rights except what Finnis claims to be the most literal textual interpretation of Aquinas when dealing with sexuality. Thomas has little to do with the matter, except to disguise the contemporary moral theology that in fact motivates the argument.

There comes a point at which a view, claiming to be interpretive of a historical tradition, both takes away and adds so much that it fails any longer reasonably to connect with what is most valuable in that tradition. In the case of new natural law, it takes much more from contemporary views than it admits, and what it retains speaks, as we will see, much more to the political crisis in legitimacy of

93 See, on this point, *id.*, p. 147.

94 See, on this point, *id.*, pp. 144–5.

95 See John Finnis, "The Good of Marriage and the Morality of Sexual Relations: Some Philosophical and Historical Observations," 42 *Am. J. Juris.* 97, 99 (1997).

96 For Finnis's critique, see *id.*; for Koppelman's argument, see Andrew Koppelman, "Is Marriage Inherently Heterosexual?" 42 *Am. J. Juris.* 51 (1997).

modern papal authority than to the deeper ambitions of historical Thomism as a public philosophy that would reasonably appeal to believers and nonbelievers alike.

The general problem with the new natural lawyers' views is shown, I believe, by the ways in which they assume and then modify the structure of Thomas's two-part argument, in particular, its first part (the search for God requiring an investigation of human nature and its natural laws). What is philosophically central to Thomas's structure is its appeal to what he took to be the best science and philosophy available, namely Aristotle, and, working within that science and philosophy, to show how it afforded the indispensable forms of reason by which we could come to know God, which is throughout the driving quest of Thomas's Christian philosophy. When Thomas thus comes to examine human nature and its natural laws, he can reasonably assume that what he finds is supported by the best science and philosophy then available, including, as we have seen, Aristotle's ethical perfectionism. But the new natural lawyers, precisely at this crucial point, not only reject Thomas's dependence on Aristotle's science and philosophy (which is certainly understandable, in light of progress in both science and philosophy since the thirteenth century) but also reject, much more fatally to their enterprise, the Thomistic aspiration to ground their new version of natural law in anything like what would be the equivalent, in contemporary circumstances, of the best available reasons of science and philosophy.

One of the most attractive features of Thomas is his ethical naturalism, the way in which he responsibly connects an understanding of human goods to what he takes to be the facts of our rational natures, the good being, as it was for Aristotle, the object of our rational desires and ends. Reasonable discussion of ethical and political issues is thus connected to the facts of our rational natures and our circumstances, leading, as we earlier saw, to the Benthamic spirit of Thomas's defense of monogamous, indissoluble marriage on consequentialist grounds. Thomas thought that his views of sexuality were consistent with the science of human nature as he understood it, and he worked out its implications with remorseless logic. He certainly did not think of his arguments as peculiarly Christian but instead ones that would appeal broadly to Jews, Muslims, and others. But the new natural lawyers abandon what was so reasonably appealing in Thomas's procedure, its attempt responsibly to show how ethical judgments connect to scientific understanding of the facts. It was only because Thomas insisted on such accountability to the best-available arguments of science and philosophy that his theology had the reasonable appeal it did not only for Catholics but also for all people sensitive to good arguments of reason.

That the new natural lawyers have given up on this Thomistic methodology is quite clear from how they reach Thomas's conclusions about sexual morality without any sense of accountability to his scientific and philosophical rigor of mind. Thomas thought of his views on sexuality as reasonable because they were rooted in or connected to a scientific understanding of our human nature, an understanding he derived from Aristotle and interpreted in terms of Aristotle's ethical perfectionism (a form of naturalism). The new natural lawyers, however, discuss sexuality in a way that affronts the imperative of Thomistic rationality. They claim to understand its normative purposes without any interest whatsoever in various forms of empirical inquiry into our human sexual natures.

At no point do they even acknowledge the empirical problem in a view of sexuality (as narrowly tied to procreation), which Freud seminally noticed was importantly not tightly tied to the reproductive cycle:

> The sexual instinct... is probably more strongly developed in man than in most of the highest animals; it has almost entirely overcome the periodicity to which it is tied in animals. It places extraordinarily large amounts of force at the disposal of civilized activity, and it does this in virtue of its especially marked characteristic of being able to displace its aim without materially diminishing in intensity.[97]

There is no discussion of the extensive research on animals versus human sexual behavior that confirms this observation,[98] or the distinctive features of human sexuality from an evolutionary perspective,[99] or of the work of researchers on human sexuality (including homosexuality) like Alfred Kinsey and his followers,[100] or of

97 Sigmund Freud, "'Civilized' Sexual Morality and Modern Nervous Illness," in *Standard Edition of the Complete Psychological Works of Sigmund Freud*, vol. 9, ed. James Strachey (London: Hogarth Press, 1959), p. 187.

98 See, on this point, Clellan S. Ford and Frank A. Beach, *Patterns of Sexual Behavior* (New York: Harper Colophon Books, 1951).

99 See Sarah Blaffer Hrdy, *Mother Nature: Maternal Instincts and How They Shape the Human Species* (New York: Ballantin Books, 1999); Sarah Blaffer Hrdy, *Mothers and Others: The Evolutionary Origins of Mutual Understanding* (Cambridge, Mass.: The Belknap Press of Harvard University Press, 2009).

100 See, for a general discussion of relevant sex researchers, Edward M. Brecher, *The Sex Researchers* (London: Andre Deutsch, 1970); Paul Robinson, *The Modernization of Sex: Havelock Ellis, Alfred Kinsey, William Masters and Virginia Johnson* (New York: Harper & Row, 1976). For relevant works of Alfred Kinsey, see Alfred C. Kinsey, Wardell B. Pomeroy, and Clyde E. Martin, *Sexual Behavior in the Human Male* (Philadelphia: W. B. Saunders, 1948); Alfred C. Kinsey, Wardell B. Pomeroy, Clyde E. Martin, and Paul H. Gebhard, *Sexual Behavior in the Human Female* (New York: Pocket Books, 1970) (originally published in 1953). For subsequent studies by researchers associated with Kinsey, see Paul H. Gebhard, John H. Gagnon, Wardell B. Pomeroy, and Cornelia V. Christenson, *Sex Offenders* (New York: Bantam, 1967); Martin S. Weinberg and Colin J. Williams, *Male Homosexuals* (New York: Oxford University Press, 1974); Alan P. Bell and Martin S. Weinberg, *Homosexualities* (New York: Simon and Schuster, 1978); Alan P. Bell, Martin S. Weinberg, and Sue Kiefer Hammersmith, *Sexual Preference: Its Development in Men and Women* (Bloomington: Indiana University Press, 1981); Martin S. Weinberg, Colin J. Williams, and Douglas W. Pryor, *Dual Attraction: Understanding Bisexuality* (New York: Oxford University Press, 1994). For illuminating biography, see James H. Jones, *Alfred C. Kinsey* (New York: W. W. Norton, 1997).

William Masters and Virginia Johnson,[101] let alone other such research.[102] The new natural lawyers offer apodictic moral certainties about gay and lesbian sex without any discussion of the extensive empirical investigations of these and other works of actual gay people[103] or works by gay people,[104] let alone of the related empirical work on gay and lesbian teenagers.[105] There is no discussion of contemporary forms of experience, including democratic political movements like feminism and gay rights that have given voice to new forms of experience and ways of life, that reasonably bear on any such inquiry in the modern world. The result is a form of ethical discourse disconnected from any responsible contemporary discussion of human sexuality, a discourse, unlike historical Thomism, that fails to take seriously the demand that its arguments rests on reasonable procedures available to all.

What the new natural lawyers innovate, in the place of Thomas's interpretation of Aristotle's ethical perfectionism, is a form of deontological ethics based on normative judgments of self-evident human goods, none of which may be violated but not all of which must be pursued or pursued in the same way. Several terminological distinctions are, at this point, apposite. Moral theories are of two sorts: teleological and deontological. Teleological theories defined right acts and institutions in terms of how they advance the realization of goods. Teleological theories differ in terms of how those goods are understood (for utilitarianism, they are pleasure or pains, or satisfactions or frustrations of desire; for perfectionism, they are excellences in the display of talents or failures to reach such standards). But teleological theories allow for the goods in question to be traded off against one another to allow for the greater net amount of good overall, which is the aim of ethics (the greatest net amount of good or evil in the world). Deontological theories, in contrast, do not define right acts or institutions in terms of such net aggregative consequences in the world but define ethical principles as reasonable constraints on action independent of such consequences, often forbidding the

[101] See William H. Masters, *Human Sexual Response* (Boston: Little, Brown, 1966); William H. Masters and Virginia E. Johnson, *Human Sexual Inadequacy* (Boston: Little, Brown, 1970); William H. Masters and Virginia E. Johnson, *Homosexuality in Perspective* (Boston: Little, Brown, 1979); William H. Masters, Virginia E. Johnson, and Robert C. Kolodny, *Heterosexuality* (New York: HarperCollins, 1994).

[102] See Philip Blumstein and Pepper Schwartz, *American Couples: Money Work Sex* (New York: William Morrow, 1983); Edward O. Laumann, John H. Gagnon, Robert T. Michael, and Stuart Michaels, *The Social Organization of Sexuality: Sexual Practices in the United States* (Chicago: University of Chicago Press, 1994).

[103] See Edward Stein, *The Mismeasure of Desire: The Science, Theory, and Ethics of Sexual Orientation* (New York: Oxford University Press, 1999).

[104] See Edward Stein, ed., *Forms of Desire: Sexual Orientation and the Social Constructionist Controversy* (New York: Routledge, 1990); John D'Emilio, *Making Trouble* (New York: Routledge, 1992).

[105] *Report of the Secretary's Task Force on Youth Suicide* (Department of Health and Human Services, 1989), esp. vol. 3, *Prevention and Intervention in Youth Suicide*.

kinds of trading off of the evils for some for the goods of others that teleological theories not only permit but also require.

The most important and influential deontological theory is that of Immanuel Kant,[106] given expression in recent moral philosophy by, among others, John Rawls,[107] Thomas Scanlon,[108] and others. Kant understands ethics in terms of our moral powers of rationality and reasonableness, the exercise of which expresses our rational dignity. Ethical principles are constraints on our conduct reasonably acceptable to and incumbent on all persons, guaranteeing appropriate equal respect for our dignity. It is this moral conception that, in politics, gives rise to constitutional principles guaranteeing respect for basic human rights, prominent among which are the rights of conscience and of speech. What distinguishes this moral conception is its political liberalism, expressed in the forms of constitutional democracy now familiar in many nations, including the United States and Britain. Its underlying principles define legitimate political power in terms of goods, like basic human rights, that all reasonable persons, understood as free and equal person with dignity, want whatever else they want. Accordingly, arguments in politics should be conducted, as both Kant and Rawls urged, in terms of public reasons available to and accessible to all, irrespective of more ultimate religious or philosophical disagreements.

The new natural lawyers are, of course, familiar with these distinct forms of moral theory and clearly want to align their views with a deontological approach along Kantian lines. This is shown by the important role ideas of dignity (in particular, of conscience) and reasonableness play in their arguments, but their alternative approach is in terms of a set of self-evident goods, subject to certain near-absolute restrictions. These goods give their views a more perfectionist character than deontological theories usually have. But because their restrictions on these goods are so absolute, their views remain, I believe, dominantly deontological. I begin with the basic goods and then turn to the restrictions.[109]

The method that the new natural lawyers choose in identifying the goods is curious. The claim is that such goods are universally implicit in our normative

106 Immanuel Kant, *Foundations of the Metaphysics of Morals*, trans. Lewis W. Beck (New York: Liberal Arts Press, 1959).

107 John Rawls, *A Theory of Justice* (Cambridge, Mass.: Harvard University Press, 1971).

108 T. M. Scanlon, *What We Owe to Each Other* (Cambridge, Mass.: Harvard University Press, 1998).

109 In fact, the new natural lawyers claim that their view is neither teleological nor deontological. See Germain Grisez, "A Contemporary Natural-Law Ethics," George P. McLean, ed., *Normative Ethics and Objective Reason* (Washington, D.C.: Paideai Publishers, 1996), pp. 241–57. It is reasonably clear why their view is not teleological, precisely because it does not allow for the trade-offs among goods that teleological theories (e.g., utilitarianism) both require and endorse. For example, new natural lawyers precisely do not allow any frustration of a basic good such as life to be justified by the pursuit of another such good. It is much less clear why the view is not deontological: it appears precisely to insist on the priority of certain reasonable (i.e., as defind according to a value-laden scale) ethical principles over any balance of teleological goods over evils. It is for this reason that I regard the new natural lawyers' views as clearly deontological and discuss them as such (i.e., as a particularly unreasonable form of deontological theory).

judgments, things that we believe are ultimately good without requiring any further justification. What is striking about the way these judgments are described is that they are self-evident, a term prominently invoked by Finnis presumably to describe his own experience. Finnis characterizes these judgments as ultimate intuitions of value, not reducible to any facts of our natures. In this way, Finnis claims to obviate the naturalistic fallacy, the mistake, famously identified by G. E. Moore in *Principia Ethica*,[110] of assuming without adequate argument that good was conceptually identical with some natural fact. Moore's fallacy is more a caution against simplistic forms of naturalism than a decisive argument against naturalism in ethics.[111] Finnis's claims of self-evidence are, however, simplistic and question begging in precisely the way that concerned Moore and are therefore not philosophically grounded. Rather, Finnis's method of argument is, no doubt unconsciously, motivated by its being the only method that allows him to rationalize normative judgment as ultimate without any concern for their factual basis. This is, of course, a recipe for legitimating possibly irrational prejudices, and it explains why Thomas himself, a supreme philosophical rationalist, did not ground his judgments of goodness in this way.

The problem is not merely a method likely to lead to irrationalism but a content that is sometimes irrationalist. It is surely plausible in the modern world that new natural lawyers should identify friendship as a human good and marriage as an important expression of that good, an improvement certainly over Thomas's more bleakly procreational sense of the good of marriage. But it is quite unreasonable, in interpreting marriage as such a good, that they should regard sexual pleasure in marriage (independent of procreation) as not only problematic but evil. In defense of their interpretation, Grisez appeals to animal biology as a reason for believing that "one-flesh union" (procreative sex in marriage) is the ultimate good of marital union. Grisez argues:

> Each animal is incomplete, for a male or a female individual is only a potential part of the mated pair, which is the complete organism that is capable of reproducing sexually. This is true also of men and women: as mates who engage in sexual intercourse suited to initiate new life, they complete each other and become an organic unit. In doing so, it is literally true that "they become one flesh."[112]

Even as a description of animal reproductive biology, this description gets the facts wrong. It fails to distinguish between the activities of animals and the functioning of its organs and other parts. When animals walk, they act, and we ascribe to them voluntary acts. But the beating of an animal's heart, an important body

[110] See G. E. Moore, *Principia Ethica* (Cambridge: Cambridge University Press, 1960) (originally published in 1903), pp. 15–16.

[111] See, on this point, Richards, *Theory of Reasons for Action*, pp. 9–10.

[112] Germain Grisez, *The Way of the Lord Jesus*, vol. 2, *Living a Christian Life* (Quincy, Ill.: Franciscan Press, 1993), p. 570.

organ, is not something that the animal voluntarily does; the heart functions, but it is not an agent. Grisez thus gets his facts wrong when he treats male and female animals as organs of some other animal or organism. Organs are parts of animals, but animals are not parts of organisms. To make his case, Grisez, irrationally, depends on a fact that does not exist. Grisez's mating couple is not an organism but two people who engage in a joint activity for a certain purpose, but they might reasonably engage in that activity for other purposes as well, as an expression of sexual love and intimacy, for example, without wanting to propagate.[113] Why, exactly, is that not a reasonable instantiation of the good of friendship or love? Such ideologically fabricated biology is of a piece with the racist biology that once rationalized antimiscegenation laws, the racist science that the U.S. Supreme Court rejected as a rational basis for laws in *Loving v. Virginia*.[114] Grisez's pseudobiology similarly rationalizes the judgment that all nonprocreational sex is intrinsically evil, demonizing intimate sexual acts of men and women, gay and straight, that express mutual pleasure, affection, and sometimes love. What racist science was to rationalizing the evil of racism, Grisez's pseudobiology is to the dehumanizing evils of sexism and homophobia.

Unfortunately, the way in which other basic goods are inferred and interpreted by new natural law is no less unreasonable. Life is certainly a basic good, as liberal political theorists have argued since Locke, a good that the state may legitimately protect on equal terms through both the criminal and civil law. But new natural lawyers take the view that, once the ovum is fertilized, life in this sense exists, and therefore abortion must be prohibited on the same terms as the criminal law of homicide prohibits murder of persons. But many reasonable people believe that an early-term fetus is not a moral person in this latter sense, lacking the appropriate capacities on the basis of which we ascribe personhood, and they deny the analogy to the criminal law of homicide precisely because it fails to take seriously the required respect for the moral voice and interests of women in deciding whether they will bear the fetus to term. New natural law takes the view that there is nothing to be discussed precisely at the point where many people believe reasonable discussion should begin.

Some of the goods inferred by new natural law, notably, religion, cannot reasonably be supposed basic goods for all persons in the modern world. Thomas Aquinas at least presented reasons, rooted in the best science and philosophy then available, for believing in the existence of God that he supposed to be compelling, on the basis of which the first part of his argument then proceeds. Although new natural lawyers might believe such arguments exist, they do not, unlike Thomas, give them any place in their structure of argument, and indeed it is doubtful that such arguments would today command the kind of reasonable philosophical

[113] See, for fuller development of this critique of Grisez, Gareth Moore, *A Question of Truth: Christianity and Homosexuality* (London: Continuum, 2003), pp. 253–73.

[114] *Loving v. Virginia*, 388 U.S. 1 (1967) (striking down Virginia's ban on interracial marriage on grounds of both equal protection and due process).

consensus they did in the thirteenth century. In any event, new natural lawyers, who claim to appeal to reasons available to all, offer us no reasons but rather self-evident judgments that, as earlier observed, rest on not looking for such further reasons. At this point, the conception of basic goods becomes obviously sectarian, appealing to basic goods that are not supported by reasons available and accessible to all.

Unfortunately, the problem may infect other goods that new natural law argues are basic. For Thomas, of course, the whole first part of his argument rests on what he took to be good reasons for believing in the existence of God and proceeds from there. He certainly did not think of any of the arguments in the first part of his structure as in any sense sectarian; they would appeal, as he hoped they would, to reasonable minds in Jews, Muslims, and others. New natural lawyers do not discuss this part of Thomas's great architecture of philosophical argument but apparently assume it. A really philosophically interesting construction of natural law would have dealt with these issues, showing which of these arguments or other arguments they depend on for their belief in the existence of God. Much has happened in science and philosophy since Thomas, some of which undermines many, though by no means all, of the traditional arguments for the existence of God. Any powerful contemporary philosophical restatement of Thomism would have to explore and discuss these issues with care. In the absence of such argument, the inference and interpretation of basic goods by new natural law assumes arguments about God and God's creative will for us his creatures (made in God's image) that probably fundamentally shape why new natural lawyers infer and interpret basic goods in the way they do. But if so, they have not done the philosophical work required to render their accounts reasonably appealing to those not already committed to Catholic belief or to any form of religious belief, which includes many reasonable people today. They have failed to offer precisely the reasonable arguments, appealing to all, which would make their Christian philosophy of interest not just to Catholics but to all democratic citizens. This is embarrassingly conspicuous in the case of the basic good of religion but may problematically infect the whole list.

(ii) Moral Absolutes

The deontological character of new natural law comes in the strong ethical constraints it imposes on any attack on a basic human good. Although it is not required that all such goods be pursued or pursued equally (while marriage is a basic good, a celibate clergy may choose to forgo marriage to better pursue other goods), new natural law imposes very strong ethical constraints on any attack on such goods, taking a life or having sex outside marriage or many forms of sex in marriage, and the like. Some narrow principles qualify this prohibitions (e.g., the principle of self-defense, where applicable, permits a taking of life that would otherwise be forbidden), but the general character of these ethical constraints is absolutist. The kinds of trade-offs among goods and evils that teleological theories permit and sometimes require is not allowed by new natural law. Its conception is therefore deontological: reasonable ethical constraints are imposed on our conduct irrespective of teleological consequences.

All reasonable deontological theories impose such constraints, but the question is whether the constraints imposed by new natural law are reasonable in the sense that the theory supposes them to be, namely supported by arguments accessible to and appealing to all, including those who are decidedly not Catholic believers. Many such reasonable people, including some Catholic believers, find some of the distinctive absolutist constraints insisted on by new natural law as lacking any rational basis, often because the goods on which such constraints defend are so problematic. Many women, including Catholic women, fail to see the ethical basis of the absolute prohibition on most forms of contraception, which certainly do not harm others (in light of overpopulation) and may enable a married couple better to care for their other children and other aims; indeed, for many women, contraception guarantees them, for the first time in human history, an appropriate respect for their dignity in deciding whether, when, and on what terms they will have children consistent with their other aims and ambitions.

3. THE SUBSTANTIVE UNREASONABLENESS OF NEW NATURAL LAW

It is against the background of the developments discussed in Chapter 1 that we can assess the substantive unreasonableness of the project of new natural law. New natural law essentially ratifies the kind of authority over these questions that Augustine and Thomas Aquinas aimed to justify, an authority made possible for them by a celibate male priesthood and a contemporary papal authority, in particular, that seeks to uphold the views on sexual morality of Augustine and Thomas. As we have seen, the role sexuality plays for Thomas is solely for propagation because sexuality is for him, following Augustine, so epistemically problematic (as he puts is, "the enjoyment of corporeal delights distracts the mind from its peak activity"[115]), and could be redeemed only by producing offspring who would support a society in which a celibate clergy would have the support and role it must have to pursue the ultimate perfectionist value of knowing God. New natural law recognizes more value in marriage (as a basic good) than Thomas did but retains the basic division of labor in Thomas's philosophical system, a noncelibate laity hierarchically subject to the authority of a celibate male clergy. Leading new natural lawyers, like Finnis, Grisez, and Robert George, are notably not celibate (all are married), but their arguments buttress essentially the moral views of the Catholic celibate clergy, in particular, those of current papal teaching. I start with the moral views of the new natural lawyers and then turn to the question of moral authority. There is a decisive objection to the enforcement

[115] Aquinas, *On the Truth of the Catholic Faith, Book 3: ... Part 2*, p. 194.

of such views through public law in constitutional democracies, namely they rest on unjust gender stereotypes that are now constitutionally condemned.

New natural lawyers sometimes recognize that Thomas's views on gender unacceptably rationalize the unjust subordination of women.[116] But their own views, grounded in the freestanding moral theology of Grisez, are themselves highly patriarchal. Germain Grisez, whose discussion is regarded as authoritative by both John Finnis[117] and Robert George,[118] thus defends at some length the proposition that, in families, "the husband-father has a special role in decision making."[119] Authority in the family is defined by what Grisez calls "their proper spheres,"[120] which is, of course, highly gendered. Although authority is "sometimes" by consensus,[121] it is clear that, for Grisez, absent consensus, "the husband-father ordinarily should decide," a proposition defended as "the irreducible core of the traditional Christian teaching which Pius XI summarizes as 'the primacy of the husband with regard to the wife and children, the ready subjection of the wife and her willing obedience.'"[122] Grisez's authority for such subordination is papal teachings, including those of John Paul II, whose views reaffirm, he argues, that a wife "remains subject to his [her husband's] rightful authority."[123] Men and women are, in marriage, "equal in dignity,"[124] but the sense of equality must be interpreted in terms of gender differences bearing on procreation rather than regarded as "a merely consensual relationship similar to other friendships, as it is by many feminists."[125] Of course, for Grisez and the other natural lawyers, such equality in difference requires as well the moral wrongness of contraception in marriage or other nonprocreative sex acts in marriage, as well as the wrongness of masturbation and, of course, abortion.[126]

How are we to understand the gender stereotypes underlying this view? I argued, in Chapter 1, that constitutional developments in a wide range of areas (e.g., extreme religious intolerance, racism, sexism) condemn persisting patterns of moral slavery that reflect historical traditions that abridge the basic human rights of groups of persons (including basic rights of conscience, speech, intimate life, and work) on the unjust ground of stereotypes that are themselves the product of such abridgment. One form of such moral slavery, now condemned by constitutional principles, is sexism, and we can understand the role of new

[116] See, on this point, Finnis, *Aquinas*, p. 171.

[117] See, e.g., John Finnis, "Natural Law Theory and Limited Government," in *Natural Law, Liberalism, and Morality*, ed. Robert P. George (Oxford: Oxford University Press, 2002), pp. 1–26, 13.

[118] See, e.g., Robert George, *In Defense of Natural Law* (Oxford: Clarendon Press, 1999), p. 161.

[119] Grisez, *Way of the Lord Jesus*, vol. 2, pp. 629–33, 629.

[120] *Id.*, p. 630.

[121] *Id.*

[122] *Id.*, p. 631.

[123] *Id.*, p. 617.

[124] *Id.*, p. 618.

[125] *Id.*, p. 619.

[126] See, on these points, *id.*, pp. 497–519, 553–752.

natural law in the construction of sexism in terms of the unjust gender stereotypes it attempts, on wholly inadequate grounds, to legitimate. It is certainly not the case that only the patriarchal celibate male priesthood of Catholicism supports a conception of gender differences that rationalizes the structural injustice of sexism. We can clarify the nature of the patriarchal view, endorsed by Grisez and others, by placing it in the context of earlier views, which have a similar structure.

Such an earlier conception was, for example, familiarly invoked by early advocates of political liberalism as a way of justifying the failure to extend liberal principles to women,[127] and it has been prominently used in political cultures otherwise committed to values of constitutional democracy and human rights to justify a subordination of women inconsistent with values. In nineteenth-century America, for example, it was Protestant thinkers like Catharine Beecher and Horace Bushnell who defended a conception of women's distinctive nature, in contrast to men's, that questioned the activism of women for their own rights, including rights of suffrage.[128]

Both Beecher and Bushnell were at sectarian religious war with the idea of basic rights claimed by and for women and, in particular, the idea of such rights asserted by and for women in the family. To make their point, they focused on one aspect of women's lives, the relationship of women as mothers to their dependent and vulnerable young children, and characterized that relationship as embodying a superior morality, one in which women approximated more closely to the self-sacrificing ideal of the life of Jesus.[129] Importantly, the alleged superior moral value of the relationship was described not from the perspective of women at all but from the perspective of the powerful feelings ("the remembrances of their almost divine motherhood"[130]) that children, as adults, have about the relationship to their mothers, who have "such ineradicable, inexpugnable possession of the life of sons and daughters."[131] This is romantic idealization in the tradition of romantic love whose appeal here rests on undoubtedly profound and widespread human experiences and feelings of stages of one's life when ego boundaries barely exist (if they exist at all) and one's experience is symbiotically one with one's primary caretaker (usually, one's mother), the stage psychoanalysts call primary love.[132] From within such intense feelings, one's mother may barely exist

[127] See, on this point, Susan Moller Okin, *Women in Western Political Thought* (Princeton, N.J.: Princeton University Press, 1979).

[128] See, for fuller discussion, David A. J. Richards, *Women, Gays, and the Constitution: The Grounds for Feminism and Gay Rights in Culture and Law* (Chicago: University of Chicago Press, 1998), pp. 144–55.

[129] See *id.*, p. 63.

[130] See *id.*, p. 172.

[131] See *id.*, p. 171.

[132] For an important treatment, see Michael Balint, *Primary Love and Psycho-Analytic Technique* (New York: Liveright, 1965), especially the articles by Michael Balint at pp. 74–90 and 109–35, and by Alice Balint at pp. 91–108. On the religious force of the romantic love tradition in nineteenth-century America, see Karen Lystra, *Searching the Heart: Women, Men, and Romantic Love in Nineteenth-Century America* (New York: Oxford University Press, 1989).

as an independent person but as an intense fantasy of almost-religious devotion; such feelings may be the basis of one's worship, as Catholic medieval spirituality apparently did, of Jesus as mother,[133] or, as nineteenth-century Protestant Americans like Beecher and Bushnell did, of one's mother as Jesus.[134]

However, feelings of romantic love, colored by sectarian religious idealization, hardly rise to the level of an argument of public reason of the sort required to justify abridgment of basic human rights. Arguments of public reason do, of course, apply to the structure of family life, including not only the relationship between spouses but also the appropriate relationship of parents to their children.[135] But the Beecher-Bushnell argument, if it can be called that, does not critically rest on the relevant features of these relationships (e.g., the liberties, opportunities, resources) to which public reasons of justice must and do attend. Nor does it bring any realism or sense of justice to women's perspectives, as persons, on their role as mothers – on mothering not as romantic fantasy but as an exercise of practical reason and intelligence; or the crippling character (for mothers and children) of what Adrienne Rich observed and criticized in the "maternal altruism . . . universally approved and supported in women."[136] Rather, Beecher and Bushnell offer a highly sectarian political epistemology of rigidly stereotypical gender roles whose force rests on chimerical fantasies like those Robert Langmuir studied in anti-Semitism. Intense feelings of identification, in which ego boundaries are barely drawn, dissolve mothers, as persons, into intrapsychic idealized images of religious devotion; fantasies, which repudiate the minimal moral requirements of respect for the separateness of persons, are made the measure of a higher morality; finally, these essentially amoral chimeria are to stand judgment over the ethical demands of equal respect for persons.

Such politically entrenched fantasies drew their reactionary point and power not only from their starkly antifeminist uses in the North (Beecher and Bushnell) but also from their interlinked proslavery, racist, and antifeminist uses in the South in, among others, works of George Fitzhugh and Louisa McCord. Both Fitzhugh and McCord condemned abolitionists for attacking the family,[137] associating slavery and the subjection of women with "relations of life, the nearest, the dearest."[138] The thought was that, under Southern slavery, blacks were, like white women, on their idealized pedestal, thought of and cared for as "almost a part of

[133] See, e.g., Caroline Walker Bynum, *Jesus as Mother: Studies in the Spirituality of the High Middle Ages* (Berkeley: University of California Press, 1982).

[134] On the background of this American development, see Ann Douglas, *The Feminization of American Culture* (New York: Knopf, 1977).

[135] See, e.g., Susan Moller Okin, *Justice, Gender, and the Family* (New York: Basic Books, 1989).

[136] See Adrienne Rich, *Of Woman Born: Motherhood as Experience and Institution*, 10th anniversary ed. (New York: W. W. Norton, 1986), p. 213.

[137] See George Fitzhugh, *Cannibals All! or, Slaves without Masters*, ed. C. Vann Woodward (Cambridge, Mass.: Harvard University Press, Belknap Press, 1960), pp. 190–8, 204–6, 213–16.

[138] See [Louisa McCord], "Uncle Tom's Cabin," 7 *Southern Q. Rev.* 81–120, 111 (n.s., 1853); also "Enfranchisement of Woman," *Southern Q. Rev.* 21 (April 1852), 233–341.

himself, a dependant to live and die with."[139] In both the Northern and Southern cases, the embattled dominant political orthodoxy, precisely when subject to reasonable doubts about the justice of its factual and normative premises, polemically inverted reality to the measure of its sectarian vision, dissolving African Americans and women into fantasies, intimately romantic parts of oneself that one may defend against critics as, literally, unjust aggressions on one's self. Arguments for justice, in this polemically irrationalist world, become invasions of privacy; ethical demands, an inferior morality (if a morality at all); claims for human rights, unnatural acts.

Beecher developed her normative conception of gender in explicit opposition to abolitionist feminism and opposed the general claims of suffrage feminism;[140] Bushnell developed his theology of gender in explicit opposition to the suffrage movement. Both argued in the tradition of Protestant theology, which has traditionally questioned the role of Mary in Catholic theology. Nonetheless, we can see in such Protestant thinkers precisely the same kinds of gender stereotypes, both idealizing and denigrating, that lie behind comparable forms of reactionary arguments against feminism that we find in Catholic thought, in particular, the version of it offered by the new natural lawyers.

The problem for new natural law is that the arguments of Beecher and Bushnell have been decisively constitutionally rejected: the normative claims of abolitionist feminism (in particular, its condemnation equally of racial and gender stereotypes) have been largely constitutionally accepted, as our earlier discussion of constitutional law makes clear, and suffrage feminism succeeded in enacting a constitutional amendment extending the right to vote to women. Their arguments were rejected for compelling normative reasons: they rested on unjust gender stereotypes whose force derived from the massive repression of voices contesting such stereotypes.

It is, from this perspective, the we can see new natural law for what it is, not a seriously argument of political theory that takes rights seriously but, like Beecher and Bushnell, an essentially reactionary attempt in contemporary circumstances to retard or turn back the claims of justice that have been recognized and constitutionalized in the United States and abroad, including feminist claims of justice to women.

It would be quite unreasonable today, as a matter of acceptably impartial scientific or moral procedures of inquiry, to limit any form of such authority, let alone authority on matters of sexual morality, exclusively to a class of persons (celibate men) who both exclude the experience of half the human race (women) and exclude further the sexual experience of most of the human race (sexually active men and women, straight and gay). It would be even more unreasonable to fix

139 See McCord, "Uncle Tom's Cabin," p. 108.

140 Catharine E. Beecher accepted the case for suffrage only when a woman satisfied property qualification requirements. See *Woman Suffrage and Woman's Profession* (Hartford, Conn.: Brown and Gross, 1871), p. 205.

one's sense of matters of fact to such facts as they may have appeared in thirteenth-century Europe with no inquiry into whatever facts may have been discovered since that time. Unfortunately, new natural law is seriously unreasonable in all these ways.

The philosophically honest way to handle this problem within Thomism would be to appeal to the best arguments of science and philosophy about matters of sexuality and gender, as other contemporary Thomists do, getting right, in a way that Thomas writing in the thirteenth century certainly does not, what human nature, including sexuality and gender, is and to work from there in developing a conception of ethics that does justice to our human nature, including our sexual nature as desiring and loving, relational, moral persons. New natural law, contrary to the philosophical integrity of Thomism, doggedly refuses to look at what the best science and philosophy tell us about sexuality and gender, instead grounding its views in self-evident judgments of basic goods that are essentially the judgments of the celibate male clergy it assumes, without good argument, to be religiously and morally authoritative. But there are quite compelling reasons such a procedure cannot be acceptable as an argument in a constitutional democracy whose principles must reasonably justify its powers to all persons, irrespective of more ultimate philosophical and religious disagreements. Such arguments must appeal to the procedures of reasoning available and accessible to all, but the procedure of new natural law rests on judgments internal to one religious tradition among others, failing to support its argument in terms of reasons available and accessible to those outside its tradition.

We need to keep clearly in mind how radically new natural law departs from Thomas's own highly scientific and philosophical procedure, one he believed any reasonable person (Muslim or Jew or whoever) could accept. The procedure of new natural law insulates itself from such critical accountability, making sectarian judgments essentially self-validating. Their procedure leads to arguments about, for example, the intrinsic wrongness of contraception that even most Catholics, let alone others, no longer find reasonable.[141] But the problem is not just that its substantive views on these and other matters fail the test of public reasons but also that they irresponsibly enforce forms of structural injustice that are now constitutionally condemned.

What makes these consequences possible is the conception of religious and moral authority, which new natural law defends, namely a rather stark form of the injustice of patriarchy, authority structured in terms of a hierarchical relationship exclusively to the voices of celibate fathers as priests. What makes such authority unjust is that it depends on unjust stereotypes of sexuality and gender that depend, in a vicious circularity, on the repression of any voice that might reasonably

[141] See, on these points, Wills, *Papal Sin*; Peter Steinfels, *A People Adrift: The Crisis of the Roman Catholic Church in America* (New York: Simon and Schuster, 2003). See also Daniel Callahan, *The Catholic Case for Contraception* (London: Arlington Books, 1969).

contest them. It is one of the distinctive features of the moral theology of Germain Grisez that he defended the church's traditional condemnation of contraception in a period, after Vatican II, when such views were under reconsideration,[142] and that he has continued to defend this view, now clearly endorsed by the papacy, joined by other new natural lawyers like John Finnis and Robert George who accept Grisez as the moral authority in this area.[143] The condemnation of contraception, as a failure to use sex procreationally, clearly rests solely on sectarian religious assumptions – on an Augustinian and Thomistic view of sexuality that is in contemporary circumstances anachronistic – and on patriarchal papal authority. The view is anachronistic because it historically assumed, as axiomatic, a patriarchal structure of sexual relationships, which we now know rests on the cultural injustice of sexism; and its concern for exclusively procreational sexuality arose in circumstances of underpopulation and massive infant and adult mortality that made having children, in a largely agrarian society, a necessity. Once these background assumptions are no longer valid, as in contemporary circumstances, there is no appealing case for the wrongness, let alone the criminalization, of contraception. The argument to the contrary rests solely on a sectarian religious authority, the papacy, which cannot be a legitimate basis for law and policy in a constitutional democracy.

What makes new natural law's view of the intrinsic evil of contraception so untenable, as a political argument to rationalize the moral condemnation and even criminalization of contraception, is not only its sectarian character but also that it depends on and reinforces long-standing cultural stereotypes whose unjust force depends on the repression of women's sexual voices and experiences. What is undoubtedly at work here, as in Beecher and Bushnell, is a highly idealized, indeed mythological conception of motherhood, one infinitely self-sacrificing and wholly disconnected from any sense of women's sexual voice and interests, voices articulated by, among others, Emma Goldman and Margaret Sanger. There is no interest in real voices and relationships, including that of a mother to her child, but rather in idealization and denigration that are the hallmarks of loss, marking a manhood achieved by replacing relationship with identification – a manhood shadowed by loss and bound to separation. Thus, when John Finnis tries to consider the good reasons a couple might have for using contraceptives (e.g., giving a better life to the fewer children they have, pursuing other interests as a couple), he dismissively claims that they have artificially narrowed the horizons of their assessment because "to know – that is, to make a *rational* judgment – that the one future embodies more premoral good than any and all of its alternatives would be to know and understand the future, both of this world and of the Kingdom, in a manner that lies utterly outside the reach of moral providence."[144]

142 Germain Grisez, *Contraception and the Natural Law* (Milwaukee, Wisc.: Bruce, 1964).

143 See Grisez, *Way of the Lord Jesus*, vol. 2, pp. 506–19. See, for acceptance of Grisez's views, Finnis, "Natural Law Theory and Limited Government"; George, *In Defense of Natural Law*, p. 161.

144 Finnis, *Moral Absolutes*, p. 19.

Finnis imposes a theologically derived absolute that reasonable persons, outside his sectarian form of faith, find incredible and cruelly callous to the real moral choices people face. There is certainly no appeal here to the kinds of facts or lived experiences of women or arguments accessible to all reasonable persons (of the sort Thomas himself clearly required) but an insular appeal to the self-evident, unreasonably anachronistic judgments of a patriarchal priesthood and its acolytes. As Kent Greenawalt has perceptively observed, the approach of the new natural lawyers to sexuality, stem-cell research, and suicide "relies on abstract, categorical modes of thought in preference to greater emphasis on qualities of lived experience and contextual distinctions drawn from that experience,"[145] a patriarchal style of thought he associates with Carol Gilligan's work on male approaches as opposed to those based on the different voice of women and others: "we can easily place traditional natural law reasoning far on the male side of the spectrum."[146]

Similar considerations underlie the way in which new natural law, following the lead of papal authority, treats abortion. Grisez, followed by Finnis and George,[147] has consistently argued that abortion is a taking of innocent life on a par with murder and should be criminal for the same reasons.[148] Grisez contends that "to question the absoluteness of the right to life of the unborn is to question the absoluteness of everyone's right to life."[149] Sandeep Sreekumar has recently shown that the claim is not reasonably tenable in terms of a critical morality based on respect for the right to life, among other basic rights.[150] We can and do

[145] Kent Greenawalt, "How Persuasive Is Natural Law Theory?" 75 *Notre Dame L. Rev.* 1647, 1672 (2000).

[146] *Id.*, 1672n93.

[147] See, for acceptance of Grisez's views, Finnis, "Natural Law Theory and Limited Government," p. 13; George, *In Defense of Natural Law*, p. 161.

[148] See Germain Grisez, *Abortion: The Myths, the Realities, and the Arguments* (New York: Corpus Books, 1970); Grisez, *Way of the Lord Jesus*, vol. 2, pp. 497–504.

[149] Grisez, *Abortion*, p. 305.

[150] See Sandeep Sreekumar, "An Argument about the Right to Life of the Foetus in Critical Morality," Ph.D. thesis, Corpus Christi College, Oxford University, Trinity Term 2005. A summary of Sreekumar's argument would be this:

> (a) a strictly jurisprudential analysis of 'rights' does not warrant the conclusion that a foetus cannot have a right to life which protects either its objective interest in life (viz., that fact that life is, on a 'thin evaluative' level, good for it), or (assuming a certain view of human identity over time) its future preference-interest, when it becomes a human being like you and me, in having remained alive as a foetus, or both but
>
> (b) a normative analysis of the values to be attributed to these respective interests shows that
>
> (ba) we can say that objective interest is valuable enough to justify anything more than a negligibly weak duty correlative to a foetal right to life only if (i) we can adduce some defensible reason for holding that human biological aliveness is in itself a locus of intrinsic value of some kind (given that Dworkin's 'sacred value' argument is logically defective, and the typical conservative assumption in the area is untenably speciesist) or (ii) we can defend the dubious position that some experiences in human

reasonably understand not only the right to life of human beings under normal circumstances (including infants and children) but also the right to life of people who are asleep or temporarily comatose and people of future generations, in terms of the normative value we place on a preference interest to remain alive, whenever such a human interest exists or should come to exist. All such claims of a right to life are normative justifiable (normatively absolute, if you will), but their critical normative justification does not reasonably support a comparable right to life of all fetuses, because such a right makes sense only on the basis of false assumptions about the value of aliveness in general (do the lives of noxious bacteria have value?) or the value of the human experiences or preference satisfactions that a fetus, when born and developed, will have. What is doing the work in Grisez's argument is not a reasonable critical morality, for the normative assumptions on which he depends are not reasonable. What is doing the work in Grisez's argument are sectarian religious assumptions, based on sexist stereotypes that idealize and denigrate women (e.g., the cult of Mary), which he accepts, as we have seen, on the basis of his faith in the patriarchal authority of the papal hierarchy.

It is striking that the interpretation accorded life as a moral absolute by the new natural lawyers, in condemning abortion, makes no mention of women, except as incidentally condemned as intending murder when they have abortions. Such silence and denial bespeak the source of the sectarian religious assumptions that motivate their views, namely unjust sexist assumptions about women's proper gender roles. The objection to abortion is thus defended not only on the ground of the right to life of the fetus but also on the ground that a woman, making the abortion choice, is not exercising her sexuality procreationally and maternally. Emily Jackson has cogently observed that the imposition on a woman, who does not want to bear or have a child, of a legal or moral duty to have such a child imposes on women and women only a compulsion to use their bodies to save another, an obligation we accept nowhere else.[151] Such injustice supports a sexist culture and psychology of "maternal self-abnegation."[152] What we believe really

life possess categorical value of the sort that necessitates our bringing into existence experiencers in whose lives those values may be actualized (in which case, of course, we also have a duty to conceive hypothetical human beings that is, pending the provision by a proponent of this view of a normatively robust difference between such entities and fetuses, as strong as any duty we have to fetuses), and

(bb) we can say that future preference-interest is valuable enough to justify anything more than a negligibly weak duty correlative to a foetal right to life if and only is we can first defend the controversial 'orexigenic' view that if a preference will be satisfied if and when it comes into existence, we ought to bring that preference into existence (and, if we can defend this view, we again stand in need of an argument that can robustly distinguish the conception of hypothetical human beings from the letting-live of fetuses).

[151] See, on this point, Emily Jackson, *Regulating Reproduction: Law, Technology and Autonomy* (Oxford: Hart Publishing, 2001), pp. 73–4, 76, 133.

[152] See *id.*, p. 3.

exercises the papacy (supported by the new natural lawyers) about abortion is its statement about women exercising their free sexuality nonprocreationally and nonmaternally, something the new natural lawyers object to generally but take particular objection to when exercised by women free of patriarchal controls on their sexuality. It is difficult to take seriously the papacy's view that is has some superior insight into the wrongness of such a taking of life and such taking of life uniquely arises at fertilization, a view neither Augustine nor Thomas shared.[153] Why dogmatically assimilate a fertilized ovum to a person without acknowledgment of the range of alternative reasonable views of the competences (e.g., sentience, brain activity, self-consciousness) of the many reasonable persons who reject such an assimilation, including many women? New natural lawyers, like Finnis, adopt their position dogmatically,[154] claiming that their case rests on natural sources of knowledge when the very lack of reasonable consensus about the weight to be given to the facts shows this is not so.[155] Their choice of fertilization is itself highly sectarian, resting on ideas of ensoulment and women's procreative duties that are not reasonably appealing views to those outside the tradition.[156] What drives their view is a highly sectarian condemnation of both contraception and abortion, which are for them instances of the same wrong. Abortion particularly exercises them because of the view of women's free sexuality it demonstrates, a conception to which traditional patriarchal conceptions of gender and sexuality take the strongest objection.

As Justice Kennedy's argument in *Lawrence* indicates, constitutional and legal recognition of the human rights of gays and lesbian came, in contrast to Great Britain and Europe, comparatively late to the United States. Justice Kennedy had earlier acknowledged the irrational cultural force of homophobia in American culture in *Romer v. Evans*, when he wrote for the Court striking down Colorado Amendment 2 on the ground that it expressed irrational prejudice. But his opinion in *Lawrence v. Texas* also takes note of American cultural homophobia, when he insists that *Bowers* must be overruled because such laws, in the context of American culture, homophobically demean the very existence of gays and lesbians, as persons incapable of love and friendship.

It is against this relatively inhospitable cultural background to arguments for gay and lesbian rights, now clearly acknowledged by arguments and decisions of the highest court of the United States, that I believe that new natural lawyers have been particularly politically and publicly active in America in opposing legal

153 See, on this point, Garry Wills, "The Bishops vs. the Bible," *New York Times*, June 27, 2004, sec. 4, at 14.

154 See John Finnis, "Abortion, Natural Law, and Public Reason," in *Natural Law and Public Reason*, ed. Robert P. George and Christopher Wolfe (Washington, D.C.: Georgetown University Press, 2000), pp. 75–105.

155 See, on this point, Wills, "The Bishops vs. the Bible."

156 See, on the sectarian character of the choice of fertilization, Ronald Dworkin, *Life's Dominion: An Argument about Abortion, Euthanasia, and Individual Freedom* (New York: Alfred A. Knopf, 1993).

recognition of gay and lesbian rights. New natural lawyers act, in an exoteric and esoteric mode of argument, the first meant for the wider culture, the second for a narrower audience of Catholic believers in papal orthodoxy. In its exoteric mode, a new natural lawyer, like John Finnis, has narrowly agreed with the holding in *Griswold v. Connecticut* but defended as well a criminal law forbidding Griswold's activities as a public promoter of contraception information and supplies,[157] and new natural lawyers have not called for the criminalization of masturbation or nonprocreational sex acts in general (straight and gay), which its views certainly might require. Rather, they have taken a public position against the Supreme Court's decisions recognizing a constitutional right to abortion services and have been particularly active in their opposition to legal recognition of gay and lesbian rights. On the issue of criminalization of gay and lesbian sex, their views differ (Finnis has argued against, Robert George has argued for); but they are all opposed to any recognition of gay rights beyond decriminalization, including antidiscrimination laws and recognition of same-sex partnerships; George has been notably active in support of a constitutional amendment banning gay marriage.[158]

The basis for all their views is the moral theology of Germain Grisez, which morally condemns contraception, abortion, nonprocreative sex acts (gay and straight), and masturbation.[159] In its esoteric mode, the new natural lawyers have attacked as equally morally evil all these modes of sexual expression, a condemnation of all sexual activity involving lesbians and gays (even those who are in the most committed sexual and/or emotional relationships), all sexual activity involving heterosexuals who are unmarried (even if they are in committed sexual and/or emotional relationships), and all sexual activity outside the missionary position involving heterosexual couples who are married, and all use of contraceptives in such sex – as well as all acts of masturbation. The selective use of its exoteric mode is largely a matter of taking on only issues where the new natural lawyers believe they stand more chance of success or at least sympathetic support and understanding. Their views on masturbation, contraception, and nonprocreative, straight sex acts are now so far outside the boundaries of reasonable public opinion that they do not say exoterically what they argue at painful length esoterically. They have been particular active against gay and lesbian rights in the United States because American culture is well behind European cultures in its historical sense of the importance of these rights, among other human rights, and in its legal and political recognition of them. Americans, who would be shocked at the criminalization of masturbation, contraception, straight nonprocreational sex acts, and even early-term abortions, have no comparable views about gay and

[157] See John Finnis, "Law, Morality, and 'Sexual Orientation,'" 69 *Notre Dame L. Rev.* 1049, 1076n68 (1994).

[158] See, on these points, discussion of chapter 1, Bamforth and Richards, *Patriarchal Religion, Sexuality, and Gender.*

[159] See Grisez, *Way of the Lord Jesus*, vol. 2, pp. 488–519, 553–752.

lesbian sex, about which they have historically known very little and what little they have known has been highly distorted by a long-standing, highly repressive culture of modernist American homophobia. It is in this environment that new natural law has seen itself as having a polemical role to play, and it has played that role aggressively.

What distinguishes George's arguments for criminalization, for example, is, I believe, how little they offer in the way of reasonable argument either about the reasonable scope of the right to intimate life or about the burden of justification that should constitutionally be required to abridge such a right. What rather distinguishes George's arguments is their question-begging character, appealing to Grisez's conception of one-flesh union and dismissing other conceptions of the basic right as illusions.[160] We have already seen that Grisez's conception rests on an alleged fact, reproductive sex as an organism, that is not a fact, justifying the abridgment of basic human rights on grounds of nothing. George adduces as authority for his position a mythological sectarian fantasy.

A new natural lawyer like Finnis, who resists George's ardor for criminalization of gay and lesbian sex, nonetheless has used new natural law to ground skepticism about laws that forbid discrimination on grounds of sexual orientation and laws that extend rights of marriage to gays and lesbians. Finnis has gone even further: defending Colorado Amendment 2, which constitutionally entrenched a prohibition on any state or local laws that forbade discrimination on grounds of sexual orientation.[161] Finnis testified in the Colorado Supreme Court to this effect and sharply criticized the views of the liberal philosopher Martha Nussbaum, that good philosophy, including Greek philosophy, did not support Finnis's allegedly philosophical arguments.[162] Unfortunately, their debate was clouded by a controversy over the proper interpretation of Plato, as if an important issue of contemporary constitutional law could or should turn on such an interpretive issue. Even if Finnis were right on the interpretive issue, it would not control the contemporary constitutional issue, which rests on the validity of the two purposes Plato cited for a prohibition of gay sex (its nonprocreative character, or its unsettling of male gender hierarchy, as one partner must take up the passive role of a woman). Neither purpose is, in contemporary circumstances, reasonably justifiable, which explains why criminalization of gay and lesbian sex has today been judicially struck down as unconstitutional.

But if these purposes are unacceptable as grounds for criminalization, they are no less acceptable as grounds for discrimination. Finnis, of course, believes that he has offered good arguments of reason why gay and lesbian sex is an evil and may

160 See Robert P. George, *In Defense of Natural Law* (Oxford, U.K.: Clarendon Press, 1999), chaps. 9, 11, 15.

161 Finnis, "Law, Morality, and 'Sexual Orientation,'" p. 11; John Finnis, "Is Natural Law Theory Compatible with Limited Government?" in *Natural Law, Liberalism, and Morality*, ed. Robert P. George (Oxford: Oxford University Press, 1996), pp. 1–26.

162 Martha C. Nussbaum, "Platonic Love and Colorado Law," 80 *U. Va. L. Rev.* 1515 (1994).

thus be discouraged, even if not criminalized, to foster an environment supportive of the only form of intimate life that for Finnis is a good, namely heterosexual marriage. But it is now widely understood, including by *The Catechism of the Catholic Church*,[163] that people do not choose their sexual orientations, and Finnis's argument seems on its own terms unreasonable in supposing that persons choose to be lesbian or gay to avoid marriage. The argument would be more plausibly made about heterosexual persons who remain single, discrimination against whom, of course, Finnis notably does not propose. A more apposite example is divorce, which certainly constitutes a threat to the indissolubility of marriage, allowing, as it does, the legal possibility of divorce and remarriage. But Finnis, who certainly regards divorce as, like gay sex, an evil, does not follow out the logic of his argument.[164] Or what about adultery, a popular vice that certainly threatens the stability of marriages? Why not legitimate discrimination against adulterers? What such failures of reason show is the homophobic irrationalism that motivates Finnis's position (only gay sex, evidently, is to be legitimately subject to discrimination), assuming we were to concede that there are good reasons for regarding gay sex as a bad thing. But of course, we should and do not concede any such thing.

Finnis's arguments do not rest on arguments of reason accessible and available to all, for, in defending new natural law, he has unmoored Thomism from the only thing that gave it philosophical interest and integrity, namely its demand that its arguments rest on the best science and philosophy available. Finnis rejects good science and philosophy for self-evident judgments based on the authority of a celibate male clergy. Accordingly, his arguments about the evil of gay and lesbian sex are not only bad arguments of public reason but also enforce what is clearly, in contemporary circumstances, a religiously sectarian conception of value, which independently violates American constitutional guarantees both of free exercise and antiestablishment. Indeed, it seems fair to say that Finnis's argumentative moves on the topic of lesbian and gay sexuality illustrate a larger point about his role in the unjust rationalization of homophobia. First, he offers, on the basis of Germain Grisez's faith-based conception of the only good sexual conduct may have, a highly sectarian, rigidly defined conception of the only sex that is moral, one limited to certain intentional attitudes in heterosexual sex in lifetime marriages.[165] These attitudes include not only procreation but also the allegedly independent expression of faithful love in lifetime marriages, the latter of which Finnis concedes to be much more common intentional attitudes (as most

[163] See *Catechism of the Catholic Church* (New York: Image, 1995), no. 2358, pp. 625–6.

[164] See, on these points, Charles E. Curran, "Sexual Orientation and Human Rights in American Religious Discourse: A Roman Catholic Perspective," in *Sexual Orientation and Human Rights in American Religious Discourse*, ed. Saul M. Olyan and Martha C. Nussbaum (New York: Oxford University Press, 1998), pp. 85–100, 92.

[165] See his article "The Good of Marriage and the Morality of Sexual Relations: Some Philosophical and Historical Observations," 42 *Am. J. Juris.* 97 (1997).

such sex is not procreative, in which Finnis includes the sex between infertile couples). But then, in an astonishing non sequitur, Finnis simply denies the evident fact that gay sex may satisfy this latter condition. At this point, there is no factual argument, or any interest in facts, as Finnis regales us – as we have seen – with unjust homophobic stereotypes of gay sex, as, in its nature, "the anonymous bathhouse encounter" or group sex,[166] or blatantly denies relevant facts (e.g., claiming that most homosexuals can easily function bisexually[167]), and preposterously regards the advocacy of the good of gay sexual relationships as morally equivalent to "a cowardly weakling [who] deliberately approves of the killings of innocent people in a terrorist massacre."[168] Such assertions merit no better label than irrationalist ranting: something that bespeaks not reason but prejudices that are immune to reason. This is shown by the way in which Finnis wants to claim intentional attitudes (without procreation) as a reasonable good of sex and then refuses to acknowledge that the argument extends to gay sex. Despite his protestations to the contrary, Finnis is wedded to a rigidly procreational conception of the good of sex, to which his sectarian religious faith, following Grisez, commits him. In defense of this conception, Finnis then asserts that gay sex cannot instantiate this good because very little of it is an expression of faithful love in lifetime marriages.[169] But again, at this point, there is no interest in facts, including growing evidence of precisely such relationships all about us. Such deep relationships are, for Finnis – and without further evidence – "illusory,"[170] "same-sex imitations or caricatures of marriage"[171]: comments that, given the longevity and commitment of many same-sex couples in the face of unremitting social hostility of the type expressed by Finnis (and, alas, countless others), can be seen only as an expression of heated, deep-seated prejudice rather than cool, reflective, rational argument. But more important, Finnis uses this irrationalist argument as his main defense of denying marriage rights to gays and lesbians. In reality, it is precisely because our traditions have so outlawed gay sex from any legitimacy, including marriage, that such social forms have made longer-term relationships so difficult to achieve, let alone sustain. Finnis's argument at this point is fatally question begging: it crucially depends on an unjust tradition it cannot and does not reasonably defend but rationalizes by bad arguments that verge on a kind of name-calling unworthy of the life of reason. It is at this point that we see so clearly that Finnis's arguments are not arguments, and certainly not good arguments, but the kind of quite bad arguments, depending on the force of unjust stereotypes (e.g., distorting facts, inverting and corrupting humane values, such as making the defense of gay love into terrorism), which rationalize and sustain irrational prejudice, in

166 *Id.*, p. 127.
167 See *id.*, pp. 123–4n108.
168 *Id.*, p. 123.
169 *Id.*, p. 130.
170 *Id.*, p. 100n11.
171 *Id.*, p. 101.

this case, the moral violence of homophobia. It is in such terms that vicious European anti-Semitism transformed the defense by European Jews of their basic human and constitutional rights into an unjust aggression that required genocide. Finnis's arguments are, at this point, viciously circular in the same way as the now constitutionally discredited forms of such arguments are in the areas of religious intolerance, race and ethnicity, and gender.

Finally, there is a new issue that has come to the forefront of public discussion in the United States, namely arguments for some measure of equal legal recognition for same-sex partnerships on par with opposite-sex relationships, including arguments for full such recognition in the form of extending to gay and lesbian partners a right to marriage. New natural lawyers have prominently not only opposed these arguments but also urged passage of a constitutional amendment that would forbid same-sex marriage anywhere in the United States. Their recent arguments are in reaction to the growing acceptance of legal recognition of such partnerships in Europe and Canada, and after some setbacks in Hawaii and Alaska, even in the United States, to wit, the decision of the Vermont Supreme Court in *Baker v. State of Vermont*[172] (leading to civil union legislation short of same-sex marriage), and, more recently, the decision of the Supreme Judicial Court of Massachusetts in *Goodridge v. Department of Public Health*[173] (under which gays and lesbians resident in Massachusetts can marry). No doubt, the growing visibility of new natural lawyers in the United States is that they offer what is alleged to be a good philosophical argument against such recognition, one that resonates with an American culture that is still quite homophobic.

What my earlier arguments clearly show is that new natural law's conception of marriage does not rest on reasons accessible and available to all but on an essentially sectarian conception of marriage based on the authority of a celibate male priesthood. On the issue of the right to marriage itself, there can be no doubt at all that precedents of the U.S. Supreme Court, including *Loving v. Virginia*,[174] *Zablocki v. Redhail*,[175] and *Turner v. Safley*,[176] regard the right to marriage, grounded in the right to intimate life, as a basic constitutional right. It is part of the moral logic of the principles protecting such basic rights, for example, the principle of free speech, that it extend to forms of speech that may be highly objectionable – for example, to subversive, racist, or sexist speech – or pornography or that the principle of religious liberty extend to all forms of conviction, good and bad. The logic of the principle of marriage as a basic

[172] *Baker v. State of Vermont*, 744 A.2d 864 (Vt. 1999).

[173] See *Goodridge v. Department of Public Health*, 798 N.E.2d 941 (Mass. 2003).

[174] *Loving v. Virginia*, 388 U.S. 1 (1967) (striking down Virginia's laws banning interracial marriage).

[175] See *Zablocki v. Redhail*, 434 U.S. 374 (1978) (striking down a Wisconsin statute that prohibited a person under a court order to support minor children from marrying without judicial permission on the ground that the means selected by the state to pursue legitimate interests of child support unduly abridged the basic right to marry).

[176] *Turner v. Safley*, 482 U.S. 78 (1987) (Missouri state prison regulation, forbidding inmates from marrying under most circumstances, is unconstitutional abridgment of basic right to marry).

right should be similar: it extends to all persons, including, as *Loving* makes clear, to interracial couples, and as *Turner* shows, to criminals. The same logic would extend, as a matter of principle, the right to marriage to same-sex couples, irrespective of the unpopularity of, or distaste for, such relationships.

Much of the debate over same-sex marriage confuses marriage as a civil and a religious union. No one is arguing that any religion must sanctify same-sex unions, though some now do so. The claim rather is that civil marriage, understood as an institution based on respect for the constitutionally guaranteed right of intimate life, must fairly extend such a basic right to all Americans on terms of arguments of public reason available to all. Richard Epstein has recently put the point cogently:

> When President Bush, for example, talks about the need to "protect" the sanctity of marriage, his plea is a giant non sequitur because he does not explain what, precisely, he is protecting marriage against. No proponent of gay marriage wants to ban traditional marriage, or to burden couples who want to marry with endless texts, taxes, and delays. All gay-marriage advocates want to do is to enjoy the same rights of association that are held by other people. Let the state argue that gay marriages are a health risk, and the answer is that anything that encourages monogamy has the opposite effect. Any principled burden of justification is not met.[177]

New natural law makes no philosophical contribution to this public debate, because, on examination, its views are essentially religiously sectarian. It condemns same-sex marriage for the same reason that it condemns contraception, masturbation, nonprocreational straight sex, abortion, and homosexuality: none of them is procreative in what new natural law takes to be the required way. But the requirement that sex be procreative is no more constitutionally reasonable than the requirement that marriage be procreative. Heterosexual couples who are childless, whether by design or by force of circumstances, are not for that reason disqualified from the right to marry, nor could they reasonably be.[178] It is not in fact our law or practice that marriage must be for procreation or procreational or that its value is only procreational. When courts have insisted on the point as a ground for refusing same-sex marriage, they have, "frankly, made up this standard out of thin air, and have applied it only to same-sex couples."[179]

The arguments of the new natural lawyers in this domain are as bad as they have proved to be elsewhere. I earlier explored their political motivations in terms of sectarian political support for gender stereotypes under constitutional attack in the United States and elsewhere. We can now reasonably extend that

[177] Richard A. Epstein, "Live and Let Live," *Wall Street Journal*, July 13, 2004, at A14.

[178] Cf. *Turner v. Safley*, 482 U.S. 78 (1987) (denial of marriage right to prison inmates, on ground that they could not procreate, held unconstitutional). For discussion, see William N. Eskridge Jr., *The Case for Same-Sex Marriage: From Sexual Liberty to Civilized Commitment* (New York: Free Press, 1996), pp. 128–30.

[179] See Evan Gerstmann, *Same-Sex Marriage and the Constitution* (Cambridge: Cambridge University Press, 2004), p. 95.

analysis to include the role of new natural lawyers in the support of the injustice of homophobia. We begin with an analysis of homophobia, as a form of sexism, then turn to the closer examination of the arguments of new natural lawyers in light of this analysis, and I offer finally some observations about why a celibate male priesthood might be so prone to be an unjust agent of such homophobia.

I understand homophobia as that expression of unjust cultural sexism, which abridges the rights of a whole class of persons, on the unjust ground of gender stereotypes that rest on the repression of the basic human rights of that class of persons, including repression of any conscience and voice that might reasonably challenge such dehumanizing stereotypes. Homophobia specifically targets the voice of gay and lesbian persons, in particular, an ethical voice that challenges the dehumanizing treatment historically inflicted on them. Homophobia historically arose because gay and lesbian sex was conceived as the unspeakable crime against nature, one that could not even be mentioned, let alone discussed. It is this crushing of any gay and lesbian voice, let alone dissenting voice, that explains the intractable depth of homophobia among other prejudices, including other forms of sexism. There has, after all, been a long history of dissent against extreme religious prejudice (anti-Semitism), as well as racism and many forms of sexism (in particular, those directed against heterosexual women). But protest against homophobia has, certainly in the United States, been only quite recent, and its legal recognition, to the extent it has occurred at all, has elicited a reactionary homophobic, violently aggressive prejudice. Unfortunately, new natural law has played an important role in legitimating such prejudice.

I believe the character of this role is illustrated by the basic human right, that to intimate life, which has been most grievously denied gay and lesbian persons. What seems reasonably clear is that the historical development of and understanding of this right as one among our basic human rights has been developed on the basis of convincing analogies to the right of conscience itself, the right protected by the argument for toleration now universally recognized as fundamental constitutional democracy, including by the Catholic Church in Vatican II.[180] It is because the right to intimate life gives expression to convictions, thoughts, emotions, and ways of life central to what gives life enduring personal and ethical meaning that this right has now been recognized as a basic constitutional right as central to the constitutionally required respect for our basic human rights as the right of conscience itself. It follows that any significant abridgment of such a right can only be constitutionally justified on the grounds of compelling reasons that are accessible to all, for example, harms like battery or killing, or values of equality rooted in justice and the like. It is because laws criminalizing contraception and abortion could not be justified on such grounds that the U.S. Supreme Court recognized that the right to intimate life was unjustly abridged by such

[180] See, for an argument along these lines, Richards, *Toleration and the Constitution*.

laws. That right has been extended recently in the United States to gay and lesbian sex, as it had been in Europe earlier, because the criminalization of such relationships did not rest on any compelling public reason. The two reasons that historically rationalized such prohibition – its nonprocreative character and its upsetting of relationships based on gender inequality or hierarchy (particularly, in male homosexual sex, in which one partner takes the passive, traditionally female role) – were both no longer publicly reasonable, as the Court had recognized in many other cases (the contraception cases had repudiated the alleged evil of nonprocreational sex as a public purpose in contemporary circumstances, and gender equality has been established as a constitutional command on par with equality among ethnic and religious groups).[181]

What shows the specifically homophobic motivations underlying new natural law is that, in contrast to Thomas's bleakly instrumental view of marriage, they recognize a basic human good, namely marriage, that clearly rests on the right of intimate life,[182] but then interpret its scope in a way that effectively protects only Thomist procreational sex in marriage, unreasonably construing both the basic right itself and the kinds of arguments that should be constitutionally required for the abridgment of such a right. Indeed, when John Finnis describes the good of marriage in esoteric writings intended for the faithful, he waxes in frankly theological terms, as if the good of sex in marriage, pace Thomas Aquinas, alone made possible the *visio Dei*:

> The revelation of God's nature. Unless God had created sex, and thus familial relationships, we could not begin to understand the meaning of "Father", "Son", Trinity, Incarnation, and adoption as children of God. By its utmost intimacy which yet preserves the individual identities and roles of those who share it, marriage (defined by negative moral absolutes in the way Grisez recalled) discloses the possibility of divine-human communion, initiated by a covenant-relationship in which we trust God will remain (faithful unconditionally, exceptionlessly, by a commitment which has the moral necessity and stability of absolute moral norms.[183]

As a Catholic critic of his church's condemnation of homosexuality recently put this point (against, among others, Finnis), it is extraordinary that so many branches of Christianity should have degenerated into fertility cults.[184] Why isn't celibacy itself on such grounds now problematic? But the real incoherence is its sectarian understanding of the good of sex. There is, on the one hand, a basic right that all persons should enjoy, and on the other hand, a class of persons who cannot or should not enjoy the benefit of such a right for no good reasons that

[181] See, on these points, Richards, *Women, Gays, and the Constitution*, pp. 362–5.
[182] See, on this point, Finnis, "The Good of Marriage and the Morality of Sexual Relations."
[183] Finnis, *Moral Absolutes*, p. 29.
[184] See Mark D. Jordan, *The Invention of Sodomy in Christian Theology* (Chicago: University of Chicago Press, 1997), p. 174.

new natural lawyers ever give or could give. This dehumanization of gay and lesbian sexuality strips gay and lesbian persons of their humanity, indulging an irrationalist prejudice that reason condemns and must condemn.[185]

Such a phenomenon requires a diagnosis of motivations. I suggest, as explanation, that it is the very absence of good reasons for such opposition that tempts thinkers to react with a homophobic condemnation in excess of any reasonable argument they can make, inventing differences that are anachronistic and, in contemporary circumstances, quite unreasonable. Why should the clergy of the Catholic Church be so tempted by sexism and homophobia? I turn to this question in the next section.

4. CULTURAL AND PSYCHOLOGICAL ROOTS

There was a radical shift between the Christianity of the second century and that of the end of the fourth century, and no figure was more powerful in engineering this shift than Augustine of Hippo. The background of this shift, decisively influential on the thought and life of Augustine, was the political decline of the Roman Empire itself, marked not only by bloody civil wars over the succession but also by the decisive political power of the Roman armies over the succession and by armies who proved increasingly unable to contain the barbarians on the borders of the empire (culminating in the sack of Rome in 410, an event that shocked the Roman world and led to Augustine's work on *The City of God*, explaining why the Catholic Church was not responsible for this catastrophe).[186] Christianity had been a distinctly minority religious preference in the second century. Although it grew steadily after that,[187] its dominance in the fourth century was due to two remarkable developments: first, the decision of Constantine in 311 that Christianity was to be the established church of the Roman Empire, receiving massive state support and patronage continuously from then forward (except for the brief three-year reign of Julian the Apostate); and second, the decision of Theodosius in 391 that all pagan practices were to be repressed coercively and that the state would use its coercive powers to support orthodox Christian views over heresies.[188] When Augustine converted to Christianity in 386, he was not sacrificing his earlier ambitions for success in the Roman political world, for he had learned from the example of Bishop Ambrose of Milan that a bishop exercised significant powers over the emperors and that the church could use the power

[185] See, for further elaboration of this argument, Bamforth and Richards, *Patriarchal Religion*, pp. 245–76.

[186] See, on these points, Peter Heather, *The Fall of the Roman Empire: A New History of Rome and the Barbarians* (Oxford: Oxford University Press, 2006).

[187] See Rodney Stark, *The Rise of Christiianity: A Sociologist Reconsiders History* (Princeton, N.J.: Princeton University Press, 1996).

[188] See Ramsay MacMullen, *Christianizing the Roman Empire A.D. 100–400* (New Haven, Conn.: Yale University Press, 1984).

of the state to enforce its views.[189] Augustine, when he became bishop of Hippo, was often successfully to appeal to imperial power to enforce his views over his enemies, including the heretical Donatists early in this career and the heretical Pelagians later in his career.[190] The great importance of Augustine, in the history of church-state relations, was his justification of the use of state power in such ways on religious grounds. It was Augustine's theory of persecution that was to justify the inquisitorial powers of the Catholic Church in the Middle Ages and later, a view that was only fundamentally reexamined and repudiated by the Catholic Church in Vatican II in 1967.[191] And it was the refutation of Augustine's theory of persecution, by Pierre Bayle and John Locke, among others, that was decisively important in the development of the institutions of constitutional democracy in which the argument for toleration has been of fundamental importance.[192]

At the heart of Augustine's theory of persecution lies his distinctive contribution to Christian theology, his doctrine of original sin. I believe that his views on this matter can be understood by closer examination of the character of his conversion to Christianity, counterpoised to the rather different conversion (to the religion of Isis) of Apuleius in his *Metamorphoses*.[193] What makes this comparison of interest is not only that Apuleius and Augustine were North African Romans but also that they shared both an education in classical philosophy (although Augustine, unlike Apuleius, did not extensively read Greek philosophy in the original) and common ambitions and achievements as rhetorician-lawyers. They also share a common sense of crisis about the lives they had once led as Roman privileged men, both highly sexual. But they take quite different paths, Apuleius into a new kind of loving sexual relationship with a woman very much his equal, Augustine into celibacy. At the heart of Augustine's different path lie his views of women.

In this connection, a Catholic nun, Karol Jackowski, recently traced the "Catholic Church's obsession with legislating sexual morality" to

> the thinking of Augustine. His most famous prayer appears to be the tormented prayer of the Catholic priesthood still: "Lord, make me chaste, but not yet." And while some church historians tend to minimize and even deny Augustine's obsession with sex, I find that his teachings prove otherwise. One has only to look at Augustine's writings (especially on original sin and the seductive nature

189 See Neil B. McLynn, *Ambrose of Milan: Church and Court in a Christian Capital* (Berkeley: University of California Press, 1994).

190 See, on all these points, Peter Brown, *Augustine of Hippo: A Biography* (Berkeley: University of California Press, 2000) (originally published in 1967).

191 See, on this history, Richard Regan, S.J., *Conflict and Consensus: Religious Freedom and the Second Vatican Council* (New York: Macmillan, 1967).

192 See, on this point, Richards, *Toleration and the Constitution*.

193 See, for fuller discussion, Carol Gilligan and David A. J. Richards, *The Deepening Darkness: Patriarchy, Resistance, and Democracy's Future* (Cambridge: Cambridge University Press, 2009).

> of woman) to see that this is clearly a man who could not, without anguish, stop thinking of sex, and could not stop blaming women for his misery.[194]

Jackowski correctly points to Augustine's quite remarkable, highly mythologized reading of the Adam and Eve narrative, a narrative the is "[t]he cornerstone of current Catholic moral theology on sex and the subordinate nature of woman."[195]

There are two roads into Augustine's pivotally important thought on this matter: first, his interpretation of the Adam and Eve narrative in *The City of God*,[196] which links a negative view of sexuality with misogyny (as Jackowski observes); and second, his exquisitely introspective exploration of his psychological development from boy to sexual man to celibate priest and bishop in *The Confessions*.[197] Both accounts support Jackowski's penetrating diagnosis of the close link between a highly negative view of sexuality and misogyny in the Augustinian view of sexuality that Thomas assumed and codified as natural law.

Augustine's interpretation of the Adam and Eve narrative places Eve in the more responsible position for Adam's disobedience, the Fall, exile, and the taint of original sin that humankind thereafter has carried in its psyche; thus, on Augustine's telling, the serpent "had a deceitful conversation with the woman – no doubt starting with the inferior of the human pair so as to arrive at the whole by stages, supposing that the man would not be so easily gullible, and could not be trapped by a false move on his own part, but only if he yielded to another's mistake."[198] It is this misogynist view of women's intrinsic inferiority to which the Fall is attributed. Before this moment, Adam and Eve did not, for Augustine, experience sexuality in the way humans now do, but a man could will erections for procreation (when needed), without any lust, just as some extraordinary people now can wiggle their ears at will or even pass air musically "without any stink."[199] The mark of the Fall, indeed its punishment, is the way sexuality now operates, "totally opposed to the mind's control, it is quite often divided against itself,"[200] that is, feeling sexual desire when one does not want to feel it and not feeling such desire when one wants to feel it. Indeed, Augustine points to the intensity of our sexual experience as a mark of our loss of rationality:

> This lust assumes power not only over the whole body, and not only from the outside, but also internally; it disturbs the whole man, when the mental emotion combines and mingles with the physical craving, resulting in a pleasure

194 Karol Jackowski, *The Silence We Keep: A Nun's View of the Catholic Priest Scandal* (New York: Harmony Books, 2004), p. 43.

195 *Id.*, p. 43. See, for an important scholarly study confirming Jackowski's analysis, Ranke-Heinemann, *Eunuchs for Heaven*.

196 See Augustine, *City of God*.

197 See Augustine, *Confessions*, trans. Henry Chadwick (Oxford: Oxford University Press, 1991).

198 Augustine, *City of God*, p. 570.

199 *Id.*, p. 588

200 *Id.*, p. 577.

> surpassing all physical delights. So intense is the pleasure that when it reaches its climax there is an almost total extinction of mental alertness; the intellectual sentries, as it were, are overwhelmed.[201]

Augustine rests his case on an experience he assumes to be universal: sexuality as a natural object of continuing shame because it involves such loss of control, including control of our rational faculties:

> In fact, this lust we are now examining is something to be the more ashamed of because the soul, when dealing with it, neither has command of itself so as to be entirely free from lust, nor does it rule the body so completely that the organs of shame are moved by the will instead of by lust. Indeed if they were so ruled they would not be *pudenda* – parts of shame.[202]

Accordingly, the only proper form of sex was that which was done with the controlled intention to procreate; sexuality without procreation or independent of such intentions was, for Augustine, intrinsically degrading, the view of sexual morality he bequeathed to the Catholic Church.

Augustine's argument, naturalistically interpreted, rests on a rather remarkable fallacy. Augustine points to two anthropological points about human sexual experience: first, humans universally insist on having sex alone and unobserved by others;[203] and second, humans universally cover their genitals in public.[204] Augustine argues that the only plausible explanation for these two facts about human sexuality is that humans experience sex as intrinsically degrading because it involves this loss of control; this perception of shame, in turn, must rest on the fact that the only proper form of sex is having it with the controlled intention to procreate; sexuality is intrinsically degrading because we tend to experience it without or independent of the one intention that alone can validate it. Assuming, arguendo, the truth of Augustine's anthropological assumptions,[205] it does not follow that humans must find sex intrinsically shameful. These facts are equally well explained by the fact that people experience embarrassment in certain forms of publicity of their sexuality, not shame in the experience of sex itself. Shame is conceptually distinguishable from embarrassment in that its natural object is a failure of personally esteemed competent self-control, whether the failure is public or private; embarrassment, in contrast, is experienced when a matter is made

201 *Id.*

202 *Id.*, p. 586.

203 *Id.*, pp. 579–80.

204 *Id.*, pp. 578–9.

205 A leading anthropological study of cross-cultural sexual practices reports that, universally, sexual intercourse occurs in private. See Ford and Beach, *Patterns of Sexual Behavior*, pp. 68–72. This is not a characteristic of animal sexual behavior: "A desire for privacy during sexual intercourse seems confined to human beings. Male-female pairs of other animal species appear to be unaffected by the presence of other individuals and mate quite as readily in a crowd as when they are alone." *Id.*, p. 71.

public that properly is regarded as private.[206] The twin facts adduced by Augustine are, indeed, better explained by the hypothesis of embarrassment, not shame. Surely many people experience no negative self-evaluations when they engage in sex in private, which is what the hypothesis of embarrassment, not shame, would lead us to expect. For example, people may experience pride in knowing that other people know or believe that they are having sex (the recently married young couple). There is no shame here, but there would be severe embarrassment if the sex act were actually observed. That people would experience such embarrassment reveals something important about human sexual experience, but it is not Augustine's contempt for the loss of control of sexual passion. Sexual experience is, for human beings, a profoundly personal, spontaneous, and absorbing experience in which they express intimate fantasies and vulnerabilities that typically cannot brook the sense of an external, critical observer. That humans require privacy for sex relates to the nature of the experience; there is no suggestion that the experience is, pace Augustine, intrinsically degrading.

If Augustine's influential view is not reasonably required by the naturalistic facts, it can reasonably be explained, as Jackowski argues, by the misogynist assumptions he brings to his understanding of sexuality. This is shown certainly by the terms of his interpretation of the Adam and Eve narrative in which women's inferiority plays the decisive role in the Fall, our sexuality tainted by its association with woman as sexual temptress irrespective of larger rational ends; indeed, our sexuality is, on this view, punishment for the Fall, our eroticism reminding ourselves of our primal disobedience. There is nothing interpretively inevitable in the approach to Bible interpretation that Augustine takes, as Elaine Pagels has made clear.[207] There is, for example, the approach of Irenaean theodicy which, to deal with the problem of evil, does not construe this and other such narratives as an original state of perfection and then fall but construes these narratives in terms of humankind gradually growing into a sense of adult ethical responsibilities, learning from mistakes and developing over time new progressive insights into ethical demands.[208] Augustine brings to the narrative a misogyny that he then finds confirmed by his interpretation of it.

The psychological roots of Augustine's misogyny are shown in the terms in which Augustine himself in *Confessions* narrates his move from sexually active man to celibate priest, a move in which his mother, Monica (a pious Catholic), plays a decisive role. What is clear in Augustine's narrative is that he had a loving affair with a woman and had a child, Adeodatus, by her: "she was the only girl for me, and I was faithful to her."[209] She was not, however, a woman of a class

[206] See, on this point, Richards, *A Theory of Reason for Action*, p. 254.

[207] See Elaine Pagels, *Adam, Eve, and the Serpent* (New York: Random House, 1988), pp. 98–126.

[208] See John H. Hick, "An Irenaean Theodicy," in *Philosophy of Religion: The Big Questions*, ed. Eleanor Stump and Michael J. Murray (Oxford: Blackwell Publishers, 1999), pp. 222–7. I am grateful for this reference to Donald Levy.

[209] Augustine, *Confessions*, p. 53.

Augustine could marry, and he separated from her so he could consider marriage in terms of the patriarchal order of the age. Monica had arranged, as patriarchal Roman women traditionally did, a suitable marriage for her son, but the girl in question would be of age in two years; meanwhile, he took another woman as his mistress.[210] Augustine's words for the separation from the woman he loved and by whom he had a beloved child speak of a traumatic break in relationship: "My heart which was deeply attached was cut and wounded, and left a trail of blood."[211] Augustine contrasts such sexual relationships to women who were illiterate with his friendships with men, which are characterized by conversation with highly literate equals, a model for intense friendships between equals that he finds fulfilled in his relationships to fellow monks, as a celibate priest, after his conversion. One of the reasons Augustine gives for coming to think of marriage as only for reproduction is that a companionate relationship based on intellectual equality is, for him, only imaginable with a man: "if God had wanted Adam to have a partner in scintillating conversation he would have created another man; the fact that God created a woman showed that he had in the mind the survival of the human race."[212]

One woman who falls outside this mold was his mother, Monica, who, though probably illiterate, conversed with her son about neo-Platonic philosophy, urging him finally to convert to Catholicism.[213] The marriage of Monica to Patricius, Augustine's father, had been, like other such marriages, an arranged affair, probably when Monica was quite young. Patricius, a pagan (he converts to Christianity only at his death), had, like other Roman men of his station, been unfaithful to Monica; and Augustine writes at some length of his violence, admiring his mother's sensitive insight into her husband's violence and her ability to calm him down:

> She knew that an angry husband should not be opposed, not merely by anything she did, but even by a word. Once she saw that he had become calm and quiet, and that the occasion was opportune, she would explain the reason for her action, in case perhaps he had reacted without sufficient consideration. Indeed many wives married to gentler husbands bore the marks of blows and suffered disfigurement to their faces. In conversation together they used to complain about their husband's behaviour. Monica, speaking as if in jest but offering serious advice, used to blame their tongues. She would say that since the day when they heard the so-called matrimonial contract read out to them, they should reckon them to be legally binding documents by which they had become servants. She thought they should remember their condition and not proudly withstand their masters. The wives were astounded, knowing what a

210 See *id.*, pp. 107–9.

211 *Id.*, p. 109.

212 Quoted in Henry Chadwick, "Introduction," *Confessions*, pp. ix–xxvi, xviii–xix.

213 See, on these points, Garry Wills, *Saint Augustine* (New York: Lipper/Viking Books, 1999), pp. 58–63.

> violent husband she had to put up with. Yet this was unheard of, nor was there ever a mark to show, that Patrick had beaten his wife or that a domestic quarrel had caused dissension between them for even a single day.[214]

Passages of this sort bespeak Augustine's remarkable sensitivity to his mother and her plight under patriarchy. On the one hand, Augustine insists that we see the violence of husbands to wives in Roman marriages, just as elsewhere he reveals how common beatings of boys like himself were by his teachers, beatings at which "our parents laughed."[215] On the other hand, Augustine admires not only his mother's close study of her husband's violence (especially triggered by verbal insults) but also her insight into how to lower its incidence. Monica may have drawn her understanding and insight, as other women have, from a religious piety centered on the Jesus of the Gospels, for example, at Matthew 5:38–42: "I tell you not to resist one who is evil. But if anyone strikes you on the right cheek, turn the other to him as well."[216] Jesus' teaching on nonviolence offers an authoritative example of such understanding and insight, one that resonated with the experience of many women under patriarchy. If the propensity of male violence under patriarchy turns on insults to one's manhood, it is precisely both not making and not responding violently to such insults (a kind of nonviolence) that may forestall or lower the incidence of the patriarchal cycle of violence.[217] Augustine's growing admiration of both his mother's life and religion makes sense against this background. It accords his mother's experience and voice a remarkable level of authority in an otherwise highly patriarchal Roman culture, including an emotional intelligence in dealing with the roots of the violence of patriarchal men. If Augustine comes to resist Roman patriarchy at all, it is clearly through his mother. In contrast, as her resistance never fundamentally questions Roman patriarchy (she accepts her servile role in marriage as in the nature of things and rationalizes her lack of verbal resistance on this ground), her son's Christianity, which he clearly learned from his mother, never extends beyond his mother's understanding. He learned of the inferior position of women from her and never fundamentally questioned it; indeed, his treatment of the Adam and Eve narrative reflects a view he learned from his mother. What greater authority could there be for his misogyny that the view of his own mother? he may well have thought.[218]

In his remarkable psychoanalytically informed biography of Augustine, Peter Brown frames the trajectory of Augustine's development in terms of his relationship to his mother, fleeing from her[219] but drawn deeply back to her, including

[214] Augustine, *Confessions*, pp. 168–9.

[215] Augustine, *Confessions*, p. 12.

[216] Quoted in David A. J. Richards, *Disarming Manhood: Roots of Ethical Resistance* (Athens: Ohio University/Swallow Press, 2005), p. 33.

[217] See, on these points, *id.*, pp. 27–40.

[218] For an express identification of his mother with Eve, see Augustine, *Confessions*, p. 82.

[219] See, on this point, *id.*, pp. 81–2.

her highly personal religion of Christian piety and her sense of her "heroes, as a man 'predestined', the course of his life already ineluctably marked out by God," one of the roots of "Augustine's grandiose theory of predestination: and, as with so many very clever people, such simple roots were all the stronger for being largely unconscious."[220] God's love for Augustine is modeled on that of his mother: "she loved to have me with her, but much more than most mothers."[221] Augustine's family was one of moderate means (support for his education and ambitions came from patrons), and his parents, both father and mother, were clearly themselves highly ambitious for their remarkably gifted son, who would rise, fired by their ambition for him, very high in the hierarchy of both the Roman church and the state of his period. Augustine condemns in his own father such ambition for his son (in contrast to his son's soul) and claims, for this reason, that he cannot be his true father (only God the father can be),[222] remarks that suggest a hostile edge in the relationship of father and son quite common under Roman patriarchy. Augustine would only come into a sense of financial independence (his father dying when he was sixteen[223]) at his mother's death (which is at the time of his conversion). Such dependence suggests what we might call a prolonged psycho-sexual adolescence; Augustine had a sexual life, but he was even then drawn to the Manichaeans, whose views are even more sexually ascetic than Christians. And at his conversion to Christianity, Augustine argues that only celibacy allows for full access to God. One thinks, in this connection, of Anna Freud's observations about "the asceticism and intellectuality of adolescence."[224]

There is a telling scene in this connection that Augustine paints about his father's pride at the bathhouse in his son's "showing signs of virility and the stirrings of adolescence, [at which] he was overjoyed to suppose that he would now be having grandchildren and told my mother so."[225] The response of Monica could not have been more different: "she shook with pious trepidation and a holy fear.... Her concern (and in the secret of my conscience I recall the memory of her admonition delivered with vehement anxiety) was that I should not fall into fornication, and above all that I should not commit adultery with someone else's wife."[226] Monica's "vehement anxiety" suggests a sexually ascetic temperament, reflecting her problems with sexuality itself, freighted, as it had been in her life with Patricius, with lack of love and with violence. An illuminating psychological analogy in mother-son relationships may be that of Gandhi to his highly idealized and very pious mother: Gandhi, as a child, competitively tried to outdo his

[220] Peter Brown, *Augustine of Hippo* (London: Faber & Faber, 1967), p. 175.
[221] Augustine, *Confessions*, p. 82.
[222] See *id.*, p. 26; see also *id.*, p. 14.
[223] *Id.*, p. 39.
[224] See Anna Freud, *The Ego and the Mechanisms of Defense*, rev. ed. (Madison, Wis.: International Universities Press, 2000), p. 153.
[225] Augustine, *Confessions*, pp. 26–7.
[226] *Id.*, p. 27.

mother in her nonviolence.[227] Augustine, finally having justified to himself the philosophical rationality of his mother's religion, adopted her religion but on terms more sexually ascetic than those by which his own highly idealized mother lived. Augustine strikingly converted, which included for him becoming a celibate priest, near his mother's death, a psychology that suggests turning to God, as the ideal friend-lover he had always sought in men and women, an idealization that covers traumatic loss – the loss of the woman he sexually loved, as well as the deaths of his beloved mother; his son, Adeodatus; and of other close friends, for whose deaths he deeply grieved, as he tells us at length.[228]

Augustine, a philosophical rationalist, had turned to Christianity only when he had found a way, through neo-Platonism,[229] to make personal sense of the Christian immaterial conception of God, as an inner voice, the voice of a perfectly sensitive and responsive lover to whom *Confessions* is passionately addressed, but a lover decidedly without a body (Porphyry wrote of the leading neo-Platonist, Plotinus, that he "seemed ashamed of being in the body").[230] It is striking, in this connection, that Augustine, like René Descartes (the father of the mind-body dualism in modern philosophy) later, had been at one point a philosophical skeptic, and he anticipated Descartes by finding a way out of global skepticism by a form of the cogito argument (not being able to doubt that, in doubting, he existed).[231] Augustine could believe in his mother's God only when, philosophically, he could make sense of the Christian God in such terms and, when, theologically, Ambrose of Milan had given him a living example of a Christian clerical life exercising responsible political authority and making metaphorical sense of both the Old and New Testament in integrated Christian terms.[232] Through these, Augustine came to the conviction, underlying his conversion, that Bible interpretation was the reasonable basis for ultimate authority in religious and ethical matters (based on the evidence of miracles and the like). What compelled him, at the moment of conversion, were the epistles of Paul, in particular, Romans, texts that he construed then as requiring celibacy as the only way

227 See Erik Erikson, *Gandhi's Truth: On the Origins of Militant Nonviolence* (New York: W. W. Norton, 1993), pp. 110–11.

228 See, e.g., Augustine, *Confessions*, pp. 56–60.

229 See, on this point, *id.*, pp. 111–32. The central text would have been Plotinus, *The Enneads*, trans. Stephen MacKenna (London: Penguin, 1991), parts of which Augustine read in Latin translation (Plotinus wrote in Greek). On the parts of Plotinus he read, see Eugene TeSelle, *Augustine the Theologian* (Eugene, Ore.: Wipf and Stock, 2002), pp. 43–5, 53, 68; John M. Rist, *Augustine: Ancient Thought Baptized* (Cambridge: Cambridge University Press, 1997), p. 188.

230 Porphyry, *The Life of Plotinus*, trans. Stephen MacKenna (Edmonds, Wash.: Holmes Publishing, 2001), p. 5.

231 See, on this point, Gareth B. Matthews, *Thought's Ego in Augustine and Descartes* (Ithaca, N.Y.: Cornell University Press, 1992). See also Gareth B. Matthews, *Augustine* (Malden, Mass.: Blackwell, 2005); Stephen Menn, *Descartes and Augustine* (Cambridge: Cambridge University Press, 2002).

232 See Neil B. McLynn, *Ambrose of Milan: Church and Court in a Christian Capital* (Berkeley: University of California Press, 1994).

of hearing God's voice within and later construed as requiring original sin and the interpretation of the Adam and Eve narrative earlier discussed.[233] The Bible interpretation in question had been reasonably contested by Christians before Augustine and would be contested by even more Christians after Augustine.[234] I agree with these critics. My interest here is in the powerful personal and political psychology that led Augustine to take the interpretive views he did and why those views were so hegemonically dominant for so long. Why, once Augustine arrived at a conception of an immaterial lover-God, did that psychologically lead him associatively (certainly not logically or philosophically) to celibacy? I believe that an account of a psychology of idealization and loss, based on regarding patriarchy as in the nature of things, explains not only Augustine's conversion but also its enormous continuing power during periods when patriarchy remained largely uncontested.

Augustine's denigration of sexuality rests on his acceptance, as axiomatic, of the highly patriarchal Roman conception of women. Honor codes exemplify the unjust demands of patriarchy on the psychology of men, a patriarchal manhood that places sons and daughters under the hierarchical authority of fathers.[235] These demands take the form of an obligatory violence directed against any voice that challenges, in particular, the strict social controls over women's sexuality (including arranged marriages) that are required to advance patriarchal dynastic ends, to wit, virginity before marriage and monogamous fidelity after marriage. A father's or brother's or lover's or husband's sense of honor, as a man, is defined in terms of his control over the chastity or fidelity of women, irrespective of personal feeling or desire. Any challenge to such control was an insult that triggered violence, as a condition of manhood under patriarchy. Later, such patriarchal conceptions (rooted in Roman patriarchy) were, in dominantly face-to-face and largely illiterate Mediterranean societies, understood in terms of how matters publicly appeared, so that men were vulnerable to dishonor because women (often, in fact, quite innocent of sexual relations) merely appeared less strictly modest and reticent in relationships to men.[236] Such masculine dishonor, sometimes arising only from gossip,[237] required violence, the killing of wives or daughters. A man's most intimate feelings and relations were, under the code of honor, subject to rules that rested as much on repression of his personal feeling and voice as they did on those of women.

Codes of honor, thus understood, are aspects of patriarchal institutions (resting on precisely the mythological idealization of gender stereotypes) that sustain forms

[233] See Augustine, *Confessions*, pp. 131, 134, 141, 153. See also, for illuminating commentary, Menn, *Descartes and Augustine*, pp. 192–206.

[234] See, on these points, Pagels, *Adam, Eve, and the Serpent*.

[235] See, on this point, Gilligan, *Birth of Pleasure*, pp. 4–5.

[236] See J. G. Peristiany, ed., *Honour and Shame: The Values of Mediterranean Society* (Chicago: University of Chicago Press, 1966), pp. 66–7.

[237] See *id.*, pp. 253–4, 256–7.

of structural injustice through violence directed against any challenge to the terms of such gender stereotypes.[238] We can still see the force of these conceptions, rooted in Roman patriarchy,[239] in the patriarchal culture of nineteenth-century Italy, imposing the kind of tragic losses and repressed voices that such objectifying gender stereotypes, as a general matter, both inflicted and covered over, namely the sacrifice of children born out of wedlock.[240] The honor code condemned as intrinsically shameful both sexual relations out of wedlock and the illegitimate children often born of such relations.[241] The honor code, enforced by local Catholic priests and the police, rationalized bullying unwed mothers to abandon children to public institutions and sometimes effectively imprisoning them in such institutions as compulsory wet nurses. The consequences for the babies were usually death.[242] Families sometimes protested such separations in terms of their "infinite grief," robbing a mother "of the dearest object of her heart,"[243] which suggests traumatizing emotional losses that must have been widespread. But such losses, consistent with the political psychology of patriarchy, were often not acknowledged but covered over with gender-stereotypical idealizations, as of the foundlings in Naples, as "children of the Madonna,"[244] most of whom in fact died. Meanwhile, their real mothers, if they were wet nurses in the foundling homes, were "treated as livestock."[245]

The atrocity of such patriarchal practices rests on such mythological idealizations in terms of gender stereotypes, denying the personal feeling and voice of the persons most afflicted by such stereotypes. The high rates of both illegitimacy and abandonment of infants during this period were common knowledge,[246] yet the underlying emotional trauma and loss could be given no voice or weight. The tragic music dramas of Giuseppe Verdi so absorbed Italians and others because they gave such powerful expression to widespread feelings that could not otherwise be acknowledged.[247]

The developmental psychology that makes possible a conception of manhood that can sustain such patriarchal demands requires traumatic separation of young

[238] See *id.*, pp. 42–53.

[239] On the continuity of these patriarchal conceptions over time, see Eva Cantarella, "Homicides of Honor: The Development of Italian Adultery Law over Two Millenia," in *The Family in Italy from Antiquity to the Present*, ed. David I. Kertzer and Richard P. Saller (New Haven, Conn.: Yale University Press, 1991), pp. 229–46.

[240] See David I. Kertzer, *Sacrifices for Honor: Italian Infant Abandonment and the Politics of Reproductive Control* (Boston: Beacon Press, 1993).

[241] See David D. Gilmore, ed., *Honour and Shame and the Unity of the Mediterranean* (Washington, D.C.: American Anthropological Association, 1987), p. 110.

[242] See Kertzer, *Sacrifices for Honor*, p. 125.

[243] See *id.*, p. 56.

[244] See *id.*, pp. 107, 122.

[245] See *id.*, p. 148.

[246] See *id.*, p. 55.

[247] See David A. J. Richards, *Tragic Manhood and Democracy: Verdi's Voice and the Powers of Musical Art* (Brighton, U.K.: Sussex Academic Press, 2004).

boys from their mothers, in contrast to the developmental continuity in such relationships allowed to girls until early adolescence, the view central to the developmental psychology of Carol Gilligan.[248] The marks of such trauma are not only loss of intimate voice and memory but also the kinds of disassociation from intimate relationship that patriarchal manhood requires. Idealizing stereotypes are, in their nature, objectifying, supported by such a psychology of disassociation that lends itself to the forms of violence required to hold such stereotypes in place in patterns of structural injustice, including the violent repression of the free sexual voice of women. These stereotypes in their nature both idealize (the good asexual woman) and denigrate (the bad sexual woman).

In this framework, women do not exist as persons with moral individuality, let alone sexual agency and subjectivity, independent of the roles assigned them by patriarchy. What Augustine could not imagine was having a loving, sexual relationship with a woman based on the kind of equal voice he assumed in his intense relationships with men. Rather, he came to regard sexual experience as such as inimical to any such relationships, which explains why, in *Confessions*, he tells a story that he increasingly identified his sexual experience as what kept him from the love of God, a love conceived on terms that dignified the lover and beloved as full persons.[249] God, who is the addressee of *Confessions*, is the most satisfying and absorbing of lovers, with whom Augustine lives in the most confidential, trusting, and loving of relationships ("physician of my most intimate self"[250]), and his love song to his lover is highly erotic:

> Yet there is a light I love, and a food, and a kind of embrace when I love my God – a light, voice, odour, food, embrace of my inner man, where my soul is floodlit by light which space cannot contain, where there is sound that time cannot seize, where there is a perfume which no breeze disperses, where there is a taste for food no amount of eating can lessen, and where there is a bond of union that no satiety can part. That is what I love when I loved my God.[251]

The developmental narrative Augustine tells so truthfully is a love story of a certain remarkable sort, revealing nakedly the developmental psychology of an infant, boy, and man that responds to traumatic breaks in real relationships by covering over the trauma with a mythologizing conception of gender that divides women into asexual good women (his mother) and sexual bad women (his lover). Although he insists at the end of his narrative that women have "an equal capacity of rational intelligence," he regards such capacity as undermined "by the sex of her body," which "is submissive to the masculine sex."[252] Women are equal, but,

248 See, on these points, Gilligan, *Birth of Pleasure*, pp. 14–17, 89–91, 161–3, 178–9, 204.
249 See, on this point, Augustine, *Confessions*, pp. 127, 134, 141, 145.
250 *Id.*, p. 180; see also *id.*, p. 202.
251 *Id.*, p. 183.
252 See *id.*, p. 302.

as sexual, unequal, a contradiction but one that Augustine's divided psychology accepts as in the nature of things, as his patriarchal mother had taught him.

What makes Augustine's conversion so psychologically interesting is that he came to it in a way that was strikingly antipatriarchal, that is, through his relationship to his mother's experience and voice, which he came to regard as ethically and religiously authoritative. Monica's personal form of Christianity led her to a remarkable understanding of and ability to deal with the Roman patriarchal violence of her husband, abilities her son clearly admired and valued. It is quite consistent with this developmental influence on her son that Augustine, in *City of God*, should offer one of the first serious and profound criticisms of Roman imperialistic violence as, more often than not, unjust both in its ends and in its means (giving rise to the just-war traditions of Western thought).[253] But Monica's insights never fundamentally questioned the Roman patriarchy she assumed to be in the nature of things, a fact clearly shown by her own role, as a Roman patriarchal mother, in arranging her son's marriage to an appropriate girl to ensure his upward mobility, even at the expense of requiring her son to give up his relationship to the only woman he ever sexually loved. Augustine shows himself very much to be a good patriarchal son when he accepts his mother's patriarchal demands, though he tells us that it broke his heart.

Augustine confesses at the beginning of *Confessions* that he adored, before his conversion, the Dido-Aeneas episode in Virgil's *Aeneid*.[254] In fact, Augustine's conversion reenacted this tragic story of love under Roman patriarchy, as he also repudiated the woman he loved because of the patriarchal demands of his mother (Monica as Venus). But Monica, unlike Venus, is, as a pious Christian woman, more of a critic of Roman patriarchal violence but, at best, a partial critic. Her son, who comes to God through Monica and often refers to God as "this dearest mother,"[255] is also at best a partial critic of Roman patriarchy. Augustine's love for his mother, who may have been the only person he ever deeply loved, must have also been ambivalent and conflicted, as is shown not only by his attempts to escape her (fleeing to Italy)[256] but also, at one point, by her throwing him out of her house because of his Manichaean views (she relented but wept constantly over his obduracy).[257] Certainly, he ultimately aligned himself with her religion, but her religion was highly patriarchal (her view of wives as servile), from which he suffered when he obeyed his mother's demands to break with the woman he loved. But Augustine insists on making himself suffer even more than his mother ever demanded of him, and certainly more than Venus ever demanded of Aeneas: he will give up sex entirely, something his mother never did, though men she

[253] See, on this point, Augustine, *City of God*, at pp. 97–9, 104, 139, 142, 154–5, 205–7, 207–12, 401.

[254] See Augustine, *Confessions*, pp. 15–16.

[255] See *id.*, p. 257.

[256] *Id.*, pp. 81–2.

[257] See *id.*, pp. 49, 56, 80–2.

much admired, like Ambrose, did.[258] Augustine not only dutifully obeyed his mother's commands, like pious Aeneas, but he set himself the competitive task to exceed her in piety, inflicting on himself, because of her, not only the loss of the woman he sexually loved but also the abandonment of sexuality itself. Augustine's radical break with his sexuality thus works in the framework of his patriarchal mother's rather inhuman demands on her son, leaving in her son a darkness visible akin to that of Virgil's Aeneas. When patriarchal demands impose on men such traumatic disruptions of real relationships, their legacy is a personal and political psychology that covers over and rationalizes the loss of real relationship with identification with patriarchal demands that refuse to be questioned and indeed wreak violence on anyone who challenges these demands (a psychology I earlier called the Gilligan-Richards thesis, see Introduction). Men, like Augustine, who have visited so much violence on their own psyches, leaving a residue of anger and rage, are vulnerable, as Romans were, to a need for violent action directed against anyone who might challenge the terrible price they have imposed on themselves to become patriarchal men. Thus, Augustine, himself once a Manichaean, confessed at the time of his conversion: "What vehement and bitter anger I felt against the Manichees!"[259]

Augustine as much plays the patriarchal Roman hero of his confessional narrative as Aeneas does in Virgil's narrative of Roman manhood. Aeneas is a heroic man because he left the woman he loved when patriarchy demanded such abandonment. At a time when the Western Roman Empire is near its end, Augustine tells a story of his own heroism, shown not only by his abandonment of the woman he loved but also of his sexuality, all as he came to believe patriarchy demanded. The Roman Empire had lived, since Augustus, under an autocratic political system in which both political and religious authority was hierarchically centered in the emperor. Since Constantine, the emperors had been largely Christian and centered on themselves the same authority over Christianity as the emperors had enjoyed over Roman pagan religion. Augustine works in the framework of this autocratic conception and calls for a heroic form of religious and political leadership, namely a celibate male priesthood, which will support such a patriarchal conception of authority even when the empire collapses, as it does during Augustine's lifetime. A member of this celibate male priesthood is "the soldier of the heavenly host,"[260] which underscores the militaristic model for patriarchal authority that he absorbed from Roman politics into his conception of the priesthood appropriate to the Christian religion. What makes such a soldier possible, whether Aeneas or Augustine, is the renunciation of sexual love.

Augustine is not the first or last sexually conflicted, highly sensitive man of genius who turned to celibacy as the only way to free himself from patriarchally

[258] See, on this point, *id.*, pp. 91–2.

[259] *Id.*, p. 160. See also *id.*, p. 254.

[260] *Id.*, p. 206.

framed sexual relationships with women that disabled him from hearing or listening to women's voices as equals. Both Tolstoy and Gandhi turn to celibacy for such reasons.[261] What is striking in thinkers of ethical genius, like Augustine, Tolstoy, and Gandhi, is that they can extend critical ethical thought to many areas but not to the patriarchal assumptions governing their most intimate sexual lives, feelings, and relationships. These they accept as in the nature of things or in the nature of sexuality. It is important to take seriously the suffering that patriarchy inflicts on men and women, in particular, highly sensitive, ethically demanding men who experience sex under patriarchy as lacking the relational personal significance and value they associate with the passionate friendship and affection of equals. We also must appreciate that the psychological basis of such sensitivity is, as it was for Tolstoy, Gandhi, and Augustine, close relationships with the highly personal religion of highly idealized mothers or maternal figures. However, because the religion of such mothers itself rests on the idealization of asexual women and denigration of sexual women, it does not fundamentally challenge the terms of patriarchy but works within its framework. The consequence for the sons of such women is that they, like their mothers, fail to resist patriarchy, which often takes the form of a celibacy announcing a new, more demanding form of patriarchy, one, in Augustine's case, that established an exclusively male, celibate, autocratic priesthood as the ultimate religious and ethical authority. This is the ultimate form of religio-ethical patriarchy, a rule of male, celibate priests to whom all others are subordinate. Its rationale and basis are a misogyny based on patriarchy, as Sister Karol Jackowski clearly sees. It is a misogyny that, in Augustine's case, he learned from his patriarchal Roman mother.

We should contrast the structure of Augustine's conversion with that of Apuleius. Augustine clearly knew Apuleius's work well, both his philosophical writings and his novel, *Metamorphoses*: "No post-classical Latin author has such a place in Augustine's writings as Apuleius."[262] Augustine himself refers to Apuleius's novel as "either fact or fiction,"[263] which suggests what it probably is, fictionalized autobiography. We cannot know, in the same way we can for Augustine, the full picture of the psychological sources bearing on Apuleius's conversion, but it is reasonable to connect the autobiographical terms of *Metamorphoses* to his marriage to an older, wealthy, educated woman, Pudentilla, who had nursed him through an illness. Such an underlying relationship clarifies the role of conversion to the Isis religion by Lucius Apuleius, as it is through Isis's sexual love, as a wife and mother, that Osiris is restored from his fragmentation into some sense of wholeness.

I believe there is good reason to think that Augustine may have modeled his *Confessions* on Apuleius's novel, as the same genre of an autobiography of

[261] See, for study of this point, Richards, *Disarming Manhood*.

[262] Harald Hagendahl, *Augustine and the Latin Classics* (Göteborg: Elanders Boktrycheri Aktiebolag, 1967), pp. 680–1.

[263] Augustine, *City of God*, p. 782.

religious conversion, albeit not fictionalized. Certainly, the text of the *Confessions* uses imagery that is self-consciously Apuleian: when Augustine describes himself as "in love with love,"[264] he is surely echoing the exquisite scene in the Cupid and Psyche story where Psyche "fell in love with Love,"[265] and the imagery of God's love is Cupid's arrow, "the arrow of your love,"[266] "you pierced my heart."[267] And Augustine's condemnation of undisciplined curiosity again self-consciously echoes the similar theme in Apuleius.[268] But the borrowings are more than stylistic and thematic. *Confessions* is a highly personal, autobiographical narrative of conversion, as is *Metamorphoses*. Both are organized around the question of love, and indeed are, in their different ways, love stories: their narratives move from sexual obsession to love, in Apuleius, from animal to human; in Augustine, from sex with women to the love of God. The Cupid and Psyche story – a love story – is as central to the novel of Apuleius as the coming to God's love, as perfect lover, is in Augustine. Augustine centers the psyche, as does Apuleius, in love: "My weight is my love."[269]

Once we see that these works as so similar, we can see as well their stark differences, which were of enormous consequence for the direction of Western culture for well more than a millennium. Whereas Augustine's conversion was rooted in his relationship to his highly idealized, asexual mother, Apuleius recovered his humanity through the sexual love of a woman who was his equal. It is striking that, to the extent that Augustinian Christianity incorporates an image of motherhood in its conception of divinity, it is through the asexual Virgin Mary, based, it has been plausibly suggested, not on the mystery religion of the highly sexual Isis but on the asexual Cybele and her violent cult of sexually self-mutilated acolytes.[270] The consequence of such idealization is not to contest patriarchy but to reinforce it, as Augustine clearly does.

I believe it is important, particularly at the present moment, to recapture the sense of a cultural period, crucial in the development of human culture, when there was a sense of open choices between two paths to a fully human life – that of Apuleius and that of Augustine. Carol Gilligan and I contest the view of late Roman sexuality that claims that there was an uncontested tendency, both philosophical and religious, in this period to an ascetic conception of human sexuality.[271] Even the best historians of this period have, I believe, been blinded by

[264] Augustine, *Confessions*, p. 35

[265] Apuleius, *The Golden Ass*, translated by E.J. Kenney (London: Penguin, 1998), p. 88.

[266] Augustine, *Confessions*, p. 156.

[267] *Id.*, p. 183.

[268] See *id.*, pp. 210–12, 215, 291.

[269] *Id.*, p. 278.

[270] See, on this point, Michael P. Carroll, *The Cult of the Virgin Mary: Psychological Origins* (Princeton, N.J.: Princeton University Press, 1986).

[271] See, for support of this essential critical point, Kathy L. Gaca, *The Making of Fornication: Eros, Ethics, and Political Reform in Greek Philosophy and Early Christianity* (Berkeley: University of California Press, 2003); Simon Goldhill, *Foucault's Virginity: Ancient Erotic Fiction and the History of Sexuality* (Cambridge: Cambridge University Press, 1995).

the hegemonic power of the Augustinian conception to read back into history an inevitability that was simply not there. The Augustinian conception was remarkably successful but not because it was reasonable, and certainly not because it reflected the dominant views of sexuality of classical philosophers or of religions like Judaism, on which Christianity claimed to be based (in fact, Christian anti-Semitism demonized the Jews precisely because Jews accepted sexuality as one of life's basic goods[272]). The ascetic Augustinian views were, in fact, sectarian and extreme even when adopted, in fact demonizing naturalistic features of human sexual experience as marks of demonic possession.[273] Augustine's preoccupation with Apuleius makes sense from this point of view, as Apuleius in *Metamorphoses* converts to a god who is a sexual and caring woman, endorsing a view of sexual love that is redemptive. The Christian attack on pagan culture was importantly on the idea that the divine could be sexual, more particularly, on women gods like Aphrodite and Isis as sexual and divine. For Augustine, the critical point is made at great length in *The City of God* in the form of an attack on Apuleius's claim that daemons or personal gods intermediate between the high God and the human experience, for such gods are, Augustine argues, in fact demons, devils.[274] Nothing is more appalling for Augustine than the rituals of pagan cults of mothers (remembered from his pre-Christian days) with their "disgusting verbal and acted obscenities."[275] What strikes us about these rhetorical rants is not only their rather posed mockery but also their underlying sense of horror and fear, centered on sexual experience in general and the sexual experience of women in particular. The triumph of Augustinian Christianity introduced anxiety into the heart of human sexual experience, an anxiety based on an uncritical acceptance of patriarchy as in the nature of things (willed by God himself, as Augustine had supposedly shown so reasonably in the psychological development frankly discussed in *The Confessions*). E. R. Dodds wrote a classic book on the anxiety he found to underlie late Roman pagan and Christian thought. We understand that anxiety in terms of the inscription of the patriarchal script of sexual love as tragic into the heart of sexuality itself.[276] It is an anxiety still, unfortunately, too much with us.

There is an uncritically tragic conception of love implicit in this psychological development, one that accepts the breaking of personal relationships as in the tragic nature of things, a burden that men in particular must accept if they are to do the work that men must under patriarchy do.[277] Augustine thus writes of his struggles before conversion as "refusing to become your soldier,"[278] so that

[272] See, on this point, Daniel Boyarin, *Carnal Israel: Reading Sex in Talmudic Culture* (Berkeley: University of California Press, 1993).

[273] See, on this point, Gaca, *Making of Fornication*.

[274] See Augustine, *City of God*, pp. 136–7, 318–26, 344–5, 351–3, 357–9, 410.

[275] *Id.*, p. 51.

[276] See E. R. Dodds, *Pagan and Christian in an Age of Anxiety* (Cambridge: Cambridge University Press, 1965).

[277] See, on this point, Richards, *Tragic Manhood and Democracy*.

[278] Augustine, *Confessions*, p. 140.

conversion, when it occurs, places him as a man finally in an appropriately patriarchal relationship to God as a patriarchal man-soldier. The celibate priest, who thus exercises patriarchal authority, is a new Aeneas, himself under patriarchal authority, hardened, as men must be, to the battles required in God's service against God's enemies.[279] It is surely not surprising that this psychology would show itself, in Augustine's case, by his making the most historically important arguments in the Christian tradition for the religious intolerance of heretics and for Christian anti-Semitism, arguments remote from the letter and spirit of the Gospels (as earlier and later Christian advocates of toleration observed).[280] I believe that the personal and political psychology earlier described clarifies the dissociative processes that make such intolerance possible and appealing. If one can justify shutting down completely the forms of sexual intimacy through which human beings experience loving connection, care, and mutual responsiveness, then one is well on one's way to shutting down the psychological basis for ethical reasoning and experience, making possible a psychology that accepts unjust stereotypes of sexuality and gender that dehumanize and thus rationalize atrocity (e.g., anti-Semitism, racism, sexism, homophobia).

We can see the force of such stereotypes (in particular, gender stereotypes) in the crucial role Augustine's interpretation of the Adam and Eve narrative plays in his conception of a human nature flawed by original sin and, for this reason, unable to exercise the moral autonomy fundamental to the kinds of liberties respect for which is fundamental to respect for human rights and the forms of constitutional government whose legitimacy rests on respect for such rights. Augustine's support for the use of Roman imperial power coercively to repress heresy is rationalized in terms of the flaw in human nature that requires such authoritarian coercive power to keep from making the mistakes, including mistakes in belief, that it cannot avoid on its own. We should be struck, in this connection, that, in contrast to Ambrose, Augustine never resisted repressive imperial policies.[281] As a modern critic of Augustine acidly observes:

> Augustine never challenged any imperial authority. After his return to Carthage in 416, he showed that he knew where authority lay, and in his last years chose to curry favor not with the wealthy aristocrats he had sought out in the 390's and 400s, but now with the hard men: the military and political enforcers Rome sent to Africa.... In his last years, Augustine resembles nothing so much as one of those pious churchmen of Francoist times, leader of a state-promoted church, followed prudently by many, despised quietly by some, and opposed fiercely by a remnant quite sure of its own fidelity to a truer church.[282]

279 See, on this point, *id.*, pp. 140, 160, 206, 254.

280 See, on this point, Richards, *Toleration and the Constitution*, pp. 85–95. See also James Carroll, *Constantine's Sword: The Church and the Jews* (Boston: Houghton Mifflin, 2001); Paula Fredriksen, *Augustine and the Jews: A Christian Defense of Jews and Judaism* (New York: Doubleday, 2008).

281 See TeSelle, *Augustine the Theologian*, pp. 272–3.

282 See James J. O'Donnell, *Augustine: A New Biography* (New York: HarperCollins, 2005), p. 225.

It is the crucial role of unjust gender stereotypes, in Augustine's thought, that explains the sense of insulted manhood that he displays at dissent from Catholic religious orthodoxy and his willingness to use and rationalize violence in repressing such dissent. Such propensities to violence are of a piece with his expression of rage, earlier noted, at pagan rituals of mother goddesses and his role as well in the repressive violence of Christian anti-Semitism (rationalizing the imposition of a servile political status on Jews because, as he put it, "The Jew is the slave of the Christians"[283]). What seems to be key to this psychology is the repressive violence directed at sexual voice and experience itself as demonic. What makes the study of this psychology in Augustine so riveting is that it displays so clearly how and why the repression of sexual voice has been so important in both the construction and transmission of various forms of structural injustice, rationalizing violence in terms of gender stereotypes that themselves rest on the repression of sexual voice. What makes Augustine an interesting example of such violent patriarchal manhood is that he carried patriarchy into his own sexuality (repressing his own sexual voice) and, for this reason, rationalized an influential cultural pattern of religious intolerance that represses any sexual voice that will not conform to his patriarchal authority. By repressing his own sexual experience, he renders himself psychologically armored against the reasonable claims of free sexual voice that would contest his views and, for this reason, rationalizes repressive violence against such views and ways of life.

Augustine himself offers a telling introspective account of the larger significance of the repudiation of sexual pleasure in his life.[284] It is not merely sexual pleasure that he disowns, but he discusses as well the need for correlative restraints on the pleasures of food and drink,[285] of smell,[286] of hearing,[287] and of seeing.[288] Such restraints lead, finally, to attacking both the arts (including the theater) and even curiosity itself.[289] If Apuleius called in the Cupid and Psyche story for a questioning of the taboo on knowing and speaking as central to the possibility of sexual love, Augustine calls, in contrast, for instituting a more radical taboo, namely on sexual pleasure itself. What follows is what a sound understanding of the human psyche would lead us to expect, a shutting down of the very sources of our relational intelligence and imagination, including our ethical intelligence. The repudiation of sexual pleasure is thus at the root of what was so dangerous in the personal and political psychology Augustine exemplifies and defends: its disassociation from real relationships and its underlying propensity to a violence – no longer controlled by ethical intelligence – against those persons or groups that threaten the legitimacy of one's repudiation.

283 Quoted in Richards, *Women, Gays, and the Constitution*, p. 403.
284 See, on this point, Augustine, *Confessions*, pp. 202–4.
285 See *id.*, pp. 204–7.
286 *Id.*, p. 207.
287 *Id.*, pp. 207–8.
288 *Id.*, pp. 209–10.
289 *Id.*, pp. 210–12.

We can see this dynamic in patriarchal psychology earlier, namely in Roman patriarchy and in Virgil's exploration of its psychology of violence.[290] In both cases, the psychology took the form of propensities to violence on outsiders or scapegoats, a violence that rationalized these propensities. This psychology of disassociation requires enemies, and the disassociation makes it easier to dehumanize them and thus to rationalize unjust violence against them. Augustine, in contrast to traditional Roman patriarchy and to Virgil's Aeneas, thought love was the central issue of a truly human life. But his search ended in something quite different, because he uncritically carried Roman patriarchy into the very heart of human sexuality, making psychologically possible a disassociation that would wreck unjust violence on any critic of its imperial demands.

The importance of this disassociation in understanding the psychology of patriarchal manhood Augustine exemplifies is, I believe, illustrated both by those who come to question this psychology (Martin Luther) and by a striking recent example of the havoc this disassociation wrecks on a responsible sense of religious ministry (the priest abuse scandals).

It clarifies this Augustinian psychology, so influential on Christian thought (Catholic and Protestant), to consider Martin Luther's sense of it from the perspective of his sense of his innovations in theology as motivated by a conversion from what he came to see as the unreasonably self-destructive demands of this psychology.[291] When Martin Luther, himself an Augustinian monk, came to question celibacy as a requirement for the priesthood,[292] he framed his general argument by a letter to his real father, who had objected to Luther's taking vows of celibacy because, he argued, his son did not fully understand how important sexuality was or would be to him.[293] Luther had come to believe that his father had been right and that his taking of the vows was a failure to stay in real relationship to a father who knew his son better than the son knew himself. Luther thus argued that the vision that had motivated his taking vows was, in fact, as his father argued at the time, "an illusion and deception."[294] The implicit contrast is between his relationship to his real father (who knew his son would require sexual fulfillment to live a good and responsible life) and the relationship to God, the mythologically idealized father whom Luther believed required celibacy. Luther thus frames his argument against celibacy, as a requirement for priestly authority, in the terms of a return to real relationship, repudiating the psychology of loss

[290] See, for fuller discussion, Gilligan and Richards, *The Deepening Darkness*.

[291] See, in general, on the close relationship of psychology and theology in Luther's life and thought, Erik H. Erikson, *Young Man Luther: A Study in Psychoanalysis and History* (New York: W. W. Norton, 1962).

[292] See Martin Luther, *The Judgment of Martin Luther on Monastic Vows*, 1521, in *Luther's Works*, vol. 44, *The Christian in Society I*, ed. and trans. Martin Atkinson (Philadelphia: Fortress Press, 1966), pp. 245–400.

[293] See Martin Luther, "To Hans Luther Wartburg, November 21, 1521," in *Luther's Works*, vol. 48, *Letters I*, ed. and trans. Gottfried G. Krodel (Philadelphia: Fortress Press, 1963), pp. 329–36.

[294] See *id.*, p. 332.

and idealization that he had earlier accepted. His implicit critique of the Augustinian psychology, which he had lived as a celibate monk, was that it arose from a traumatic breaking of real personal relationships, a psychic loss that showed itself in a disassociation from one's voice and experience, rationalized by idealization that covered over lack of relationships. The consequence was a kind of motivated stupidity that cuts one off not only from others but also from oneself.

A former Catholic priest, Eugene Kennedy, has recently explored another dimension of this Augustinian psychology, namely the idealization of mothers (as asexual) and the denigration of sexual women. Augustine's developmental psychology from sexual man to celibate monk shows such a process of traumatic loss of separation from the woman he sexually loved and from his idealized mother on her death. Consistent with the views of Sister Jackowski, Kennedy argues that the psychology of celibacy in Catholic priests often rests on intense, highly idealized relations to their mothers that reflects a lack of real relationship either to them or to women generally, an idealization, arising from loss and a wounded sexuality, that rationalizes today the unjust patriarchal authority of the priesthood in matters of gender and sexuality.[295] This deeply patriarchal psychology so idealizes a conception of self-sacrificing, indeed asexual, motherhood (expressed in the role of the Virgin Mary in Catholic piety) that the resulting Catholic moral teaching cannot take seriously the decision of real women to have an abortion, thus transforming a responsible moral decision by women into murder in service of a sectarian conception of fetal life. We can also see the harmful consequences of this psychology today in the way the celibate male clergy of the Catholic Church has failed responsibly to respond to the priest abuse scandal, denying not only what has long been before their eyes (and is now before the eyes of the world) but also their own complicity in sustaining a psychology of the priesthood that imposes unreasonable demands of celibacy.[296] The traumatic breaking of real relationships expresses itself in a psychology of disassociation that, as in the recent report on long-standing patterns of child abuse in Catholic Ireland, disclosing something everyone knew and yet refused to know.[297] It is when Catholics come responsibly to face this problem that they sometimes lose faith not only in the priesthood but also in religion itself.[298] The problem, however, is not Christianity as such, for the teaching of Jesus of Nazareth suggests skepticism about the role patriarchy plays in our lives. The problem is the role that patriarchy has uncritically played in the formation of forms of Christianity, including, in Catholicism, an exclusively male, celibate, patriarchal priesthood. Indeed, from

[295] See, on this point, Eugene Kennedy, *The Unhealed Wound: The Church and Human Sexuality* (New York: St. Martin's Press, 2001), pp. 60–2, 128–32.

[296] See Bamforth and Richards, *Patriarchal Religion*, pp. 320–32.

[297] See Sarah Lyall, "Blaming Church, Ireland Details Scourge of Abuse," *New York Times*, May 21, 2009, at A1, A4; see also John Banville, "A Century of Looking the Other Way," *New York Times*, May 23, 2009, at A21.

[298] See, on this point, William Lobdell, *Losing My Religion: How I Lost My Faith Reporting on Religion in America – and Found Unexpected Peace* (New York: Collins, 2009), pp. 215–51.

the perspective of a religious Christian, like Fyodor Dostoyevsky, it is the authority that historical forms of Christianity accorded to patriarchy that would rationalize, and, for Dostoyevsky, had rationalized churches to exercise an authority like the Grand Inquisitor to condemn the teaching of freedom and equality of a Jesus of Nazareth himself.[299] From this perspective, the critique of patriarchy may be a religious obligation on believing Christians if they take seriously what continues to move them and moved Dostoyevsky, the life and teaching of Jesus of Nazareth.

[299] See Fyodor Dostoyevsky, *The Brothers Karamazov*, trans. David McDuff (London: Penguin, 1993), pp. 283–304.

CHAPTER 5

FUNDAMENTALISM AMONG PROTESTANTS

Protestant fundamentalism in the United States must be understood within the larger framework of the distinctive history and culture of the Protestant churches in contrast to Roman Catholicism. Only when we are quite clear about this larger framework can we both understand and critically assess such fundamentalism, as it both arises very much within that framework and yet incoherently questions and abandons what has made that framework so valuable not only as an interpretation of Christianity but also in the historical growth and development of the principles and institutions of constitutional government, including the argument for toleration. I begin with a discussion of this larger framework and then turn to the nature of the claims that fundamentalism makes within this framework. My critique then examines closely various dimensions of its internal incoherence (including its lack of attention to the life and teachings of Jesus of Nazareth) and its substantive unreasonableness. I then offer a diagnosis of its roots in a reactionary patriarchal culture and psychology.

1. PROTESTANTISM AND CONSTITUTIONAL DEMOCRACY

Human culture, which had been oral, was transformed by the emergence of literacy and written texts.[1] The very capacity to think of oneself as part of a culture is delimited not by the exigencies or oral memory but by the written texts that today preserve the content of the culture. Cultural homogeneity may still be very great, indeed greater than in the oral period, for a small and exclusive literate elite may, as in ancient Babylonia and Egypt, use a theocratic hierarchy to enforce forms of economic and political domination that had been previously impossible.[2] But the presence of a written tradition introduces the possibility of divisive cultural controversy over the meaning of the written texts that convey the tradition. In

[1] For an overview of the literature on this topic, see Walter J. Ong, *Orality and Literacy* (London: Methuen, 1982).

[2] See, in general, Jack Goody, *The Domestication of the Savage Mind* (Cambridge: Cambridge University Press, 1977).

favorable historical circumstances, such controversy is unleashed with cultural consequences as transformational as those associated with the emergence of literacy itself.

The culture of the West, the culture that we associate with the philosophical genius of ancient Greece and the religious genius of Judaism and Christianity, unleashed these controversies in a way not seen in such comparable high cultures as China.[3] The culture of the West has been decisively shaped by two historical moments, one fatally integrative, the other creatively divisive, both of which permanently established forms of interpretive controversy over authoritative texts as part of the very foundations of that culture.

The first such moment grew out of the decision to build Christian culture on two kinds of synthesis: Old Testament putative history and prophecy, as supposedly fulfilled by the New Testament elaborating the uniquely Jewish conception of a personal and ethical God who acts in and through history,[4] and the assimilation of intellectual achievements of the pagan culture that the new culture supplanted.[5] Thus, for example, in both his *Confessions* and *The City of God*, Augustine uses typological Bible criticism, learned from Ambrose of Milan, to interpret and integrate the meanings of the Old and New Testaments, and he then applies this synthesis to interpret God's will acting through history.[6] And in *The Trinity*, he discusses central theological questions in the context of interpretations of the integrated meanings of biblical texts and the great texts of pagan philosophy – in particular, the neo-Platonism of Plotinus.[7] This remarkable synthesis of complex texts, interpretive techniques (biblical typology), and background philosophical doctrines reveals a distinctively Western style of complex interpretive synthesis wedded to a linear historical self-consciousness. Augustine's synthesis also fatally included, as we have seen (Chapter 4), something he assumed to be in the nature of things, once Catholicism was made the established church of the Roman Empire, namely a close working relationship of church and state that included the legitimation of state power to persecute heretics, repress pagan religions, and keep the Jews in a subordinate status as the moral slaves of Christians.

[3] See J. H. Plumb, *The Death of the Past*, pp. 62–101 (Boston: Houghton Mifflin, 1971).

[4] See, e.g., Dan Jacobson, *The Story of the Stories: The Chosen People and Its God* (New York: Harper & Row, 1982); Robert Alter, *The Art of Biblical Narrative* (New York: Basic Books, 1981).

[5] See Charles N. Cochrane, *Christianity and Classical Culture* (London: Oxford University Press, 1944); George Santayana, *The Life of Reason*, vol. 3, *Reason in Religion*, pp. 69–177 (New York: Dover, 1982); Hans Blumenberg, *The Legitimacy of the Modern Age*, trans. Robert M. Wallace (Cambridge: Massachusetts Institute of Technology Press, 1983); Étienne Gilson, *God and Philosophy* (New Haven, Conn.: Yale University Press, 1941). On the transition from pagan to Christian culture in late antiquity, see E. R. Dodds, *Pagan and Christian in an Age of Anxiety* (New York: W. W. Norton, 1965); Peter Brown, *The Making of Late Antiquity* (Cambridge, Mass.: Harvard University Press, 1978).

[6] Augustine, *Confessions*, bks. 11–12; Augustine, *City of God*, trans. Henry Bettenson (Harmondsworth, U.K.: Penguin, 1972).

[7] Augustine, *The Trinity*, vol. 8, *Augustine: Late Works*, trans. John Burnaby (Philadelphia: Westminster Press, 1955).

Thomas Aquinas, drawing on Aristotle, works very much within this Augustinian framework (Chapter 4).

The second great moment arises in the Protestant Reformation in divisive disagreements within Christianity over the terms and content of the interpretive integration of its authoritative texts. Martin Luther and John Calvin, whose movements are fueled by the more widespread literacy made possible by the printing press and by the translation of the Bible into the vernacular,[8] propose alternative models for the exegesis of authoritative biblical and philosophical texts, models calling for a more democratic and democratizing priesthood of all believers no longer subject to the ultimate hierarchical authority of a celibate male priesthood that had been defended, as we have seen, by Thomas Aquinas (Chapter 4).[9] A new Erasmian philosophy of interpretation, humanist in inspiration,[10] calls for the text of the Bible to be read more historically in light of an authentic primitive Christianity before it was corrupted by an unbiblical Roman Catholic Church.[11] The domination of the Christian tradition by Aristotle (reflected in Thomas Aquinas) is gradually eroded, giving way to a more voluntarist, nominalist theology and, if anything, a more Augustinian integration of Christian and pagan texts[12] (one, however, that perpetuates the Augustinian theory of persecution in both Luther and Calvin, justifying the persecution not only of Catholics but also of other Protestants and the subordination of Jews[13]). The earlier Christian interpretive integration provides the context for continuing discussion of the meanings of diverse texts; the Reformation introduced a new kind of discussion of metainterpretive questions concerning how such texts should be interpreted. These debates energize, in turn, new forms of interest in and cultivation of the nature of reasonable belief and knowledge, including the authenticity of different sources of knowledge and the proper ways of acquiring knowledge of the past, the present, and the future, as well as scientific method and historiography, so characteristic of the modern mind.[14] Indeed, it is these Reformation debates

8 See Elizabeth Eisenstein, *The Printing Press as an Agent of Change*, 2 vols. (Cambridge: Cambridge University Press, 1979).

9 See Ronald H. Bainton, "The Bible in the Reformation," in *The Cambridge History of the Bible*, vol. 3, ed. S. D. Greenslade (Cambridge: Cambridge University Press, 1963), pp. 1–37; Normans Sykes, "The Religion of Protestants," in *id.*, pp. 175–98.

10 See Louis Bouyer, "Erasmus in Relation to the Medieval Biblical Tradition," in *The Cambridge History of the Bible*, vol. 2, ed. G. W. H. Lampe (Cambridge: Cambridge University Press, 1969), pp. 492–505.

11 See Eisenstein, *Printing Press as an Agent of Change*, vol. 1, pp. 164–450.

12 See Perry Miller, *The New England Mind: The Seventeenth Century* (Cambridge, Mass.: Belknap Press of Harvard University Press, 1939), pp. 3–35. On the influence of nominalist theology, see Arthur O. Lovejoy, *The Great Chain of Being* (Cambridge, Mass.: Harvard University Press, 1936), pp. 163, 332–3.

13 For the views of the Protestant reformers, see J. E. E. D. (Lord) Acton, "The Protestant Theory of Persecution," in *The History of Freedom and Other Essays* (London: Macmillan, 1907).

14 See, e.g., Barbara J. Shapiro, *Probability and Certainty in Seventeenth-Century England* (Princeton, N.J.: Princeton University Press, 1983); Henry G. Van Leeuwen, *The Problem of Certainty in English Thought, 1630–1690* (The Hague: Martinus Nijhoff, 1970).

that vitalize the modern philosophy, searching for reliable bases of knowledge, which we conveniently but misleadingly date from René Descartes and Baruch Spinoza.[15]

The most radical and liberating reexamination of the Augustinian synthesis was made possible by the ways in which Protestantism legitimated a democratic and democratizing appeal to the conscience of each person as a rational and reasonable moral agent, contrasting the simple and elevated nonviolence, charity, inclusiveness, and humanity of the Christian Gospels with the inquisitorial political violence of the dominant Catholic and Protestant traditions, both appealing to the authority of Augustine. It was from such a democratically empowered sense of conscience that the argument for toleration arose among radical Protestants, including, notably, Pierre Bayle and John Locke,[16] who rejected the Augustinian theory of persecution as inconsistent with the basic values of rational and reasonable freedom, respect for conscience itself. The association of religious conscience with ethical imperatives is, of course, pervasively characteristic of the Judeo-Christian tradition and its conception of an ethical God acting through history.[17] Locke and Bayle are religious Christians in this tradition. They regard themselves as returning Christianity to its ethical foundations (reminding Christians, for example, of the toleration of the early patristic period).[18] Both support their arguments, in part, with exegesis in Bible interpretation.[19] Disagreements in speculative theology, which had grounded Augustinian persecutions for heresy, were, for them, patent betrayals of essential Christianity; they disabled people from regulating their lives by the simple and elevated ethical imperatives of Christian charity illustrated by the life and teachings of Jesus of Nazareth.

Thus, the deepest motivations of Locke's and Bayle's arguments for the inalienable right to conscience are a new interpretation of what ethics is and how it connects to religion and politics. To be precise, Locke connected a free conscience to the capacity of persons to reason about the nature and content of the ethical obligations imposed on persons by a just God,[20] and he thought of

15 See Richard H. Popkin, *The History of Scepticism from Erasmus to Spinoza* (Berkeley: University of California Press, 1979).

16 See, for fuller discussion of Bayle and Locke, David A. J. Richards, *Toleration and the Constitution* (New York: Oxford University Press, 1986), pp. 88–102. For discussion of other Protestants as well, see Perez Zagorin, *How the Idea of Religious Toleration Came to the West* (Princeton: Princeton University Press, 2003).

17 See, on the distinctive force of this conception and its sharp repudiation of different conceptions of divinity in surrounding culture, Henry N. Schneidau, *Sacred Discontent: The Bible and Western Tradition* (Baton Rouge: Louisiana State University Press, 1976).

18 See, e.g., Pierre Bayle, *Philosophique Commentaire sur ces paroles de Jesus Christ "Constrain-les d/entrée," Oeuvres Diverses de Mr. Pierre Bayle*, vol. 2 (A la Haye: Chez P. Husson et al., 1727), pp. 357–560, 387–8.

19 *Id.*, pp. 367–92; John Locke, *Works of John Locke*, vol. 6, *A Letter Concerning Toleration; A Second Letter Concerning Toleration; A Third Letter Concerning Toleration; A Fourth Letter for Toleration* (London: Thomas Davison, 1823), pp. 1–574, 37–8.

20 See, in general, John Colman, *John Locke's Moral Philosophy* (Edinburgh: Edinburgh University Press, 1983). On Locke's theocentrism and ethics of moral independence, see John Dunn, "From Applied Theology to Social Analysis," in *Wealth and Virtue: The Shaping of Political Economy*

these obligations as centering on a core of minimal ethical standards reflected in the Gospels.[21] Bayle regarded independent conscience both as the mode of knowledge of ethical principles and as the agency by which persons incorporated them in the intentional structure of their ends (later called by Kant a good will).[22] Ethics, for Bayle (as for Kant), is only a vital force in one's life when one independently and reasonably acknowledges its principles oneself and imposes them on one's life. Respect for the right to conscience ensures, for Bayle and Locke, that speculative theological disagreements do not distort the central place of this conception of ethics in what both regarded as true religion. Bayle, who rejoiced in paradox, put the point bluntly. Beliefs in speculative religion did not ensure salvation.[23] Such beliefs were often brigaded with the greatest irreligion, that is, barbarous failures of ethical obligation and Christian charity (religious persecution); moreover, disbeliefs in such truths, even atheism, were consistent with decent conduct.[24] Respect for conscience, which ensures that such corrupting theological conceptions are not enforced by law, thus yields both a truer religion and a truer and more practical ethics.

This conception – that ethical independence and the right to conscience are mutually supportive – leads to the most radical departure of this argument from other political traditions, namely Locke's seminal principle that religious ends (as opposed to broad secular ends – life, liberty, and property or happiness) are not and must not be a legitimate state concern.[25] This argument was naturally opposed as undermining public morality and political stability, especially when it was later elaborated by Thomas Jefferson and James Madison to require disestablishment (in Virginia and under the First Amendment of the U.S. Constitution).[26] Political experience had associated religion with state coercive and other support, so that many wondered how a state could be stable when all religions were independent of it. Both Locke and Bayle argue, in response, that a peaceful civility can be restored only when Augustinian persecution is abandoned; persecution itself

in the Scottish Enlightenment, ed. Istvan Hont and Michael Ignatieff (Cambridge: Cambridge University Press, 1983), pp. 119–35.

21 See John Locke, *The Reasonableness of Christianity*, ed. I. T. Ramsey (Stanford, Calif.: Stanford University Press, 1958).

22 Bayle, *Philosophique Commentaire*, pp. 367–72, 422–33.

23 As Bayle stated in his *Pensees Diverses sur la Comete*, "L'home n'agit pas selon ses principles"; see Walter Rex, *Essays on Pierre Bayle and Religious Controversy* (The Hague: Martinus Nijhoff, 1965), p. 55.

24 Bayle set forth this point in the provocative paradox that mere belief in speculative truths does not lead to ethics, and may, if idolatrous (lacking in true faith), be worse than atheism. See *id.*, pp. 51–60. Human nature is so complex, for Bayle, that, though atheistic beliefs may mandate immorality, atheists do not always act that way; *id.*, pp. 62–5. Conversely, though religious beliefs may mandate morality, believers may act immorally.

25 The statement of this principle is the subject of the first *Letter Concerning Toleration, Words of John Locke*, vol. 6, pp. 5–58.

26 For example, opposition to total disestablishment of the Anglican Church in Virginia, led by Patrick Henry and Richard Henry Lee, centered on the idea that some form of multiple establishment was necessary to preserve public morality in the state. See H. J. Eckenrode, *Separation of Church and State in Virginia* (New York: De Capo Press, 1971), p. 74.

creates the instabilities of intractable sectarian conflict.[27] Past political experience was, for Locke and Bayle (and for Jefferson and Madison), a poor guide once the Reformation unleashed the metainterpretive diversity of religious thought. Indeed, for them, such political experience was itself based on an unsound theory of intolerance and on a corrupt conception of public morality, rooted in Augustine's legitimation of the enforcement of Catholicism through the Roman Empire and its successor states, an enforcement that had corrupted both politics and Christianity. The warning drawn from past political experience proved, of course, wrong. The argument for the right to conscience did not undermine public morality; it led to a new conception of what ethics and democratic politics are, made possible by the ethical independence that respect for conscience fosters.

In particular, Locke (in contrast to Bayle) integrates a general contractarian theory of constitutional democracy with the right to conscience. Thus, the central concerns of Locke's *Second Treatise of Government* are twofold: circumstances that release citizens from the moral obligation to obey the law and further circumstances that justify the right to rebel.[28] Locke understood release from the moral obligation to obey to be the necessary, but not sufficient, condition of the right to rebel; the right to rebel arises when moral obligations are released but also demands that independent requirements of respect for rights of innocent third parties and feasibility be met. The historical novelty of Locke's argument should not be underestimated. Certainly, earlier political theory and practice recognized the legitimate power of resistance to tyrannous monarchs. But Locke localizes such power not in the other ordained institutions of government (e.g., parliament) but directly in the people themselves. The violation of their rights justifies both release from moral obligation of fidelity to law and the right to rebel. The conception of the sovereignty of the people and their basic human rights is expressed by Locke through the idea of a social contract understood both historically and hypothetically. The hypothetical formulation is the one of continuing interest; it is the Lockean idea further interpreted and deepened by Jean-Jacques Rousseau,[29] Immanuel Kant,[30] and John Rawls.[31] Locke's form of the hypothetical contract is a criterion of justice: the justice of government, one of the necessary conditions for the moral obligation to obey the law, is interpreted against the benchmark of whether all persons subject to the government would, consistent with their inalienable human rights, find the government more acceptable than the state of nature. Locke regards the inalienable right to

[27] For Locke, see, e.g., *Words of John Locke*, vol. 6, pp. 7–9; for Bayle, see *Philosophique Commentaire*, pp. 415–19.

[28] See the discussion of Locke's argument in David A. J. Richards, *A Theory of Reasons for Action* (Oxford: Clarendon Press, 1971), pp. 152–7.

[29] Jean-Jacques Rousseau, "The Social Contract," in *The Social Contract and Discourses*, trans. G. D. H. Cole (New York: Dutton, 1950).

[30] Immanuel Kant, "Concerning the Common Saying: 'This May be True in Theory, but It Does Not Apply in Practice,'" in *Kant's Political Writings*, ed. Hans Reiss, trans. H. B. Nisbet (Cambridge: Cambridge University Press), pp. 61–92.

[31] John Rawls, *A Theory of Justice* (Cambridge, Mass.: Harvard University Press, 1971).

conscience as among the central human rights, whose violation by the state is unjust by the test of the hypothetical contract. The inalienability of the right follows, for Locke, from its protection of the highest-order interests of persons in the freedom and rationality by which they come to know themselves as ethical being – a control that persons cannot ethically surrender to anyone, including the state.[32]

The arguments of *Second Treatise* and *Letters Concerning Toleration* are, thus, intimately joined. The violation of the right to conscience is, by the test of the hypothetical contract, unjust, with necessary implications for both moral release from fidelity to law and the justification of rebellion. The intimacy of the link can be understood in terms of the way Locke, in contrast to Bayle, connects the inalienable right to conscience (a value both Locke and Bayle share) to the moral sovereignty of the people, bearers of basic human rights, over legal and political community, a sovereignty that justifies Locke's political theory of democratic constitutionalism, the right of the people in appropriate circumstances not only to revolt but also to establish democratically accountable constitutional institutions whose legitimacy rests on the better protection of basic human rights. The founders of the American Constitution self-consciously appeal to this conception, "We the People," as the ground for the legitimacy of the Constitution proposed to and ratified by the American people in 1787–9, and it is the people, consistent with this Lockean conception, who demand that its first amendments, the Bill of Rights of 1791, protect basic human rights, prominent among which is the First Amendment, guaranteeing a right to conscience that requires respect for religious liberty and forbids the establishment of religion, and guarantees free speech and press.[33]

Later constitutional developments in the United States, including the antebellum struggles over the place of slavery under the Constitution as well as more recent struggles, are best understood in terms of this background of the Lockean conception of constitutional democracy, testing the legitimacy of political power in terms of whether such power appropriately respects the moral sovereignty of the people. It is not surprising that, because this conception arose from the role of conscience in radical forms of Protestantism, such forms of American Protestantism (e.g., Baptists, Quakers) played important roles in the support and development of American constitutional principles and institutions. It is precisely such radical Protestants that American constitutional principles of religious liberty protected from other more Augustinian Protestants, and their support for such principles fostered the growing acceptance of such principles eventually by all states. And in the most divisive national debates about the meaning of fundamental constitutional principles, some of the most courageous and progressive arguments have been made by radical Protestants. The Quakers, for example,

32 For the central importance of religious toleration in Locke's political thought, see Dunn, *The Political Thought of John Locke* (Cambridge: Cambridge University Press, 1969).

33 For fuller defense, see David A. J. Richards, *Foundations of American Constitutionalism* (New York: Oxford University Press, 1989).

included the Grimké sisters, protesting American slavery and racism as well as the subjection of women and sexism, and Martin Luther King, a Baptist minister, appealed to the basic right to conscience in supporting his demands for a right to free speech that would protect his movement of nonviolent protest of American racism with all its transformative consequences both for American law and politics.[34]

America is, of course, today a much more religiously diverse nation than it was at its founding. But even then, it was much more religiously diverse than many European nations, including diverse denominations of Protestants, as well as Catholics and Jews, and the American doctrine of religious liberty has, if anything, fostered such diversity over time.[35] Living under the doctrine also afforded liberal Catholic scholars like John Courtney Murray an experience on the basis of which they forged neo-Thomist arguments that eventually persuaded the leadership of the Catholic Church to abandon its Augustinian theory of persecution in favor of the respect for religious liberty, as a basic human right, enshrined in Vatican II. Such basic rethinking of Catholic doctrine did not, however, extend to traditional Catholic teaching on matters of gender and sexuality, a view defended, as we have seen, by the new natural lawyers (Chapter 4). If the fundamentalism of new natural law is norm based, a source-based fundamentalism to similar effect has arisen among some Protestants long historically committed to the right to conscience, a commitment very much in tension, as we must now explore, with their current views.

2. CONTEMPORARY FUNDAMENTALIST PROTESTANTISM

The two leading historical studies of the development of American Protestant fundamentalism, by Ernest R. Sandeen[36] and George M. Marsden,[37] trace its roots to one of the most Augustinian forms of American Protestantism, the Reformed Calvinist theology of the Princeton Seminary that appealed to the literal terms of biblical authority as a bulwark against new forms of Bible interpretation,[38] including not only the postmillennial social gospel of Walter Rauschenbusch (that inspired both Reinhold Niebuhr and Martin Luther King)[39] but also the German forms of Bible interpretation that American fundamentalists, in the wake of German atrocities in World War I, construed as an expression of Nietzsche's

34 See, in general, David A. J. Richards, *Disarming Manhood: Roots of Ethical Resistance* (Athens: Ohio University/Swallow Press, 2005).

35 See Sydney E. Ahlstrom, *A Religious History of the American People*, 2nd ed. (New Haven, Conn.: Yale University Press, 2004).

36 Ernest R. Sandeen, *The Roots of Fundamentalism: British and American Millennarianism 1800–1930* (Chicago: University of Chicago Press, 1970).

37 George M. Marsden, *Fundamentalism and American Culture*, 2nd ed. (New York: Oxford University Press, 2006) (originally published as *Fundamentalism and American Culture: The Shaping of Twentieth Century Evangelicalism 1870–1925* [New York: Oxford University Press, 1980]).

38 See, e.g., Sandeen, *Roots of Fundamentalism*, pp. 103–31.

39 Marsden, *Fundamentalism and American Culture*, pp. 91–2.

critique of the ethics of Christianity itself.[40] It was evidence of deterioration, reflected in World War I, that made attractive to fundamentalists a premillennial reading of the prophecies of the New Testament, including dispensations that predicted troubles, including the return of the Jews to Israel, as a prelude to the second coming of Jesus (postmillennial readings claimed the second coming of Jesus had already occurred or was occurring as we realized the ethical dimensions of his teachings in social and political reform).[41] Fundamentalism, as an interdenominational development in Protestantism, centered on five interpretive claims on the method, authority, and substance of Bible interpretation: "(1) the inerrancy of Scripture, (2) the Virgin Birth of Christ, (3) his substitutionary atonement, (4) his bodily resurrection, and (5) the authenticity of the miracles."[42]

The alleged literalism of such interpretive claims was defended, as one would expect in an American political culture in which Protestant conscience played such a formative role, in terms of its appeal to the democratic common sense of each believer as opposed to hierarchical authority of a celibate priesthood, which Catholicism had placed between the Bible and the believer.[43] On this Baconian view, the Bible was interpreted as stating facts in the same way that empirical science called for stating and assembling facts, in effect eliminating from both the indispensable role that hypothesis or theory construction plays in organizing and explaining and indeed predicting facts. Charles Darwin's theory of evolution could thus be dismissed as not science but hypothesis, and the factual claims of Genesis could be taken as science.[44]

The appeal for fundamentalists of such claims of literal interpretation was not, however, either as democratic or as rooted in reasonable common sense as they supposed. Both the force and the substance of their fundamentals arose from the Augustinian assumptions of original sin and Augustine's associated reading of the Adam and Eve narrative (see Chapter 4). It is because our natures, in particular, our gendered and sexual natures, are, as Augustine argued, so corrupt, that fundamentalist readings of the Bible are, on this view, so urgently required.[45] The 1878 Niagara Creed, one of the formative statements of fundamentalist thought, explicitly states these assumptions and their consequences:

> We believe that man, originally created in the image and after the likeness of God, fell from his high and holy estate by eating the forbidden fruit, and as the consequence of his disobedience the threatened penalty of death was then and there inflicted, so that his moral nature was not only grievously injured by the fall, but he totally lost all spiritual life, becoming dead in trespasses and sins and subject to the power of the devil . . .

40 *Id.*, pp. 161, 169, 213–14.

41 On premillennial thought, its sources, and impact, see Sandeen, *Roots of Fundamentalism*, pp. 11–12, 13–14, 22, 62, 222–4, 227–8.

42 Marsden, *Fundamentalism and American Culture*, p. 117; see also *id.*, p. 167.

43 See, on this point, *id.*, pp. 7–8, 14, 19–20, 55–62, 110–18, 169, 174, 212–14, 216–21.

44 On science versus hypotheses, see *id.*, pp. 19–20, 120–1, 174, 212–13, 216–21.

45 See, on this point, Vincent Crapanzano, *Serving the Word: Literalism in America from the Pulpit to the Bench* (New York: New Press, 2000), pp. 16, 91–2, 147, 152, 165, 173–4.

> We believe that, owing to his universal depravity and death in sin, no one can enter the kingdom of God unless born again; and that no degree of reformation however great, no attainment of morality however high, no culture however attractive, no humanitarian and philanthropic schemes and societies however useful, no baptism or other ordinance however administered, can help the sinner to taken even one step toward heaven; but a new nature imparted from above, a new life implanted by the Holy Ghost through the Word, is absolutely essential to salvation.[46]

It is these assumptions that explain why fundamentalist thought has been so obsessed with preserving a reading of Genesis, which contains the Adam and Eve narrative, as science. It is a narrative very much read as rationalizing a male reactionary discourse,[47] God the Father, as patriarch, setting the terms of both gender and sexuality (the serpent)[48] in terms of quite rigid gender roles.[49] Eve's fault was, on this patriarchal view, trusting her own experience as opposed to the word of God the Father,[50] reflecting a deep distrust among fundamentalists of experience, including moral experience. One honest fundamentalist man, Paul, interviewed by Vincent Crapanzano in his remarkable study, explained that a literal reading of the Bible appealed to him precisely because he no longer needed himself to decide what was right.[51]

Of the five theses of fundamentalism, only one – belief in the Virgin Birth – is explicitly about gender and sexuality. What belief in the Virgin Birth suggests, however, is the role of patriarchal idealization in fundamentalist thought, an idealization that covers loss of real relationships.[52] It reveals the reactionary impulses that drive this form of fundamentalist Protestantism, namely preserving the patriarchal order of things that they find in their way of reading the Bible, including the subordination of women and the sharp moral condemnation of practices that, for them, exemplify a sexual freedom inconsistent with such subordination, in particular, abortion and gay and lesbian sexuality (one fundamentalist group advocates the death penalty for homosexuality[53]).

Protestant fundamentalism claims to be an expression of the democratic exercise of free conscience and reasonable common sense. It is, however, neither democratic nor reasonable – its allegedly literal readings are driven by Augustinian assumptions it brings to the text and never critically examines. But much more significantly for its putative Protestantism, its driving ideology undermines its respect for the democratic conscience of the women and men who reasonably disagree with its fundamentalist interpretations by excluding them from any

46 Quoted in appendixes in Sandeen, *Roots of Fundamentalism*, pp. 273–4.
47 Crapanzano, *Serving the Word*, pp. 23–4.
48 See *id.*, pp. 29–30, 134, 147, 165.
49 See *id.*, pp. 139–40, 147.
50 See *id.*, p. 152.
51 See *id.*, pp. 105–16.
52 See, on such patriarchal idealization, *id.*, pp. 140, 142.
53 *Id.*, pp. 50–1.

religious authority whatsoever. Its fundamentalist moral certainty about the subordination of women arises from its certainty that women must be excluded from the ministry, all incoherently rationalized in terms of the priesthood of all believers. The Southern Baptist Convention's Resolution No. 5, "On the Priesthood of the Believer," passed in 1988, thus reads:

> WHEREAS, The Priesthood of the Believer is a term which is subject to both misunderstanding and abuse; and
>
> WHEREAS, The doctrine of the Priesthood of the Believer has been used to justify wrongly the attitude that a Christian may believe whatever he so chooses and still be considered a loyal Southern Baptist; and
>
> WHEREAS, The doctrine of the Priesthood of the Believer can be used to justify the undermining of pastoral authority in the local church,
>
> Be is therefore RESOLVED, That the Southern Baptist Convention . . . affirm its belief in the biblical doctrine of the Priesthood of the Believer (1 Peter 2:9 and Revelation 1:6); and
>
> Be it further RESOLVED, That the doctrine of the Priesthood of the Believer in no way contradicts the biblical understanding of the role, responsibility, and authority of the pastor which is seen in the command to the local church in Hebrews 13:17, "Obey your leaders, and submit to them; for they keep watch over your souls, as those who will give an account," and
>
> Be it finally RESOLVED, That we affirm the truth that elders, or pastors, are called of God to lead the local church (Acts 20:29).[54]

Harold Bloom observes, "There is no single Baptist principle . . . that has not been twisted or abrogated by the Fundamentalist Convention,"[55] an incoherence in Baptist principles motored by rhetorical strategies that polemically transform reasonable doubt about traditional views of gender and sexuality into grounds for exclusion and dehumanization.[56] We need now to examine more critically the internal and external unreasonableness of such fundamentalist Christianity and, following Bloom, to investigate what could motivate such a betrayal of the democratic morality of Protestant Christianity.

3. A CRITIQUE OF PROTESTANT FUNDAMENTALISM

Protestant fundamentalism is, in contrast to the new natural lawyers, source based: it draws its authority from a literal reading of biblical texts. But there are three grounds on which we may reasonably question its authority: first, its

54 Quoted in Harold Bloom, *The American Religion: The Emergence of the Post-Christian Nation* (New York: Touchstone, 1992), p. 226.

55 Bloom, *American Religion*, p. 227.

56 See, on this point, Carl L. Kell and L. Raymond Camp, *In the Name of the Father: The Rhetoric of the New Southern Baptist Convention* (Carbondale: Southern Illinois University Press, 1999).

failure to take seriously the life and teaching of Jesus of Nazareth; second, its failure to take seriously the corrupting role of patriarchy in the transmission of the Christian tradition; and third, its uncritical dependence on Augustinian assumptions, including his theory of persecution and his role in the formation of Christian anti-Semitism.

a. The Historical Jesus

The contemporary scholarly consensus crucially sees the historical Jesus as a pious, learned Jew of his culture and period, acutely conscious of the prophetic tradition of moral protest that he elaborates, whose life had analogues in his period (Honi, Hanina, and others) and whose teachings were largely within the range of views current in intertestamental Judaism,[57] including the influence on Jesus' teaching of Hillel.[58] It is a feature of such pious Judaism that it essentially focuses on the trusting relationship to God conceived as a loving, caring person, not on the theological propositions of later Christian belief.[59] Geza Vermes powerfully shows, in this connection, how Jesus avoids, in addressing God, "the divine epithet, 'King'" predominant "in ancient Jewish literature"[60]; rather, "the Synoptic Gospels depict him as addressing God, or speaking of him, as 'Father' in some sixty instances, and at least once place on his lips the Aramaic title, *Abba*."[61] God is addressed as an approachable, solicitous, and loving father, one concerned above all with staying in a relationship to his erring children, those outcasts whom "'decent' Jews despised and relegated to pariah status."[62] To their query about his joining a meal given by a publican and attended by many of his colleagues, Jesus

[57] Among important studies along these lines are Geza Vermes, *Jesus the Jew: A Historian's Reading of the Gospels* (Philadelphia: Fortress Press, 1981) (originally published in 1973); Vermes, *Jesus and the World of Judaism* (London: SCM Press, 1983); Vermes, *The Religion of Jesus the Jew* (Minneapolis: Fortress Press, 1993); Vermes, *The Changing Faces of Jesus* (New York: Viking Compass, 2001); David Flusser, *Jesus* (Jerusalem: Magnes Press, Hebrew University, 2001); David Flusser, *Judaism and the Origins of Christianity* (Jerusalem: Magnes Press, Hebrew University, 1988); Paula Fredriksen, *From Jesus to Christ*, 2nd ed. (New Haven, Conn.: Yale University Press, 2000); Paula Fredriksen, *Jesus of Nazareth, King of the Jews: A Jewish Life and the Emergence of Christianity* (New York: Alfred A. Knopf, 2000); E. P. Sanders, *Jesus and Judaism* (Philadelphia: Fortress Press, 1985); Sanders, *The Historical Figure of Jesus* (London: Allen Lane, 1993); John P. Meier, *A Marginal Jew: Rethinking the Historical Jesus*, vol. 1, *The Roots of the Problem and the Person* (New York: Doubleday, 1991); Meier, *A Marginal Jew: Rethinking the Historical Jesus*, vol. 2, *Mentor, Message, and Miracles* (Doubleday: New York, 1993);. Meier, *A Marginal Jew: Rethinking the Historical Jesus*, vol. 3, *Companions and Competitors* (New York: Doubleday, 2001); David Daube, *The New Testament and Rabbinic Judaism* (Peabody, Mass.: Hendrickson, 1998); A. N. Wilson, *Jesus: A Life* (New York: Fawcett Columbine, 1992).

[58] See, on this point, Flusser, *Judaism and the Origins of Christianity*, pp. 509–514; Vermes, *Religion of Jesus the Jew*, pp. 40–1.

[59] See, for a good examination of this contrast, Walter Kaufmann, *Critique of Religion and Philosophy* (Princeton, N.J.: Princeton University Press, 1958), pp. 278–85.

[60] Vermes, *Religion of Jesus the Jew*, p. 152.

[61] *Id.*

[62] Vermes, *Changing Faces of Jesus*, p. 174.

justified his presence by identifying his host and his host's colleagues as those who are spiritually ill and in need of a physician (Mark 2:17; Matthew 9:12; Luke 5:31). There is also a specific report that he allowed a prostitute ("a woman of the city who was a sinner"; Luke 7:37, 39; cf. Mark 14:3; Matthew 26:6–7) to anoint him. Jesus' practice of accepting the companionship of the despised was sufficiently common knowledge to endow him with the name "friend of tax-collectors and sinners" (Matthew 11:19; Luke 7:34). If his mission as healer and exorcist was for the sick and the possessed, he understood himself as primarily bringing God's love to those in the most spiritual need: "I came not to call the righteous, but sinners" (Mark 2:17; Matthew 9:13; Luke 5:32). The overriding concern was the miserable and helpless: "I was sent only to the lost sheep of the house of Israel" (Matthew 15:24); "Go to the lost sheep of the house of Israel" (Matthew 10:6). As Vermes puts the point:

> [Jesus] is depicted in the Synoptics as the compassionate, caring, and loving pilot and shepherd who, imitating the merciful, caring, and loving God, guides those most in need, the little ones (Matt. 18:10), the sinners, the whores, and the publicans, toward the gate of the Kingdom of the Father.[63]

Jesus' sense of God, as loving and caring father of his erring children, was interpreted by the Jewish philosopher, Martin Buber, as a model for love in an I-Thou personal relationship:

> and now one can act, help, heal, educate, raise, redeem. Love is responsibility of an I for a You: in this consists what cannot consist in any feeling – the equality of all lovers, from the smallest to the greatest and from the blissfully secure whose life is circumscribed by the life of one beloved human being to him that is nailed his life long to the cross of the world, capable of what is immense and bold enough to risk it: to love *man*.[64]

Buber, interpreting Jesus' sense of relationship to God as a loving father, construes such a loving relationship as one of equality and reciprocity: "everyone can speak the You and then becomes I; everyone can say Father and then becomes son; actuality abides."[65] How are we to understand the sense in which Buber, interpreting Jesus, suggests that what under patriarchy (father-child) is a form of hierarchy is, rather, a loving and caring relationship of equality and reciprocity (a person in love being father and son)? Both Buber and Jesus are surely contesting the patriarchal framing of the relationship, for if even the father-son pairing must ultimately be understood as in developmental service of a loving and caring relationship of equals, then hierarchy must yield to relational care, sensitivity, and concern – including concern for voice – in all relationships.

63 *Id.*, p. 220.
64 Martin Buber, *I and Thou*, trans. Walter Kaufmann (New York: Charles Scribner's Sons, 1970), pp. 66–7.
65 *Id.*, p. 117.

The power of Buber's reading of Jesus is the way it clarifies the remarkable role women play in his life and ministry in ways that are, if anything, very much in tension with patriarchal conceptions of gender. In the Synoptic Gospels, Jesus is pictured as showing reserve, verging on hostility, to his family, including his mother, Mary. Mark (3:21) bluntly reports that Jesus' family held him to be mad, to the point that they wanted forcibly to remove him from his public ministry. Elsewhere we are informed that his mother and brothers expected preferential treatment from Jesus, for example, that he would interrupt his teaching when they arrived. Jesus rejected such treatment: "Who are my mother and my brothers?" he asked. Pointing to his disciples, he declared them, metaphorically, his "mother" and "brothers" (Mark 3:31–5; Matthew 12:46–50; Luke 8:19–21). Further, although Jewish men, including holy men, were expected to marry, everything points to Jesus as an unmarried, celibate man, including Matthew 19:12 ("eunuchs such as make themselves eunuchs with a view to the kingdom of heaven").[66] In these respects, Jesus does not conform to a patriarchal conception of gender – he refuses to accept the authority of his own family of origin and does not define himself by his authority within a family.

Jesus takes, nonetheless, a remarkable interest in women, as persons, and they take an interest in him. Women not only were disciples[67] but also were among the most faithful of his disciples, holding onto their relationship to Jesus in a way that men did not. Although male disciples abandoned Jesus after his arrest, or even denied him (Peter), women were with him at his death, as Mark (15: 40–1) recounts: "Now there were also women, looking on from a distance, among whom were Mary from Magdala, Mary the mother of James the Younger and Joses, and Salome, who, when he [Jesus] was in Galilee, followed him and served him, and many other [women] who had come up with him to Jerusalem [for the feast of the Passover]."[68] Moreover, it is to a group of these faithful women that, at his tomb and later, resurrection experiences were first granted, only to be initially disbelieved by the terrified male disciples (see Mark 16:1–14; cf. Matthew 28:1–10; Luke 24:1–49). The interest of women in his teaching is portrayed as something that legitimately engages their intelligence as persons, as Jesus defends Mary's listening to his teaching from her sister Martha's distracted insistence that Jesus patriarchally tell Martha to help her in the womanly tasks of serving (Luke 10:38–42).

Jesus clearly teaches and ministers to women in ways that speak to their subjective experience, including their experience of suffering as women, even when they are traditional outcasts. The experience of women, as equally subject to God's loving attention as men, is thus a frequent subject of both the parables

[66] For a good discussion, see Meier, *Marginal Jew*, vol. 1, pp. 332–42 (for comment on Matthew 19–12, see pp. 342–3).

[67] See, on this point, Meier, *Marginal Jew*, vol. 3, pp. 73–80.

[68] See *id.*, p. 75.

and judgment sayings of Jesus,[69] and of his ministering concern. Jesus cures the daughter of a Syro-Phoenician woman, though, as a foreign woman she would normally be supposed to be an unclean Gentile with whom a Jewish man should not talk (Mark 7:24–30; Matthew 15:21–8); he cures Peter's mother-in-law (Mark 1:29–31; Matthew 8:14–15; Luke 4:38–9); he heals a crippled woman on the Sabbath (Luke 13:10–17); Jesus cures a woman, suffering from menstrual flows, who, though ritually unclean, touches him, then brings the daughter of Jairus back to life (Mark 5:21–43; Matthew 9:18–26; Luke 8:40–56); and Jesus is so moved by the grief of the widow of Nain that he brings her son back to life (Luke 7:11–17).[70] Jesus also accepts and defends as blessed a sinning woman (most likely a prostitute) who has anointed and kissed his feet (Luke 7:36–50), and he speaks at length to a ritually unclean, sinning woman from Samaria at a well and brings her to faith (John 4:7–42).[71]

The conversation with the woman at the well displays not just unusual openness and interest but also capacities of psychological penetration, as Jesus speaks "to a woman whom he had never met before and appear[s] to know everything about the emotional chaos of her life . . . images which cannot be dispelled by scholars calling into question their historical plausibility."[72] A. N. Wilson brilliantly connects such remarkable insight into and sympathy with women with the ways in which women, as feminists, have read the Gospels as calling for forms of political liberation:

> The words of Jesus to the daughter of Jairus were taken up as a rallying-cry among nineteenth-century feminists. "Damsel arise!" were words which emblazoned colleges and schools which, for the first time in history, had been founded with the specific purpose of educating women. This was not completely fanciful. By contrast with St. Paul and the early Christians, Jesus neither feared women, nor treated them as a sub-species. It would appear that he was prepared to defy convention in this regard and to befriend women in a time and place where the sexes were not supposed to mix on socially equal terms. Some of his closest associates were women.[73]

Jesus is, of course, a man, but the interpretive issue raised by his attitude toward women is the critical position to patriarchy that his attitude suggests. Certainly, his defense of the woman taken in adultery calls for skepticism about one of the roots of patriarchal violence, namely violence against women who transgress patriarchal demands placed on their sexuality (John 8:1–11). As one careful student of the historical Jesus concludes, his teaching, at a minimum, "entailed a certain

[69] For a good discussion, see Ben Witherington III, *Women and the Genesis of Christianity* (Cambridge: Cambridge University Press, 1990), pp. 52–64.

[70] See, for illuminating discussion of these forms of the ministry of Jesus, *id.*, pp. 74–7.

[71] See, for good discussion of both these events, *id.*, pp. 65–74.

[72] Wilson, *Jesus*, p. 5; see also pp. 67–8.

[73] *Id.*, p. 151.

reformation of the patriarchal structure of society."[74] If we take seriously, as contemporary feminist Bible scholars do, the degree to which Jesus' critique of patriarchy was diluted by the sexism of his later followers – who, ministering largely to highly patriarchal Greco-Roman audiences of potential converts, chose as canonical texts and traditions those closer to the patriarchal assumptions of their audiences – a reasonable case can be made that the historical Jesus' critique of patriarchy was probably much more profoundly radical.[75]

One way of understanding the roots of what is ethically radical in Jesus is to relate his attitude to women to his conception of God, which is itself remarkably antipatriarchal. Jesus always speaks, as we have seen, of God as a loving father, but, as Buber's interpretation of Jesus shows, gender as such plays no fundamental role in his understanding of the relationship as one of reciprocal intimate love and care between equals. Jesus' thought on this point is traditionally Jewish: Moses thus speaks to God of his loving demands as maternal, "Did I conceive all these people? Did I give birth to them, that you should say to me, 'Carry them in your bosom, as a nurse carries a sucking child,' to the land that you promised on oath to their ancestors" (Numbers 10:11).[76] Isaiah describes not only the human response to God in terms of a woman in labor (Isaiah 12:8, 21:3, 26:17) but also God's prophetic love: "I will cry out like a woman in labor, / I will gasp and pant" (Isaiah 42:14;[77] see also Isaiah 40:11: "He will feed his flock like a shepherd;/he will gather the lambs in his arms, / and carry them in his bosom, and gently lead the mother sheep"[78]); a Qumran hymn speaks of God's love as maternal: "And as a woman who tenderly loves her babe, so does Thou rejoice in them."[79] Consistent with this Jewish way of thinking, all the important features that Jesus ascribes to a loving God are exactly those that Sara Ruddick describes as maternal care, a loving care that holds on to relationship to another, despite frustrations and disappointments, to serve the ends of love – protection, growth, and ethical acceptability.[80] What is remarkable in Jesus' conception of God is how his loving care shows itself to sinners who have not yet repented and the extent to which Jesus defines his life and teaching in precisely such terms, never breaking relationship to those who have failed his hopes for them but rather defining the value, indeed

74 See Witherington, *Women and the Genesis of Christianity*, p. xiv; see also p. 15.

75 See, for plausible arguments along these lines, Rosemary Radford Ruether, *Sexism and God-Talk: Toward a Feminist Theology* (Boston: Beacon Press, 1993); Elisabeth Schussler Fiorenza, *Jesus: Miriam's Child, Sophia's Prophet* (New York: Continuum, 1994); Fiorenza, *In Memory of Her: A Feminist Theological Reconstruction of Christian Origins* (New York: Crossroad, 2002); Fiorenza, ed., *Searching Scriptures*, vol. 1, *A Feminist Introduction* (New York: Crossroad, 1993); Fiorenza, ed., *Searching the Scriptures*, vol. 2, *A Feminist Commentary* (New York: Crossroad, 1994).

76 See *The New Oxford Annotated Bible* (New York: Oxford University Press, 1991), p. 181. For relevant commentary, see Aaron Wildavsky, *The Nursing Father: Moses as a Political Leader* (University: University of Alabama Press, 1984).

77 See *New Oxford Annotated Bible*, p. 923.

78 See *id.*, p. 918.

79 Cited in Vermes, *Religion of Jesus the Jew*, p. 177.

80 Sara Ruddick, *Maternal Thinking: Toward a Politics of Peace* (Boston: Beacon Press, 1989).

the power of love, to be its willingness to stay in loving relationship above all when the beloved fails one. Jesus starts, it seems, from the microcosm of caring love that Ruddick describes (something he must have experienced in his own life as the son of a remarkable mother and/or father) and then writes it at large into a sense of ethics and religion that understands its demands in the terms of the loving care of God in the protection, growth, and ethical acceptability of his recalcitrant children as interpreted historically (as a record of their advances to and digressions from growth to moral maturity as a people) through the prophetic tradition, which Jesus assumes and elaborates. We can never know what jolted Jesus to move from microcosm to macrocosm, but if, as historians of Jesus believe, his father, Joseph, was dead by the time of Jesus' ministry,[81] the traumatic loss of a beloved father, who imparted to his son a God of maternal care, may figure in the tensions that propelled him from his family to his public ministry. Jesus has, as Buber shows, redefined the scope and demands of ethical concern between and among persons, made in God's image, as a loving concern that is equally available to all persons, certainly to women at least as much as men. As Erik Erikson, the psychoanalyst and historian, perceptively observed about Jesus: "one cannot help noticing, on Jesus' part, an unobtrusive integration of maternal and paternal tenderness."[82]

Consider, from this perspective, Jesus' teachings about nonviolence: namely the Sermon on the Mount (Matthew 5:7). In particular, the text directly relevant to nonviolence is Matthew 5:38–42:

> You have heard that it was said "An eye for an eye and a tooth for a tooth." But I tell you not to resist one who is evil. But if anyone strikes you on the right cheek, turn the other to him as well. If anyone wants to sue you and take away your tunic, let him have your cape, too. If anyone presses you into service to go one mile, go with him two. Give to him who ask you for a loan, and do not refuse one who is unable to pay interest.[83]

The text is followed by Matthew 5:43–8:

> You have heard that it was said "You shall love your neighbor and hate your enemy," but I tell you to love your enemies and pray for those who misuse you. In this way you will become sons of your heavenly Father, who causes the sun to rise upon both good and evil men, and sends rain to just and unjust alike. If you love only those who love you, what reward have you? Do not the tax gatherers do the same? And if you greet only your brethren, what extra are you doing? Do not the heathen do the same? Be true, just as your heavenly Father is true.[84]

81 See, e.g., Flusser, *Jesus*, p. 28.
82 Erik H. Erikson, "The Galilean Sayings and the Sense of 'I,'" 70 *Yale Rev.* 321, 349 (1981).
83 W. E. Albright and C. S. Mann, *The Anchor Bible: Matthew* (New York: Doubleday, 1971), p. 68.
84 *Id.*, p. 71.

The familiar King James translation of 5:48 is: "Be ye therefore perfect, even as your Father in heaven is perfect."[85]

The sense of the mandate "not to resist one who is evil" but rather "to turn the other [cheek]" is presumably meant as an example of what Jesus means by telling his disciples "to love your enemies" (the sermon is addressed to Jesus' disciples, whereas, in teaching the general public, he uses parables). Such substantive normative demands on oneself are companioned by Jesus' skepticism about normative judgments on others at Matthew 7:1–5:

> Do not sit in judgment, lest you yourself be judged, for you will be judged by the same standard which you have used. Why look at the splinter in your brother's eye, if you do not take notice of the beam in your own? How dare you say to your brother, "Let me take the splinter out of your eye", when all the time there is a beam in your own eye? Casuist! First remove the beam from your own eye, and then you will see clearly in order to remove the splinter from your brother's eye.[86]

There are compelling reasons for believing that the historical Jesus could not have meant Matthew 5:36–42 to forbid the role that the principle of self-defense plays in criminal law. As David Daube has persuasively argued, Jesus invokes an eye for an eye not as a principle of criminal law but in terms of the developing tradition of Jewish civil law, in which varying monetary damages were assigned for different kinds of injuries. Jesus does not question this tradition as applied to injuries but questions the view of the tradition that it extends to insults as well, including the Near Eastern insult of striking the right cheek with the back of the hand.[87] Perhaps, as Joachim Jeremias argues, Jesus is speaking not of a general insult but "of a quite specific insulting blow: the blow given to the disciples of Jesus as heretics."[88] In any event, Jesus is addressing "the urge to resent a wrong done to you as an affront to your pride, to forget that the wrongdoer is your brother before God and to compel him to soothe your unworthy feelings; and it advocates, instead, a humility which cannot be wounded, a giving of yourself to your brother which will achieve more than can be achieved by a narrow justice."[89]

In light of Daube's analysis, we can reasonably interpret the antithesis of Matthew 5:43–4 ("You have heard that it was said 'You shall love your neighbor and hate your enemy,' but I tell you to love your enemies and pray for those who misuse you.") in terms of Jesus' rejection of the Essene teaching that commanded such hatred.[90] Paradoxically, the Essenes accepted a teaching of nonretaliation

[85] The Bible authorized King James Version (Oxford: Oxford University Press, 1998).

[86] Albright and Mann, *Anchor Bible: Matthew*, p. 83.

[87] See, on this point, *id.*, p. 69n39.

[88] Joachim Jeremias, *The Sermon on the Mount* (London: Athlone Press, 1961), p. 27.

[89] Daube, *New Testament and Rabbinic Judaism*, pp. 258–9.

[90] See, on this point, W. D. Davies, *The Setting of the Sermon on the Mount* (Cambridge: Cambridge University Press, 1964), p. 427.

analogous to that of Jesus, but that teaching was a strategic expression of apocalyptic faith that, at the last judgment, God himself would wreck vengeance on such hated enemies of the light.[91] John the Baptist, Jesus' mentor, may have been associated with the Qumran Essenes, but the fact that his message, like that of Jesus, appealed to the entire Jewish people, including sinners, suggests that, by the time he appears in the Gospels, John was no longer a member of the secretive, monastically self-isolated sect.[92] Both John and Jesus may have been celibate men, like the Essenes, but Jesus, unlike the ascetic John, embraced open-table fellowship with all as a distinctive feature of his ministry, a "bon vivant existence with robbers and sinners . . . more scandalous and ominous than a mere matter of breaking purity rules dear to . . . the Pharisees,"[93] a scandal captured at Matthew 11:19, "For the Son of Man came eating and drinking, and you say: 'Behold an eater and drinker, a friend of toll collectors and sinners.'"[94] Accordingly, what distinguishes Jesus' commands "not to resist one who is evil" and "turn the other [cheek]" is the way he grounds its motivations in an inclusive caring love that here asks men in particular to question the force of the Mediterranean honor code in their lives, whose demands require that insults to manhood unleash a cycle of violence. Such honor codes are framed in terms of patriarchal gender stereotypes, and the violence is the way such stereotypes are enforced, for the violence is keyed to threats to honor defined by patriarchy. Jesus, here as elsewhere, is asking men to question the role such violence plays in their sense of manhood.

As we have seen, one of the remarkable features of Jesus' life and teaching was its ethical sensitivity to the plight of women usually covered over by patriarchal gender stereotypes that silence women's voices by a violence unleashed by any threat to such stereotypes, a theme touched on in his defense from stoning of the woman taken in adultery (John 8:1–11). Such gender stereotypes repress men's voices and the extent to which the conventional political force of such stereotypes rests on the violent repression of any voice of a man that would reasonably contest the demands such stereotypes unjustly impose both on men and women. The incident of the adulteress is put in particularly poignant terms as Jesus confronts a culture of patriarchal male hypocrisy with a question that calls for a voice in patriarchal men that they do not usually confront:

> Then the scribes and the Pharisees led forward a woman who had been caught in adultery, and made her stand there in front of everybody. "Teacher," they said to him, "this woman has been caught in the very act of adultery. Now, in the Law Moses ordered such women to be stoned. But you – what do you have to say about it?" (They were posing this question to trap him so that they could have something to accuse him of.). But Jesus simply bent down and started drawing on the ground with his finger. When they persisted in their

[91] See, on these points, Flusser, *Judaism and the Origins of Christianity*, pp. 193–201.

[92] See Vermes, *Changing Faces of Jesus*, p. 275.

[93] Meier, *A Marginal Jew*, vol. 2, p. 149.

[94] Cited at *id.*, pp. 148–9.

> questioning, he straightened up and said to them, "The man among you who has no sin – let him be the first to cast a stone at her." And he bent down again and started to write on the ground. But the audience went away one by one, starting with the elders; and he was left alone with the woman still there before him. So Jesus, straightening up, said to her, "Woman, where are they all? Hasn't anyone condemned you?" "No one, sir," she answered. Jesus said, "Nor do I condemn you. You may go. But from now on, avoid this sin." (John 8:3–11)[95]

There is a Socratic inwardness in Jesus' questioning of these patriarchal men (exemplifying the principle of Matthew 7:1–2, "Do not sit in judgment, lest you yourself be judged, for you will be judged by the same standard which you have used"), one that lays bare voices and desires in men that the injustice of patriarchy violently represses. It is their inability to answer Jesus' searching question as he turns from them, "drawing on the ground with his finger," that gives voice to the silenced voices in the male psyche that patriarchy violently represses in accord with the demands of the honor code. That code wreaks havoc, of course, on any woman who deviates from its demands, as the stoning of an adulteress shows. Jesus' ethically rooted forgiveness in this case may have been so threatening to the sexism of the early church that it was not accepted into the canon until a more tolerant period.[96] Its profound interest to the present argument is how, combined with the prohibition on violence between men in Matthew 5:43–4, it confronts us with the ways in which patriarchal conventions of manhood depend on a violence unleashed by any threat to the gender stereotypes on which the stability of patriarchy depends, whether violence against women or violence between men. In both cases, Jesus shows how patriarchal violence rests on the repression of a free ethical voice.

No aspect of Jesus' life and teaching was more important than his own insistence on the free prophetic ethical voice that, consistent with the tradition of the prophets on which he relied,[97] he himself developed and displayed with an authority that "astonished" his audiences, "for he taught them as one that had authority, and not as the scribes" (Mark 1:22).[98] The historical Jesus may have regarded himself as an eschatological prophet like Elijah[99] and have discovered his own remarkable prophetic voice in relationship to a conception of a God whose loving care inspired that voice. Jesus' approach to disagreement with his teaching or his actions was that of a teacher; when such disagreement with him expresses itself in the political violence that ultimately ended his life, he asks

[95] See Raymond E. Brown, *The Anchor Bible: The Gospel According to John I–XII* (New York: Doubleday, 1966), p. 332.

[96] See, on this point, *id.*, p. 335.

[97] On this tradition, see Abraham Heschel, *The Prophets* (New York: Perennial Classics, 2001).

[98] King James Version.

[99] See, on this point, Meier, *A Marginal Jew*, vol. 3, pp. 495, 623.

poignantly: "Are ye come out as against a thief with swords and staves for to take me? I sat daily with you teaching in the temple, and ye laid no hold on me" (Matthew 26:55).[100] Jesus, like Socrates, whose method of indirection and introspective inwardness he resembles, died for his beliefs and teachings, himself the victim of unjust political violence directed against a voice interpreted as challenging that injustice, under the terms of Roman law that "instigators of a revolt, riot, or agitators of the people" were to be "either crucified, thrown to wild animals, or banished to an island."[101]

Roman political authority was, of course, itself highly patriarchal, resting on a conception of patriarchal manhood that made possible a military life and rule that legitimated aggressive war, imperial rule, and the enslavement of defeated peoples on which the Roman imperium and economy depended.[102] The Roman governor of Judea, Pontius Pilate, who condemns Jesus to death probably at the insistence of the Sadducee temple officials who were corruptly complicitous with Roman rule, exemplifies such patriarchal hierarchy and violence – a servile devotion to his superiors, contempt for the people he ruled, cowardice, and cruelty.[103] Jesus may have been as much critical of the patriarchal violence of Rome as he was or would have been of the forms of it in Jewish culture, including those forms that would later develop into the violence of the Zealots in the First Jewish Revolt (66–70 CE) to which the Romans would respond within forty years of the death of Jesus with the ultimate destruction of the second temple in 70 CE, leading to the Diaspora.[104] The death of the historical Jesus thus exemplifies what may have been one of his distinctive teachings: that the violence of patriarchal manhood in any of its forms requires the unjust repression of free ethical voice.

b. Patriarchal Formation of Christian Tradition

Protestant fundamentalism rests on a reading of the New Testament that pays little or no attention to the life and teaching of the historical Jesus, which suggests, as I have argued, a deep skepticism about precisely the patriarchal assumptions on which fundamentalism rests, including its exclusion of women from the ministry. Such fundamentalism is incoherent with what should, on internal biblical grounds, be the best evidence of the life and teaching of the founder of

100 King James Version.

101 Cited at p. 166, Flusser, *Jesus*, p. 16.

102 See, on these points, Richard Alston, "Arms and the Man: Soldiers, Masculinity, and Power in Republican and Imperial Rome," in *When Men Were Men: Masculinity, Power and Identity in Classical Antiquity*, ed. Lin Foxhall and John Salmon (London: Routledge, 1998), pp. 205–23; Aldo Schiavone, *The End of the Past: Ancient Rome and the Modern West*, trans. Margery J. Schneider (Cambridge, Mass.: Harvard University Press, 2000); Carol Gilligan and David A. J. Richards, *The Deepening Darkness: Patriarchy, Resistance, and Democracy's Future* (Cambridge: Cambridge University Press, 2009).

103 For an illuminating discussion, see Flusser, *Jesus*, pp. 155–73.

104 On the Zealots and Jesus' relation to them, see Meier, A *Marginal Jew*, vol. 3, pp. 205–8, 565–9.

Christianity, Jesus of Nazareth, namely the four gospels, and for this reason is deeply unreasonable.

To the extent that fundamentalism claims biblical support, it primarily draws authority not from Jesus but from other texts of the New Testament, in particular, the letters of Paul.[105] Christianity is a historical religion, and, of all the texts in the Hebrew and Christian Bibles, some of the texts of the New Testament are among the most historically reliable, as they were written much closer to the alleged historical events than most biblical texts, certainly, most of the texts of the Hebrew Bible.[106] Because the authentic Pauline letters are the earliest Christian texts we have (written before any of the Gospels), they are among the most reliable, certainly, about the earliest views of Christian believers after the death of Jesus.[107] However, there are several historical difficulties with the appeal to Paul in interpreting Jesus. First, several of the letters, including one on which fundamentalists depend as the ground for their literalism, are not authentic.[108] Second, Paul never knew Jesus personally, unlike the apostles and other followers, but he claimed to know him through visions. Third, in contrast to the apostles, who thought of Christianity as a sect in traditional Judaism, Paul conceived of his mission as one to Gentiles, many of whom were not Jews, and came to regard Christianity as not requiring traditional Jewish practices, including circumcision and observance of dietary laws.[109] With the destruction of temple Judaism by the Romans and the murder and disruption of the Jewish Christians in Jerusalem, Paul's mission to the Gentiles became Christianity, though a form of Christianity discontinuous with its roots in the historical Jesus. Fourth, because of the character of Paul's mission and his audience, there are good reasons for historical skepticism about the authority of his view of Christianity when his view contrasts sharply with the life and teachings of Jesus of Nazareth.

The main reason for this skepticism is the antipatriarchal character of the life and teaching of Jesus of Nazareth, and yet the hegemonic authority of patriarchal assumptions in the ancient Roman world,[110] the world of the Gentiles that Paul took as the audience for conversion to Christianity. Paul, who never knew Jesus and had come to reject the traditional Judaism in which he once devoutly believed, innovates a mission to the Gentiles based on his highly personal

[105] See, on this point, Crapanzano, *Serving the Word*, pp. 57, 75–7, 84–7.

[106] See, for an excellent study of this matter, Robin Lane Fox, *The Unauthorized Version: Truth and Fiction in the Bible* (New York: Alfred A. Knopf, 1992).

[107] See, e.g., Garry Wills, *What Paul Meant* (New York: Viking, 2006).

[108] See, on this point, Fox, *Unauthorized Version*, pp. 131–6.

[109] See, for good studies of Paul, Alan F. Segal, *Paul the Convert* (New Haven, Conn.: Yale University Press, 1990); Jacob Taubes, *The Political Theology of Paul*, trans. Dana Hollander (Stanford, Calif.: Stanford University Press, 2004); Samuel Sandmel, *The Genius of Paul: A Study in History* (Philadelphia: Fortress Press, 1979); Daniel Boyarin, *A Radical Jew: Paul and the Politics of Identity* (Berkeley: University of California Press, 1994); Wills, *What Paul Meant*.

[110] On Roman patriarchy and its role in the formation of Christianity, see Gilligan and Richards, *The Deepening Darkness*.

interpretation of Jesus, and one that could only reasonably appeal to non-Jews in the ancient world to the extent it was consistent with the highly patriarchal assumptions about religion and politics dominant in the ancient Roman world. The passages in the authentic Pauline letters, to which fundamentalists appeal as authority for their views of gender and sexuality, reflect these assumptions and must be read skeptically for this reason, in particular, when they distort and even betray precisely the ethical impulses of freedom and equality that are so distinctive of the antipatriarchal life and teachings of Jesus of Nazareth himself. If anything, the problem of patriarchy, in the transmission of authentic Christianity, was very much heightened over time, in particular, when Christianity becomes under Constantine and his successors the established church of the Roman Empire, becoming more Roman than Christian.[111]

c. *Dependence on Augustine*

It is remarkable to contrast the historical Jesus with the form Christianity took after it became the established church of the Roman Empire. I have already discussed at some length (Chapter 4) Augustine's role in establishing, building on Roman political and religious models, a male celibate priesthood that was highly patriarchal, religious authority being placed in this priesthood that successfully appealed, as Augustine often did, to imperial authorities to enforce its view of religious truth. We must now explore further Augustine's role in justifying religious persecution and the role he played in Christian anti-Semitism. Why the Christian obsession with the Jews?

The crux of the problem was this. Politically entrenched conceptions of truths (enforced, for example, by the Roman emperors) had, on the basis of the Augustinian legitimation of religious persecution, made themselves the measure both of the standards of reasonable inquiry and of who could count as a reasonable inquirer of truth. But such political enforcement of a conception of religious truth immunizes itself from independent criticism in terms of reasonable standards of thought and deliberation. In effect, the conception of religious truth, though perhaps having once been importantly shaped by more ultimate considerations of reason, ceases to be held or to be understood and elaborated on the basis of reason.

A tradition that loses the sense of its reasonable foundations will stagnate and depend increasingly for allegiance on question-begging appeals to orthodox conceptions of truth and the violent repression of any dissent from such conceptions (treating them as a kind of disloyal moral treason). The politics of loyalty rapidly degenerate into a politics that takes pride in widely held community values solely because they are community values. Standards of discussion and inquiry become increasingly parochial and insular and serve only a polemical role in the defense

[111] See, on this point, *id.*

of the existing community values; indeed, they become increasingly hostile to any more impartial reasonable assessment in light of independent standards.[112]

Such politics tends to degrade to forms of irrationalism to protect its essentially polemical project: opposing views relevant to reasonable public argument are suppressed, facts distorted or misstated, values disconnected from ethical reasoning, and ultimately, deliberation in politics is denigrated in favor of violence against dissent and the aesthetic glorification of such violence. Paradoxically, the greater the tradition's vulnerability to independent reasonable criticism, the more likely it is to generate forms of political irrationalism (including scapegoating of outcast dissenters) to secure allegiance.

I earlier called this phenomenon the paradox of intolerance.[113] A certain conception of religious truth was originally affirmed as true and politically enforced on society at large because it was supposed to be the epistemic measure of reasonable inquiry (i.e., more likely to lead to epistemically reliable beliefs). But the consequence of the legitimation of such intolerance was that standards of reasonable inquiry, outside the orthodox measure of such inquiry, were repressed. In effect, the orthodox conception of truth was no longer defended on the basis of reason but was increasingly hostile to reasonable assessment in terms of impartial standards not hostage to the orthodox conception. Indeed, orthodoxy was defended as an end in itself, increasingly by nonrational and even irrational means of appeal to community identity and the like. The paradox appears in the subversion of the original epistemic motivations of the Augustinian argument. Rather than securing reasonable inquiry, the argument has cut off the tradition from such inquiry. Indeed, the legitimacy of the tradition feeds on irrationalism precisely when it is most vulnerable to reasonable criticism, contradicting and frustrating its original epistemic ambitions (thus the sense of paradox in such self-defeating epistemic incoherence).

The history of religious persecution amply illustrates these truths – and no aspect of that history more clearly so than Christian anti-Semitism. The relationship of Christianity to its Jewish origins has always been a tense and ambivalent one.[114] The fact that many Jews did not accept Christianity was a kind of standing challenge to the reasonableness of Christianity especially in its early period

[112] See, in general, John Hope Franklin, *The Militant South, 1800–1861* (Cambridge, Mass.: Harvard University Press, Belknap Press, 1956); Bertram Wyatt-Brown, *Honor and Violence in the Old South* (New York: Oxford University Press, 1986); cf. W. J. Cash, *The Mind of the South* (New York: Vintage Books, 1941).

[113] See David A. J. Richards, *Women, Gays, and the Constitution: The Grounds for Feminism and Gay Rights in Culture and Law* (Chicago: University of Chicago Press, 1998), pp. 42–4.

[114] For a useful study of the early Christian period, see John A. Gager, *The Origins of Anti-Semitism: Attitudes toward Judaism in Pagan and Christian Antiquity* (New York: Oxford University Press, 1983). The classic general study is Leon Poliakov, *The History of Anti-Semitism*, vol. 1, trans. Richard Howard (New York: Vanguard Press, 1965); vol. 2, trans. Natalie Gerardi (New York: Vanguard Press, 1973); vol. 3, trans. Miriam Kochan (New York: Vanguard Press, 1975); vol. 4, trans. George Klin (Oxford: Oxford University Press, 1985).

(before its establishment as the church of the late Roman Empire) when Christianity was a proselytizing religion that competed for believers with the wide range of religious and philosophical alternative belief systems available in the late pagan world.

In his recent important studies of anti-Semitism,[115] the medievalist Gavin Langmuir characterizes as anti-Judaism Christianity's long-standing worries about the Jews because of the way the Jewish rejection of Christianity discredited the reasonableness of the Christian belief system in the pagan world. Langmuir argues that the Christian conception of the obduracy of the Jews and the divine punishment of them for such obduracy were natural forms of anti-Judaic self-defense, resulting in the forms of expulsion and segregation from Christian society that naturally expressed and legitimated such judgments on the Jews.[116] In contrast, Langmuir calls anti-Semitism proper the totally baseless and irrational beliefs about ritual crucifixions and cannibalism of Christians by Jews that were "widespread in northern Europe by 1350";[117] such beliefs led to populist murders of Jews usually (though not always) condemned by both church and secular authorities. Their irrationalist nature requires, Langmuir suggests, a distinguishing name, chimeria, suggesting, from the Greek root, "fantasies, figments of the imagination, monsters that, although dressed syntactically in the cloths of real humans, have never been seen and are projections of mental processes unconnected with the real people of the outgroup."[118]

Building on Langmuir's insights, I believe my argument more deeply explains both the resistance of the Jews to Augustinian orthodoxy and why that orthodoxy turned on them so viciously, with such catastrophic consequences for the Jews in twentieth-century Europe, the cradle of Christian civilization.

The Jews should be understood as a remarkable example of the personal and political psychology of resistance, grounded in the protection of intimate personal life, including sexual love and relationship. The priesthood in the Judaism of the temple, before the Diaspora, was not celibate; celibacy was advocated only by sects, like that of Qumran, opposed to dominant Jewish belief and practice. After the Diaspora, temple rituals and the associated priesthood play no role in rabbinical Judaism, as Jewish belief and practice increasingly centers in the home and the synagogues where the Hebrew Bible is studied under teachers, rabbis, chosen by believers; rabbis, like other Jewish men, marry and have family lives. Sexual love and family relationships are at the center of Jewish belief and practice, including religious commandments for husbands to give pleasure in sex to their

115 See Gavin I. Langmuir, *Toward a Definition of Antisemitism* (Berkeley: University of California Press, 1990); Langmuir, *History, Religion, and Antisemitism* (Berkeley: University of California Press, 1990).

116 See Langmuir, *Toward a Definition of Antisemitism*, pp. 57–62.

117 *Id.*, p. 302.

118 See *id.*, p. 334.

wives on the Sabbath.[119] Martin Buber thus, as we have seen, philosophically explicates the Jewish sense of God in terms of a relational and loving care and sensitivity of one human, made in God's image, to another. Because Jews do not believe in an afterlife, there is little temptation to denigrate the legitimate pleasures of body and mind of this world in light of the next.[120] Although Jewish women in the Diaspora were not permitted to be rabbis, they play, in contrast to many Christian women, powerful roles not only in their families (including its religious life) but in business, as Jewish men were expected to study Talmud. Under the anti-Semitic laws in Christian Europe, Jewish men were also excluded from many forms of profession, including the military, which further accentuated the cultural differences between Jewish and Christian conceptions of manhood and womanhood.[121]

The remarkable tradition of Jewish resistance to Augustinian Christianity is, I believe, best explained as a resistance to Christianity's denigration of sexual life and relationships. I have no doubt that Jews as well objected to many theological views of the hegemonic Christianity that enveloped them, for example, the Trinity, the Virgin Birth, Jesus as the incarnation of God, an afterlife, and the like, beliefs that would have struck many Jews of the period of Jesus as forms of pagan belief, not consistent with the ethical monotheism of the Hebrew Bible. But it was the role these beliefs played, in legitimating Augustine's disavowal of sexual love and relationship, which, I believe, explains the resistance of Jews, a resistance held and maintained against extraordinary pressures and constraints. There is not just the joyous eroticism of the Song of Songs in the Hebrew Bible but the Bible's antimythological narratives (contesting the mythological religions around them[122]) as well as anti-idealizing narratives, for example, its remarkable sense of human frailty before the ethical demands of God, a frailty sometimes explored with an astonishingly artistic narrative complexity that prefigures the novel.[123] Even the leaders whom God favors (e.g., David) are notably flawed,

[119] See, on these and related points, Daniel Boyarin, *Carnal Israel: Reading Sex in Talmudic Culture* (Berkeley: University of California Press, 1993).

[120] But see, for a recent study of resurrection beliefs in classical Judaism, Jon D. Levenson, *Resurrection and the Restoration of Israel: The Ultimate Victory of the God of Life* (New Haven, Conn.: Yale University Press, 2006).

[121] See, on these points, Daniel Boyarin, *Unheroic Conduct: The Rise of Heterosexuality and the Invention of the Jewish Man* (Berkeley: University of California Press, 1997).

[122] See, on this point, Herbert N. Schneidau, *Sacred Discontent: The Bible and Western Tradition* (Baton Rouge: Louisiana State University Press, 1976); Moshe Halbertal and Avishai Margalit, *Idolatry*, trans. Naomi Goldblum (Cambridge, Mass.: Harvard University Press, 1992). See also Dan Jacobson, *The Story of Stories: The Chosen People and Its God* (New York: Harper & Row, 1982). On these mythological religions, see Henri Frankfort, *Kingship and the Gods: A Study of Ancient Near Eastern Religion as the Integration of Society and Nature* (Chicago: University of Chicago Press, 1948); Henri Frankfort, H. A. Frankfort, John A. Wilson, and Thorkild Jacobsen, *Before Philosophy: The Intellectual Adventure of Ancient Man* (Baltimore: Penguin, 1961).

[123] See, on this point, Robert Alter, *The Art of Biblical Narrative* (New York: Basic Books 1981). See also Moshe Halbertal, *People of the Book: Canon, Meaning, and Authority* (Cambridge, Mass.: Harvard University Press, 1997).

highly sexual, and subject to betrayal and loss;[124] and even God has his frailties (e.g., anger).[125] And the refusal of God to permit Abraham's sacrifice of his son[126] bespeaks a larger view of the ethics of loving relationships in the family that questions the sacrifice of children, a Jewish view that would suggest why the orthodox Christian view of God's sacrifice of his son would, to say the least, not appeal to Jews. Idealization arising from loss – a feature of Augustinian orthodox Christianity – would be questioned by Jews as religious and ethical demands of a loving God, and clarifies the basis of their resistance to Christian demands. Indeed, I would say, for this reason, that the Jews are perhaps the first example in human history of such a long-lasting resistance group, clarifying how important such associational activity is to the power and persistence of such resistance.

Historical Judaism, like all other religions and cultures that we know of, itself embodied patriarchal features. Its historical exclusion of women from study of the Torah established, at the core of the religion, a patriarchal hierarchy, rationalized on the sexist ground that "[a]nyone who teaches his daughter Torah, teaches her lasciviousness."[127] And although the starkly homophobic prohibitions of Leviticus 18:22[128] and 20:13[129] are today reasonably understood, by Jewish Bible scholars among others, as applicable only in certain places and circumstances, the historical tradition of rabbinical Judaism did not qualify its homophobic teaching in the way reasonable contemporary Bible interpretation supports.[130] In contrast, the celebration by Judaism of the sexual body and its antiheroic conception of manhood placed it in opposition to the dominant patriarchal conception of Christianity, and it is appeal to such values that underlies the growing reasonable internal criticism by Jews of both the sexist and homophobic features of its

124 See 1–2 Samuel and 1 Kings 1–2.

125 See Genesis 18:23–33 (Abraham persuades God to moderate what Abraham regards as his excessive anger against Sodom: "Will thou also destroy the righteous with the wicked?" Genesis 18:23 [Authorized King James Version]).

126 See Genesis 22.

127 Quoted in Boyarin, *Carnal Israel*, p. 171.

128 "You shall not lie with a male as one lies with as woman: it is an abomination," Leviticus 18:22, in Jacob Milgrom, *Leviticus 17–22: The Anchor Bible* (New York: Doubleday, 2000), p. 1515.

129 "If a man lies with a male as one lies with a woman, the two of them have done an abhorrent thing; they must be put to death – the bloodguilt is upon them," Leviticus 20:13, in *id.*, p. 1727.

130 For such an interpretation by a leading Jewish scholar, see Milgrom, Leviticus 17:22, pp. 1515, 1565–70, 1727, 1749–50, 1785–8 (prohibitions applicable only in Israel and only in circumstances when necessary to increase population; thus, they are not applicable when population control is urgent and when gay and lesbian Jewish couples can adopt children, an option not historically available). For Mary Douglas's pathbreaking arguments about the limited and differing application of the biblical prohibitions (the most demanding ones, like Leviticus 20:13, only applicable to the sacred space of the priesthood of the temple), see *Leviticus as Literature* (Oxford: Oxford University Press, 1999); see also Douglas, *In the Wilderness: The Doctrine of Defilement in the Book of Numbers* (Sheffield, U.K.: Sheffield Academic Press, 1993). For a similar argument by an Orthodox Jewish rabbi, see Rabbi Steven Greenberg, *Wrestling with God and Men: Homosexuality in the Jewish Tradition* (Madison: University of Wisconsin Press, 2004).

historical tradition, a criticism that has been much more difficult certainly for Augustinian Christianity.[131]

It is precisely because Jewish resistance took the form that it did (defending both the sexual body and an antiheroic conception of manhood) that Augustinian Christianity, centered in the repression of sexual voice, turned on the Jews with such repressive force. The entire role of grace in Augustine's thought, interpreting Paul, arises from the doctrine of original sin that Augustine finds in the Adam and Eve narrative, rejecting sexuality because it blocks access to God. The Pauline attack on the role of law in Judaism, which subjects sexual love to ethical constraints and reasoning underlying the law, arises from what Jews found so unreasonable, the rejection of sexuality because it blocked access to God.[132] The Jews accept no such doctrine of original sin because God is known through, among other human goods, the good of sexual love. The role of law is to address our rational autonomy, offering reasonable constraints within which we should pursue this good. From the Jewish point of view, it is the Christian repudiation of sexuality, which is so unreasonable and so difficult to comply with, that explains the role of grace in Pauline/Augustinian Christianity: only the love of God makes such asceticism possible. Augustine's search in *Confessions* for a more perfect lover (which he finds in an incorporeal God) makes sense against this background. When the Jews reject this conception of God as unreasonable (because grounded in an unreasonable understanding of human sexuality), their view stands as a stinging rebuke to Augustinian Christianity, to which Augustine takes the sharpest objection. Augustine made this point in terms of "carnal Israel," explaining: "the Jews . . . prove themselves to be indisputably carnal."[133] Augustine's repressive ire much more targeted heretical Christians (e.g., the Donatists, the Pelagians). In contrast to John Chrysostom and Ambrose, Augustine called for an end to violent assaults against synagogues, Jewish property, and Jewish persons, which he did not when it came to pagans or Christian heretics. But Augustine wanted the Jews to survive only on terms of subordination, which would make of their obduracy an example to all others.[134] Augustine thus called for a legally enforced moral slavery of the Jews, a degradation of whole classes of persons to

[131] For an illuminating historical study of Jewish views of sexuality, see David Biale, *Eros and the Jews: From Biblical Israel to Contemporary America* (New York: Basic Books, 1992). On the problematic stance of the contemporary hierarchy of the Catholic Church, see Nicholas Bamforth and David A. J. Richards, *Patriarchal Relgiion, Sexuality, and Gender: Critique of New Natural Law* (Cambridge University Press, 2007). On the psychological space for liberal views in traditional religions, see Tova Hartman Halbertal, *Appropriately Subversive: Modern Mothers in Traditional Religions* (Cambridge, Mass.: Harvard University Press, 2002).

[132] On Paul's life and thought, see Sandmel, *Genius of Paul*; Boyarin, *A Radical Jew*; Alan F. Segal, *Paul the Convert: The Apostolate and Apostasy of Saul the Pharisee* (New Haven, Conn.: Yale University Press, 1990); Taubes, *Political Theology of Paul*.

[133] Cited in Boyarin, *Carnal Israel*, p. 1.

[134] See, on this point, James Carroll, *Constantine's Sword: The Church and the Jews: A History* (Boston: Houghton Mifflin, 2001), pp. 208–19. See also Paula Fredriksen, *Augustine and the Jews*, pp. 272–7, 320.

a servile status (including imposing limits on access to influential occupations, intercourse with Christians, living quarters, and the like) justified, as it expressly was, by Augustine, in the quite explicit terms of a legitimate slavery: "The Jew is the slave of the Christian."[135]

It is this cultural background of enforced moral slavery – supported, as it was, by orthodox Christianity (both Catholic and Protestant) – that explains, I believe, the development of even more lethal forms of anti-Semitism in the modern period. Augustinian intolerance was, as we have seen, highly patriarchal and thus gendered. The repression of sexual voice in himself made Augustine extraordinarily sensitive, as a patriarchal man, to any questioning of the terms of his repression; and no group raised such questions more forcefully than the Jews – thus, "carnal Israel." Augustine, however, operated in an ethical system that imposed Christian limits on the persecution of the Jews. But in the modern period, a leader like Hitler, inspired by Nietzsche's legitimation of hatred of Christianity (much deeper than any animus against the Jews),[136] believed in no such limits, and yet accepted and popularized an aggressive form of political anti-Semitism, supported by a crackpot racist science, that drew its appeal from the highly patriarchal form of anti-Semitism Europe inherited from Augustine. It was, for an anti-Semite like Hitler, Jewish resistance in matters of sexuality and even gender that was the target of his genocidal rage, a rage elicited by the humiliation of German manhood at Versailles and directed at the traditional scapegoat for such reverses, the Jews whose resistance was what made them so wounding to German manhood.[137]

No group responded with more enthusiasm to emancipation and the promise of political liberalism than the Jews of Germany and Austria-Hungary.[138] The problem, however, was that what counted as political liberalism was fundamentally flawed. For one thing, Augustinian Catholic and Protestant Christianity – with its history of anti-Semitism – continued to enjoy state support and endorsement. For another, the dominant conception of manhood remained highly patriarchal, formed on classical models like Aeneas in politics and military life and Augustine in religion. There is a fundamental contradiction between democratic liberalism (with its central conviction of equal voice) and patriarchy (the

135 Cited in Langmuir, *History, Religion, and Antisemitism*, p. 294.

136 See, on the hatred underlying asceticism, especially, Christian asceticism, Friedrich Nietzsche, *On the Genealogy of Morals*, trans. Douglas Smith (Oxford: Oxford University Press, 1996), pp. 77–136. Nietzsche criticizes the Jews largely because they prepare the way for Christianity. See *id.*, pp. 35–6. To the extent that the Jews are less ascetic than Christians, they are, for Nietzsche, in fact less objectionable than Christians.

137 On the powerful role of patriarchal conceptions of gender in Hitler's fascism, see Claudia Koonz, *Mothers in the Fatherland: Women, the Family, and Nazi Politics* (New York: St. Martin's Press, 1987); Claudia Koonz, *The Nazi Conscience* (Cambridge, Mass.: Belknap Press, Harvard University Press, 2003).

138 See, in general, Amos Elon, *The Pity of It All: A Portrait of the German-Jewish Epoch, 1743–1933* (New York: Picador, 2002).

hierarchical arrangement of the authority of father-priests over sons, daughters, and wives). The enthusiasm of the Jews for this form of liberalism thus carried with it very real dangers, as it rested on a patriarchal conception that could easily turn on them, as it had throughout the history of hegemonic Augustinian Christianity.

Perhaps the worst danger was that successful assimilation to such a political and religious culture would compromise the very resistance of the Jews to its unjust demands. Freud himself puzzled over the ferocity of the political anti-Semitism that he saw gathering force in Germany and Austria, observing that the more Jews assimilated to German culture and thus the less the differences (if any) between Jews and non-Jews, the more ferocious the anti-Semitism, as if the irrationalism of anti-Semitism expressed "the narcissism of small differences."[139] What Freud did not see was the patriarchal strand in anti-Semitism, which I have traced back to Augustinian orthodoxy, namely that it arose from the traumatic renunciation of sexual love and connection required for the heroism of manhood, whether in politics or in religion. Freud could not see the problems in this patriarchal conception, including its dangers to the Jews, because he had, under the pressure of assimilation, come to accept a form of it in his psychology.

What made Hitler's political anti-Semitism so powerful in Germany and Austria was the highly gendered form of anti-Semitism that Hitler both drew on and fomented, which, through the experience of traumatic loss and German defeat in World War I, made possible a psychology that created an enemy within, a scapegoat, whose fault was their resistance and history of resistance to dominant arrangements. It was the sense of humiliated patriarchal manhood that expressed itself in the role violence and the glorification of violence played in Hitler's fascism, both at home and abroad, with Hitler himself taking the role of an autocratic Roman emperor, with ultimate patriarchal authority over politics and religion.

Of course, some Jews, notably Theodore Herzl, saw the looming danger of political anti-Semitism in European politics quite early on at the time of the Dreyfus Affair and called for a political resistance, Zionism, a liberal Jewish state in which Jews could live as equals and that would not depend on continuing trust in the flawed liberalism of France, Germany, or Austria.[140] And others, like Hannah Arendt, understood, before it was too late, the genocidal intentions of German fascism, and fled to the United States, writing one of the best studies of totalitarianism in Germany and the Soviet Union,[141] and asking the hard questions

[139] On this point, see Sigmund Freud, "Civilization and Its Discontents," in *Standard Edition of the Complete Psychological Works of Sigmund Freud*, ed. and trans. James Strachey (London: Hogarth Press, 1961), vol. 21, p. 114; see also *Moses and Monotheism* (1964), vol. 23, p. 91.

[140] See Amos Elon, *Herzl* (New York: Hold, Rinehart and Winston, 1975); Geoffrey Wheatcroft, *The Controversy of Zion: Jewish Nationalism, the Jewish State, and the Unresolved Jewish Dilemma* (Reading, Mass.: Addison-Wesley, 1996).

[141] See Hannah Arendt, *The Origins of Totalitarianism* (New York: Harcourt Brace Jovanovich, 1973). On Arendt's early life, education (including her affair with the philosopher Martin Heidegger), and fleeing from Germany to the United States, see Elisabeth Young-Bruehl, *Hannah Arendt: For Love of the World* (New Haven, Conn.: Yale University Press, 1982), pp. 5–163.

about why there was not more resistance by Jews.[142] But even Herzl and Arendt fail to understand the role of patriarchy in the political anti-Semitism they otherwise so brilliantly analyzed and resisted.

We should be struck that the most notable forms of Christian resistance to fascist violence did not come from a reading of religious texts, let alone from theology. For example, Dietrich Bonhoeffer initially thought that Christian texts required pacifism.[143] His change in view, a view that led him actively to support the abortive plot to kill Hitler, arose from the call of his lived moral experience in confronting Hitler's murderous regime, an experience that required him "to see the great events of world history from below, from the perspective of the outcast, the suspects, the maltreated, the powerless, the oppressed, the reviled – in short, from the perspective of those who suffer."[144] Among those experiences were his relationships in his family, in particular, to his mother and grandmother, who experienced Hitler's anti-Semitic policies as an outrageous break with long-standing, humane ethical relationships to Jews (his brother-in-law was, in fact, a leader of the plot to kill Hitler and certainly confronted Bonhoeffer with the genocidal reality of Hitler's programs).[145] Conversely, nothing in the Huguenot theology of the French minister André Pascal Trocmé called for pacifism in general or active resistance to the enforcement of Hitler's anti-Semitic programs in Vichy, France. But both his relationship to his mother and his relationship to his Italian, rather nonreligious wife (who insisted that Jewish children be given refuge and help in escaping from the police rounding them up for transport to camps in Germany) fundamentally clarify how Trocmé took the important role he did in resisting Hitler's anti-Semitic programs.[146]

These examples suggest that resistance becomes psychologically and ethically possible when the human psyche finds its voice in experiences of ethical presence in relationship to other loving attentive persons and their voices. It is when men hold on to the truth of that ethical voice in relationship that they come to question and reject conceptions and practices, like conventional manhood and womanhood, that not only are false by that test but also require the suppression of truthful voice. What underlies the psychology and ethics of resistance is the voice of the psyche revolting at conceptions and practices that rest on lies and must, to survive, kill the psyche's sense of relational truth and presence.

142 See Hannah Arendt, *Eichmann in Jerusalem: A Report on the Banality of Evil* (New York: Penguin, 1992).

143 See, on this point, John W. deGruchy, ed., *The Cambridge Companion to Dietrich Bonhoeffer* (Cambridge University Press: Cambridge, 2002), p. 158.

144 Dietrich Bonhoeffer, *Letters and Papers from Prison*, ed. Eberhard Bethge (New York: Touchstone Books, 1971), p. 17.

145 See, on these points, Renate Bethge, "Bonhoeffer's Family and Its Significance for His Theology," in *Dietrich Bonhoeffer – His Significance for North Americans*, ed. Larry Rasmussen (Minneapolis: Fortress Press, 1990), pp. 1–30.

146 See, on these points, Philip P. Hallie, *Let Innocent Blood Be Shed: The Story of the Village of Le Chambon and How Goodness Happened There* (New York: Harper & Row, 1979).

The response of Protestant fundamentalism to such questioning was to adopt an interpretive attitude to biblical texts not resting on those texts (which could more reasonably be interpreted in other ways), but uncritically to assume long-standing patriarchal Augustinian assumptions that led it to find in the text what such assumptions, now very much under reasonable challenge, required it to find. It is for this reason that fundamentalist insistence on the scientific truth of the creation narrative in Genesis, a persistent theme in fundamentalist advocacy from the 1920s until today, is so important in their sense of themselves. It is not the science that really interests them but the highly patriarchal reading of the narrative that they absorbed from Augustine's interpretation of the Adam and Eve narrative. It is because the Augustinian interpretation plays such an important role in their sense of themselves (supporting a misogynist reading of original sin, which, in turn, rationalizes their way of reading the Bible to support patriarchy) that they so desperately insist on scientific creationism or, if not that, intelligent design.[147] But what in culture and psychology supported such a development?

4. DIAGNOSIS: PATRIARCHAL CULTURE AND PSYCHOLOGY

Protestant fundamentalism is, I have argued, internally incoherent and substantively unreasonable. But its very insistence on a fundamentalist certainty about issues of gender and sexuality that are, in fact, subject to reasonable doubt exposes, I believe, its cultural and psychological roots, to which I now turn.

It was a long-standing feature of the Protestant challenge to hegemonic Roman Catholicism to point to the Christian Gospels as a way of challenging what the papal hierarchy and its acolytes had made of Christianity. There was no more politically and constitutionally important such challenge than of radical Protestants like Bayle and Locke who forged the argument for toleration in part on the ground that nothing in the Gospels supported the inquisitorial violence legitimated by the theory of Augustinian persecution that had been accepted by both Catholics and Protestants. It was very much on the same basis that the radical abolitionists (including the abolitionist feminists) questioned the role of patriarchy in traditional Christianity, including its legitimation of slavery and racism and the subjection of women and sexism. Their arguments included novel forms of Bible interpretation in the free and reasonable voice of an abolitionist feminist woman like Sarah Grimké, who challenged the traditional patriarchal reading of the Adam and Eve narrative, and, later, similar such arguments by Elizabeth Stanton and others in her *Woman's Bible*.[148]

It is not difficult to see why Christian women, once they came to see patriarchy as a moral and political evil resting on the repression of women's free and ethical voices, would find the Christian Gospels so reasonably supportive of their critique.

[147] See, in general, Ronald L. Numbers, *The Creationist: From Scientific Creationism to Intelligent Design* (Cambridge, Mass.: Harvard University Press, 2006).

[148] See, on these points, Richards, *Women, Gays, and the Constitution*.

As I earlier argued, the best evidence we have about the historical Jesus is that he was remarkably critical of then dominant patriarchal practices. At a minimum, anyone who takes seriously the historical Jesus must also entertain reasonable doubts about dominant patriarchal arrangements whether in religion or politics or culture more generally.

Nothing could more profoundly challenge the uncritical role patriarchy had played in the formation and transmission of the Christian tradition than the appearance in Protestant America in the nineteenth century, in the midst of volcanic struggles over American slavery and racism, of such voices and antipatriarchal voices of free and reasonable women at that. It bespeaks how important Augustinian patriarchy had become in American Protestant Christianity that the response to these voices should be a kind of cultural panic attack, an attack manifested, of course, in the development of Protestant fundamentalism but also in much broader developments in American culture at the end of the nineteenth and beginning of the twentieth centuries.

The breadth and depth of these developments is shown by the ways in which the radical abolitionist feminism of the Grimké sisters and Elizabeth Stanton, including its critique of Protestant Christianity, was marginalized and largely silenced to forge larger alliances with much more conventional white women, some of them quite racist, which would make possible the growing appeal and eventual success of suffrage feminism, as women secured the right to vote by constitutional amendment in 1920. The triumph of suffrage feminism, which had required the silencing of the free voices of women (questioning patriarchal conceptions of both sexuality and gender) like Victoria Woodhull, Margaret Sanger, and Emma Goldman, accomplished very little in terms of the critique of racism and sexism of the abolitionist feminists. It was only in the civil rights movement of the 1960s that such free and reasonable voices again challenged American patriarchy.

The decline of abolitionist feminism into suffrage feminism shows the impact of the panic attack on women of serious challenges by Christian women to the patriarchal assumptions of Protestant Christianity. Ann Douglas has shown how American women accommodated themselves to the largely patriarchal terms of religious authority in Protestant America in the nineteenth century,[149] forging an alliance between women and the Protestant clergy in which Protestant Americans like Catharine Beecher and Horace Bushnell resisted women's rights in favor of the idealization of women's self-sacrifice, identifying a mother's love with Jesus[150] and finding a religious virtue in submission.[151] It was precisely the way in which Sarah Grimké or Elizabeth Stanton themselves engaged in Bible

149 See Ann Douglas, *The Feminization of American Culture* (New York: Alfred A. Knopf, 1977).

150 See, on this point, Richards, *Women, Gays, and the Constitution*, pp. 145–9.

151 See, on contemporary forms of this way of thinking, R. Marie Griffith, *God's Daughters: Evangelical Woman and the Power of Submission* (Berkeley: University of California Press, 1993); Brenda E. Brasher, *Godly Women: Fundamentalism and Female Power* (New Brunswick, N.J.: Rutgers University Press, 1998).

interpretation, as an expression of the basic human right to conscience, that elicited such panic in both women and men, like Beecher and Bushnell. But the very terms of the Protestant patriarchy they accepted and idealized had increasingly identified Christianity with women, which was paradoxically all too close to the kind of authority Grimké and Stanton wanted women to enjoy as interpreters of a Christian tradition that had, in their views, been distorted by patriarchy. By the end of the nineteenth century, there was a pervasive cultural panic among Protestant Christians at such feminization of American Christianity that took the form of a reassertion of patriarchal authority over religion and culture, all in the name of a muscular (i.e., manly) Christianity.[152]

It is important to see how culturally pervasive such stereotypes of male authority were in this period, powerfully influencing and shaping the life and views of the great American philosopher and psychologist William James,[153] and the rather imperialistic politics of Theodore Roosevelt, including his enthusiasm for both the Spanish-American War and for entering World War I (in which he lost one of his beloved sons).[154] The American panic was specifically exercised by and targeted the feminization of what were regarded as male roles, and it took on a specifically homophobic nuance after the Wilde trials in Britain in 1895 in which Oscar Wilde's public defense of his homosexual lifestyle scandalized both Protestant Britain and America – a man treating another man as a woman.[155] Even at Harvard, the great American philosopher, George Santayana, experienced such homophobic isolation and denigration, including from William James;[156] and James extended such denigration to his great novelist brother, Henry.[157]

It is unsurprising, against this background, to find the terms *effeminacy* or *effeminate*, or similar terms (*sissy*), so widely and publicly used during this period as critical terms about what a man was not to be or could not be.[158] In particular, a true man could not accord authority to women,[159] and the nineteenth-century feminization of American Protestantism was a peril in religion,[160] including the ordination of women as ministers during this period.[161] Jesus, in particular, was not "effeminate or weak" but "the supremely manly man."[162]

152 See, e.g., Clifford Putney, *Muscular Christianity: Manhood and Sports in Protestant America, 1889–1920* (Cambridge, Mass.: Harvard University Press, 2001).

153 See, for an excellent general study, Kim Townsend, *Manhood at Harvard: William James and Others* (Cambridge, Mass.: Harvard University Press, 1996).

154 See, for an illuminating study, Edward J. Renehan Jr., *The Lion's Pride: Theodore Roosevelt and His Family in Peace and War* (New York: Oxford University Press, 1998).

155 See Richards, *Women, Gays, and the Constitution*, pp. 314–17.

156 See Townsend, *Manhood at Harvard*, pp. 145–9.

157 See *id.*, pp. 71–2.

158 See, e.g., Putney, *Muscular Christianity*, pp. 12, 20, 39, 41, 42, 48, 75, 92, 94, 104, 106, 130, 163, 180, 206.

159 See, on this point, *id.*, pp. 31, 37, 48, 79.

160 See *id.*, pp. 73–8.

161 See *id.*, pp. 80–1.

162 Quoted in *id.*, p. 92.

Protestant fundamentalism crucially arose as one important and, as it turns out, enduring expression of this much wider cultural panic, enduring long after other expressions of this panic were forgotten or became culturally much less pervasive. Such fundamentalism arose, as the powerful historical studies of Betty DeBerg[163] and Margaret Bendroth[164] make quite clear, as a reactionary expression of the wider cultural panic of Protestant Americans at both the feminization of American religion and the specific challenge by antipatriarchal women, like Sarah Grimké and Elizabeth Stanton, to the patriarchal traditions of Bible interpretation that had dominated traditional Christianity. The movement was certainly not monolithic. Dwight Moody, one of its leading preachers, was open to women preaching, and women did play important roles early on, albeit increasingly subordinate to male ministers; and some Evangelical women powerfully challenged on biblical grounds the growing sexism at the heart of fundamentalism.[165] But the terms of American fundamentalism were increasingly set in stone by the belligerent rhetoric of its leading preachers like Billy Sunday:

> Jesus was a scrapper, and his disciple Sunday would destroy the notion that a Christian must be "a sort of dishrag proposition, a wishy-washy sissified sort of galoot that lets everybody make a doormat out of him." "Lord save us from off-handed, flabby-cheeked, brittle-boned, weak-kneed, thin-skinned, pliable, plastic, spineless, effeminate ossified three-karat Christianity." Sunday wanted to kill the idea "that being a Christian takes a man out of the busy whirl of the world's life and activity and makes him a spineless, effeminate proposition." He struck a Rooseveltian note in his assertion: "Moral warfare makes a man hard. Superficial peace makes a man mushy"; and he summed up his temper when he confessed: "I have no interest in a God who does not smite."[166]

The tone here is belligerently reactionary, what Richard Hofstadter saw as "a desire to strike back against everything modern – the higher criticism, evolutionism, the social gospel, rational criticism of any kind. In this union of social and theological reaction, the foundation was laid for the [100 percent] mentality."[167]

What is at the heart of this mentality is a patriarchal psychology I have explored earlier: a long-standing culture and psychology of moral slavery of groups of persons, resting on the unjust suppression of any reasonable voice that might protest such slavery. Anti-Semitism, as we have seen, arose from the culture and psychology Augustine defended and exemplified. The culture was patriarchal Roman political culture that rested on the suppression of the free voices, including

[163] See Betty A. DeBerg, *Ungodly Women: Gender and the First Wave of American Fundamentalism* (Macon, Ga.: Mercer University Press, 2000).

[164] See Margaret Lamberts Bendroth, *Fundamentalism and Gender: 1875 to the Present* (New Haven, Conn.: Yale University Press, 1993).

[165] See Janette Hassey, *No Time for Silence: Evangelical Women in Public Ministry around the Turn of the Century* (Grand Rapids, Mich.: Academic Books, 1986).

[166] Richard Hofstadter, *Anti-Intellectualism in American Life* (New York: Vintage Books, 1963), p. 119.

[167] *Id.*, p. 121.

sexual voices, of those who might reasonably challenge its unjust demands. The psychology was Augustine's own break with loving relationships with real women, a loss and disassociation that expressed itself in identifying with his patriarchal role, including anger at those who challenged this role. The Jews were one natural object of Augustine's anger because their conception of sexual love so challenged the terms of sexual loss and disassociation Augustine imposed on himself. What reveals the force of this culture and psychology is its suppression of reasonable doubt about its own doctrines (e.g., transubstantiation, the Virgin Birth), its violence repression of protesting voice, and its psychological stance of believed certitudes, including its grounds for repression. Precisely the reasonable voices such a tradition most needs are, paradoxically, repressed (the paradox of intolerance, as I earlier called it).

We can see this culture and psychology in the formation and endurance of Protestant fundamentalism, shown quite clearly in the belligerent violence of the insults of Billy Sunday and his contemporary epigones at supposed enemies (always the unmanly or effeminate, explicitly or implicitly) and in its contempt for the reasonable argument that has always distinguished American Protestantism, a contempt Mark Noll has called "the scandal of the evangelical mind"[168] and Richard Hofstadter analyzes as one of the cultural supports for American persecutory anti-intellectualism.[169] As Noll acutely observes, such anti-intellectualism abandons the demands of the thoughtful moral independence of Protestant conscience and individuality (that led to the argument for toleration and its elaboration in democratic constitutionalism) for something much easier and more popular: "it is a very easy matter simply to adopt the herd instincts of mass popular culture."[170] The obverse side of such denigration of reason is the glorification, even idealization of violence, Jesus the advocate of nonviolence becoming, for Billy Sunday, "Jesus the scrapper." Such anti-intellectualism feeds into an increasingly popular American sectarian politics in which cynical politicians both massage and encourage such forms of fundamentalism, and certainly never challenge it.[171] Such pandering has become common both among Democrats and Republicans, as Ronald Dworkin recently observed about the issue of gay marriage, an important issue in the presidential election of 2004:

> In spite of all the attention to the issue, neither candidate seemed even to notice, let alone reply to, the careful case made by Chief Justice Margaret Marshall of the Massachusetts Supreme Court that the widely shared principles of her state's constitution required her to decide that gay marriage be permitted

[168] See Mark A. Noll, *The Scandal of the Evangelical Mind* (Grand Rapids, Mich.: William B. Eerdmans, 1994).

[169] Hofstadter, *Anti-Intellectualism in American Life*, pp. 55–141.

[170] Noll, *Scandal of the Evangelical Mind*, p. 34.

[171] See, on this point, Kevin Phillips, *American Theocracy: The Peril and Politics of Radical Religion, Oil, and Borrowed Money in the 21st Century* (New York: Viking, 2006); Damon Linker, *The Theocons: Secular America under Siege* (New York: Doubleday, 2006).

> no matter how offensive that might seem to most people. Her decision was treated simply as an event that might be capitalized on by one side and might embarrass the other, with no apparent concern about whether her claim that established principles required that decision was right. After all the shouting and denouncing, there can be only a tiny number of American who have any idea what the legal argument was about.[172]

"Shouting and denouncing" bespeaks the pervasiveness of the problem I am describing and explaining: American politics at the level of football cheers and boos, the more aggressively masculine and polemical, the better.

American Protestant fundamentalism arose in a period of panic over issues of gender, religion, and culture, more generally, and historians noted its continuing appeal and force throughout the twentieth century, including what Richard Hofstadter observed: "the emergence of a kind of union, or at least a capacity for co-operation between Protestant and Catholic fundamentalists, who share a common Puritanism and a common mindless militancy on what they imagine to be political issues, which unite them in opposition to what they repetitively call Godless Communism."[173] It is not surprising that Protestant fundamentalism retained its appeal during a period of increasing national ferment on issues of race and gender,[174] and that it became culturally and politically important in a period quite like its period of origin, a cultural panic about issues of gender, in particular, that arose in response to the cumulative political and constitutional successes of the civil rights movement of the 1960s, followed by the anti–Vietnam War movement; the emergence of second wave, rights-based feminism; and the gay rights movement (Chapter 1).[175]

If the stability of patriarchy and its associated evils arises from the repudiation of sexual love (the love laws), the basis of resistance to patriarchy is a moral argument against the dehumanizing abridgement of basic human rights and a psychology moved by this moral argument because it protects and secures something rooted in the human psyche, namely loving sexual relationships, the sacrifice of which is at the center of the patriarchal heart of darkness. I have argued that what makes the movements of the 1960s and later so historically remarkable is that, for the first time in American constitutional history, their resistance to the evils of anti-Semitism, racism, sexism, and homophobia arises from an antipatriarchal ethical voice and that their constitutional successes reflect the impact on our public law of an emancipated ethical voice arising from resistance to the role the patriarchal love laws play in sustaining such irrational prejudices (Chapter 1).

172 Ronald Dworkin, *Is Democracy Possible Here? Principles for a New Political Debate* (Princeton, N.J.: Princeton University Press, 2006), pp. 5–6.

173 Hofstadter, *Anti-Intellectualism in American Life*, pp. 140–1.

174 See, for a good general study, Joel A. Carpenter, *Revive Us Again: The Reawakening of American Fundamentalism* (New York: Oxford University Press, 1997).

175 See Marsden, *Fundamentalism and American Culture*, pp. 231–60.

Such resistance rests on a normative conception of free and equal democratic voice that is, I believe, fundamentally at odds with the traditional place of patriarchy in our lives. Indeed, I would generalize the point in terms of a contradiction, both normative and psychological, between democracy and patriarchy. Constitutional democracy, as Americans understand and value it, has at its core a normative conception of respect for equal human rights that include, prominently, equal respect for free voice speaking from conviction, a right protected constitutionally in the United States by the guarantees of the First Amendment (including the protection of conscience from improper exercises of state power in a secular state and the protection of speech expressing conscience). Such guarantees of free and equal voice are in tension with the hierarchical conception of authority patriarchy requires, in which authority comes from the patriarch, not from the free and equal voice of each person. Indeed, the stability of patriarchy rests on the violent denial and abridgment of such voices, in particular, those voices that would most reasonably challenge its supposed authority.

If I am right about this tension, indeed contradiction between democracy and patriarchy, then resistance movements to the continuing role of patriarchy in our lives must be regarded as both democratic and democratizing: they both assert a basic right to equal voice and deliberatively seek to persuade others to eliminate patriarchal institutions that rest on an antidemocratic suppression of voice. What makes such resistance psychologically possible and appealing – in the face of the traditional power of patriarchy – is the way it gives expression to a free and equal voice that breaks the silence that patriarchal objectification imposed on the psyche, breaking the taboo on seeing, knowing, and speaking of one's love and lover. We resist because only through resistance can we come to know and realize the value of loving relationship in a human life.

I have already argued on these grounds that the Jews were such a resistance group, because they resisted conversion to Augustinian Christianity and held to the place of sexuality in their lives against Christian asceticism. I believe, however, that the argument is quite general: the radical abolitionist movement in the antebellum United States, with its resistance both to American racism and sexism, appealed not only to the moral argument against abridgment of basic human rights but also to an underlying psychology in which the resistance of women, white and black, to traditional patriarchy played a pivotal role, often empowering resistance as well in the men like William Lloyd Garrison who inspired and supported them.[176] And the reemergence of radical abolitionist arguments in the civil rights movements of the 1960s and later in the United States is powerfully explained in the terms of the analysis, including the impact of these movements on American constitutional law (Chapter 1). It is in light of the challenge of these constitutional developments to American patriarchy

176 See, for fuller defense of these claims, Richards, *Women, Gays, and the Constitution*.

that we can understand the reactionary force of religious fundamentalism in the United States.

The reactionary appeal of contemporary Protestant fundamentalism makes sense as an expression of the culture and psychology of an embattled manhood subject to these difficulties, taking the psychological form of a certitude about issues of gender and sexuality now clearly subject to reasonable doubt, perhaps more clearly so than ever before in American history. The issue of abortion and its constitutional protection in *Roe v. Wade* have provoked so sharp a reaction among Christian fundamentalists because of the symbolism about a woman's free sexuality that abortion expresses for them: "women are more promiscuous, they argue, because abortion allows them to avoid the consequences of their sin."[177] And gay and lesbian sexuality has been such a target for their anger because it involves forms of intimate sexual love that challenge patriarchal conceptions, patriarchal conceptions that have uncritically dominated Augustinian Christianity for much too long. The uncritical denunciation of gay marriage, to which Dworkin referred earlier, bespeaks the wider appeal of such patriarchal conceptions that so easily and mindlessly attack a group so easily demonized and so widely misunderstood and misrepresented.

The forms of sexism and homophobia, underlying such fundamentalist anger and denunciation, are contemporary expressions of the same culture and psychology within Augustinian Christianity that supported its anti-Semitism, resting also on a moral slavery directed precisely at reasonable voices that challenge that repressive conceptions of gender and sexuality central to Augustinian Christianity. The Jews of Israel play an important role in premillennial fundamentalist Bible interpretation, as prelude to the second coming, but their role continues to be one played according to a Christian script of their proper role and destiny, as continuing moral slaves of Christians. The same repressive impulses are now quite forthrightly directed by fundamentalist Protestants against both straight women and against gay men and lesbians, who challenge in their own voices and lives the continuing political force of patriarchal conceptions of gender that are both unreasonable and unjust.

Against the background of the history of reactionary Protestant fundamentalism that I have sketched, it is not surprising that some of its worst impulses of uncritical denunciation should be directed at gays and lesbians. American homophobia has been around for a very long time, and it has entered more deeply into the sense of American manhood than we would certainly like to think, a manhood that has long defined itself patriarchally, cutting men off from loving relationships with both women and men, and thus finding unthinkable what is, in fact, conspicuously around us – men and women who find themselves in passionate and

[177] Christel Manning, *God Gave Us the Right: Conservative Catholic, Evangelical Protestant, and Orthodox Jewish Women Grapple with Feminism* (New Brunswick, N.J.: Rutgers University Press, 1999), p. 199.

enduring love for each other, as individuals, unburdened by gender stereotypes that objectify and falsify. It is the supreme paradox that such love could be so falsified by a fundamentalist Protestant Christianity that includes, in the life and teachings of Jesus of Nazareth, so moving a plea for loving ethical relationships with those his culture conventionally regarded as unclean outcasts, precisely the role fundamentalists forge for gays and lesbians.[178] This is bad ethics and worse Christianity.

[178] See, on this point, Garry Wills, *What Jesus Meant* (New York: Viking, 2006), pp. 32–9.

CHAPTER 6

MORMON FUNDAMENTALISM

Mormon fundamentalism arises, like Protestant fundamentalism, very much within the framework of American Protestantism. It is, however, much earlier, arising from the ferment of early nineteenth-century American Protestantism, a ferment very much made possible by the role of the inalienable right to conscience in the argument of toleration that had been constitutionalized at the federal level by the First Amendment (including its free exercise and antiestablishment clauses) and that was increasingly accepted at the state level, as states abandoned established churches. But although Mormonism was made possible by the right to conscience, its exercise of that right took a very different turn from the role that the right to conscience played in other forms of more orthodox Protestantism. The role the right to conscience played in American Protestantism expressed itself in support for and elaboration of the constitutional principles that rested on that right and other such basic human rights. Mormonism, as we shall see, took a very different form, much more self-consciously and explicitly patriarchal than other forms of Protestantism and, for this reason, not only hostile to constitutional democracy but also explicitly theocratic. I begin with a discussion of the sources and nature of Mormon fundamentalism and then turn to a discussion of both the incoherence and the unreasonableness of its dominant contemporary form; finally, I examine the culture and psychology that supports such Mormon fundamentalism and conclude with some larger points about the role a hierarchically ordered male priesthood plays both in this and in the other forms of American fundamentalism examined in this work.

1. MORMON FUNDAMENTALISM

Mormonism is a source-based fundamentalism, like more orthodox Protestant fundamentalism, but its sources include not only the biblical texts, Hebrew and Christian, to which Protestants appeal but also at least three other texts that, for Mormons, fulfill and supplant the others. These texts are *The Book of*

Mormon, *Doctrine and Covenants*, and *The Pearl of Great Price*,[1] and they are almost entirely the work of Joseph Smith, the prophet who founded and led Mormonism until his murder in Carthage, Illinois, by a violent mob in 1844 (to be succeeded by Brigham Young, who led Mormons to Utah). There are few founders of religions about whom we know as much as Joseph Smith, and the best, most illuminating historical study remains Fawn M. Brodie's remarkable *No Man Knows My History*.[2] What makes this work so impressive is that it is a labor of brilliantly intelligent rational love, astute and penetrating in its treatment of historical materials but deeply sympathetic to Joseph Smith as the charismatic and appealing man he obviously was, a work that Brodie paid a real human price to write (she was excommunicated from the Mormon Church for writing it).[3] There are other useful books on Smith by good historians and more conventional Mormons than Brodie,[4] but they lack the human dimension that makes Brodie's treatment so compelling, penetrating, loving, and respectful.

Brodie places Joseph Smith very much in his historical context in upstate New York in the 1820s, where, consistent with the elaboration of the right to conscience and growing acceptance of the disestablishment of religion, Americans experienced a heady freedom in experimenting with new forms of religious life, including several new sects founded, remarkably, by women, including "Ann Lee, who called herself the reincarnated Christ and who with her celibate communists [the Shakers] had fled New England's wrath"[5] and, "twenty-five miles from Joseph Smith's home[,] . . . Jemima Wilkinson, the 'Universal Friend,' who thought herself to be the Christ . . . [and] governed her colony by revelations from heaven."[6] Male prophets also appeared:

> In the same decade that young Joseph announced his mission, William Miller proclaimed that Jesus would visit the earth in March 1843 and usher in the millennium. . . . John Humphrey Noyes was converted to the theory that the millennium had already begun, and laid plans for a community based on Bible communism, free love, and scientific propagation. Matthias strode about New York City brandishing a sword and seven-foot ruler, shouting that he had come to redeem the world.[7]

1 See Joseph Smith, *The Book of Mormon, Doctrine and Covnenants, The Pearl of Great Price* (Salt Lake City: Church of Jesus Christ of Latter-Day Saints, 1973).

2 Fawn M. Brodie, *No Man Knows My History: The Life of Joseph Smith* (New York: Vintage, 1995) (originally published 1945).

3 See, for a range of views, Newell G. Bringhurst, ed., *Reconsidering No Man Knows My History: Fawn M. Brodie and Joseph Smith in Retrospect* (Logan: Utah State University Press, 1996).

4 See Richard L. Bushman, *Joseph Smith and the Beginnings of Mormonism* (Urbana: University of Illinois Press, 1984); Richard Lyman Bushman, *Joseph Smith: Rough Stone Rolling* (New York: Alfred A. Knopf, 2005).

5 Brodie, *No Man Knows My History*, p. 12.

6 *Id.*, p. 13. See, on this remarkable period of ferment in American cultural history, Robert H. Abzug, *Cosmos Crumbling: American Reform and the Religious Imagination* (New York: Oxford University Press, 1994).

7 Brodie, *No Man Knows My History*, p. 15.

Both the teaching and the following of Matthias, who was to meet Joseph Smith, clarify the wider cultural roots that gave rise to both Matthias's and Smith's Mormonism: Matthias was particularly furious that women, like Ann Lee and Jemima Wilkinson and others, were beginning to exercise antipatriarchal religious authority,[8] usurping the traditional prerogative of the male Calvinist clergy.[9] His teaching correspondingly called for a return to the patriarchal model of the Old Testament prophets,[10] including arranged marriages[11] (he married off his own daughter to a follower[12]). Matthias, like Smith, was reacting to the Evangelical teaching of Charles Finney and his followers; in particular, both Matthias and Smith were "plebeian Christians [who] detested above all the Finneyites' tinkering with the traditional father-centered family and the traditional father-centered family and the customary, scripturally approved roles of men and women."[13] The reactionary psychology of patriarchy under threat underlying Matthias's teaching showed itself in his violence against both women and children,[14] his self-regard as having the legitimate power to take the wife of a follower as his own sexual partner and wife,[15] his indulgence in other sexual irregularities,[16] and that he possibly poisoned a follower.[17] Matthias's group "never became more than a marginal cult," but "[i]n the hands of more inspired and capable organizers – above all the Mormons Joseph Smith and Brigham Young – revelations not entirely unlike those of Matthias survived public hostility to carve out an important place among America's churches."[18]

What made Joseph Smith so different from Matthias was, as Fawn Brodie argues, the sympathetic and enthusiastically supportive audience he enjoyed for his ostensible revelations from most of his family, including his father and mother, and the remarkable young woman with whom he fell in love and married, Emma Smith, who faithfully transcribed some of Smith's earliest revelations (as he orally imparted them to her).[19] The life of Smith's parents, Lucy and Joseph Sr., had been ones largely of crushing economic failure and loss in a period of new economic and religious freedoms that made such freedoms all the more threatening and fearful. Smith's early life with Emma went little better. Smith's revelations were of a new patriarchal order in which he was the prophet of a

[8] See, on this point, Paul E. Johnson and Sean Wilentz, *The Kingdom of Matthias: A Story of Sex and Salvation in 19th-Century America* (New York: Oxford University Press, 1994), pp. 80, 82, 90, 92, 93.
[9] *Id.*, p. 55.
[10] *Id.*, p. 96.
[11] *Id.*, p. 119.
[12] *Id.*, pp. 124–5.
[13] *Id.*, p. 10.
[14] *Id.*, pp. 49–50, 59, 70–1, 113, 124.
[15] *Id.*, pp. 122–3.
[16] *Id.*, p. 123.
[17] *Id.*, pp. 138–41.
[18] *Id.*, p. 172.
[19] See, on this point, Brodie, *No Man Knows My History*, pp. 89–90, 97.

new American religion, based on the narrative of *The Book of Mormon*, which was to forge a new chosen people on the model of the lost tribes of Israel that had ended up in America, where they were defeated and destroyed. Smith's revelations deeply moved his broken parents because they showed that their own defeat and loss made sense as the birth of a new magical patriarchal order[20] in which men like his father would be leading patriarchs (as, in fact, Smith Sr. was in his son's new religion[21]), and women like his mother, Lucy, would find in her son's revelations validation of her own mystical personal religion, "intimate and homely, with God a ubiquitous presence invading dreams, provoking miracles, and blighting sinners' fields," a friendly God "[h]er children probably never learned to fear."[22] Both of Smith's parents had had their own mystical visions, which explains the role of visions in Smith's own life and the receptiveness of his family to them.[23] What Smith intuitively sensed was a need in his parents, his wife, himself, and many others, a need borne of new freedoms that not only destabilized traditional roles and expectations but also made loss all the more inexplicable and threatening. As Brodie sharply observes, "[Smith's] mission should be to those who found religious liberty a burden, who needed determinate ideas and familiar dogmas, and who fled from the solitude of independent thinking."[24] Once Smith embarked on this venture and received the faithful support and understanding of those he loved (in particular, the loving faith of his wife), there was no going back, as he himself was gradually transformed by their belief in him into a growing conviction that would, over time, become the "magnificent self-assurance"[25] of an earthy, sensual, successful man and leader:

> [People] built for him, preached for him, and made unbelievable sacrifices to carry out his orders, not only because they were convinced he was God's prophet, but also because they loved him as a man. They were as elated when he won a wrestling match as they were awed when he dictated a new revelation. They retold tales of his generosity and tenderness, marveling that he fed so many of the poor . . . , and that he entertained friend and enemy alike. He was a genial host, warmhearted and friendly to all comers, and fiercely loyal to his friends.[26]

Mormonism was self-consciously modeled on ancient Israel, the communal identity of a chosen people, patriarchally ruled and ordered at the level both of religion and of family life. Indeed, Smith worked out the logic of patriarchy more consistently than did his ancient Jewish models. Whereas the priesthood in ancient

[20] On the cultural background of Mormonism, see D. Michael Quinn, *Early Mormonism and the Magic World View*, rev. ed. (Salt Lake City: Signature Books, 1998).

[21] See Brodie, *No Man Knows My History*, p. 163.

[22] *Id.*, p. 5.

[23] *Id.*, pp. 411–12.

[24] See *id.*, p. 91.

[25] See *id.*, p. 294.

[26] *Id.*

Judaism was a hereditary clan, Smith democratically extended the priesthood to all men,[27] who are priest-patriarchs as heads of families and as the priesthood of the religion. But this apparently democratic priesthood is exclusively male and is theocratically ordered in terms of the ultimate patriarchal authority of Joseph Smith, including his authority over succession. Again, Smith remorselessly works out the logic of patriarchy, making very clear that he regards it as inconsistent with democracy either in religion or in politics.[28] It is when, consistent with his repudiation of democracy, he ordered the printing presses of opponents destroyed that Americans came to see and increasingly war on a theocratic religion so hostile to constitutional democracy.[29]

But Smith's greatest problem, both internally among fellow Mormons and externally with the wider American society, arose from another of his remorseless elaborations of the logic of patriarchy, his doctrine and practice of plural wives, or polygamy. Smith's sense of mission arose, as we have seen, from the enthusiastic support of his own family. His own earthy, intimate sense of religion was imparted to him through the mystical personal religion of his mother, God as a friend to the sources of human achievement and happiness, including material prosperity and sexual fulfillment in family life. And Smith's sense of himself as a prophet arose indispensably from the loving faith in him and his mission of his wife, Emma. No background could be further from the ascetic renunciation of sexuality and loving relationship central, as we have seen, to Augustinian Christianity, and Smith, for this reason, abandoned original sin and its associated negative view of human sexual desire.[30]

Smith abandoned without apparent sense of loss or compunction the Augustinian background that we have seen to be so important in understanding the fundamentalisms of both norm-based Catholic new natural law and source-based Protestant literalism. But this almost carefree abandonment, although it embraces a sense of the good of sexuality much more indebted to traditional Judaism than to Christianity, does not question the traditional role of patriarchy in orthodox Christianity. Indeed, Smith's own rewriting of the Genesis narrative quite clearly, like Augustine and later orthodox Christianity, places responsibility for the Fall squarely on Adam's violation of his patriarchal duty, namely listening to his wife:

> And unto Adam, I, the Lord God, said: Because thou hast hearkened unto the voice of they wife, and has eaten of the fruit of the tree of which I commanded thee, saying – Thou shalt not eat of it, cursed shall be the ground for they sake; and in sorrow shalt though eat of it all the days of they life.[31]

27 *Id.*, pp. 99–100.

28 See, on this point, *id.*, pp. 285, 364.

29 See, on this point, *id.*, pp. 367–79.

30 See, on this point, *id.*, pp. 187–93.

31 Joseph Smith, *The Pearl of Great Price*, *Moses*, pp. 9–10.

If anything, Smith adopts a more extreme form of patriarchy, indeed more extreme than the form of it Smith took as a model in the polygamy of the patriarchs of the Hebrew Bible (Jacob's polygamous marriages particularly absorbed Smith[32]). Smith's revelation of plural marriage, a perquisite of the highest Mormon priesthood (including himself), includes the right to take the wives of others, which was not a right of the Jewish patriarchs. The difference, of course, is the kind of ultimate patriarchal authority Smith arrogated to himself and a few others, not subject to any other authority.

What is quite remarkable about Mormonism in the history of religion is the way a conception of patriarchy is worked out with such remorseless logic, one that precisely arose from a repudiation of the less patriarchal forms of religion that were developing around it.[33] What made this psychologically and normatively possible for Smith was his own homely earthiness, including his sensuality and love of sexual pleasure as male perquisites, and his absolute conviction of the patriarchal essence of his new religion and his own absolute patriarchal authority over its deepest meaning. Smith had by now enjoyed the faithful support not only of his family of origin and his beloved wife but also of a movement of devoted followers, who had followed and obeyed him despite many reverses and the growing hostility of the surrounding Christian culture, in which the right to conscience and the argument of toleration played roles it had ceased to play among Mormons. His intoxicating sense of success, rooted in the earthy materialism and sensuality of his message that appealed to many, was that of a man of considerable physical charm ruling communities "overflowing with women who idolized him"[34] and "in 1835, after eight years of marriage to a woman somewhat his senior, Joseph began to yearn for variety and adventure."[35] In the best of circumstances, propensities of male sexual narcissism are difficult for men even to recognize, less alone criticize or regulate. Smith, a highly sexual and charismatically attractive man, yielded utterly to those propensities and lived them out lavishly, finding in the logic of patriarchy "that for a prophet it is easier to change marriage laws than to contravene them."[36]

The logic of patriarchy placed a hierarchical priesthood of fathers over all others and authorized a sexual life consistent with such hierarchical perquisites. Women exist not as moral agents in patriarchy but rather to serve and support patriarchally defined ends, including arranged marriage for dynastic or other such ends. Smith's conception of his own absolute and ultimate patriarchal authority, combined with his robust sexual interests in women not his wife, expressed itself in a revelation of plural marriage that he kept secret for a long period

32 Brodie, *No Man Knows My History*, p. 298.

33 On Smith's repeated references to his establishing the true patriarchal order of marriage, see *id.*, pp. 252, 297–9, 300, 340–1.

34 *Id.*, p. 186.

35 *Id.*, p. 187.

36 *Id.*

(indeed, publicly lying and getting others to endorse his lies) but acted on, taking possibly as many as fifty such wives, some already married to other men.[37] As one would expect in such an extreme expression of religious patriarchy, women's voice and interests were not sought or consulted, but women were told what their place was in the divine order required of them, namely plural marriage to Smith or one of his circle of leaders. The many women who accepted that role regarded it as their religious duty and did their patriarchal duty as Smith, their adored leader for so long, defined it for them.[38] Smith's hold over such women and their husbands and/or fathers was so strong that they would agree, one father breaking with his daughter over her refusal to become one of Smith's wives.[39] Like parents in Catholic families whose sons were abused by priests, fathers regarded Smith as the true father, aligning themselves with him rather than with their children.[40] All these marriages, like other marriages by Mormon priests, were regarded as celestial marriages for eternity and ordained by God (having children, so allowing yet-unborn souls to be saved). "The endowment ceremony [in Mormon ritual] was essentially fertility worship"[41]; its secret rituals "transformed the Mormon Church into a mystery cult."[42] It was the religious mandate behind celestial marriages that led them to be categorically distinguished by Smith from prostitution or adultery, which were morally condemned with the same ardor as more conventional Christians condemned such acts.[43] Because the women believers thus propositioned were told by Smith that refusal was religiously damnable, their consent was, to say the least, coerced and exploitative.[44]

Smith's own marriage to Emma had once been unusually loving and devoted, but plural marriage, as Smith defended and practiced it, inflicted the same traumatic loss on women that patriarchal institutions always did. This psychology of loss was covered over by the idealization of self-sacrifice and self-abnegation by women. One Mormon politician called this women's purification:

> Every law of the gospel has a trial connected with it, and the higher the law the greater the trial; and as we ascend nearer and nearer to the Lord our God we shall have greater trials to content with in purifying ourselves before Him. He has helped us this far.... [W]hen our sisters seek unto Him He ... gives them strength to overcome their selfishness and jealousy.... You, sister, whose

[37] See *id.*, pp. 334–47.

[38] See, on this point, Sarah Barringer Gordon, *The Mormon Question: Polygamy and Constitutional Conflict in Nineteenth Century America* (Chapel Hill: University of North Carolina Press, 2002), p. 96.

[39] Brodie, *No Man Knows My History*, pp. 321–2.

[40] See, on this point, Nicholas Bamforth and David A. J. Richards, *Patriarchal Religion, Sexuality, and Gender: A Critique of New Natural Law* (Cambridge: Cambridge University Press, 2008), pp. 326–7.

[41] Brodie, *No Man Knows My History*, p. 279.

[42] *Id.*, p. 282.

[43] See, on this point, *id.*, p. 373.

[44] *Id.*, pp. 337–8.

> husbands have taken other wives, can you not bear testimony that the principle has purified your hearts, made you less selfish, brought you nearer to God and given you power you never had before?[45]

Such purification, as Sarah Gordon acutely observes, "had the effect of distancing husbands and wives. Their focus turned to celestial glory rather than earthly satisfaction."[46] Some Mormon women, notably Smith's wife, Emma, never accepted polygamy, and her spirited resistance confronted Smith with an experience rare for him, the authority of a loving woman's voice challenging both his teaching and his life.[47]

We have earlier seen the psychological roots of patriarchy, the traumatic loss of real relationship leading to identification with patriarchal voice expressing itself in violence against any challenge to its authority (the Gilligan-Richards thesis, in Introduction). We can discern these psychological roots here, as the traumatic break in relationships expressed itself in Smith's endorsement of violence against his enemies, as "a second Mohammed."[48] Smith, for example, may have ordered the assassination of Lilburne Boggs, governor of Missouri (the attempt resulted in injuries, not death[49]). The same anger was now directed at women like Emma who raised their voices in resistance in precisely the way that elicits patriarchal violence. Smith had the revelation of plural marriage put in written form in 1843 in what is now section 132 of *Doctrine and Covenants*, but Mormon leaders followed Smith in continuing publicly to deny polygamy between 1835 and 1852, when it was finally admitted.[50] Smith's section 132 appealed to the authority of the ancient Jewish patriarchs and ended specifically by ordering Emma to agree or perish: "And I command mine handmaid, Emma Smith, to abide and cleave unto my servant Joseph and to none else. But if she will not abide this commandment she shall be destroyed, saith the Lord; for I am the Lord they God, and will destroy her if she abide not in my law."[51] There is something touching and vulnerable in seeing the thundering certitudes of this prophet of the religion of patriarchy combined with a plea that his wife remain loyal to him (as she did until his death) and putting in God's mouth (not speaking in his own voice) a threat of destruction of the woman he once loved and may still have loved. We need to remind ourselves, at the end, that, during this period, Smith did acknowledge doubts about how and why his mission should have been taken so seriously,[52] and

45 Quoted in Gordon, *Mormon Question*, p. 101.
46 Gordon, *Mormon Question*, p. 101.
47 Brodie, *No Man Knows My History*, pp. 340–2.
48 *Id.*, p. 230.
49 *Id.*, pp. 323, 330–2.
50 *Id.*, p. 321.
51 Smith, *Doctrine and Covenants*, p. 244.
52 See Brodie, *No Man Knows My History*, pp. 295–6.

that he was, at the last, himself the victim of homicidal violence and, earlier, of tarring and feathering.[53]

It is important to keep in mind that the Mormons lived largely in a close-knit, highly regulated community with one another, a community that had bonded around the patriarchal, theocratically defined authority accorded Joseph Smith and a small circle of leaders around him that brooked no dissent. It is a feature of the social psychology of such groups that the apparent disconfirmation of the prophecies central to its belief system may, in appropriate circumstances of support from other believers, lead to ways of rationalizing such apparent disconfirmation as consistent with some other, perhaps larger, prophetic truth.[54] In such circumstances, disconfirmation may strengthen belief. The murder of Joseph Smith was interpreted by his followers as a martyrdom in the long tradition of such martyrs in the history of more orthodox Christianity, and the unrelenting persecution to which Mormons were subject further supported this interpretation for the mainstream group of believers who were to follow the leadership of Brigham Young to Utah.[55] Smith's wife, Emma, notably refused to follow Young, in part because Young accepted her husband's revelation of plural marriage.

Mormonism, in the form Smith founded and Young organized and defended in Utah, centered on a fundamentalism based on the source-based revelations of Joseph Smith as recorded in the three texts he left to posterity, *The Book of Mormon*, *Doctrine and Covenants*, and *The Pearl of Great Price*. What is quite central to this fundamentalism is the extreme form of patriarchy that Smith came to regard as at the heart of his revelation, one that established a theocratic religion and politics, ruled by a hierarchically ordered male priesthood, and an associated family life of celestial marriage in which, as we have seen, polygamy played an important role. The subordination of women to the authority of men was central, requiring women to live as polygamous wives bearing and raising children in what was essentially a modern fertility cult. Women had value solely within this order of things, sexually available to men, as fertile wives and mothers of children. Nothing was more crucial or more institutionally important to Mormon fundamentalism than its hierarchical male priesthood, and its total repudiation of the idea – already very much present when Smith formed his distinctive views – that the right to conscience, so central to Protestant Christianity, extended on equal terms to women, including the right of women themselves to be ministers or priests

53 *Id.*, p. 119.

54 See, for a general treatment of this phenomenon, Leon Festinger, Henry W. Riecken, and Stanley Schachter, *When Prophecy Fails: A Social and Psychological Study of a Modern Group That Predicted the Destruction of the World* (New York: Harper Torchbooks, 1964) (originally published in 1956).

55 See, for Mormon official statements to this effect, Smith, *Doctrine and Covenants*, pp. 252–6. See also R. Laurence Moore, *Religious Outsiders and the Making of Americans* (New York: Oxford University Press, 1986), pp. 25–47.

or even prophetesses (as Ann Lee and Jemima Wilkinson and Anne Hutchinson had been).

2. THE UNREASONABLENESS OF MORMON FUNDAMENTALISM

We must assess Mormon fundamentalism as it currently exists, as the religious and political force it is in contemporary circumstances. An important aspect of its patriarchal character in the nineteenth century had been its endorsement of polygamy. What, then, are we to make of the apparent abandonment of the institutional Mormonism founded by Joseph Smith and Brigham Young of polygamy? Its repudiation is expressed by one of the few bits of the three texts authored by Joseph Smith that are not by Smith, namely the "Official Declaration," which now ends *Doctrine and Covenants*. The declaration, issued in 1890 by Wilford Woodruff, in his capacity as president of the Church of Jesus Christ of Latter-Day Saints, begins by noting press reports that the Mormon Church had recently solemnized some forty or more plural marriages. Woodruff attests that the charges are false and that the one such marriage alleged to have taken place in the Endowment House in Salt Lake City, Utah, was done without his knowledge and, on learning of it, he ordered the Endowment House taken down. Woodruff then explains:

> Inasmuch as laws have been enacted by Congress forbidding plural marriages, which laws have been pronounced constitutional by the court of last resort, I hereby declare my intention to submit to those laws, and to use my influence with the members of the Church over which I preside to have them do likewise.
>
> There is nothing in my teachings to the Church or in those of my associates, during the time specified, which can be reasonably construed to inculcate or encourage polygamy; and when any Elder of the Church has used language which appeared to convey any such teaching, he has been promptly removed. And I now publicly declare that my advice to the Latter-day Saints is to refrain from any marriage forbidden by the law of the land.[56]

The declaration ends with a motion, unanimously adopted, by the church at the assembly of its General Conference, accepting the "declaration concerning plural marriages as authoritative and binding," appealing to Woodruff's authority as "the only man on the earth at the present time who holds the keys of the sealing ordinances."[57]

The history of the crisis and conflict between institutional Mormonism and American constitutionalism between 1852 and 1890 has been well told by Sarah Gordon,[58] and Woodruff clearly phrases his "Official Declaration" as compelled

[56] Smith, *Doctrine and Covenants*, p. 257.
[57] *Id.*
[58] See Gordon, *Mormon Question*.

by authoritative judgments of the U.S. Supreme Court, which refused constitutionally to protect Mormon polygamy. Consistent with Mormon theocracy, acceptance of the declaration is justified on the basis of Woodruff's hierarchical authority, standing by legitimate succession in the shoes of the prophet himself, Joseph Smith.

Woodruff offers no theological argument of any kind, which has certainly led at least forty thousand Mormon fundamentalists to continue the practice of polygamy, sometimes inflicting murder on women whose crime was raising their voices in resistance to such practices,[59] and recently being prosecuted in Texas for the sexual abuse of young girls.[60] It is historically quite plausible that celestial marriage was at the very heart of Joseph Smith's revelation of a remorselessly consistent patriarchal religion,[61] and thus interpretively to construe Woodruff's declaration as, at best, an effort to preserve what could be saved from constitutionally legitimate destruction in Mormonism, namely all its institutions of patriarchal religion that were not in conflict with constitutional principles, including separation of church and state, or not within the legitimate constitutional power of the state or federal government to forbid. The state of constitutional law, at the time of Woodruff's declaration, allowed the state to forbid polygamy because American courts had come to accept the judgment of Francis Lieber that polygamy was inconsistent with sound principles of liberal government.[62] There is reason to doubt whether American hostility to Smith's Mormonism represented the clear and coherent working out of anything like the abolitionist feminist view that sexism was and should be as much a moral and constitutional evil as racism, a view that was to inform American constitutional interpretation only much later (see Chapter 1). John Stuart Mill, an advocate of equality like the abolitionist feminists, had indeed condemned the hypocrisy of the American persecution of Mormons because it condemned the Mormons for a sexism of which Americans were mindlessly guilty throughout their cultural and political life (including depriving women of the right to vote).[63] But in the admittedly incoherently democratic and patriarchal features of mainstream American common sense of the late nineteenth century, Mormon polygamy had so provocatively challenged this common sense that our highest courts had come to regard it as legitimately subject to state condemnation.

On this interpretation of Woodruff's declaration, the supreme patriarch of the Mormon Church was cutting his losses. It would have been very much in the

59 See Jon Krakauer, *Under the Banner of Heaven: A Story of Violent Faith* (New York: Anchor Books, 2004).

60 See Stephanie Simon, "Legal Fights Strain Polygamist Sect," *Wall Street Journal*, May 11, 2009, at A5.

61 See, e.g., Gordon, *Mormon Question*, pp. 28, 96–107.

62 See, on this point, Gordon, *Mormon Question*, pp. 66, 81, 140–1, 272n47.

63 See, on this point, David A. J. Richards, *Women, Gays, and the Constitution: The Grounds for Feminism and Gay Rights in Culture and Law* (Chicago: University of Chicago Press, 1998), p. 451.

temporizing spirit of Joseph Smith himself, who repeatedly lied and convinced others to lie publicly, that polygamy was not in fact a Mormon tenet during a period when it clearly was. If Smith could so shrewdly lie, waiting for the day when he could go public, why couldn't or wouldn't Woodruff do something similar, holding, as he does, "the keys of the sealing ordinances,"[64] ordinances secretly imparted to his leadership circle by Smith himself. For these reasons, Harold Bloom offers the following prediction: "I cheerfully do prophesy that some day, not too far on in the twenty-first century, the Mormons will have enough political and financial power to sanction polygamy again. Without it, in some form or other, the complete vision of Joseph Smith never can be fulfilled."[65]

There is a constitutional problem, however, with Bloom's argument: American constitutional law has come to accept the view of the abolitionist feminists that sexism is a constitutional evil for the same reasons as racism (Chapter 1).[66] It is thus no longer hypocritical, as Mill argued, but a matter of constitutional principle to argue that polygamy violates the now-compelling secular state purpose of reinforcing the subjection of women. Polygamy, as traditionally understood and certainly as the Mormons understood it, reinforced such unjust gender roles and thus cannot be regarded as a constitutionally reasonable form of intimate life consistent with these principles. As Nancy Rosenblum has observed:

> Despite rare exceptions, patriarchy has been the dominant form of polygamy. It has never had its basis in reciprocity or friendship, not even ideally. Its justification has never been the expansiveness of affection or cooperation. It has rested on ideological or spiritual accounts of male authority and female subjection, on status associated with numbers of wives, and of course on beliefs about male sexual power (or the need to temper women's sexual power) and male entitlements. It is doubtful that the known doctrinal supports for polygamy could be rehabilitated and made congruent with democratic sex.[67]

Compelling secular arguments of gender equality thus reasonably support in contemporary circumstances the limitation of the right to marriage to monogamous couples.

But it is precisely such constitutional developments that render substantively unreasonable not only Mormon polygamy but also the forms of Mormon fundamentalism that remain very much alive. The patriarchal subordination of women is the heart of the matter, a doctrine Smith announced in a November 1835 public statement: "Wives, submit yourselves unto your husbands, as unto the Lord, for the husband is the head of the wife, even as Christ is the head of the

[64] Smith, *Doctrine and Covenants*, p. 257.

[65] Harold Bloom, *The American Religion: The Emergence of the Post-Christian Nation* (New York: Touchstone, 1992), p. 123.

[66] See, on this point, Richards, *Women, Gays, and the Constitution*, pp. 199–287.

[67] See Nancy L. Rosenblum, "Democratic Sex: *Reynolds v. U.S.*, Sexual Relations and Community," in *Sex, Preference, and Family: Essays on Law and Nature*, ed. David M. Estlund and Martha C. Nussbaum (New York: Oxford University Press, 1997), p. 80.

Church. . . . Wives, submit yourselves unto your own husbands, as it is fit in the Lord."[68] It is this subordination that excludes women from the priesthood and subjects them to the authority of their priest-husbands or priest-fathers, and these men in turn to the authority of their male superiors in the hierarchy, with Joseph Smith's successor at the pinnacle. Women's status is patriarchally defined by their roles as fertile wives and mothers, expressed through the Mormon theological doctrine of "gaining entry to life for the spirits of the unborn,"[69] which explains contemporary Mormon condemnation of both abortion and contraception, and its opposition to forms of gay and lesbian life. Its opposition to gay marriage has been particularly strident and effective, as Mormon money apparently tipped the balance in the California referendum banning gay marriage.[70]

Smith's deeply patriarchal religious imagination expressed itself in the brooding sense of the presence and weight on us of the unbaptized dead (whom Mormons regard themselves as under obligation to baptize[71]), as well as the unborn, whom Mormons have an obligation to bring to life and baptize as Mormons. It is through giving life and weight and presence to such theologically imagined metaphysical beings that Smith rationalized to himself and others sectarian demands that were archaic and anachronistic even when he lived, and that are certainly so today.

What makes these source-based fundamentalist views so unreasonable today is precisely their failure to take seriously women (whether straight or lesbian) or gay men as the bearers and sources of human rights. What gave these fundamentalist views some appeal in the early nineteenth century was an American religious and political culture that was still, as Mill observed, quite patriarchal (albeit less patriarchal than the Mormons), though the Mormon valuation of sexual love in the nineteenth century evidently extended to same-sex relationships.[72] As American constitutional and ethical values have become less patriarchal, Mormonism publicly limited the institution (polygamy) that most conspicuously challenged such values but aligned itself with other patriarchal features of American culture, including the adoption of expressly homophobic views that arguably are foreign to its earlier traditions.[73] Mormon assimilation to mainstream American values has included the abandonment of some of its worst and best features. In contemporary circumstances, the residual fundamentalism of Mormonism is even more incoherent and substantively unreasonable.

[68] Brodie, *No Man Knows My History*, pp. 182–3.

[69] Bloom, *American Religion*, p. 118.

[70] See Mark Schoofs, "Mormons Boost Antigay Marriage Effort," *Wall Street Journal*, Sept. 20–1, 2008, at A8; Jesse McKinley and Kirk Johnson, "Mormons Tipped Scale in Ban on Gay Marriage," *New York Times*, Nov. 15, 2008, at pp. A1, A11.

[71] See, on this point, Bloom, *American Religion*, pp. 118–23.

[72] See, on this point, D. Michael Quinn, *Same-Sex Dynamics among Nineteenth-Century Americans: A Mormon Example* (Urbana: University of Illinois Press, 1996).

[73] See *id.*

It is incoherent because, of all the alleged fundamentalist interpretations of Christianity we have studied, it is the most at odds with any reasonable understanding of the life and teachings of Jesus of Nazareth, which were, as we have seen, remarkably antipatriarchal (Chapter 5). And in its contemporary mainstream form, Mormonism incoherently insists on its patriarchal character but without the doctrine of celestial marriage that was at the heart of Joseph Smith's revelation of patriarchal religion, as, for Smith, men could become gods only through such marriage to women who understood their ordained role as the moral slaves of such gods.[74] This is the Mormonism not of its founder but of public relations, "Mormonism lite." If Mormons cannot reasonably live by their prophet's life and teachings, they need to be wholly more critical of the role patriarchal assumptions continue to play in their lives and convictions. Their prophet was nothing if not authentic and full hearted. They are neither.

And Mormonism is substantively unreasonable because it fails to respect the most important and enduring constitutional values Americans enjoy, namely the basic human rights of all persons, including women and gay men. Certainly, its fundamentalist views on gender and sexuality cannot today be a constitutionally reasonable basis for laws and policies.

3. PATRIARCHAL CULTURE AND PSYCHOLOGY: THE ROLE OF A PRIESTHOOD

We have now seen, in the norm-based fundamentalism of new natural law and the source-based fundamentalisms of both Evangelical Protestantism and Mormonism, the importance of a patriarchal all-male priesthood, one that crucially excludes from the ministry or priesthood or role of prophet any women or man who would challenge patriarchy. Despite all the other differences among all these approaches, an all-male priesthood organizes and explains their common fundamentalism in contemporary circumstances. It is because of the continuing role of an all-male priesthood in all these ostensibly Christian religions that, despite all their other differences, they converge on a fundamentalist certainty about gender and sexuality, including the subordination of women and the intrinsic wrongness of contraception, abortion, and all forms of nonprocreational sex – most notably, gay and lesbian sex. If this can happen with Christianity, whose founder was so critical of patriarchal institutions and attitudes, presumably it can happen with any religion when its teachings are placed in the hands of an all-male priesthood. We should recall that patriarchy is defined in terms of the hierarchical authority of fathers as priests over women and girls as well as men and boys. What we have come to see, in the course of our closer study of three forms of Christian fundamentalism, is not only the role such patriarchy plays in the fundamentalist reaction to the developments of Chapter 1 but also the underlying psychology of

74 See, on this point, Bloom, *American Religion*, p. 108.

traumatic loss that, in each case, supports a personal and political psychology that regards patriarchy as in the nature of things, indeed as God's law.

What makes the study of the life and teaching of Joseph Smith so illuminating, from this perspective, is the insight it gives us into the psyche and relationships that both give rise to and sustain a patriarchal culture. Religious patriarchy in ancient Judaism, as we have seen, never existed in the form Joseph Smith invented, and under the circumstances of the elaboration of the Protestant right to conscience and the argument for toleration in the early days of the American republic, religious patriarchy in Protestantism was itself in question. Smith and his family had suffered losses from the new religious and economic freedoms of the period, including the loss of the traditional patriarchal authority of the learned Calvinist ministry, as new experiments in religious life arose from the right to conscience that was increasingly constitutionally entrenched, including religions founded by women. It is the sense of his own father's humiliating failures and losses and his own early failures that set the stage for Smith's revelations, in which Smith, as prophet and ultimate patriarch, imagined and elaborated over time the extreme religious patriarchy that is Mormonism. Smith's revelations both expressed and confirmed the visions both his father and mother had experienced but gave those visions a new form and object, in which Smith and his father had the authority of the ancient Jewish patriarchs, and Smith's mother and wife would see a son and husband who were not broken, humiliated, and lost but the final authority on a new way of life. Rather extreme gender idealization covers and rationalizes the losses Smith and his family had experienced, as Smith defined a new idealized identity for himself as a patriarchal man and for his mother and wife as patriarchal women.

An idealized patriarchal priesthood has psychological appeal against the background of such a sense of traumatic loss. The traumatic loss experienced by Smith and his family is, from this perspective, like that experienced by Augustine. Although Smith and Augustine could not, in other respects, be more different, what they both experienced was a devastating traumatic loss, and both found in an idealized sense of themselves as patriarchal father-priests a hierarchical authority that expressed itself in violence against any expression of dissent. Although Augustine's path called for sexual asceticism, Smith's clearly did not, but it did require a patriarchal authority that led him to break with the wife whom he had once loved and who had long loved and supported him, identifying himself with a patriarchally imagined voice endorsing exploitative and coercive sex with women. Smith could no more live in equal relationship to a free woman than could Augustine. It was such a patriarchal structuring of relationship that both required and fed off the loss of loving relationship, and that was so threatened, as Protestant American fundamentalists certainly were, by gender equality.

What Smith remarkably brought to his new patriarchal religion was a very American sense of the earthy comforts of material well-being, achievement, and sexual pleasure over which Augustinian Christianity had cast a pall of doubt and even guilt. Unburdened by these doubts, Smith unleashed and explored his sexual psyche as a patriarchal man, following out with remorseless psychological and normative logic a patriarchal conception of marriage that gave the support of heaven to the demands of his sexual desires for women, celestial marriage.

What made this religion enduring, in a way comparable religious cults arising in this period (Matthias) were not, was the creation of a hierarchically ordered priesthood with authority over doctrine and rituals; a priesthood and an organizational framework that gave Mormonism a structure of collective authority that in turn gave it stability and continuity; and in view of its prophetic origins, even a doctrine of continuing prophecy that could, when necessary, adjust the claim of the religion to the most exigent demands of the surrounding political and constitutional culture (publicly abandoning even polygamy, and later its racism). It is the capacity of Mormonism to adjust to and even define the patriotic values of material prosperity, competitive achievement, and sensual family life of American culture that led Harold Bloom, following Leo Tolstoy, to call Mormonism the American religion.[75]

But there is one value in American constitutional culture to which Mormonism has always been antagonistic, though its creation was made possible through it, namely the role of the right to conscience and the argument for toleration in American constitutionalism. The radical patriarchy of Joseph Smith was deeply intolerant and, because theocratic, antidemocratic. The adjustments of Mormonism to American constitutional culture have been considerable, which shows how increasingly powerful and authoritative that constitutional culture is. But contemporary Mormon fundamentalism places it at odds with the development of constitutional principles that increasingly question patriarchy (Chapter 1). It is not surprising that Mormonism, born in the revival of an archaic religious patriarchy, should react so savagely and unjustly to these developments. What we need, however, to see clearly is how deep the clash is – as deep, surely, as the clash of nineteenth-century Mormon polygamy with American constitutionalism. Only now, contemporary Mormonism, which strives to be mainstream American, is no longer the unjustly persecuted but itself one of the persecutors, aroused, as the culture and psychology of patriarchy always is, to repress the voice and authority of free men and women who raise reasonable doubts about patriarchy.

What Mormon fundamentalism shares with Catholic and Protestant fundamentalism is this reactionary impulse. Their common fundamentalism is the certainty they ascribe to the subordination of women and to moral judgments about the wrongness of contraception, abortion, and nonprocreational sex. Their common vehicle is an all-male patriarchal priesthood. What explains both, however, is the patriarchal psychology of traumatic loss, which expresses itself in an identification with the gender stereotypes of manhood and womanhood that

75 See Bloom, *American Religion*, pp. 16, 21, 97.

rationalize both their common fundamentalism and vehicle. Most important, my account of the psychology of patriarchy – both personal and political – explains why claims of gender equality are regarded as so threatening and indeed are the targets of a repressive violence that is not supported by reason. It is this psychology that explains how fundamentalist views that are, on internal and external grounds, so unreasonable can thus enjoy the psychological appeal that they do. If I am right about this, it shows that such views are – notwithstanding what fundamentalists think – matters of faith and not reason. It also shows something of extraordinary importance for American constitutional law, a matter we will examine in Part III.

PART III

FUNDAMENTALISM IN LAW AND RELIGION

CHAPTER 7

PATRIARCHAL ROOTS OF CONSTITUTIONAL FUNDAMENTALISM

My argument in Part II has shown how three theologically quite different forms of Christianity have come to share a fundamentalism in matters of gender and sexuality that is, on internal and external grounds, unreasonable and thus lacks a rational basis to justify laws and policies in a secular democracy like ours. It is also a common feature of all these religious fundamentalisms that they do not see themselves as unreasonable, so it has been a matter of argument, the argument of this book, to show that, on examination, they are unreasonable.

The gap between their self-understanding and reality raises a psychological question: what psychology disables otherwise reasonable people from not seeing the character of their own views? There is a psychology that explains the gap; namely the three forms of religious fundamentalism share a common patriarchal psychology of traumatic loss of real relationship leading to identification with a patriarchally imagined voice that expresses itself in violence against any voice that would raise reasonable doubts about the justice of patriarchy. Such patriarchy expresses itself in an all-male hierarchical priesthood, which limits authority in matters of religion and ethics to highly patriarchal men. Such patriarchal arrangements rest on the repression of the dissenting voices of those who might raise reasonable doubts about such arrangements, including, of course, free straight and lesbian women as well as gay men. I have called moral slavery the status of subordination in which such groups are held under patriarchy.

There is a further important question to which we must now turn: how and why have these otherwise-disparate forms of religious fundamentalism come to share a common political position and to enjoy the kind of political support they have had? I answer this question in this chapter in two stages. First, I offer an account of how and why they have formed a political alliance along the lines they have. Second, I offer an explanation of how and why they have been as successful as they have been, arguing that 'originalism' in constitutional interpretation has been the ideological mask of neutrality that has allowed fundamentalists to enjoy the support they have. On examination, 'originalists' offer a view of constitutional interpretation that is as unreasonable in law as fundamentalism is in religion.

'Originalism' has enjoyed the appeal it has as a defense of patriarchal values now under reasonable attack. The unreasonableness of 'originalism' is not seen because it expresses the same patriarchal psychology that disables religious fundamentalists from appreciating the unreasonableness of their views. Its advocates do not see its problems as a theory of constitutional interpretation because, as I show, they are themselves psychologically in thrall to forms of fundamentalist religion that they are unable to question but consider themselves as required to defend aggressively against what they see as illegitimate threats to their authority as patriarchal men.

1. THE POLITICAL ALLIANCE OF RELIGIOUS FUNDAMENTALISTS

The three forms of fundamentalist religion I have discussed now at some length (Catholic new natural law, Protestant fundamentalists, and Mormons) disagree on so much that the question naturally arises as to how and why they have come to agree, as they have, on matters of gender and sexuality in a way they have (endorsing the subordination of women and morally condemning contraception, abortion, and gay and lesbian sex acts and lifestyles). What I believe my argument has shown is that their convergence on these issues has little to do with their religion in general or their Christianity in particular, for their views are so unreasonable even as interpretations of their religions that many deeply religious people have difficulties connecting their religious beliefs to the normative judgments that fundamentalists ascribe with such apodictic certainty to such religious beliefs and traditions. What, then, explains their convergence in normative judgments? What I believe my argument has shown is that the convergence arises from the role patriarchy has uncritically played in the interpretive attitude these fundamentalists have brought to their religious traditions: they have come to agree on these matters because they uncritically bring a patriarchal lens to bear on their religious traditions.

But fundamentalists have gone well beyond such convergence in religious conviction: they have converged as well on a political alliance with one another that has aggressively sought to bring their convictions to bear on American politics and law, indeed, even on judicial appointments to our courts, in particular, the U.S. Supreme Court. As I have argued at some length, it cannot be because their common views on matters of sexuality and gender are reasonable, because their normative arguments are, in fact, unreasonable both on internal and on external grounds. What can explain their failure to see this, and their aggressive attack on the now constitutionally recognized rights of fellow Americans (e.g., a woman's right to an abortion protected by *Roe v. Wade*)? I have argued that what explains this development is its underlying patriarchal psychology. Because religious fundamentalists have so uncritically interpreted their religious traditions through a patriarchal lens, they have come to see cases like *Roe* and related cases recognizing the constitutional rights of gays and lesbians (*Romer v. Evans* and

Lawrence v. Texas) as threats to their forms of patriarchal religion. Like all such threats to a patriarchally defined sense of honor, fundamentalists have aggressively mobilized to repress the antipatriarchal voices that have been accorded the political and constitutional resonances and successes they have enjoyed.[1]

There is, however, a further question, to which we must now turn: how and why have such fundamentalists enjoyed the level of political and even constitutional support they have? If their normative views are as unreasonable as I have argued they are, why have they enjoyed the level of support they have, as seen, for example, in the important political role they played in the elections and administrations of President Ronald Reagan, President George H. W. Bush, and, more recently, President George W. Bush? As I earlier observed, we can trace the aggressive reemergence of religious fundamentalism into American politics to the period of division among liberals that arose during the 1960s and later, when the alliance between Martin Luther King Jr. and then president Lyndon Johnson, leading to the stunning political successes of the civil rights movement, collapsed over the Vietnam War, which Johnson, tragically, supported and King opposed. What King saw that Johnson could not was that the same implicit questioning of patriarchy that mobilized the civil rights movement also questioned the patriarchal violence of an unjust war like that in Vietnam. King, however, was murdered, and his astonishing heritage of nonviolence was covered over in the American public mind by race riots. It was in this confused environment that religious fundamentalism aggressively entered into American politics, mobilized by attempts to limit further advances in racial equality (the attack on affirmative action) and, in particular, in angry reaction to successes of the antiwar and feminist movements and to claims of the incipient gay rights movement.

We can see this problem most starkly in the role that religious fundamentalists have played, often quite successfully, in the aggressive mobilization of political coalitions that aim to reverse any political or constitutional advances in the recognition of the rights of gay and lesbian persons. As Tina Fetner has shown in her important study *How the Religious Right Shaped Lesbian and Gay Activism*,[2] early on in the period after World War II, when advocacy for gay rights first emerged in the United States and had some modest political successes, religious fundamentalists – who were always larger in numbers and much better funded – aggressively and often successfully reversed such political successes, for example, as in Anita Bryant's Save Our Children campaign that repealed an ordinance protecting gays from discrimination in Dade County, Florida. And well before any state had moved to extend partnership or marriage rights to gay and lesbian couples, religious fundamentalists not only successfully secured state constitutional amendments forbidding such rights but also convinced many states and

[1] See, for a good general study, Dagmar Herzog, *Sex in Crisis: The New Sexual Revolution and the Future of American Politics* (New York: Basic Books, 2008).

[2] Tina Fetner, *How the Religious Right Shaped Lesbian and Gay Activism* (Minneapolis: University of Minnesota Press, 2008).

even Congress and then President Clinton to pass "defense of marriage" statutes, denying any federal or state recognition of gay marriage. Once the highest court of Massachusetts extended the right of marriage to gay and lesbian couples under state constitutional law, religious fundamentalists then got President George W. Bush to propose a constitutional amendment that would forbid gay marriage anywhere in the United States.

Religious fundamentalists would not have enjoyed this level of political success, as Mormons did in spending huge sums of money to mobilize majorities in California to ban gay marriage by constitutional amendment,[3] if their fundamentalist normative views did not resonate with other Americans. There is a continuing problem of patriarchy in American culture: what I later define as the democratic dilemma in the twenty-first century. It is most starkly posed by advocacy of gays and lesbians for political and constitutional recognition of their basic human rights. Homophobia is much more culturally entrenched in the United States than it is in Britain and Europe, revealed by the fact that Americans, in contrast to Europeans, were not allowed even to hear arguments for gay rights until after World War II;[4] and the federal government, even well after World War II, uncritically endorsed homophobic exclusions from equal citizenship in the domains of immigration, military service, and welfare in a period when exclusions on grounds of race and gender were increasingly rejected.[5] American feminism has, in contrast, existed at least since the abolitionist feminists in the antebellum period, whose rights-based feminism was embraced by many American women and men during and after the 1960s.[6] Although *Roe v. Wade* has long been challenged by religious fundamentalists, it thus continues to enjoy the support of most Americans in a way gay rights does not.[7] Arguments for gay and lesbian rights, including rights to marriage, remain so incendiary for Americans because they challenge a patriarchal conception of manhood and womanhood that remains entrenched in the incoherent American understanding of marriage defined by patriarchal ideals at war with the reality of American emotional individualism (leading to the highest divorce rates in the world).[8] The American understanding of marriage as patriarchal may also be connected to an American religiosity

[3] See Mark Schoofs, "Mormons Boost Antigay Marriage Effort," *Wall Street Journal*, Sept. 20–1, 2008, at A8; Jesse McKinley and Kirk Johnson, "Mormons Tipped Scale in Ban on Gay Marriage," *New York Times*, Nov. 15, 2008, at A1 and A11.

[4] See, on this point, David A. J. Richards, *The Sodomy Cases: Bowers v. Hardwick and Lawrence v. Texas* (Lawrence: University Press of Kansas, 2009), pp. 11–31.

[5] See, on these points, the brilliant historical argument of Margot Canaday, *The Straight State: Sexuality and Citizenship in Twentieth-Century America* (Princeton: Princeton University Press, 2009).

[6] See, for a general study of these developments, David A. J. Richards, *Women, Gays, and the Constitution: The Grounds for Feminism and Gay Rights in Culture and Law* (Chicago: University of Chicago Press, 1998).

[7] See, on these points, Nathaniel Persily, Jack Citrin, and Patrick J. Egan, *Public Opinion and Constitutional Controversy* (New York: Oxford University Press, 2008), pp. 80–107, 234–66.

[8] See Andrew J. Cherlin, *The Marriage-Go-Round: The State of Marriage and the Family in America Today* (New York: Alfred A. Knopf, 2009).

that remains uncritically patriarchal, never questioning what patriarchy requires never be questioned. American fundamentalists have achieved the levels of support they have because their very moral aggressiveness in proselytizing against gay rights psychologically supports and invigorates not only their own but also still-widely-held patriarchal assumptions of others, effectively repressing reasonable doubts about views that are, in fact, unreasonable.[9]

As I have observed, it is a symptom of the patriarchal psychology of religious fundamentalists that they do not see – or, seeing it, do not acknowledge – the sectarian roots of their normative views (Evangelicals, for example, sometimes do not publicly admit the biblical basis of their views[10]). If these views are, as I have argued, sectarian, how it is that the larger society can fail to see this? Once again, patriarchy seems to be at work here, as much a continuing problem outside religion as it is in religion. But the problem of patriarchy has also been further aggravated in the United States by the ways in which both politicians and constitutional lawyers have allowed patriarchy to distort their understanding of American constitutional law, subverting precisely the constitutional traditions they have sworn to uphold.

Judicial appointments have become a particularly incendiary focus for such activism of religious fundamentalists. Many religious fundamentalists have taken as a focus of their activism the overruling of *Roe v. Wade* and have brought pressure particularly on Republican presidents (including President Reagan and the two Presidents Bush, father and son) to appoint judges who would overrule *Roe*. Because of the public support *Roe* in fact enjoys (many Republicans are pro-choice), Republican presidents have not appointed new judges that did overrule *Roe* in the way their fundamentalist supporters wanted, but they have, perhaps cynically, appointed enough to keep the issue very much politically alive in their fundamentalist supporters. Because gay rights in general (and gay marriage in particular) do not enjoy this level of support, the dominant ideology of the Republican Party has again focused on a certain kind of judicial appointment hostile to advancing gay rights. Because Republicans are in fact divided on social issues, Republican apologists can distinguish Democrats' acceptance of gay rights from their judicial imposition, claiming that their position opposes only the latter, as if human rights of small, despised minorities are best vindicated through majoritarian democratic politics rather than through judicial review. The architects of this cynical policy continue to appeal to it today as President Obama has appointed a new justice to the Supreme Court of the United States.[11]

9 On the psychology of this phenomenon, see Leon Festinger, Henry W. Riecken, and Stanley Schachter, *When Prophecy Fails: A Social and Psychological Study of a Modern Group That Predicted the Destruction of the World* (New York: Harper Torchbooks, 1964); Leon Festinger, *A Theory of Cognitive Dissonance* (Stanford, Calif.: Stanford University Press, 1957), pp. 21, 200–2, 246–59.

10 See, on this point, Fetner, *How the Religious Right Shaped Lesbian and Gay Activism*, pp. 71, 95.

11 See, e.g., Karl Rove, "Republicans and Obama's Court Nominees," *Wall Street Journal*, May 7, 2009, at A15; Charlie Savage, "Conservatives Map Strategies on Court Fight," *New York Times*, May 17, 2009, at 1 and 20.

It was during the administration of President Ronald Reagan that the political alliance between religious and legal fundamentalism took the form of then attorney general Ed Meese's endorsement of 'originalism' as the only valid mode of constitutional interpretation, expressed in the successful nomination to the Supreme Court of Antonin Scalia and the abortive nomination of Robert Bork. Politicians have gotten so far with this argument because their preferred method of constitutional interpretation, 'originalism,' masks what is really at stake. To understand this phenomenon, we must more closely examine the role patriarchal psychology plays in leading advocates of 'originalism.' As we shall see, it is religious fundamentalism that underlies and supports 'originalism.'

2. THE LINK BETWEEN RELIGIOUS AND CONSTITUTIONAL FUNDAMENTALISM

It is not surprising that there should be connections between the culture and psychology of religious fundamentalisms and that of constitutional fundamentalism, 'originalism.' I have already argued that 'originalism' is, on close examination, a deeply unreasonable theory of constitutional interpretation (Chapter 2). It does not explain what its ostensible advocates do, as they often fail to follow its mandates and follow its mandates only so highly selectively as to suggest prejudice and whim, not reason in law. Yet, as we have also seen, its leading advocate, Judge Antonin Scalia, often quite intemperately attacks those who take much more reasonable interpretive positions than his own. He not only does not see how unreasonable his position is but also quite aggressively, even violently, attacks those who reasonably disagree with him. His very vehemence makes Scalia attractive not only to fundamentalists but also to journalists who find his frankness newsworthy in a way they do not justices who are more self-critical and judicial.[12] Taking a page from our study of religious fundamentalism, where we saw a similar gap between beliefs and reason, could psychology help us come to terms with these phenomena? Are there connections, in fact, between religious and constitutional fundamentalism?

The two clearly 'originalist' justices currently on the Supreme Court, Antonin Scalia and Clarence Thomas, exemplify such connections. Scalia's father was a professor of Italian literature at Brooklyn College. Scalia attended both Jesuit high school and college, and then, after studying abroad, Harvard Law School. After graduation from law school, he married Maureen McCarthy, with whom he has raised nine children.[13] The seriousness of Scalia's conservative Roman

[12] See Adam Liptak, "On the Bench and Off, the Eminently Quotable Justice Scalia," *New York Times*, May 12, 2009, at A14 and A16.

[13] See Richard A. Brisbin Jr., *Justice Antonin Scalia and the Conservative Revival* (Baltimore: Johns Hopkins University Press, 1997), p. 12. On the impact of this religious and family background on Scalia's judicial philosophy, see George Kannar, "The Constitutional Catechism of Antonin Scalia," 99 *Yale L.J.* 1297 (1990); Donald L. Beschle, "Catechism or Imagination: Is Justice Scalia's Judicial Style Typically Catholic?" 37 *Villanova L. Rev.* 1329 (1992).

Catholicism is evident in an article by him on the relationship of his religious convictions to his work as a constitutional judge.[14] Scalia observes that, in view of his 'originalism,' the constitutionality of the death penalty is clear; but he notes the church's current view that the death penalty is morally wrong, and, if he regarded that view as binding, he would have to resign his job as a constitutional judge on the issue of the death penalty. Thankfully, for Scalia, he does not regard the church's current view as having sufficient continuity to be binding, and therefore he can decide death penalty cases in line with his 'originalism.' The contrast, for Scalia, is to "such other hard Catholic doctrines as the prohibition of birth control and of abortion,"[15] which, being long entrenched, are binding. The consequence is clear: Scalia, in view of his acceptance as binding of these doctrines, could not decide constitutionally that these acts were protected. Scalia also notes in passing his conviction that the "tendency of democracy to obscure the divine authority behind government should not be resignation to it, but the resolution to combat it as effectively as possible,"[16] and his view that public acknowledgment of God should not raise constitutional questions.

Scalia's admission shows that he accepts, as morally binding on his conscience, the Catholic Church's fundamentalist views on both the subordination of women and the intrinsic wrongness of contraception, abortion, and nonprocreational sex. There are, of course, many Catholics who regard such fundamentalist views as deeply unreasonable, some of whom (e.g., Gary Wills[17] and Charles Taylor[18]) share the view taken in this book, namely that such views are so internally and externally unreasonable that they are not morally binding on Catholics or anyone else. But Scalia accepts the moral teaching on these matters of the papacy; that is, Scalia accepts something like the views of the new natural law lawyers. Scalia thus may believe, as the new natural law lawyers do, that these views are matters of reason, not of faith. His very willingness to say that he could not conscientiously decide a Supreme Court case contrary to his church's teaching says as much. So, Scalia has frankly both acknowledged his acceptance of the fundamentalism of the new natural law lawyers and has stated that he regards such fundamentalism in religion as binding on him as a judicial interpreter of the U.S. Constitution. In short, Scalia, who is nothing if not honest, maps his religious fundamentalism onto his constitutional fundamentalism. The connection is a matter not of inference but of clear statement by Scalia about Scalia.

Clarence Thomas's education was, if anything, even more religiously Catholic than that of Scalia, including not only high school and college, but, in between, studying for the priesthood at a Catholic seminary; like Scalia, he eventually

[14] See Antonin Scalia, "God's Justice and Ours," 123 *First Things* 17 (2002).

[15] See *id.*, p. 20.

[16] See *id.*, p. 19.

[17] See, e.g., Gary Wills, *Head and Heart: American Christianities* (New York: Penguin, 2007), pp. 523–46.

[18] See Charles Taylor, *A Secular Age* (Cambridge, Mass.: Belknap Press of Harvard University Press, 2007), pp. 498–9, 503–4, 645–6, 767.

studied at a leading secular American law school, Yale, from which he graduated.[19] Thomas was questioned at his Senate Judiciary Committee hearings about his natural law views, from which he distanced himself,[20] and he did not, unlike Bork, go public about his 'originalism.' Shrewdly dodging these issues (as his handlers in the Bush administration advised him to do) and manipulating Anita Hill's accusations of sexual harassment in his favor led to his confirmation by the Senate.[21]

In his autobiography, *My Grandfather's Son: A Memoir*,[22] Thomas tells a story of the loss of a father (whom he never knew) and of a mother with whom he did not live. Such loss is filled not by a loving relationship but by the harsh demands and actions of his maternal grandfather ("the patriarch of our family"[23]), with whom Thomas lived. The developmental psychology is classically patriarchal. The traumatic breach in loving relationship with his mother is resolved by a passionate identification with his grandfather's patriarchal demands. The narrative is one of his grandfather's relentless demands and deep disappointment when Thomas leaves his training for the priesthood; the grandfather's hurtful harshness to his grandson includes throwing Thomas out of the house and later refusing to attend his graduation from Yale Law School. Thomas's response is an even more radical identification with his grandfather: "his hardness had hardened my own heart."[24] It reflects this process of identification with the aggressor that, when Thomas thinks about the roots of his own views on race (including his opposition to busing as a remedy for unconstitutional forms of racial segregation), he traces them to his grandfather's views.[25] The very unconventionality of such views among black people supports Thomas's sense – when expressly ratified by his grandfather – of the rightness of his own increasingly conservative views in part because they are so unconventional; as Thomas himself puts the point:

> I'd complained to him [his grandfather] about how badly I was being treated because of my views. "Son, you have to stand up for what you believe in," he said. It was just that simple, for it was just what Daddy [his grandfather] had done his whole life. Those were the words I needed to hear. Now he would never say them to me again.[26]

In fact, his grandfather had just died. That loss, over which Thomas admits he "had no control over [his] grief,"[27] reinforces Thomas's identification with what he

[19] See Andrew Peyton Thomas, *Clarence Thomas: A Biography* (San Francisco: Encounter Books, 2001), pp. 69–72, 81–108, 114–18.

[20] See Scott Douglas Gerber, *First Principles: The Jurisprudence of Clarence Thomas* (New York: New York University Press, 1999), pp. 40–7.

[21] See Jane Mayer and Jill Abramson, *Strange Justice: The Selling of Clarence Thomas* (Boston: Houghton Mifflin Company, 1994).

[22] Clarence Thomas, *My Grandfather's Son: A Memoir* (New York: HarperCollins, 2007).

[23] *Id.*, p. 52.

[24] See *id.*, p. 113.

[25] *Id.*, p. 104.

[26] *Id.*, p. 169.

[27] See *id.*, p. 168.

imagines to be his grandfather's patriarchal voice. In fact, his real grandfather may have been more emotionally complex than his grandson imagines, a fact shown by something Thomas has difficulty understanding, his grandfather's nonjudgmental affection for Thomas's own child, an affection he never expressed to Thomas himself.[28]

It is after his grandfather's death, and shortly after his grandmother's, that Thomas confesses to being drawn back to the Catholic faith of his childhood. Strikingly, he characterizes his rebirth of religious faith in terms of his patriarchal identification: "By running away from God, I had thrown away the most important part of my grandparents' legacy."[29] And at the moment President George H. W. Bush introduced Thomas to the American people as his nominee to the Supreme Court, Thomas writes: "I thought of my wife, my grandparents, and all the other people who had helped me along the way, especially the nuns of St. Benedict the Moor and St. Pius X."[30] The continuing psychological force of such patriarchal identification shows itself in the way Thomas identifies with another wounded patriarch, Bork, and his travails during the hearings on his appointment to the Supreme Court,[31] and to characterize what he regards as his own unjust treatment during his hearings in terms of a rather grandiose identification with the sufferings of Jesus.[32] His confirmation for the Supreme Court was, Thomas writes, God's will: "Thanks to God's direct intervention, I had risen phoenixlike from the ashes of self-pity and despair, and though my wounds were still raw, I trust that in time they, too, would heal."[33] Strikingly, Thomas, like Augustine earlier, expresses his identification with Jesus not with his antipatriarchal compassion for outcasts, including outcast women, but with being a Christian soldier.[34] Women, Thomas observes at one point, can hardly be regarded as being as oppressed as he was:[35] he is thinking, of course, only of himself as a black man, as if black women did not exist. There is a striking lapse in ethical intelligence here and a resulting lack of moral feeling for anyone's suffering but his own. The wounds experienced by so patriarchal a man as Thomas never heal. The force of such an exquisitely observed patriarchal psychology is shown in what Thomas recognizes as his dominant moral vice, his anger. What he does not see, because his patriarchal psychology requires that he not see, is that his anger is directed at anyone who dissents from his highly patriarchal views.

There is nothing in Roman Catholicism as such that leads to or justifies 'originalism,' and there have certainly been Catholic justices who have not been 'originalists,'[36] including notably Justice Anthony Kennedy, who wrote the

[28] See *id.*, pp. 111–12.
[29] *Id.*, p. 184.
[30] *Id.*, p. 214.
[31] See *id.*, pp. 323–4.
[32] See *id.*, pp. 254–5.
[33] *Id.*, p. 282.
[34] See, on this point, *id.*, pp. 233–4.
[35] See, on this point, *id.*, pp. 98–9, 165.
[36] See, e.g., on Justice Murphy, Beschle, "Catechism or Imagination."

opinion for the Supreme Court in *Lawrence v. Texas*. Justice Thomas's interest in natural law embraces Locke,[37] which, as I suggested in Chapter 2, should lead to repudiation of 'originalism.' What moves Scalia and Thomas to 'originalism' is a certain view of the founders that is, I believe, motivated by the culture and psychology of patriarchy that have been the subject of this book.

Why should 'originalism' thus appeal to Scalia, an Italian American, and Clarence Thomas, an African American? It might be thought that, if anything, members of groups that have been unjustly racialized – both Italian Americans and African Americans – would resist an interpretive attitude to law that could not do justice under law to such injustice.[38] But there is always a risk that the pressure to assimilate to a dominant culture silences such resistance. Sigmund Freud, for example, puzzled over the ferocity of the political anti-Semitism that he saw gathering force in Germany and Austria, observing that the more Jews who assimilated to German culture and thus the less the differences (if any) between Jews and non-Jews, the more ferocious the anti-Semitism, as if the irrationalism of anti-Semitism expressed "the narcissism of small differences."[39] What Freud did not see was the patriarchal strand in anti-Semitism, which I have traced back to Augustinian orthodoxy, namely, that it arose from the traumatic renunciation of sexual love and connection required for the heroism of manhood, whether in politics or in religion. Freud could not see the problems in this patriarchal conception, including its dangers to the Jews, because he had, under the pressure of assimilation, come to accept it as natural.[40] Resistance to injustice may be compromised when it is grounded in assimilation to an ostensibly liberal political culture that is, in fact, compromised by its patriarchal institutions and assumptions. Freud's resistance to anti-Semitism was compromised by the way he assimilated the dominant patriarchal assumptions of his place and period, leading him in his psychology to read patriarchy as nature, thus compromising the resistance that was never more needed than in his place and period.

Such assimilationist pressures are very powerful in the United States, and particularly so for otherwise ethnically marginalized groups. Scalia, for example, comes from an unusually learned Italian American background (his father was a professor of Italian literature). Both this background and his religious education (until law school) may have set him apart from other Italian Americans, whose aims may have been more defined in terms of economic mobility and success. This kind of scholarly idealism, when combined with a passionate desire

[37] See, on this point, Gerber, *First Principles*, pp. 40–7.

[38] On the racialization of Italian Americans, see David A. J. Richards, *Italian American: The Racializing of an Ethnic Identity* (New York: New York University Press, 1999).

[39] On this point, see Sigmund Freud, "Civilization and Its Discontents," in *Standard Edition of the Complete Psychological Works of Sigmund Freud*, ed. and trans. James Strachey (London: Hogarth Press, 1961), 21:114; see also *Moses and Monotheism* in *Standard Edition of the Complete Psychological Works of Sigmund Freud*, ed. and trans. James Strachey (London: Hogarth Press, 1964), 23:91.

[40] See, on this point, Gilligan and Richards, *The Deepening Darkness*.

to become American, led to an identification with America's founders, but understood patriarchally in the way Scalia learned from his religion. Assimilation on such terms is an all too common and understandable human psychology, particularly appealing when it opens up avenues of success and recognition not otherwise available. Success, as we earlier saw with Mormonism's founder Joseph Smith, has a way of psychologically shoring up and supporting the certitudes of overweening ambition, in particular, when they sustain a sense of one's manhood and are uncritically applauded and honored for this reason (both President Bush and presidential candidate John McCain acclaimed Scalia as their ideal of a good constitutional judge). Such certitudes are as unreasonable in religion as they are in constitutional law, but the psychology of manhood I am discussing quite sincerely affirms its certitudes, turning violently, as Scalia does, as we saw in Chapter 3, on the culture that reasonably questions them. We should understand in this way why Scalia has found it so easy to become a polemically aggressive spokesman in America's culture wars, not only against the straight and lesbian women and gay men whose rights have recently been recognized but also in a war on the culture of the American law school, which Scalia so passionately resents, both because he came from it and probably always felt so denigrated by it. Thus, a man of learning allies himself with the anti-intellectualism of Protestant Evangelicals, consumed by ambition and success, by the patriarchal rage that fuels, as we saw in Chapter 3, Scalia's emotional tone and animus in the dissenting opinions when the Supreme Court extended constitutional rights and guarantees to women (straight and lesbian) and gay men.

We can see the workings of this psychology very well in the hostility of both Thomas and Scalia to affirmative action plans for law schools, from which both of them possibly profited.[41] Their objections are not grounded in compelling constitutional objections to the often-quite-reasonable programs law schools have adopted but rather suggest the tangled psychology of a humiliated manhood that leads them passionately to identify not with the real experience of racialization of their own ethnic groups but with an idealized American manhood that takes offense at any challenge to its patriarchal authority. Clarence Thomas's autobiography illustrates this tangled psychology. Thomas blames Yale Law School, where he was a law student, for admitting him on terms of affirmative action, on two grounds. First, teachers and students regarded all such students as "somehow inferior."[42] Second, because of affirmative action at Yale, grades of students like Thomas who benefited from such programs were not treated on the same basis as comparable grades of non–affirmative action students, so that Thomas could not get a job with any of the firms with whom he interviewed. Neither argument

[41] See, e.g., *Grutter v. Bollinger*, 539 U.S. 306 (2003) (Michigan Law School affirmative action program held constitutional), opinion of Scalia, with whom Thomas joins, and opinion of Thomas, with whom Scalia joins, both concurring in part, dissenting in part).

[42] Thomas, *My Grandfather's Son*, p. 75.

is reasonably compelling. On the first point, Thomas notes at least one Yale professor who certainly did not treat him as inferior.[43] On the second, an alternative explanation for his job-hunting problems in the private market of law firms is not Yale's affirmative action program, but American racism. But, more important, it was precisely because Thomas had gone to Yale that John Danforth, who was then "serving as Missouri's attorney general,"[44] was willing to hire him. There is little doubt that it was the Yale education, about which Thomas complains so bitterly, that led to the willingness of people in public life, including notably John Danforth, to give Thomas jobs in the public sphere, including, eventually, both his chairmanship of the Equal Employment Opportunity Commission and his judicial appointments to both the D.C. Circuit and the Supreme Court of the United States. There is thus something deeply unreasonable in Thomas's rage at Yale, which his patriarchal psychology explains. There is certainly nothing in good historical argument that supports Thomas's views on affirmative action. Yet Thomas continues to justify his 'originalism' as the only way to constrain constitutional interpretation,[45] when in fact his 'originalism' has no reasonable basis in history but is a ruse covering highly personal, idiosyncratic views and life experiences of a kind that have no place in reasonable constitutional interpretation.

It is not good interpretive argument that leads to 'originalism,' for the 'originalists' offer no such argument (see Chapter 2). Something else moves them, a psychology that attracts them and their audiences, an imaginative transformation of America's Lockean Constitution into what Locke regarded as the antithesis of liberal thought and practice – Robert Filmer's patriarchalism (Chapter 3). Locke's argument for liberal constitutionalism aimed to refute Filmer's defense of absolute monarchy, deriving lineally from the authority of Adam. Locke's conception is that each generation of the living must test the legitimacy of political power in terms of its own moral conception of inalienable human rights, the right to conscience prominent among them. His argument for the right to revolution against the Stuart monarchy was that it had abridged basic human rights, including the right to conscience. Accordingly, the monarchy was legitimately overthrown to establish a limited monarch and House of Commons that would better respect human rights.

What moves the 'originalists' is not good argument, but the psychologically compelled imagination that moves patriarchal men and women everywhere: the need to sustain the hierarchical authority of a patriarchal father over all others as the model for authority. In the case of both Justices Scalia and Thomas, what made this possible was their religious fundamentalism, which appears in both cases to be something very like the new natural law view of Catholicism. Scalia is quite frank on this point: nothing in the authoritative moral tradition

[43] See *id.*, pp. 74–5.

[44] *Id.*, p. 87.

[45] See Justice Clarence Thomas, "How to Read the Constitution," *Wall Street Journal*, Oct. 20, 2008, at A19.

of Catholicism could be inconsistent with his interpretation of the American constitution. If there were a conflict, Scalia would conscientiously have to resign. Scalia avoids any conflict by adopting a constitutional theory, 'originalism,' that allows him to deny that anything in the Constitution denies the subordination of women or protects the constitutional right of intimate life that the Supreme Court has extended to contraception, abortion, and gay and lesbian sex acts. The appeal of 'originalism' for Justice Thomas rests on a similar view. What grounds their interpretive attitude is not good argument, for there is no such argument. What explains the appeal to them of these views is the patriarchal culture and psychology of their religious fundamentalism. But the appeal of 'originalism' extends not just to Scalia and Thomas but also to the politicians and political constituencies who supported their appointment; indeed, President George W. Bush pointed to Justice Scalia as his model of a good constitutional judge,[46] the kind of person Bush would want to appoint to our highest court (more on this shortly).

The background of such appeal is precisely the convergence of the forms of religious fundamentalism discussed in Part II that have united as a political movement around their certainty about the subordination of women and the intrinsic evil of contraception, abortion, and nonprocreational sex (in particular, gay and lesbian sex). It may be a matter of regret for many orthodox and unorthodox believing Christians that such Christian groups have come to accept views that are, on internal and external grounds, so unreasonable. But in religious matters, there is room for faith beyond reason, which certainly entitles religious fundamentalists to respect for their views and their right to conduct their own lives accordingly. What my argument in Part II shows, however, is that religious fundamentalists (e.g., the new natural law lawyers) claim that their views not only are reasonable but also are supported on secular grounds that appeal to the reason of all, religious and nonreligious people alike (e.g., as Thomas Aquinas believed about his arguments; see Chapter 4). It is this belief that leads them and other fundamentalists to argue that their fundamentalist views are a legitimate basis for law in a secular democracy, like the United States, constitutionally committed by the First Amendment of its Bill of Rights neither to abridge rights of religious free exercise nor to establish any religion. What my argument also has shown was that religious fundamentalists misunderstand the basis for their views, which are certainly not supported by the kinds of reasons required to justify laws in a religiously and morally pluralistic culture like that of the United States. Rather, their views rest on a sectarian religious faith, a faith – being unreasonable – that cannot legitimately be the basis for law. So, there is a problem, a deep constitutional problem, with the political role religious fundamentalists have come to play in American politics.

46 See, on this point, "Did Bush Promise to Appoint a Justice Like Scalia," http://mediamatters.org/items/w005101300005.

It surely bespeaks something normatively deep about American constitutionalism that even advocates of fundamentalism in both religion and law agree with the rest of us that laws in the United States cannot rest solely on sectarian religious faith not reasonably shared in the society at large. Why this deep consensus? The consensus certainly does not forbid religious argument at large, for often such argument can be (as it often has historically been) a way of making a claim that is reasonably compelling or can be seen as compelling from a range of perspectives, religious and philosophical. It is, however, a quite different matter to ground law and public policy in considerations that move only a sectarian view, religious or nonreligious, for example, "a view that acts are immoral, based on a religious point of view and detached from any perspective about harm in this life that would be sufficient to justify a prohibition or regulation."[47] Such an impulse is deeply antidemocratic in the way theocracies are antidemocratic. It does not take seriously the democratic demand that the power of the state must, in principle, be justified in terms of reasons that can appeal to the convictions of all. This is the requirement that John Rawls, following Immanuel Kant, called public reason.[48] It is the attitude toward others that expresses respect for them as equal bearers of human rights in our common democratic enterprise.

Both religious and legal fundamentalism are deeply mistaken in supposing that their views meet this requirement. They do not meet it, as I have argued, on both internal and external grounds. Their views are grounded not in reasons that all persons can share but on sectarian faith. Indeed, it is precisely their fundamentalism about a certain range of issues (the subordination of women, the intrinsic evil of contraception, abortion, and gay and lesbian sex) that reveals their sectarianism. Reason is in its nature open to argument and experience; the fundamentalist stance as certain shows reason not to be the basis of their views. It is the very refusal to subject such views to reason that makes them so constitutionally untenable and may explain why they aggressively impose their views on others through politics. The imposition itself is an act of dictatorial will. It treats fellow citizens not as democratic equals but as servile subjects to a theocratic authority. That such a view should have gotten so far in American politics shows something troubling about the continuing power of patriarchy even in a constitutional democracy as developed as the United States. That so many Americans cannot even see the problem defines, I believe, the problem.

'Originalism' has come to enjoy the political support it does, for example, among politicians in the Republican Party, because it leads to what appears to its

[47] Kent Greenawalt, *Religion and the Constitution*, vol. 2, *Establishment and Fairness* (Princeton, N.J.: Princeton University Press, 2008), p. 535. See also, for general exploration of when religious argument does not violate this requirement, Kent Greenawalt, *Religious Convictions and Political Choice* (New York: Oxford University Press, 1988); Greenawalt, *Private Consciences and Public Reasons* (New York: Oxford University Press, 1995); Greenawalt, *Religion and the Constitution Volume 2*, pp. 450–537.

[48] See, e.g., John Rawls, *Collected Papers* (Cambridge, Mass.: Harvard University Press, 1999), pp. 573–615.

advocates to be a neutral and attractive constitutional theory that gives untrammeled expression to fundamentalist religious views in American politics. But on examination, these fundamentalist views are themselves religiously sectarian; and 'originalism' is a deeply unreasonable approach to constitutional interpretation precisely because of why it appeals to fundamentalists: namely it allows them to read out of the Constitution not only its secular basis but the protection on fair terms of the basic constitutional rights of women (straight and gay) and gay men. Religious fundamentalism and 'originalism' in law are thus connected, both rooted in the patriarchal personal and political psychology that wars on any threats to its traditional place in American culture. And patriarchy is certainly at threat, as the constitutional developments discussed in Chapter 1 express, as I have argued, a criticism of patriarchy as in contradiction to American constitutionalism.

The situation would be bad enough if only two justices of the Supreme Court were 'originalists.' It has now become, however, alarming because of the important role fundamentalists have played among the constituencies that elected George Bush president of the United States. It is to satisfy them that Bush declared in public that his model for a good constitutional judge was Justice Scalia. With the death of Chief Justice Rehnquist and the retirement of Justice O'Connor, Bush successfully appointed two justices, both Roman Catholics, Chief Justice Roberts (to replace Rehnquist) and Justice Alito (to replace O'Connor). Although Justice Roberts denied at his hearings that he was an 'originalist,' Justice Alito did not.[49] These two justices – joined by Justices Scalia, Thomas, and Kennedy – overruled or sharply limited an earlier 5–4 opinion striking down as unconstitutional a ban on late-term abortions.[50] Ronald Dworkin has recently argued that Justice Kennedy's opinion for the Court casts doubt on Kennedy's own role in reaffirming the central principle of *Roe v. Wade*.[51] What makes Dworkin's criticism so forceful is that Kennedy's opinion gives weight to the interest in potential life defined in terms of "the bond of love the mother has for her child"[52] and negligible weight to the well-supported medical view of the health interests of women in having this procedure. As Justice Ginsberg observed acidly in her dissent, the opinion of the Court gives decisive weight to essential stereotypical claims of women's role, as mothers, over the real women who decide conscientiously that they do not want a child and whose health makes this procedure the better choice (over another procedure that, just as gruesome, the Court has allowed).[53] In effect, the Court allows its imagination of an idealized, selfless, and

49 See, on this point, Ronald Dworkin, *The Supreme Court Phalanx: The Court's New Right-Wing Bloc* (New York: New York Review Books, 2008), pp. 32–3.

50 See *Gonzales v. Carhart*, 550 U.S. 124 (2007) (federal prohibition on late-term prohibition unconstitutional because there are no clear advances to mother's health and it expresses respect for potential life). Cf. *Sternberg v. Carhart*, 530 U.S. 914 (2000) (state prohibition on late-term abortions, without exception for mother's health, held unconstitutional).

51 See Dworkin, *The Supreme Court Phalanx*, pp. 37–45.

52 *Gonzales v. Carhart*, 550 U.S. at 159.

53 See *id.* at 182–5.

asexual good mother – on the model in Catholic piety of the Virgin Mary (who would not want or would regret this procedure) – to erase the painful health risks to which real women will be exposed who do not want a child and cannot have a procedure that would remove those risks. It is plausible that the five justices in the majority, including Justice Kennedy, have allowed their sectarian ideals as patriarchal Catholic men about women as self-sacrificing mothers illegitimately to be the basis for their decision. The point is not that they are all Catholics,[54] but the basis of their constitutional judgment is a sectarian judgment not shared by many reasonable Americans, Catholic and non-Catholic. What is alarming is that the appointment of two new justices, one quite conservative and the other an 'originalist,' may have tipped the balance of the Supreme Court in a more 'originalist' and certainly more conservative direction (influencing even a non-'originalist' justice like Kennedy), thus compromising the judicial protection of basic human rights.

More recently, in *District of Columbia v. Heller*, the same group of justices held that the Second Amendment of the Bill of Rights protected a personal right of self-defense that was violated by a District of Columbia ban on handgun possession; the ban made it a crime to carry an unregistered firearm and allowed the police chief to issue one-year licenses but required lawfully owned firearms to be unloaded or disassembled or bound by a trigger lock or similar device.[55] What makes this opinion remarkable, as both Justice Stevens and Justice Breyer observed in dissent, is that it flies not only in the face of the text of the Second Amendment (whose preface speaks of "[a] well regulated Militia, being necessary to the security of a free State") but also in the face of what we know of its background history.[56] The opinion of the Court was written by Justice Scalia, but because of the text and history Stevens and Breyer point to, it is not 'originalist' at all. It reads, rather, as precisely the kind of appeal to unenumerated basic rights (here, the right of self-defense)[57] or an appeal to changing moral values[58] that Scalia disdained on alleged 'originalist' grounds when it came to protecting a

[54] See, for critique of this claim, John Yoo, "Partial-Birth Bigotry," *Wall Street Journal*, Apr. 28–9, 2007, at A8.

[55] *District of Columbia v. Heller*, 128 S. Ct. 2783 (2008).

[56] See, on this point, Saul Cornell, *A Well Regulated Militia: The Founding Fathers and the Origins of Gun Control in America* (Oxford: Oxford University Press, 2006); H. Richard Uviller and William G. Merkel, *The Militia and the Right to Arms; or, How the Second Amendment Fell Silent* (Durham, N.C.: Duke University Press, 2002). For an illuminating discussion of both the historical and the policy issues relating to gun control, see Mark V. Tushnet, *Out of Range: Why the Constitution Can't End the Battle over Guns* (Oxford: Oxford University Press, 2007). For commentary, see Sanford Levinson, "Guns and the Constitution: A Complex Relationship," *Reviews in American History*, March 2008, at 1–14.

[57] See, for this reading, Cass R. Sunstein, "Second Amendment Minimalism: *Heller* as *Griswold*," 122 *Harv. L. Rev.* 246 (2008); Jess Bravin, "Rethinking Original Intent," *Wall Street Journal*, March 14–15, 2009, at W3. See also Akhil Reed Amar, "*Heller, HLR*, and Holistic Legal Reasoning," 122 *Harv. L. Rev.* 145 (2008).

[58] See, for this reading, Reva B. Siegel, "Dead or Alive: Originalism as Popular Constitutionalism in *Heller*," 122 *Harv. L. Rev.* 191 (2008).

basic human right to intimate life that would extend to women and gays and lesbians. But even thus understood, what moves the opinion is not a reasonable contemporary understanding of the role of self-defense as a way of protecting, when necessary, one's human rights to goods like life (a right all persons enjoy) or text and history but the patriarchal lens the majority brings to reading text and history. Scalia's thus writes of the right very much as a patriarchal man: the "defense of self, family,"[59] or "hearth and home."[60]

Justice Breyer, in dissent, adduces evidence about domestic violence as a contemporary problem,[61] a problem that might lead to a less patriarchal understanding of the law of self-defense, for example, the human right of a woman to protect herself, when necessary, from violence and dehumanizing forms of degradation. Growing understanding of the plight of battered women in violently patriarchal marriages certainly has led to shifts in the normative and even legal understanding of the requirements of self-defense; courts have struggled, for example, with the question of what weight should be given to the experience of battered women in responding (sometimes homicidally) to what they perceive, not unreasonably, as escalating threats from their husband.[62] Such an understanding might lead one reasonably to question whether handguns in homes really advance aims of self-defense (as opposed to aggravating interspousal violence whether by husbands or wives). The majority opinion does not grapple with these moral complexities.

What controls the majority opinion is a patriarchal imagination not of the moral right to self-defense but of a man's honor and the legitimacy of violence when one's honor is at threat. At work here is the patriarchal psychology of the gun lobby framing gun risks,[63] not a deliberative judgment about human rights at threat in the modern world. But such codes of honor are highly gendered, legitimating violence against any threat to patriarchal control. Reasonable gun control regulations in contemporary circumstances are thus transformed into an attack on manhood – by which Scalia means patriarchal manhood. If defending male honor is what really is at stake here, striking down such reasonable gun control laws may legitimate such codes of honor and thus exacerbate the problem of interspousal violence, which often arises from a woman's resistance to such patriarchal control.

59 *Id.*, p. 2817.
60 *Id.*, p. 2821.
61 *Id.*, p. 2855.
62 On these shifts, see Sanford H. Kadish, Stephen J. Schulhofer, and Carol S. Steiker, *Criminal Law and Its Processes*, 8th ed. (New York: Aspen, 2007), pp. 750–74.
63 See, on this point, Dan M. Kahan and Donald Braman, "More Statistics, Less Persuasion: A Cultural Theory of Gun-Risk Perceptions," 151 *U. Pa. L. Rev.* 1291 (2003). For commentary, see Sanford Levinson, "What Follows Putting Reason in Its Place? 'Now Vee May Perhaps To Begin, Yes?'" 151 *U. Pa. L. Rev.* 1371 (2003). See also Dan M. Kahan, David A. Hoddman, and Donald Braman, "Whose Eyes Are You Going to Believe: *Scott v. Harris* and the Perils of Cognitive Illiberalism," 122 *Harv. L. Rev.* 838 (2009).

When a patriarchal psychology in these ways increasingly controls opinions of our highest court, Americans have reason, on the basis of their deepest constitutional values of respect for human rights, to resist. It is, as we have seen, a crucial feature of patriarchal culture and psychology that it repressively targets the voices of the women and men who would most reasonably raise doubts about its claims. If a majority of the Supreme Court has become or might become hostage to this psychology, our highest court will no longer protect the basic human rights of all against irrational prejudice but will itself become the agent of such prejudice. There is no greater threat to the legitimacy of the Supreme Court, as history clearly shows.

Chief Justice Roger Taney in *Dred Scott v. Sanford* led a majority of the Supreme Court, on such 'originalist' grounds, not only to entrench slavery both in the states and in the territories but also to exclude people of color from the protections of the U.S. Constitution.[64] Better lawyers than Taney, notably Abraham Lincoln, condemned his 'originalism' because it indulged America's most debased impulses, its racism, at the expense of the text and history that appealed to universal human rights as a powerful constitutional counterweight to such impulses. The condemnation by Lincoln and others of Taney's 'originalism,' as betraying democratic constitutionalism, precipitated the constitutional crisis that led to the Civil War.[65]

Our contemporary experience with the revival of 'originalism' is not dissimilar. Even its leading advocates do not consistently apply it, for such consistency would undermine the legitimacy of cases – like those repudiating state-imposed racial segregation – that such advocates are eager to endorse. We are thus left with a deeply unreasonably interpretive attitude that is applied aggressively only to those developments in constitutional interpretation that question traditional patriarchal views of sexuality and gender, thus perhaps inadvertently revealing the root of the problem. Lincoln's criticism of Stephen Douglas for indulging racism applies to politicians who indulge sexism and homophobia today: "He is blowing out the moral lights around us. . . . [H]e is, in my judgment, penetrating the human soul and eradicating the light of reason and the love of liberty in this American people."[66] It is shocking that the party of Lincoln should have become the political agent of such unreason.

[64] See *Dred Scott v. Sanford*, 60 U.S. (19 How.) 393 (1857). For a penetrating critique of the opinion, see Don E. Fehrenbacher, *The Dred Scott Cases: Its Significance in American Law and Politics* (New York: Oxford University Press, 1978).

[65] On Lincoln's critique of *Dred Scott* and its role in precipitating the Civil War, see David A. J. Richards, *Conscience and the Constitution: History, Theory, and Law of the Reconstruction Amendments* (Princeton, N.J.: Princeton University Press, 1993), pp. 41, 54–7, 81.

[66] Quoted in Richards, *Conscience and the Constitution*, p. 55.

CHAPTER 8

FUNDAMENTALISM IN RELIGION AND LAW: A CRITICAL OVERVIEW

I have offered a normative critique and cultural and psychological diagnosis of American fundamentalism in religion (the Catholic new natural lawyers, Protestant Evangelicals, and Mormons) and constitutional law (the 'originalists'). What are the larger implications of my analysis for the understanding and evaluation of American culture, politics, and constitutional law, and for fundamentalism generally, including the forms of it that flourish abroad? I begin in this chapter with a comparison of my analysis to two important recent investigations of American fundamentalism, one by a cultural anthropologist (Vincent Crapanzano), the other by a constitutional lawyer (Cass Sunstein); my discussion of Sunstein leads to how we should understand and evaluate the election and presidency of Barack Obama in light of my general argument. Then, I explore the implications of the kind of overview on fundamentalism in religion and law that I propose, in particular, for central issues in American constitutional law. Finally, in the Conclusion, I address what light my account casts on fundamentalisms both at home and abroad and what I call the twenty-first-century dilemma of American democracy – patriarchy.

1. CRAPANZANO AND SUNSTEIN ON FUNDAMENTALISM

There are two recent accounts of American fundamentalism that inspired my interest in this topic. The first, by the cultural anthropologist Vincent Crapanzano,[1] investigated fundamentalism in religion and constitutional law together. The second, by Cass Sunstein, a constitutional lawyer,[2] focused exclusively on reasons for rejecting the right-wing ideology on constitutional interpretation of the 'originalists.'

[1] See Vincent Crapanzano, *Serving the Word: Literalism in America from the Pulpit to the Bench* (New York: New Press, 2000).

[2] See Cass R. Sunstein, *Radicals in Robes: Why Extreme Right-Wing Courts Are Wrong for America* (New York: Basic Books, 2005).

The great interest in Crapanzano's pathbreaking study was not only in his attempt to unite American fundamentalism in religion and law under a common analytical framework but also in the remarkable insights he achieved into one of the forms of American religious fundamentalism, namely, Protestant Evangelicals. Crapanzano's sensitive use of the anthropological method of participant observation of Protestant fundamentalism led fundamentalists to speak to him with unusual candor, suggesting many of the features of such fundamentalism that I elaborate in my own analysis. These include the highly patriarchal character of both what it brings to the interpretation of scripture and what, in consequence, it finds there, and the important role in its highly conservative, indeed reactionary fundamentalism on issues of gender and sexuality of a highly misogynist interpretation of original sin. It was reading Crapanzano that led me to realize how much Protestant fundamentalism depended on the Augustinian doctrine of original sin and his associated theory of persecution, and thus to begin to see the connections between the culture and psychology underlying this form of fundamentalism and that underlying both the new natural lawyers and the Mormons.

But although Crapanzano certainly tried to organize his argument around a common analytical framework on fundamentalism in religion and law, he confesses not succeeding in finding any comparable explanation for 'originalism' to that which he found for Protestant fundamentalism.[3] I disagree with him precisely on this point, and one of the motivations of this study was to show, as I have tried to do, the common culture and psychology that underlies fundamentalism in both religion and law. My argument has moved beyond Crapanzano in two dimensions: first, it used a common background framework of patriarchal culture and psychology to explain not only fundamentalist Protestantism but also the new natural lawyers and contemporary Mormonism; and second, it extended the analysis to links between fundamentalism religion and 'originalism' in law.

There have been two important recent studies of the political alliance between otherwise quite different American religions and their increasingly important impact on American politics and constitutional law.[4] What I have tried to show is the underlying patriarchal culture and psychology that supports such alliances, and their impact, in particular, on American constitutional interpretation and ongoing political struggles over such interpretation. 'Originalism' could not have arisen or had the support it has enjoyed if it did not both express and support long-standing patriarchal assumptions in American culture that exist in tension with our democratic constitutionalism. My argument in this book has hopefully introduced a new explanatory and normative dimension into understanding how such religious alliances arise and are sustained and their impact not only on constitutional law but on American politics generally. Because I am a constitutional

[3] See, on this point, Crapanzano, *Serving the Word*, pp. 297, 326.

[4] See Damon Linker, *The Theocons: Secular America under Siege* (New York: Doubleday, 2006); Kevin Phillips, *American Theocracy: The Peril and Politics of Radical Religion, Oil, and Borrowed Money in the 21st Century* (New York: Viking, 2006).

lawyer, my focus here has been on American fundamentalist religions – their alliances with one another and their impact on fundamentalism in constitutional law, but the account clearly throws light as well on the linkages of such religious fundamentalisms to American politics generally, both at home and abroad.

If I am right on this point, we need, if anything, more, not less, rigorous interdisciplinary work on interpretation in religion and law as a unified study. Crapanzano, a cultural anthropologist, brilliantly showed how powerful such interdisciplinary work can be when it comes to studying American religion. What we need now is to carry his analysis further, as I have tried to do, not only in other forms of religious fundamentalism but also into the very heart of American constitutional interpretation. If I am right about this, there lies before us an important research project that calls for the resources of the university to begin taking law as seriously as they are already taking religion. We need to bring the study of law out of law schools into the university generally, and we need to bring into American law schools the best of university scholarship forging interdisciplinary methods alone adequate to dealing with law at the high level of intellectual and ethical responsibility its study requires both of its teachers and its students.

The scope of Cass Sunstein's study is, on the one hand, much narrower than mine or Crapanzano's: namely, it is a critique of what he takes to be the unacceptable ideology of judging sponsored by the 'originalists,' rather than an investigation of fundamentalism in both religion and law and their connections. On the other hand, his critique of 'originalism' extends into other fields besides constitutional privacy, and indeed is, if anything, critical of both the principle of constitutional privacy (claiming nothing in history supports the principle[5]) and certainly its application to abortion,[6] though evidently not to contraception and gay and lesbian sex.[7] I agree with much of Sunstein's critique of 'originalism' in general and its views of areas outside constitutional privacy, for example, its failure to attend to the history supporting the constitutionality of affirmative action[8] and its influence in the Supreme Court's recent cutting back on the power of Congress over the interpretation of the commerce clause.[9]

But his narrow views of constitutional privacy, as well as of free speech (limited, he argues, to political speech),[10] rest on often quite badly argued judgments (as if it were self-evident that free speech embraces only political speech, when its clearest and most demanding historical application was to religion).[11] Almost everything

[5] Sunstein, *Radicals in Robes*, p. 88.

[6] *Id.*, pp. 19, 104–9.

[7] *Id.*, pp. 98–9.

[8] *Id.*, pp. 137–42.

[9] *Id.*, pp. 235–41. For a brilliantly reasonable and persuasive critique of these decisions, see John T. Noonan Jr., *Narrowing the Nation's Power* (Berkeley: University of California Press, 2002).

[10] See Sunstein, *Radicals in Robes*, p. 229.

[11] See on this point, David A. J. Richards, *Toleration and the Constitution* (New York: Oxford University Press, 1986).

Sunstein says about constitutional privacy is put in terms of conclusory judgments, all the more conclusory when badly argued or completely unargued. The claim, for example, that nothing in history supports constitutional privacy is clearly wrong: as I showed in Chapter 1, there are compelling historical reasons, rooted both in the founding and in antebellum debate over the wrongness of slavery, for regarding the right to intimate life as a basic human right that is constitutionally protected. Such unargued assertions in this domain are, nonetheless, put in polemically strong terms: Sunstein is, for example, quite "confident" that the right to privacy should never apply to commercial sex,[12] a matter about which even a conservative jurist like Charles Fried recently expressed compelling reasons to the contrary.[13] And the principle of constitutional privacy should not judicially be extended to gay marriage,[14] but the judgment merely echoes the dominant view of politicians, giving no reasons.

Sunstein claimed to be taking up a moderate position between the extreme right-wing 'originalisms' and a group of thinkers he calls perfectionists, including Dworkin certainly and, I assume, myself. But his general arguments for this position conflates reasonable conceptions of judicial decision making proceeding case by case with the much less reasonable celebration, as a virtue, of the incomplete theorization of interpretations of constitutional law.[15] There are two problems with Sunstein's plea for incomplete theorization. First, it is not clear that, on examination, it really recommends anything much different from the perfectionist views he criticizes.[16] Second, to the extent it does recommend something different (e.g., Sunstein's critique of constitutional privacy), it is not only interpretively and normatively wrong but also undercuts the grounds for a convincing critique of fundamentalism in law.

Fundamentalism in law is not deplorable merely because it invents a history of the founders that is usually bad history, nor because, as Sunstein makes clear, it fails to attend to the often-powerful arguments of critical historiography that run directly against its highly conservative conclusions. It does all these bad things, and more. But we cannot either understand what motivates such an unsound theory of constitutional interpretation, or why such a view has the appeal it does, unless we take seriously its roots in a patriarchal culture and psychology now very much under critical attack. What has brought fundamentalism in law, 'originalism,' to center stage in American constitutional law and politics is its very specific onslaught on both the suspectness of gender and sexual orientation and the principle of constitutional privacy, principles that are, as I and others have

12 Sunstein, *Radical in Robes*, p. 97; see also *id.*, p. 102.

13 Charles Fried, *Modern Liberty and the Limits of Government* (New York: W. W. Norton, 2007), pp. 130–8.

14 Sunstein, *Radicals in Robes*, p. 127.

15 See, for his general defense of this position, Cass R. Sunstein, *One Case at a Time: Judicial Minimalism on the Supreme Court* (Cambridge, Mass.: Harvard University Press, 1999).

16 For a revealing examination along these lines, see Ronald Dworkin, *Justice in Robes* (Cambridge, Mass.: The Belknap Press of Harvard University Press, 2006), pp. 66–72.

argued, both interpretively and normatively sound, resting on the deepest principles of democratic voice that actuate our constitutionalism. For the first time in American history, as I argued in Chapter 1, the voices of women (straight and lesbian) and gay men were accorded their basic rights of dissent from the injustice of American patriarchy, including the love laws (forbidding sexual intimacy across the patriarchally enforced boundaries of religion, ethnicity, and gender). The normative appeal of their resistance is shown by their increasingly successful critique of the role the love laws played in the patriarchal support of the structural injustices of extreme religious intolerance (anti-Semitism), racism, sexism, and homophobia. What explains both the motivations and the appeal of fundamentalism in law (like the related fundamentalisms in religion) is a reactionary response to these developments, deriving from the hold patriarchy continues to exercise over American manhood and womanhood. The kind of contempt for reason, which all fundamentalisms reflect and indeed take pride in, itself requires explanation and critique, in particular, when we are dealing with the role of reason in the fuller protection of the basic human rights guaranteed to all by the principles of American constitutionalism.

I have defined patriarchy in terms of the hierarchical authority of priest-fathers over all others, mothers and daughters as well as sons, an authority maintained by the suppression of the voices that would most reasonably contest and resist such authority. Women lack independent moral voice and agency in this conception; they play a role and a crucial one in patriarchy, but one defined by the subordination and lack of voice that sustains such arrangements. Because authority in general (in religion and law) is filtered solely through patriarchal men, who make God and ethics in their image, the reasoning of women, rooted in their experience, is devalued and denied in favor of an idealization of good patriarchal women that requires the denigration of bad women, neither of whom is real. What threatens patriarchy is reasoning that takes seriously the reasoning and experience of real women, which explains why fundamentalisms crucially exclude women from the authority of a priesthood, preferring rather an echo chamber of endlessly repetitive patriarchal voices. 'Originalism' expresses its patriarchal roots by giving a patriarchal interpretation to the founders as, essentially, patriarchal men, giving us highly specific orders that we must follow slavishly, no matter how unreasonable. The founders, on this view, were not only men but patriarchal men, and their authority for us must be that of patriarchs. Fidelity to their authority requires that we never regard antipatriarchal women (straight or lesbian) or gay men as having voices and reasoning that shape the meaning of constitutional principles. That is, for fundamentalism in law, the heart of the matter. This ideological war on reason is at the heart of the psychology of patriarchy, all the more so when the voices so reasonably contest long-standing patriarchal practices that are inconsistent with democratic principles.

A view, so contemptuous of reason, has a way of making good reasons less compelling as grounds for constitutional interpretation, appealing, in its place, to uncritical ideological conceptions of political preference or taste. Sunstein's criticisms of decisions outside constitutional privacy suggest the impact of such lowering of standards of reason on justices who are not 'originalists' and who should not, therefore, be drawn to interpretive views resting on bad history, or a rule-based jurisprudence that distorts our history and the role principles have played in understanding and making sense of that history both over time and in contemporary circumstances. But we cannot understand the power 'originalism' has unless, pace Sunstein, we take seriously its patriarchal roots, which remakes authority in its own self-referential image, ordering us to obey or defer to such authority, not, in particular, to be open to or to listen to reason, the reason of each and every person subject to law. Its ultimate polemical redoubt is, in the name of a history that does not exist and an authority that is undemocratic, to express contempt for the demands of reason in constitutional law – which is itself a work of democratic reason calling for respect for universal human rights. It is in this sense catastrophic.[17]

The worst that can be said of incomplete theorization in Sunstein's views – and they are central to what is original in his views – is that, in the interest of some conception of political consensus, we should not press the demands of reason as far as theorists like Dworkin and myself urge. But what leads us to press the case for reason, including appeal to deeper moral and political theories, is precisely what affronts us in the fundamentalisms about us, in particular, the fundamentalism in law. It is surely important that this fundamentalism – despite its internal incoherence and substantive unreasonableness – has been as appealing as it is, indeed, that 'originalists' like Justice Scalia could be held up by President Bush as a model of judicial integrity, one that he sought to emulate in his appointments to the Supreme Court of the United States, or that candidate John McCain in the presidential campaign of 2008 held up as his model for such appointments should he be elected. Why so appealing, indeed so praised, as if 'originalism' were not only common sense, but an ideal of judicial impartiality? When political judgments are so unreasonable, we need, as a condition of our intellectual and ethical responsibilities as a free people, more profound critique, not less – certainly not a search for compromise with precisely the political judgments that are so flawed by irrationalism. We need both critique and diagnosis.

The appeal to the founders is what 'originalism' plays on, but, in fact, it not only makes no reasonable sense of their remarkable enduring contribution to democratic constitutionalism but also falsifies their contribution, by remaking Lockean democrats into Filmerian patriarchs. What is astonishing is how a patriarchal culture and psychology can so mindlessly imagine the founders in this way. This is why, I believe, a diagnosis in terms of a reactionary patriarchal culture

[17] See, for extensive defense of this conception of American constitutionalism, David A. J. Richards, *Foundations of American Constitutionalism* (New York: Oxford University Press, 1989).

and psychology is so called for. Patriarchy has lasted for so long, including under American constitutionalism, because it has thus repressed and marginalized the voices of those who would most reasonably contest and resist its demands. But patriarchy is inconsistent with the normative principles of democratic constitutionalism, which explains why it has recurrently expressed itself in American constitutional history by seeking to remake American constitutionalism in its own patriarchal image, draining our constitutional project of its ethical demands, grounded in an enlarging and deepening respect for basic human rights. As I earlier observed (Chapter 7), this was the moral basis of Lincoln's indignation, indeed sense of disgust, at the uncritical 'originalism' of *Dred Scott v. Sanford*, entrenching slavery in the territories in an obscene violation of the Constitution's demand that the national government respect universal human rights. Patriarchy thus made psychologically possible the aggressive expression of ignoble impulses of American proslavery racism as what the Constitution demanded, precipitating the Civil War. Contemporary 'originalism' is yet another expression of this deeply American, self-blinding, reactionary dynamic. We need to see it for what it is, and demand the one thing it cannot endure, accountability to reason on terms that respect the basic human rights that are constitutionally protected. At this point, Sunstein's undertheorization is precisely what we do not need, indeed, what it is irresponsible to think we do need.

2. THE PROMISE OF BARACK OBAMA FOR DEMOCRATIC CONSTITUTIONALISM

Cass Sunstein has published a more recent book that deepens his critique of 'originalism,' as well as an interpretive approach he calls Burkean, in light of the kinds of perfectionist arguments he had earlier sought to avoid.[18] His central concern in that book, quite consistent with my own argument here, is that constitutional law be a check on biases and prejudices, including the cascades of majoritarian animus to minorities that disfigure our democracy (opposition to gay marriage is one of his examples).[19] There is much to admire in this book, not least the way in which Sunstein interprets his undertheorization thesis more strategically as in ultimate service of perfectionist principles.

The interest of this more recent book is that it sheds reasonable light on the constitutional views of Barack Obama, currently president of the United States, who evidently became a close friend of Sunstein during the period that they both taught at the University of Chicago Law School (Sunstein now works as an adviser in the White House on leave from his current appointment at the Harvard Law

[18] See Cass R. Sunstein, *A Constitution of Many Minds: Why the Founding Document Doesn't Mean What It Meant Before* (Princeton, N.J.: Princeton University Press, 2009).

[19] See *id.*, pp. 169–73.

School, and he has been nominated to run the Office of Information and Regulatory Affairs in the White House Office of Management and Budget[20]). Obama has himself made quite clear his own constitutional views, which are critical of 'originalism,' and indeed, while a senator, he opposed the judicial appointments both of Chief Justice Roberts and Justice Alito because their views were either 'originalist' or too sympathetic to 'originalism.'[21] His opposition to Roberts, who appeared at his hearings to be moderate, appears now to be well supported by the chief justice's quite right-wing conservatism on the Court.[22] Obama saw clearly what others did not. This raises and should raise for us psychological questions about why Obama has, unlike other more conventional American politicians (including Democratic politicians), had the intelligence to see through the ways in which patriarchy masks itself from the sober and reasonable assessment of what Americans should demand from their constitutional judges.

Both of Sunstein's books discussed earlier clarify how and why Obama has been so critical of 'originalist' interpretive views, why indeed he actively opposed judicial appointments motivated by such views, and why his own judicial appointments will be of persons who reject 'originalism.' Sunstein's name has prominently been mentioned as someone Obama might at some point appoint to the Supreme Court, and both of Sunstein's books make clear why such an appointment might, for Obama, be so sensible.

The argument of this work further supports the position of Barack Obama on these matters and casts a flood of light on two important questions that Obama's appeal should lead us to ask. First, what is it in Obama's developmental background and life that have made him such an intelligent and penetrating moral leader on 'originalism' and other questions? Second, why Obama's appeal now? Both questions require us to see what is so clearly before us but has been so little seen: Obama is conspicuously not a patriarchal man.

The remarkable manhood of Barack Obama suggests he is as forward looking on issues of gender as on issues of race, transcending old categories and inviting new understanding and debate. This is apparent in the number of talented women he has appointed to his administration, including Hillary Clinton as secretary of state, and in his recent nomination of Sonia Sotomayor as a justice of the U.S. Supreme Court. But I am struck as well by his commitment to listening across conventional political divisions and his desire to forge a politics not based on demonizing enemies. Obama resists hierarchy politically (placing one group over another), because his psychology is not internally divided by the gender binaries of more patriarchal men (e.g., a masculine reason [or mind] over a

[20] See John D. McKinnon, "Businesses Encouraged by Nominee for Regulatory Czar," *Wall Street Journal*, May 13, 2009, at A4.

[21] See, for Obama's own stated views, Barack Obama, *The Audacity of Hope* (New York: Three Rivers Press, 2006), pp. 79, 89–97.

[22] See Jeffrey Toobin, "No More Mr. Nice Guy: The Supreme Court's Stealth Hard-Liner," *New Yorker*, May 25, 2009, pp. 42–51.

feminine passion [or body]). For the same reason, Obama is less vulnerable than more patriarchal men to perceived insults to honor that reflexively elicit violence (thus, his resistance to the Iraq misadventure).

Obama's background and life story suggest some of the paths to democratic manhood that Carol Gilligan and I have observed in men who come to resist patriarchy by staying in real relationship to beloved figures (often mothers) who resist patriarchy and by seeking and finding an intimate life in relationship to a partner they regard and treat as an equal.[23] On my view, there is no psychologically more important and liberating form of resistance to patriarchy than breaking the patriarchal love laws that forbid intimate connections across the barriers of religion, race, or gender. It is precisely such connections that make possible a psychology that sees how false and unjust the patriarchal stereotypes of manhood and womanhood are, making possible a sense of ethics and politics more justly responsive to the voices and experiences of the individual women and men who resist the injustice of patriarchy (which represses and indeed wars on these voices).

Obama's predecessor, George W. Bush, was a patriarchal man, "burdened" (as Maureen Dowd observed) "by the psychological traits of an asphyxiated and pampered son."[24] This psychology expressed itself in the way Bush linked the militant defense of the patriarchal family (proposing a constitutional amendment to ban gay marriage) to leading the nation into an unjust war in Iraq on the basis of perceived insults to our national honor (September 11).

Obama has a very different developmental history. Obama barely knew his father, though he had a lively imagination about him; indeed, when he did actually meet his rather controlling father on a short visit to Honolulu, he soon "began to count the days until my father would leave."[25] Obama developed his liberal and humane values in relationship with his mother and her parents, Toot and Gramps. Obama's mother broke the patriarchal love laws by falling in love with and marrying a man of color (after divorce from him, she was to fall in love and marry another man of color), and Obama clearly came to see and understand her as a real woman with sexual interests, including "fantasies that had been forbidden to a white middle-class girl from Kansas, the promise of another life, warm, sensual, exotic, different."[26] It was Obama's mother who, as a boy, woke him early to teach him his English lessons for three hours before he went to school, a regime at which the young Barack bridled; her defense was, "This is no picnic for me either, buster."[27] Obama later learned from his mother that his father abandoned the marriage in part because his Kenyan family

[23] See Gilligan and Richards, *The Deepening Darkness: Patriarchy, Resistance, and Democracy's Future* (Cambridge: Cambridge University Press, 2009); see also Richards, *Disarming Manhood: Roots of Ethical Resistance* (Athens: Ohio University/Swallow Press, 2005).

[24] Maureen Dowd, "The Long, Lame Goodbye," *New York Times*, Jan. 18, 2009, Week in Review, at WK 15.

[25] Obama, *Dreams from My Father*, p. 68.

[26] *Id.*, p. 124.

[27] *Id.*, p. 48.

patriarchally "didn't want Obama blood sullied by a white woman."[28] Obama thus experienced firsthand both his mother's resistance to the patriarchal love laws and his father's lack of resistance, opening his heart and mind to what makes such resistance so liberatory yet so difficult and lack of resistance sometimes so tragic. What such resistance makes psychologically possible is breaking through the ethnic and other stereotypes that unjustly divide through love of another as an individual. It was in loving relationship to such a resisting woman that Obama came to accord authority to her liberal and humane values, including the moral authority of women's voices and experiences. Obama dealt with the experience of loss (the loss of his father, the feeling of separation as a man of color from his white mother and grandparents) not through identification with patriarchal stereotypes of manhood but by staying in relationship to the real, individual people whom he loved and loved him. Both his mother and Toot were strong, adventurous women, loving men while holding to their own ambitions and sense of themselves (Toot had earned more money than her husband). Obama stayed in loving relationship to unidealized real women (including a mother who did not sacrifice her sexual or her intellectual life); his mother, an anthropologist, may have imparted to her son an interpretive ability not to confuse culture and nature, and thus to be sensitive to the ways in which the unjust power of patriarchy rests on this confusion. Through his mother and grandmother, Obama came to his own vibrant relationship with a woman clearly his equal. In *Dreams from My Father*, he identifies a "strong, true love" with an equal as what saves men from the "male cruelties" that destroyed his father.[29] In doing so, he shows us a manhood that is democratic, not patriarchal.

In his thinking about his economic policies, for example, Obama's ethical intelligence frames issues in terms of how his policies on education would impact someone in his grandmother's situation[30] or crystallizes hard ethical choices about health care in terms of a moving description of his grandmother at the end of her life,[31] or his mother's struggles with her health insurance as she died of ovarian cancer,[32] or thinks of gender equality in terms of the importance to him of his wife earning more than he during certain years, when "she carried us."[33] And when he defended his pro-choice views on abortion in a commencement speech at Notre Dame, he insisted "that this heart-wrenching decision for any woman is not made casually. It has both moral and spiritual dimension."[34] More patriarchal

[28] *Id.*, p. 126.

[29] *Id.*, p. 429.

[30] See David Leonhardt, "After the Great Recession: An Interview with President Obama," *New York Times Magazine*, May 3, 2009, pp. 36–41, 76, 87, at p. 39.

[31] See *id.*, p. 76.

[32] See President Barack Obama, info@barackobama.com, May 20, 2009, e-mail calling for support of his health-care policy.

[33] See Leonhardt, "After the Great Recession," p. 76.

[34] See Peter Baker and Susan Saulny, "At Notre Dame, Obama Calls for Civil Tone in Abortion Debate," *New York Times*, May 18, 2009, pp. A1 and A3, at p. A1.

men do not speak or think in this way about the moral authority for them of women's voices and experiences.[35]

Obama's inaugural speech made clear the power of democratic manhood to deepen our democracy. While defining our nation's challenge – both at home and abroad – as one of building on "the sacrifices borne by our ancestors," he did not idealize American history. In asking us to "choose our better history," he asked us to remember what we have learned as a people who "have tasted the bitter swill of civil war and segregation." For Obama, responsibilities arise from relationships, and he emphasizes those not celebrated; "men and women obscure in their labor – who have carried us up the long, rugged path towards prosperity and freedom." His responsibility to his Kenyan father extends from "the small village where my father was born," to understanding how and "why a man whose father less than 60 years ago might not have been served at a local restaurant can now stand before you to take a most sacred oath." But his understanding of responsibility directly reflects what he owes his remarkable single mother as well as Toot and Gramps, as he calls on the American people to show "a parent's willingness to nurture a child." He asks us to remember and build on not falsifying ideals but real relationships: "these men and women [who] struggled and sacrificed and worked till their hands were raw so that we might live a better life." He calls for new forms of deliberative political intelligence, drawn from real debate between equals in service of real values, "honesty and hard work, courage and fair play, tolerance and curiosity, loyalty and patriotism." For Obama, as a democratic man, these values demand the inclusion of all people, "the God-given promise that all are equal, all are free, and all deserve a chance to pursue their full measure of happiness," a promise he extends to "nonbelievers": and one he finally defines in terms that dissolve "the lines of tribe," so that "our common humanity shall reveal itself." In contrast, Obama rejects as "childish things" a polarized and reactionary American politics that feeds on exclusion, "the petty grievances and false promises, the recriminations and worn-out dogmas that for far too long have strangled our politics."[36]

Both the style and content of the inaugural address echo, probably self-consciously, the speeches of Lincoln – for Lincoln, the appeal to our universal values of human rights against the antidemocratic values of the proslavery South; for Obama, "the rule of law and the rights of man": against a reactionary right-wing fundamentalist politics based on "the old hatreds."[37] There is both moral passion and the most sober analytical reason in Obama as there was in Lincoln, both men joining emotion and thought in the service of realizing a more perfect

[35] For further exploration of this psychological point about antipatriarchal men, discussing, from this perspective, the psychologies of Garrison, Tolstoy, Gandhi, Martin Luther King, and Churchill, see Richards, *Disarming Manhood*.

[36] See the address "All This We Will Do," *New York Times*, Jan. 21, 2009, at P2.

[37] *Id.*

union. What strikes me at this moment in American history is the transformative power of democratic manhood. By challenging patriarchal gender binaries and hierarchies, it shows us how childishly undemocratic we have been and brings real democracy again within our political grasp. Only a manhood resisting patriarchy can understand and advance democracy.

My extended analysis of the patriarchal psychology underlying the appeal of both religious and legal fundamentalism clarifies why a democratic man like Obama, himself a resister of patriarchy, should have become a national moral leader opposing 'originalism.' He can see what more patriarchal men cannot, how undemocratic 'originalism' is, how locked into an echo chamber of anachronistic patriarchal voices unresponsive to the claims of democratic reason for gender equality. Obama's plea for empathy in judges is neither pragmatic nor unprincipled in the way conservatives suppose,[38] but in service of the enduring values of equal liberty of democracy itself. What is deplorable in this conservative criticism is the way it assumes, tracking the gender binary, that a good constitutional judge must sharply demarcate reason from emotion in a way no good judge ever has or could, appealing to an indefensible conception of disassociated manhood as the measure of good constitutional interpretation.[39] What is so remarkable about Obama is that he sees such patriarchal assumptions for the corruption of our constitutional democracy that they are and, in the form of the 'originalists,' have been.

Obama's speech to the Senate, explaining why he would vote against the nomination of Roberts, confirms the probing ethical and political intelligence underlying his rejection of 'originalism.' Obama accepts that Roberts "loves the law" and would "deeply respect the basic precepts that go into deciding 95 [percent] of the cases that come before the federal court," cases in which "both a Scalia and a Ginsburg will arrive at the same place most of the time." What worries Obama, however, is "those 5 [percent] of hard cases" where matters are less clear and a good judge must go beyond clear and uncontroversial rules of decision (e.g., "whether affirmative action is an appropriate response to the history of discrimination in this country" or "whether a general right of privacy encompasses a more specific right of women to control their reproductive decisions"). In these cases, "the critical ingredient is supplied by what is in the judge's heart," by which Obama means a sense of the values of justice in our constitutional tradition, "evening out the playing field between the strong and the weak." What Obama finds in Roberts's record is his protection of the strong as opposed to the weak, including, in particular, his dismissal both "of efforts to eradicate the remnants of racial discrimination" and "concerns that it is harder to make it in this

[38] See David Lewis Schaefer, "When It Comes to Judges, 'Pragmatic' Means Unprincipled," *Wall Street Journal*, May 9–10, 2009, at A13; John Hasnas, "The 'Unseen' Deserve Empathy, Too," *Wall Street Journal*, May 29, 2009, at A15.

[39] I am grateful to Donald Levy for suggesting this point to me.

world and in this economy when you are a woman rather than a man."[40] What Obama objected to in Roberts was precisely his patriarchal disassociation from the resisting voices of both people of color and women, challenging injustices rooted in patriarchy. What rationalizes such disassociation is the gender binary (reason, as masculine, versus emotion, as feminine). What makes Obama so psychologically remarkable among American political leaders is not only that he sees the gender binary as the problematic criterion for judicial impartiality it is but that he sees the appeal to it as an illegitimate way of rationalizing constitutional injustices rooted in patriarchy. Obama broke through the disassociation himself when he voted against the nomination of Roberts precisely because Roberts lacks "heart," namely a sense of justice appropriately sensitive to the moral voices of those groups traditionally silenced by patriarchy.

We can see such intelligence as well in Obama's recent choice of Sonia Sotomayor, a Hispanic woman, as his nominee to the Supreme Court of the United States, a person who shares features of Obama's psychological development (loss of a father and loving care by a mother devoted to the educational advancement of her children) and his antipatriarchal perspective on constitutional interpretation.[41] Sotomayor is on record, questioning, in her own words, "whether [in] ignoring our differences as women or men of color we do a disservice both to the law and society."[42] What she clearly means is that judges, who take seriously their different relationship to patriarchy (as a member of a group unjustly treated), may be more likely to interpret our constitution as a more just response to all voices, resisting the ways in which patriarchy silences the resisting voices of groups that have been unjustly dehumanized. It shows the psychological roots of 'originalism' in the reactionary demands of patriarchal manhood, suppressing voices that resist the injustices patriarchy inflicts, that conservative objection to Sotomayor's nomination takes the form of Newt Gingrich's hypothetical: "Imagine a judicial nominee said 'my experience as a white man makes me better than a Latina woman.' Wouldn't they have to withdraw?"[43] Gingrich speaks in and from the echo chamber of patriarchal privilege that cannot even imagine the justice of resisting voices, and their relevance to more impartial and just constitutional interpretation. In this hermetically sealed Orwellian world that distorts truth to the demands of unjustly entrenched power, sensitivity to precisely an unconstitutional motive like racism and sexism is transformed into racism and sexism,[44] and the questioning by a woman judge of men is denigrated as "blunt

[40] See Barack Obama, "Why Obama Voted against Roberts," *Wall Street Journal*, June 2, 2009, at A21.

[41] I am writing this in early June 2009.

[42] Quoted in Jess Bravin, "Legal Realism Informs Judge's Views," *Wall Street Journal*, May 28, 2009, at p. A3.

[43] Quoted in Jonathan Weisman and Naftali Bendavid, "Battle over Sotomayor Heats Up," *Wall Street Journal*, May 28, 2009, at A3.

[44] See, for an example of this point, Raymond Hernandez and David W. Chen, "Nominee's Links with Advocates Fuel Her Critics," *New York Times*, May 29, 2009, at A1 and A14; David D.

and testy" in a way the comparable questioning of a man never is.[45] What is clearly at stake here is a perceived threat to the gender binary, as it is precisely at the points that Sotomayor resists the binary and for this reason is a better judge of constitutional law that she is condemned as unjudicial. It is a symptom of how powerful the patriarchal psychology behind 'originalism' has become in the United States that Sotomayor, a nonpatriarchal woman, is mindlessly accused of racism when former Chief Justice William Rehnquist and current Chief Justice John Roberts, both patriarchal white men, were nominated despite records including a racist defense of separate but equal (Rehnquist) and "a crusader's zeal in his efforts to role back the civil rights gains of the 1960s and '70s – everything from voting rights to women's rights" (Roberts).[46] Obama's importance to democracy is that he sees such irrationalism for what it is (voting against the nomination of Roberts) and has nominated Sotomayor at least in part because resistance to the gender binary suggests to him a person likely for that reason to be a better constitutional judge.

It is too early to know how transformative Obama's presidency will be on American political and constitutional culture. And there is reason to worry that even so democratic a man as Obama may for a mixture of prudential reasons and residual patriarchal anxieties not always lead in the ways his conscience may and should require (e.g., on gay marriage).[47] Even here, however, Obama has pledged to listen to all voices, including those who disagree with him, which puts in a different light Obama's choice to bring a fundamentalist pastor into the inauguration ceremony or his appeal to those conservative African Americans in California who joined with the Mormons to repudiate gay marriage.

Lincoln again may be a good comparison. Lincoln was always antislavery, but he knew that his political cause, as a democratic politician, was hopeless if he challenged as well (as radical abolitionists like Garrison and Lydia Maria Child had) the racism so broadly shared both in the North and South. Lincoln in much of his career accepted this racism as axiomatic, though during the Civil War he also evinced a capacity for reflective moral growth, questioning his racism in light of the experience of black soldiers fighting courageously and decisively for the Union cause.[48] Obama is certainly less homophobic and more morally reflective than most American politicians but, as a democratic politician, may feel that,

Kirkpatrick, "A Judge's Focus on Race Issues May Be Hurdle," *New York Times*, May 30, 2009, at A1 and A8.

45 See, on this point, Jo Becker and Adam Liptak, "Assertive Style Raises Questions on Demeanor," *New York Times*, May 29, 2009, at A14. Judge Calabresi, a colleague of Sotomayor on the Second Circuit Court of Appeals, there observed: "Some lawyers just don't like to be questioned by a woman.... It was sexist, plain and simple."

46 Charles M. Blow, "Rogues, Robes and Racists," *New York Times*, May 30, 2009, at A19.

47 See, e.g., Sheryl Gay Stolberg, "Gay Issues in View, Obama Is Pressed to Engage," *New York Times*, May 7, 2009, at A1 and A21.

48 See, on this point, David A. J. Richards, *Conscience and the Constitution: History, Theory, and Law of the Reconstruction Amendments* (Princeton, N.J.: Princeton University Press, 1993), pp. 111–12.

like Lincoln, he cannot, without much worsening of things all around, challenge the degree to which Americans remain quite homophobic in their attitudes. He may, therefore, as Lincoln did with racism, not challenge homophobia as much as liberals like myself would like. Indeed, if Obama possesses as democratic a psychology as I have argued he does, the successes that his resistance to patriarchy makes possible in deepening and extending our democracy may, precisely because they place patriarchy in such threat, elicit reactionary forces that may defeat even him and our hopes for him. We don't know, and we won't know for some time. But even on the limited record before us, it is surely remarkable that it should be this man with this background that should, more than any other comparable political figure, have so bravely and intelligently confronted and resisted the essentially patriarchal appeal of 'originalism.'

But why should Obama have the appeal that he has had now, at precisely this point in our cultural and political history as a people? Obama's voice, as a man of color, has had the democratic resonance it has had for the American people in a way surely made possible by the voice of Martin Luther King Jr. My point is not only that King's greatest political successes – passage of the Civil Rights Act of 1964 and the Voting Rights Act of 1965 – laid the framework that made possible a democracy that could elect Barack Obama. Equally important, Obama, like King, found a moral voice that appealed across the racial and other barriers that have historically divided and polarized Americans on the basis of a more democratic vision of our constitutionalism, a political value that unites all Americans. American liberalism, whose political problems can be traced to the tragic division of King and Lyndon Johnson over the Vietnam War, has found in Obama a political leader apparently able to bridge these divisions. Obama, a less patriarchal man than even Martin Luther King,[49] found his voice, as an expression of his developmental psychology, more deeply in relationship to the antipatriarchal women and men who nurtured and loved him and in egalitarian relationship to the woman he loves as a partner in public and private life. Obama's remarkable appeal arises at the end of the long period from Ronald Reagan to George Bush, both of whom put a smiling patriarchal face on a reactionary conservatism that has largely governed American political life, a moment when the aggressive defense of patriarchal family values and unjust war abroad culminated in disastrously improvident regulation of the American economy, abuses of power that began under and derived from the reactionary patriarchal politics of Reagan.[50]

Americans were jarred awake from the patriarchal disassociation that had governed American politics for much too long and saw what was now so clearly before their eyes, leading them to be open to questioning a conservatism that

[49] On King's struggles with patriarchy, both in his political and in his personal life, see Richards, *Disarming Manhood*, pp. 131–80.

[50] On the roots of our current economic crisis in Reagan's policies, see Paul Krugman, "Reagan Did It," *New York Times*, June 1, 2009, at A21.

rested on patriarchal assumptions that divided Americans from one another and gave rise to a sense of humiliated manhood (after September 11) that expressed itself in an aggressive war in Iraq that was both unwise and unjust. Obama, who opposed the Iraq war and 'originalism,' appealed to the deeper democratic values that now united and moved Americans and posed a plausible alternative, calling for a deepening and extending of our democracy consistent with the values and achievements of the political movements for human rights of the 1960s and later, including Johnson's long-forgotten War on Poverty. The psychology of resistance that was the basis of these movements continued in the United States during the period of conservative dominance, still very much alive though much more marginal to our politics that it should have been (thus, the irrationalist demonizing of liberalism). Obama's appeal shows how alive this psychology was now in him and Americans generally. It was no longer plausible, as it had once been, to denigrate the remarkable ethical and political achievements of the 1960s and later as "sex, drugs, and rock 'n' roll,"[51] because the freeing of moral voice from patriarchal constraints (exemplified by Obama himself) resonated with and invigorated a free moral voice now more alive in us, and more correspondingly critical of the patriarchal obfuscation and distortion that had malformed our politics for too long. Obama's voice found the resonance it did because it gave expression to a psychology of resistance that was now – to the surprise of many – deeper and more broadly shared among Americans and for this reason responsive to Obama's more democratic appeal as an alternative to the disastrous policies at home and abroad of political conservatism. The elephant in the room, so to speak, had been patriarchy. Obama, a democratic man made possible by the developments in American culture since the 1960s, critically showed us what we had become and showed us what we could and must be.

3. IMPLICATIONS FOR CONSTITUTIONAL LAW AND POLITICS

What are the implications of my argument for constitutional law and politics? Some of these implications will already be clear, and others can be reasonably inferred. My focus here is on bringing together the two strands of my argument – fundamentalism in religion and in law – to consider what they suggest about central issues of contemporary constitutional interpretation I have not yet discussed.

I have offered my critique of patriarchy not only as an external ethical criticism of our culture's long-standing complicity with it but also as an internal criticism of the role patriarchy has, in my view, played in retarding or frustrating the elaboration of our most fundamental constitutional principles grounded in the fuller protection of the basic human rights owed all persons. Indeed, the view I have defended here is that patriarchy explains the role the condemnation of moral

[51] See, on this point, Gilligan and Richards, *The Deepening Darkness: Patriarchy, Resistance, and Democracy's Future*, pp. 257–63.

slavery plays in the Reconstruction Amendments, and that therefore the account of patriarchy I offer is the best interpretation of the things those amendments condemn in American politics, namely a politics actuated by irrational prejudices that are an expression of long-standing American traditions of moral slavery. One of the ways of coming to understand and evaluate a view of constitutional interpretation is to explore its implications, to carry its analysis further, and thus to appreciate what is its explanatory and normative power.

The most reasonable way to proceed, in thus evaluating the theory I propose in this book and have defended in a number of other books, is to ask what sense it makes of how we should understand and interpret perhaps the most innovative feature of American constitutionalism, the constitutional principles of the First Amendment that require respect for religious free exercise and condemn the establishment of religion. My own view has long been that these guarantees are the most structurally important substantive guarantees of human rights in the U.S. Constitution,[52] and I am concerned now with asking how these guarantees should be understood and interpreted in light of the argument of this book.

What is, of course, central to my account is that patriarchy offers the best theory of the constitutional principles of the Reconstruction Amendments, and thus that combating patriarchy should be regarded as a compelling secular state purpose, indeed, the best explanation of why the constitutional condemnation of extreme religious intolerance (anti-Semitism), racism, sexism, and homophobia are compelling secular state purposes. This analysis has important implications for the reasonable interpretation of the religion clauses in contemporary circumstances. I begin with free exercise and then turn to antiestablishment.

My former colleagues Christopher Eisgruber and Lawrence Sager argue in a recent book that the religion clauses should be understood in terms of two central principles. First, no one within the reach of the Constitution should be devalued on the account of the spiritual foundations of her or his commitments. Second, all persons should enjoy broad rights of free speech, personal autonomy, associative freedom, and private property.[53] Their argument is unusual in American constitutional scholarship: it is both historically well informed and even better normatively well grounded in ways that not only clarify the work of the Supreme Court in interpreting the clauses but, in the matter of constitutionally compelled free exercise exemptions from laws, afford a more reasonable and explanatory account of what the Court has done than the Court itself. Because the account is as explanatory and normatively powerful as it is, it also addresses the more controversial interpretations of the religion clauses of the Supreme Court, including the current Court, in ways that are both critical and convincing.

52 See Richards, *Toleration and the Constitution*.

53 Christopher L. Eisgruber and Lawrence G. Sager, *Religious Freedom and the Constitution* (Cambridge, Mass.: Harvard University Press, 2007).

There is, however, one aspect of their account that I want to explore in the light of the argument of this book, namely their robust defense of the autonomy of religions to determine the qualifications of clergy, including limiting the clergy to men.[54] Eisgruber and Sager defend and endorse this principle as an instance of "the same important constitutional principle, namely, that there are a variety of personal relationships in which members of our political community are free to choose their partners, associates or colleagues without interference from the state."[55] My former colleagues observe that one law professor (Ira Lupu) has argued that churches should have the right to decide for themselves whom to admit as members, but that, once having made that decision, they be obliged to respect antidiscrimination laws with regard to treatment of their members. On this view, because the Catholic Church permitted women to join, it could not constitutionally discriminate against its women when choosing priests.[56] My colleagues find this "a strange view: Why concede to the Catholic church the freedom to exclude persons on the basis of gender, but not permit the Church to assign differentiated roles of leadership on the basis of gender?"[57] Rather, they argue that "the Constitution itself guarantees churches (and other associations, both secular and religious) the freedom to select leaders and officers on the basis of their constitutive principles,"[58] even if their selection involves discrimination on the ground of race or gender that violates Title VII of the Civil Rights Act of 1964 (from which religions are exempt and, for Eisgruber and Sager, must be exempt constitutionally).[59]

If my analysis is correct, combating patriarchy is itself a compelling secular state purpose because it best explains why combating extreme religious intolerance, racism, sexism, and homophobia are compelling state purposes. But as we have seen in our analysis of fundamentalist religions, it is the patriarchal nature of an all-male clergy (sometimes celibate, as in Catholicism; sometimes not, as in Protestantism and Mormonism) that explains the dogmatic and reactionary fundamentalism on issues of gender and sexuality. It is therefore reasonable to argue that such patriarchal authority is responsible for a range of irrational prejudices that are now constitutionally condemned as a basis for laws and policies on secular grounds rooted in the Constitution itself. If this is right, why is it not constitutionally reasonable to insist that such patriarchal religions not be exempt from antidiscrimination laws?

[54] See *id.*, pp. 51, 57, 63–5, 225–6, 250.

[55] *Id.*, p. 65.

[56] See *id.*, pp. 65–6. The article discussed is Ira C. Lupu, "Free Exercise Exemptions and Religious Institutions," 67 *Boston U. L. Rev.* 391, 435–8 (1987). For a view more in line with the one taken by Eisgruber and Sager, see Douglas Laycock, "Towards a General Theory of the Religion Clauses: The Case of Church Labor Relations and the Right to Church Autonomy," 81 *Columbia L. Rev.* 1371 (1981).

[57] See Eisgruber and Sager, *Religious Freedom and the Constitution*, p. 66.

[58] See *id.*, p. 250.

[59] *Id.* See, for a similar account, Kent Greenawalt, *Religion and the Constitution*, vol. 1, *Free Exercise and Fairness* (Princeton, N.J.: Princeton University Press, 2006), pp. 378–86.

There is a form of the argument I am exploring that has already been proposed, widely discussed, and largely rejected at least in the United States, namely Catherine MacKinnon's argument that the right of free speech protected by the First Amendment should be interpreted not to bar censorship of hard-core pornographic materials that promote violence against and the degradation of women. MacKinnon's argument was that combating sexism (including its violence against and degradation of women) was a compelling state purpose and that, therefore, whatever values of free speech attached to hard-core pornography should yield to combating sexism. I, like others, have questioned MacKinnon's argument both for its underestimation of the free speech values of erotica (in particular, for groups like gay men whose sexuality was repressed and silenced) and for its claim that censorship of such material would combat sexism, when, in fact, as happened in Canada, laws based on MacKinnon's views would be used not against the mainstream, popular heterosexual pornography MacKinnon despises, but against groups (like gays and lesbians) whom MacKinnon would want to protect from such gender-based repression.[60]

The general form of MacKinnon's argument is that the protected rights of the First Amendment (including not only free speech but also religion and conscience more generally) should yield to the compelling secular state purposes, including combating sexism, that have now been recognized as constitutionally compelled. My own account would suggest that if a form of MacKinnon's general argument were ever valid, it would not be the application of the argument that she defends but its application to a case like subjecting the core evil of patriarchal religions (an all-male clergy) to antidiscrimination laws, as Lupu proposed. Patriarchy, as I have suggested, is not reasonably required by any of these religions and forges attitudes that, ostensibly rooted in religion, crucially legitimate a range of irrational prejudices that are now constitutionally condemned as a basis for laws and politics. In contrast to MacKinnon's proposal, the application of antidiscrimination laws to limitations of religious clergy to only men does not compromise the compelling secular purpose it claims to advance: it advances it quite reasonably. If I am right about the pivotal importance in contemporary America of patriarchal religion in legitimating sexism, then the proposal quite directly addresses the root of the problem, the role that religions in the modern world play in supporting forms of fundamentalism that aggressively attack the basic human rights of women (straight and lesbian) and gay men.

But it is difficult to see how a principled liberalism could accept the general form of MacKinnon's proposal and its plausible application, as I have suggested, to the violation by religions of antidiscrimination principles. Liberalism requires, as one of its foundational principles, equal respect for all forms of conscience, whether or not the convictions conscientiously held include endorsement of basic

60 See, for further development of this argument, David A. J. Richards, *Women, Gays, and the Constitution: The Grounds for Feminism and Gay Rights in Culture and Law* (Chicago: University of Chicago Press, 1998), pp. 242–3.

constitutional principles, including those that condemn the expression through law or policy of extreme religious intolerance (anti-Semitism), racism, sexism, and homophobia.[61] If we thus constitutionally protect such anti-Semitic or racist or sexist or homophobic convictions, we cannot, as a matter of principle, not protect the organizational liberty, rooted in conscience, that gives expression to such irrational prejudice, to wit, the limitation of clergy exclusively to men, even when a limitation on such organizational liberty is justified as a way of combating irrational prejudices rooted in patriarchy.[62] In fact, many religions, even ones with all-male clergy, question their historical complicity with great evils like anti-Semitism, as, for example, many Catholics now do.[63] And even as highly patriarchal a religion as Roman Catholicism has given up what many once thought to be its distinctive position on the legitimacy of religious persecution. The church abandoned this position in Vatican II largely under the influence of American Catholic priest-scholars like John Courtney Murray; building on American liberalism, Murray questioned his church's illiberalism and persuaded its leaders to accept the argument for toleration, central to constitutional liberalism. The Catholic Church should certainly have gone further in its reforms, rethinking, as many Catholics believe, its anachronistic views of gender and sexuality (see Chapter 4). But if a patriarchal religion like Catholicism could think itself into liberal change on one major issue, why not on another? Certainly, if the argument of this book is reasonably persuasive, it might lead many religious people themselves to question more critically the grounds that both gave rise to and sustain an all-male clergy. If the grounds are no stronger than an accommodation of the religion to then hegemonically dominant patriarchal patterns, such an accommodation may now be questioned as unreasonable, in particular, when more authoritative features of the tradition (e.g., the antipatriarchal teachings of Jesus of Nazareth) support such questioning.

What is important is that liberal constitutional principles never be compromised, which includes guaranteeing the basic rights of the First Amendment to all religions, including fundamentalist ones, but also subjecting such fundamentalist religions to precisely the criticism they richly deserve. I've tried to exemplify such criticisms in the argument of this book, questioning the unjust role patriarchy has played in the formation and perpetuation of both orthodox and unorthodox forms of Christianity. But such criticisms can have the reasonable force they should

[61] See David A. J. Richards, *Free Speech and the Politics of Identity* (Oxford: Oxford University Press, 1999).

[62] For a related case, in which the Supreme Court unanimously upheld such a right to exclude people when rooted in free speech values, see *Hurley v. Irish-American Gay, Lesbian and Bisexual Group of Boston (GLIB)*, 515 U.S. 557 (1995) (state antidiscrimination law cannot constitutionally be applied to the decision of private group sponsoring a parade not to permit gays and lesbians to carry signs with whose message the private group disagreed).

[63] See, e.g., James Carroll, *Constantine's Sword: The Church and the Jews: A History* (Boston: Houghton Mifflin, 2001).

have only if all views, religious and secular, are freely expressed and debated on terms of equal respect for all persons.

It does not follow that all decisions, including employment decisions, of religions must or should be exempt from antidiscrimination norms. Not all of the employment decisions of religions implicate the core values of autonomy that decisions on clergy do, and the argument for constitutional exemption applies only here but no further. In these further areas, in which people are employed in secular roles to serve secular needs, the legitimate scope of antidiscrimination norms should prevail.

Nor does it follow that a nonsectarian, noncommercial group like the Boy Scouts should enjoy a constitutionally protected right to discriminate against gay men, as a 5–4 majority of the Supreme Court mistakenly held in *Boy Scouts of America v. Dale*,[64] exempting the Boy Scouts from a state antidiscrimination law forbidding discrimination on the ground of sexual orientation. Andrew Koppelman and Tobias Wolff are surely right that the state was pursuing legitimate antidiscrimination interests, supported by compelling state purposes, condemning homophobic violence ensuring "that one of the central institutions of the socialization of youth – as a matter of fact, the largest youth organization in the country – is available to all boys in a nondiscriminatory fashion."[65] And the statute did not prevent groups with strongly held discriminatory ideas from uniting and disseminating them. The discriminatory policy hurt the young who participate in Scouting, and it was not endorsed by many members. There was no interest of either religious free exercise or free speech at stake in the case: Scouting was nonsectarian and was not organized around any message concerning sexuality.

But if the argument I offer should not compromise constitutionally protected values of religious free exercise or free speech in their proper domain, it suggests reasons for a more expansive interpretation of the antiestablishment prohibition of the First Amendment. Eisgruber and Sager root the antiestablishment clause in state-endorsed disparagement of any religion or other conviction, identifying the constitutional concern in "the vulnerability of conscience to discrimination or mistreatment."[66] Accordingly, they are much more concerned, than other recent commentators like Noah Feldman,[67] about state-endorsed religious symbols.[68] But they are also concerned with state resources going to religion when two conditions are not satisfied: first, those receiving such resources must enjoy a reasonable

[64] *Boy Scouts of America v. Dale*, 530 U.S. 640 (2000).

[65] See Andrew Koppelman with Tobias Barrington Wolff, *A Right to Discriminate? How the Case of Boy Scouts of America v. James Dale Warped the Law of Free Association* (New Haven, Conn.: Yale University Press, 2009), p. xiv.

[66] Eisgruber and Sager, *Religious Freedom and the Constitution*, p. 203.

[67] See Noah Feldman, *Divided by God: America's Church-State Problem – and What We Should Do about It* (New York: Farrar, Straus and Giroux, 2005).

[68] For their critique of Feldman on this point, see Eisgruber and Sager, *Religious Freedom and the Constitution*, pp. 153–6.

secular alternative to available religious options; and second, government must avoid playing favorites among religions.[69]

My argument powerfully supports the concern of Eisgruber and Sager that these antiestablishment principles not be compromised, including both their concern about state-endorsed religious symbols and their critique of the recent Supreme Court decision allowing state tax money to support tuition vouchers largely used at religious schools.[70] If my argument is right, patriarchal religion plays in the United States an important role in sustaining a range of now constitutionally condemned evils – extreme religious intolerance (anti-Semitism), racism, sexism, and homophobia. It is one thing to extend to these religions the basic guarantees of liberty that all Americans should and must enjoy, but it is quite another that they should enjoy state endorsement. As Kent Greenawalt has perceptively observed:

> If a dominant [constitutional] principle now is that people should be considered as equal regardless of race, gender, ethnic origin, sexual preference, or religious identity, the sense of exclusion engendered by government expressions of religious ideas is a cause for serious concern, whatever the intensity of the feelings of most outsiders.[71]

In light of my argument about the powerful role patriarchy plays in American religion and its resulting support of secular evils now constitutionally condemned, state endorsement of religion should, if anything, be of greater constitutional concern than it has ever been. For the same reasons, the use of state resources to support religious education should be more not less constitutionally problematic when, in light of my argument, we can reasonably see that such resources support teachings that combat compelling secular purposes that are now constitutionally guaranteed. Indeed, in light of my analysis, the whole question of tax exemptions for religions, many of whom support patriarchal values, should be rethought.

The American constitutional tradition of religious liberty rests on the argument for toleration.[72] Its principle of antiestablishment was a uniquely American innovation, innovated by Jefferson and Madison, elaborating the radical Protestant argument that it was the close symbiotic relationship of church and state since Constantine made Christianity the established church of the Roman Empire that led not only to undermining and subverting democracy but also to the degradation of Christianity from the humane ethics of the Gospels to the tyrannies of the Inquisition. When Jefferson and Madison called for a sharper separation of religious and political power in the antiestablishment principle, they were concerned

[69] See, on these conditions, *id.*, pp. 203–4.

[70] See *Zelman v. Simmons-Harris*, 536 U.S. 639 (2002). For their critique, see Eisgruber and Sager, *Religious Freedom and the Constitution*, pp. 212–17.

[71] Kent Greenawalt, *Religion and the Constitution*, vol. 2, *Establishment and Fairness* (Princeton, N.J.: Princeton University Press, 2008), p. 465.

[72] See, on this point, Richards, *Toleration and the Constitution*.

that, learning from this historical experience, religion in general (and Christianity in particular) be so separated from the state that the democratic impulses in Christianity would be harnessed to support constitutional democracy, and constitutional democracy would itself thus better satisfy its conditions of legitimacy, that political power would respect the basic human rights of all persons subject to such power.

If my argument is correct, patriarchy is in tension with democracy, and patriarchal religion is certainly not in service of the democratic impulses in Christianity, which it unreasonably ignores when it does not repress. It is precisely this form of religion that the American principle of antiestablishment was concerned with separating from state endorsement or support. It is for this reason that we need now, perhaps more than ever, to insist that the antiestablishment tradition not be compromised in the way it has been both by the Supreme Court and by constitutional scholars. Otherwise, what we have in the United States is not the separation of church and state that leading founders like Madison and Jefferson believed would promote both a more democratic state and more democratic religion. Rather, we have a de facto establishment of religion like the established churches found in Europe, only without the kind of democratic control over such established churches (e.g., the Anglican church in Great Britain, the Lutheran church in Sweden), which ensures that they support secular aims like gender equality or justice to homosexuals. We have, in short, what our Constitution forbids: an establishment of sectarian, undemocratic religion without the democratic accountability that can alone justify such established religions in the modern world. This is disastrous for American constitutional ideals of both religious liberty and of gender equality. It casts in doubt what is, in fact, one of America's most enduring contributions to democratic constitutionalism: free exercise and antiestablishment, largely because our generation, under the influence of 'originalism,' has proved incompetent to understand, preserve, and protect what the enduring achievements of our founders were. Europeans for this reason justly question an American democratic constitutionalism in which antidemocratic fundamentalist religions have achieved such power over our politics and even our constitutionalism.

It is in this area, as much as constitutional privacy, that we must worry about the role 'originalism' plays in current constitutional interpretation. Justice Scalia has, for example, quite directly appealed to his fundamentalist religious convictions as the ground for endorsing constitutional interpretations that closely link the state and religion:

> The reaction of people of faith to this tendency of democracy to obscure the divine authority behind government should not be resignation to it, but the resolution to combat it as effectively as possible. We have done that in this country (and continental Europe has not) by preserving in our public life many visible reminders that – in the words of the Supreme Court opinion

> from the 1940's – "we are a religious people, whose institutions presuppose a Supreme Being." These reminders include: "In God we trust" on our coins, "one nation, under God" in our Pledge of Allegiance, the opening of sessions of our legislatures with a prayer, the opening of sessions of my Court with "God save the United States and this Honorable Court," annual Thanksgiving proclamations issued by our President at the direction of Congress, and constant innovations of divine support in the speeches of our political leaders, which often include, "God bless America." All of this, as I say, is most un-European, and helps explain why our people are more inclined to understand, as St. Paul did, that government carries the sword as "the minister of God," to "execute wrath" upon the evildoer.[73]

Scalia made these arguments in print in 2002, and not all of them referred to Supreme Court cases already decided. One of them, the inclusion of "under God" in the Pledge of Allegiance, would come before the Supreme Court only in 2004, when a majority of the Court refused on standing grounds to decide whether the inclusion violated the establishment clause.[74] Interpretive doubts might be raised about all the cases Scalia discussed in 2002, including his reckless discussion of his views about a case not yet decided but certainly likely to be decided.

We see yet again the incoherence of the 'originalism' that Scalia has espoused. Historical argument, which 'originalism' regards as the measure of valid constitutional interpretation, argues that the founders regarded the Constitution as secular and put in place the two religion clauses of the First Amendment (free exercise and antiestablishment) to ensure that political power be limited to secular ends – life, liberty, and the pursuit of happiness – ends on which persons from diverse religious and philosophical backgrounds could reasonably agree.[75] Historical argument is thus playing no role in Scalia's attempt more closely to ally the state and religion, for history is, on this issue, clearly against the views he takes. This shows, yet again, how intellectually incoherent 'originalism' has become in contemporary American politics and law. It lacks support in the only thing the view claims can legitimately support constitutional interpretation. The tradition that a historically sensitive judge should value and uphold is ignored whenever it comes in conflict with personal sectarian convictions that have no place in constitutional interpretation.

73 Antonin Scalia, "God's Justice and Ours," 123 *First Things* 17, 19–20 (2002).

74 See *Elk Grove Unified School District v. Newdow*, 542 U.S. 124 (2004).

75 See, for recent historical defenses of this general position, Frank Lambert, *The Founding Fathers and the Place of Religion in America* (Princeton, N.J.: Princeton University Press, 2003); Lambert, *Religion in American Politics: A Short History* (Princeton, N.J.: Princeton University Press, 2008); Gary Wills, *Head and Heart: American Christianities* (New York: Penguin Press, 2007); Forrest Church, *So Help Me God: The Founding Fathers and the First Great Battle over Church and State* (Orlando: Harcourt, 2007); Martha C. Nussbaum, *Liberty of Conscience: In Defense of America's Tradition of Religious Equality* (New York: Basic Books, 2008).

Both the substance of his views (so clearly tied to his own religious convictions) and his recklessness bespeak how unapologetically, even arrogantly faith-driven, Scalia's 'originalism' is and how rooted in patriarchal religion, which leads not only to Scalia's attack on the principle of constitutional privacy but also to his views on the interpretation of the religion clauses, which precisely unite what our constitutional tradition separated. What is evident here, as elsewhere, is the patriarchal culture and psychology underlying 'originalism' that polemically remakes constitutional democracy in its own undemocratic image. All the marks of patriarchal psychology are on display: not only a mindless lack of self-doubt, but a strutting pride in one's incoherent certainties, a repressive contempt for those who raise reasonable doubts, and a religiously sectarian endorsement of American state violence, "the sword as 'the minister of God,' to 'execute wrath' upon the evildoer."

CONCLUSION

PATRIARCHY AS THE AMERICAN DILEMMA: FACING THE PROBLEM OF FUNDAMENTALISM AT HOME AND ABROAD

We have now closely studied American fundamentalisms in both law and religion and their connections. What have we seen, and how can we understand what we have seen?

What we have seen in both religion and law is something paradoxical. On the one hand, fundamentalism expresses an interpretation of religion and law in terms of an unquestioned and unquestionable certainty about original meaning. On the other hand, there is little or no interest in the historical context that gave rise to religion or law and certainly no interest at all in the changes in context that might reasonably inform its interpretation over time. Fundamentalism thus rests on an original meaning but takes little or no interest on what contextually informs meaning both at one period and over time. What is going on here is a kind of abstraction and reification of meanings as certain and a refusal to even entertain reasonable debate and discussion about the meanings taken as certain. Indeed, the position is even more paradoxical. Fundamentalisms violently repudiate and seek to repress precisely the dissenting voices to their certainty about original meaning that would most reasonably inform the search for meaning. This theme runs through my entire examination of the fundamentalisms both in American religion and in American law.

The incoherence runs even deeper. The original meanings that fundamentalists agree on and are the basis of their alliances in American politics center not on logical or analytical truths or factual matters about which there is reasonable consensus but precisely on traditional views of sexuality and gender as if they could not be reasonably doubted or debated. But they are very much in reasonable doubt. Indeed, well beyond that, many of these views rest on anachronistic views that many Americans believe cannot be justly enforced through law. The Supreme Court of the United States has agreed with them, deeming the enforcement of such views through law unconstitutional (see, e.g., Chapter 1).

Once we see such claims of certainty about original meaning as paradoxical in the ways I have outlined, we must ask a psychological question: how can people believe or claim to believe such things and then unite around such beliefs as the basis for the increasingly aggressive role fundamentalists have played in American politics? What marks such incoherent beliefs is disassociation, which explains a certainty disengaged from any sense of the responsibilities of reason. My argument has been that such disassociation arises from a psychology of traumatic breaks in personal relationships that lead to identification with the patriarchal voice that requires such breaks. It is identification with an imagined patriarchal voice that explains the disassociation from reason and human connection that makes fundamentalism psychologically possible. It also explains why fundamentalists are so hostile to any reasonable voice that challenges their certainty. The trauma, underlying patriarchy, expresses itself in fear of and anger at any voice that reasonably challenges patriarchal demands, in particular, the love laws, which forbid precisely the human connections that reveal the lies that sustain patriarchy.

My argument has been that this psychology underlies the continuing appeal of patriarchal religion for Americans, and that this psychology explains as well the appeal of 'originalism' in law. In both cases, a deeply unreasonable view has the appeal it does not on its merits, as a religious or legal argument, but in service of the imperatives of patriarchal psychology: imagining that authority in religion or law is defined by a despotic father insensitive to the voice and experience of anyone who resists his authority. It is for this reason that fundamentalist certitude in religion and law repudiates reasonable doubt about its claims, indeed wars on such claims. Such claims threaten to break through the disassociation that supports fundamentalist beliefs. This explains the fear and anger that underlie the polemics of fundamentalists. It is precisely the reasonable views that expose the incoherence that sustains this psychology that must be denigrated or quashed without any reason given or expected. It is against such a sense of threat that religious fundamentalists, otherwise theologically so different, unite in solidarity against threats to patriarchal manhood or womanhood, repressing their doubts in group solidarity and aggressive political action.

Madison's theory of faction in *The Federalist No. 10* is relevant to understanding why this political dynamic is so worrying in a constitutional democracy like the United States. Madison argued that the design and justification of the federal system must be tested by whether constitutional structures (including federalism) so limited the expression of faction in democratic politics that such politics might better satisfy the normative aims of government: respect for human rights and pursuit of the public interest. Madison was a deeply democratic thinker, but he saw clearly that democratic politics, of the sort that the American Constitution contemplated, would be illegitimate if they unleashed without any constraints the forces of what he called, following David Hume, faction.

Madison was not a moral skeptic: he and other leading founders had no doubt that ethical thinking (including human rights) had an objective basis. The theory of faction, in Hume and Madison, has nothing to do with moral skepticism. It is rather concerned with the effects of group psychology on distorting ethical thinking. Because politics was a form of group activity, Hume endorsed the "maxim, that, in contriving any system of government, and fixing the several checks and controls of the constitution, every man ought to be supposed a knave, and to have no other end, in all his actions, than private interest."[1] Hume squared this maxim of his political science with his moral and political philosophy of sympathetic benevolence by noting how "somewhat strange" it is that the "maxim should be true in *politics* which is false in *fact*."[2] And he explained the truth of the maxim in politics by facts of group psychology that are central to political life:

> Men are generally more honest in their private than in their public capacity, and will go to greater lengths to serve a party, than when their own private interest is alone concerned. Honour is a great check upon mankind: but where a considerable body of men act together, this check is in a great measure removed, since a man is sure to be approved of by his own party, for what promotes the common interests; and he soon learns to despise the clamours of adversaries.[3]

Hume further analyzed these facts of political psychology as factions, of two different kinds: personal (i.e., familial or clan based) and real (those from interest, from principle, and from affection).[4]

Madison not only was a much more democratic thinker than Hume but also was much more engaged with the Lockean view of basic human rights as the test of legitimate politics. But his experience had confirmed the good sense of Hume's political science when it came to the design and justification of a constitution like that of the United States. Democracy would, if anything, give even more extensive scope to the role of groups in politics than less democratic forms of government (like Great Britain at the time of the founding). Nothing more worried Madison than that the very scope that democratic constitutionalism would give to the formation and expression of factions might undermine its very legitimacy. The very definition he gives of faction in *The Federalist No. 10* suggests what was worrying him: "By a faction, I understand a number of citizens, whether amounting to a majority or a minority of the whole, who are united and actuated by some common impulse of passion, or of interest, adverse to the rights of other citizens, or to the permanent and aggregate interests of the community."[5] From the perspective of Madison's belief in respect for basic human rights as the test of legitimacy in politics, what worried him was that, in a democracy, the group psychology of faction might lead to factions in politics that were hostile to the human rights of those who were outsiders to the faction. The aim of the argument is to show that democracy, as structured by the federal system, would minimize or cabin this threat. But, the argument of *The Federalist No. 10* only works on the

[1] Quoted in David A. J. Richards, *Foundations of American Constitutionalism* (New York: Oxford University Press, 1989), p. 35.
[2] Quoted in *id.*, p. 35.
[3] Quoted in *id.*, p. 35.
[4] Quoted in *id.*, p. 35.
[5] Jacob E. Cooke, ed., *The Federalist* (Middletown, Conn.: Wesleyan University Press, 1961), p. 57.

assumption that majority factions at the state level would be minority factions at the national level and, through the structures of delegation and representations of the federal system, would not have unfettered opportunity to govern at the federal level but would have to find common grounds with other minority factions, thus leading to greater respect for human rights and respect for the public interest.

But there is a startling non sequitur at the heart of Madison's argument; namely, nothing in the argument deals with the problem of superfactions at both the state and national levels: factions that are a dominant majority at both levels of government. Two such factions come to mind: racism (which Madison at the Constitutional Convention referred to as "a ground of the most oppressive dominion ever exercised by man over man"[6]) and an extreme form of religious intolerance like anti-Semitism. Both white people and Christians were in the majority at both the state and the national levels, and both groups, as history clearly shows, were capable of forming factions "adverse to the rights of other citizens," for both racism and anti-Semitism dehumanize people of color and Jews and thus rationalize atrocities. Nothing in Madison's argument in *The Federalist No. 10* deals with this problem, which explains his despairing private letters to Jefferson around the time of the Constitutional Convention about what he regarded as fundamental defects in the Constitution.[7] Such defects proved disastrous, as the interlinked questions of American slavery and racism could not be resolved constitutionally, leading to the national tragedy of internecine civil war. Strikingly, the Reconstruction Amendments corrected many of the defects that worried Madison, not least by the abolition of slavery, federal guarantees of the protection of human rights at the state and national levels, and federal guarantees against the political expression of the majority factions that so worried Madison (e.g., racism)[8] .

Madison had justified the Constitution of 1787 to the American people on the ground that it would better protect human rights than alternatives like the British Constitution, against which Americans successfully revolted in 1776. In fact, on the issue of slavery and racism, it did no such thing, allowing a majority faction like American racism not only to entrench slavery in the South but also to dominate American national politics. In contrast, Great Britain would democratically abolish slavery in 1833, a comparison that particularly galled a constitutionalist like Abraham Lincoln. On the most important issue of human rights in the nineteenth century (the abolition of slavery), the British Constitution had proved more legitimate than that of the United States.[9]

Madison's argument in *The Federalist No. 10* is a defense of a democratic politics structured by the federal system. It does not address the power of

[6] Quoted in David A. J. Richards, *Conscience and the Constitution: History, Theory, and Law of the Reconstruction Amendments* (Princeton, N.J.: Princeton University Press, 1993), p. 24.

[7] On these letters, see Richards, *Conscience and the Constitution*, pp. 22–3.

[8] See, on these points, *id.*

[9] See, on this point, Richards, *id.*, pp. 52–3.

judicial review, which had been separately defended by Hamilton in *The Federalist No. 78*. It is striking that, in the wake of World War II, this power of judicial review played an increasingly important role in addressing precisely the superfactions that so worried Madison, in particular, the Supreme Court's role in identifying and striking down laws and policies that express racism, and its protection both against the states and national government of the guarantees of religious liberty in the First Amendment (the free exercise and antiestablishment clauses), which render anti-Semitism as constitutionally odious as racism.

The argument of this book about the patriarchal roots of American fundamentalism clarifies, I believe, the group psychology of faction. The underlying patriarchal psychology of fundamentalism is one of traumatic breaks in personal relationships that lead to an identification with patriarchal voice and a resulting disassociation that not only cannot connect with reasonable dissenting voices but also seeks to repress them. It is this psychology that explains how diverse forms of fundamentalism bond around their common repression of antipatriarchal dissenters, and how and why their increasingly aggressive role in American politics is essentially reactionary, seeking to reverse or to retard any further political or constitutional recognition of the justice of their claims. It is also explains why its response to reasonable doubt expresses itself in what Leon Festinger observed in religious cults whose central prophecies had been disproved, namely a need for proselytizing (which had not existed before): the support of other people being required to sustain belief in a way it had not earlier been psychologically necessary.[10] What Festinger analyzed as a cult phenomenon appears writ large in the aggressive political activism of American religious fundamentalists, as they seek not only in one another but also in the larger society the kind of support that allows them and others to rationalize to themselves what is in fact unreasonable. The very political successes of such fundamentalists embolden them, exemplifying in our politics what Madison so feared in democracy, the power of majoritarian religious factions to subvert ethical conscience, indeed dehumanizing outsiders. The interest of my analysis (the Gilligan-Richard thesis) is to trace the roots of this problem of personal and political psychology to patriarchal norms and values that uncritically sustain this psychology and to bring to light the dimensions of the problem as a challenge to the very legitimacy of our constitutional democracy.

[10] See Leon Festinger, H. Riecken, and S. Schachter, *When Prophecy Fails* (Minneapolis: University of Minnesota Press, 1956); Leon Festinger, *A Theory of Cognitive Dissonance* (Stanford, Calif.: Stanford University Press, 1957), pp. 21, 200–2, 246–59. For relevant commentary and later developments in social psychology, see Michael A. Hogg and Joel Cooper, eds., *The Sage Handbook of Social Psychology: Concise Student Edition* (Los Angeles: Sage Publications, 2007), pp. 3–23; Arnoldo Rodrigues and Robert V. Levine, *Reflections on 100 Years of Experimental Social Psychology* (New York: Basic Books, 1999), pp. 82–113; Lauren Slater, *Opening Skinner's Box: Great Psychological Experiments of the Twentieth Century* (New York: W. W. Norton, 2004), pp. 113–32. On ethical issues, see James H. Korn, *Illusions of Reality: A History of Deception in Social Psychology* (Albany, N.Y.: State University of New York Press, 1997), pp. 81–96.

The constitutional successes of the civil rights and other movements were made possible by the antipatriarchal voices these movements brought to bear on American public life – the voices of people of color and the voices of free women speaking about the ethical importance to them of choice in matters of reproductive autonomy and the voices of gays and lesbians speaking of their desire for intimate life and their claim to the right to intimate life that all other Americans enjoyed as a birthright of freedom (Chapter 1). It is precisely their resistance to the patriarchal love laws that drew the ire of religious fundamentalists, for their fundamentalism rested on a patriarchal repression of such voices. In effect, such fundamentalists live in a patriarchal echo chamber, speaking and hearing only an imagined patriarchal voice in which women do not exist as real persons and moral agents. Such a voice sustains rigidly defined gender stereotypes as the measure of authority in religion and in law. Because no man has ever had an abortion, the issue is judged only from the patriarchal perspective of stereotypes of good, self-sacrificing, asexual versus bad, selfish, sexual women. Fetuses become persons. Women are required to sacrifice self (as men are in war), as if one could be an ethical person without a sense of self. And women who choose to have abortions are transformed from real women responsibly coping with difficult moral choices about relationships into an unreal stereotypical image of bad (because sexual) women, indeed, mothers who monstrously murder their children (see Chapters 1 and 4 on this point).

Madison had acutely observed that religion – so far from being a constraint on majority factions – was often its worst expression: "The conduct of every popular assembly acting on oath, the strongest of religious Ties, proves that individuals join without remorse in acts, against which their consciences would revolt if proposed to them under the like sanction, separately in their closets."[11] As Madison clearly sees, it is the nature of group psychology in politics that explains how it is that people with a sense of conscience can, under the dynamic of such psychology, "join without remorse in acts" that would revolt them if considered by them as individuals "separately in their closets." It is this that renders fundamentalist politics, precisely when successful, so disassociated – success feeding the disassociation.

It is bad enough that such religious factions mobilize through political action against constitutionally recognized rights. What makes them constitutionally toxic is when such views are read into constitutional interpretation in the form of 'originalism.' We have seen that the modern judiciary, interpreting the Reconstruction Amendments, has responsibly addressed the problem of majority factions that Madison worried would democratically express their will through politics violating constitutional guarantees of basic human rights. 'Originalism' – which draws its appeal from its connections to religious fundamentalism – effectively shrinks constitutional interpretation to the measure of religious faction. Precisely

[11] Quoted in Richards, *Foundations of American Constitutionalism*, p. 37.

the worst demons of faction – that Madison argued democratic constitutionalism could and must tame – run riot.

We saw a form of this in our examination of the dissenting opinions of Justice Scalia, usually joined by Justice Thomas, examined and discussed in Chapters 3 and 7. The intemperate, angry, and dismissive tone of these opinions bespeaks the underlying patriarchal anger and fear. Both content and tone become particularly strident in connection with opinions that recognize the constitutional rights of gays and lesbians (e.g., *Romer v. Evans, Lawrence v. Texas*). My earlier discussions of the analogy between anti-Semitism and homophobia bring out the psychology underlying such opinions. Homophobia plays the same role for fundamentalist Christians that anti-Semitism once played in Christianity generally. Christian anti-Semitism was based on sectarian religious views aimed at a group that conspicuously fail to convert to Christianity or the Augustinian views of Christianity about sexual asceticism as the necessary path to God, precisely because such a form of dissenting convictions raised doubts about the reasonable appeal of Christian orthodoxy. Correspondingly, what makes the successful claim of gays and lesbians to recognition of their rights such a target of Christian fundamentalist rage is that they resist, on grounds of conscience, the sectarian religious views that condemn them and, like Jews, refuse to convert but rather forge responsible forms of intimate life that reject the view of sexuality that Augustine of Hippo read into the Christian tradition. Anti-Semitism has, since the Holocaust, been largely discredited among Christians. But if homophobia comes to very much the same thing, it is shocking that current Supreme Court justices should be so much in thrall to religious fundamentalism that they can intemperately express rather than reasonably contest the expression of such a constitutionally condemned religious faction in politics. 'Originalism' is the public mask judges wear covering their complicity. We need to see them for what they are and reject them as irresponsible guardians of our constitutional traditions.

It is only when we bring the lens of gender to bear on the psychology underlying fundamentalism that we can expose what sustains it: not good argument or reasonable faith but a repressive fear and anger that targets, as unmanly or unwomanly, anyone who resists the rigidly binary gender stereotypes that enforce patriarchal demands. The polemics of gender thus divide Americans from one another and from their common humanity, the moral bedrock of both Christianity and constitutional democracy.

The focus of my attention in the argument of this book has been on the tension, indeed contradiction between patriarchy (which motivates fundamentalism in American religion and law) and our constitutional democracy. My aim is to confront Americans with our own psychological and moral contradictions, which I connect to the continuing power of patriarchal religion in America. It is because the legitimacy of constitutional democracy rests on the protection of basic human rights, including the equal right to conscience and voice, that patriarchy, which rests on the hierarchical authority of the voice of priest-fathers, is in such contradiction with the deepest values of our constitutionalism. My argument is thus, importantly, not an argument of external criticism, grounded in liberal political theory, of our legal system. Rather, because liberal values are internally central to the legitimacy of American constitutionalism, the argument is an internal criticism of the political and constitutional role fundamentalism has come to play in American public life, pointing out how and why its reactionary motivations (protecting patriarchal practices justly under increasingly successful constitutional attack) are so constitutionally problematic.

Although my attention here has been to fundamentalisms under American constitutionalism, there is good reason to believe that my methodological approach can be fruitfully applied elsewhere. There is now a historically informed, comparative field that studies common patterns of democratization and de-democratization in various periods and places.[12] Such study reveals not a linear mechanism but an ongoing process of progress and reversal, in which the suppression of independent groups, the elimination of inequalities, and the integration of trust networks in politics play important roles. These processes are democratizing or de-democratizing to the degree that they advance or retard political relations between the state and the citizens that are extended broadly, equally, and lead to protected, mutually binding deliberation.[13] Fundamentalisms, as I have analyzed them, are de-democratizing: they entrench the political power of groups independent of the state that not only do not consult other groups but also treat them unequally. We have already seen this in the impact of American religious fundamentalisms both on our politics and on our constitutional law. The analysis can plausibly be extended to forms of constitutionalism similar to that of the United States in which increasingly powerful fundamentalist movements threaten constitutional legitimacy. For example, Martha Nussbaum's *The Clash Within* argues that the emergence of Hindu fundamentalism, as a force in Indian politics, is in precisely the tension with Indian secular constitutionalism that American fundamentalisms are with American constitutionalism.[14] Patriarchy is, of course, culturally universal, and the Hindu caste system, with its love laws (limiting marriage, usually arranged, to one's caste), is deeply patriarchal. It is not therefore surprising that a reactionary movement of Hindu political fundamentalism (Hindutva) should have arisen in India, and not only, as Nussbaum shows, fomented unjust violence against anyone (Muslim, Hindu, or Christian) who challenges this patriarchal system but also become increasingly powerful politically (even leading India for several years). What is central to Nussbaum's argument is the degree to which such religious fundamentalism, when it becomes

[12] See Charles Tilly, *Democracy* (Cambridge: Cambridge University Press, 2007); Tilly, *Contention and Democracy in Europe, 1650–2000* (Cambridge: Cambridge University Press, 2004); Tilly, *Trust and Rule* (Cambridge: Cambridge University Press, 2005).

[13] See Tilly, *Democracy*, pp. 13–14.

[14] See Martha C. Nussbaum, *The Clash Within: Democracy, Religious Violence, and India's Future* (Cambridge, Mass.: The Belknap Press of Harvard University Press, 2007).

politically aggressive, threatens the legitimacy of India's secular constitutionalism. Thus, as Brenda Cossman and Ratna Kapur have argued, the Indian Supreme Court has failed to take seriously how much Hindutva undermines the constitutional legitimacy of India as a secular state.[15] If they are right, Indian experience confirms the argument of this book, namely that patriarchal practices, when under challenge from the demands of a democratic constitutionalism based on respect for universal human rights, give rise to reactionary fundamentalisms that are increasingly in tension with the demands of a secular democratic constitutionalism. The problem is not uniquely American, and my argument shows that patriarchal love laws are at the heart of the problem.[16]

The debates in India over its secular constitution may be contrasted with the comparable European and also Turkish debates about prohibitions of wearing Muslim headscarves or burkas[17] either in schools (headscarves in France, the jihab[18] in Great Britain) or in general (burkas in a proposed law in the Netherlands). For an American, the insistence in France that the Muslim headscarf and the Jewish yarmulke are explicitly prohibited in public schools (along with large Christian crosses) does not, as the French suppose, advance legitimate secular ends but rather compromises legitimate rights of free exercise on a basis that appears sectarian, not secular. A voluntarily accepted religious obligation of public modesty, expressed through wearing headscarves, is a free exercise right, and there is no compelling purpose that justifies a prohibition. Modesty is not inconsistent with gender equality, for example. In effect, the drive for assimilation in France and elsewhere is imposing on recent immigrants requirements of dress that are mere matters of majoritarian style.[19]

My argument suggests that the very future of democracy, not just in the United States but everywhere, requires a much more critical study and understanding of the degree to which patriarchy is in tension with democracy, because the psychology that supports patriarchy gives rise to reactionary fundamentalisms that war on the resistance of free democratic voice to unjust patriarchal demands on both women and men. Gender equality, a demand of democratic constitutionalism, threatens patriarchy, which in turn gives rise to reactionary fundamentalism. If the problem is a common, even universal, as it may well be, the project of democratic constitutionalism requires that gender equality be taken more seriously, including empowering the democratic voices of men and women resisting

[15] See Brenda Cossman and Ratna Kapur, *Secularisms's Last Sigh? Hindutva and the (Mis)Rule of Law* (Oxford: Oxford University Press, 2001). See also Anuradha Dingwaney Needham and Rajeswari Sunder Rajan, eds., *The Crisis of Secularism in India* (Durham, N.C.: Duke University Press, 2007).

[16] See also Ratna Kapur, *Erotic Justice: Law and the New Politics of Postcolonialism* (London: Glasshouse Press, 2005).

[17] This is a full garment covering the body and all of the face but the eyes.

[18] This clothing does not cover the face but does cover the body and head.

[19] See, for further discussion, Martha C. Nussbaum, *Liberty of Conscience*, pp. 346–53.

patriarchy.[20] We cannot understand the psychological dimensions of the problem for democracy unless and until we bring the lens of gender to bear on understanding our contemporary plight, a plight in which anything may be discussed but the degree to which our mind and hearts are imprisoned by rigid gender stereotypes that cut us off from our ethical intelligence, our humanity.

What lies at the heart of our problem is a continuing feature of many religious traditions, namely the religious authority accorded an all-male priesthood hierarchically ordered over boys and men, girls and women. Both the orthodox and unorthodox Christian fundamentalisms we have examined in some depth show how pivotally important an all-male priesthood has been in remaking even so antipatriarchal a person as Jesus of Nazareth in their patriarchal image. If this can happen in Christianity, it can, of course, happen to any religion – Jewish, Islamic, Hindu, Buddhist, or whatever. What sustains such authority is what corrupts it: because it arises from ignoring and indeed repressing the free moral voices and experiences of well more than half the human race, it lacks ethical force and can sustain itself only by warring on the voices that resist its unjust authority. Such patriarchal religion thus corrupts an ethics of equal respect and, in turn, democracy, which requires equal respect. Accordingly, if democracy and human rights now have a universal moral appeal, we must, as a human species, examine more critically the forms of patriarchal religion that are so contradictory both to democracy and to human rights.

In the United States, for example, constitutional guarantees of both religious liberty and antiestablishment have given rise to a particularly robust and diverse range of religious views. Precisely because of the respect constitutionally accorded religious conscience in the United States, the role of patriarchy in American religions may have become more deeply entrenched than it might have been in a constitutional democracy, like Britain or Sweden, in which an established church has been more accountable to democratic values. But as I argued earlier, gender equality is also now a compelling secular purpose under American constitutional law, and the American law of religious liberty can and must take more seriously the weight to be accorded such a compelling state purpose, in particular, in the greater weight that should be accorded antiestablishment values. Americans as a people, many of whom are religious, must also responsibly exercise their democratic freedom in insisting that their still patriarchal churches responsibly rethink their views in the light of democratic values. Many of these churches at earlier points justified slavery and racism as the word of God. In light of our growing public understanding of these as secular evils that violate deeper constitutional values of respect for human rights, very few churches do so any longer. There is every reason to think that a similar process can reasonably lead many of these churches to rethink not only their understanding of religion but also

20 See, for an illuminating general study, Helen Irving, *Gender and the Constitution: Equity and Agency in Comparative Constitutional Design* (Cambridge: Cambridge University Press, 2008).

their understanding of constitutional law. We can, however, begin this process only when we understand the dimensions of the problem. This book is very much an effort in this spirit and to this end.

But the account I have offered does not only illuminate internal constitutional debates whether in the United States or India. It also floods light on the patterns of violence, rooted in a sense of manhood whose honor rests on violence in support of forms of structural injustice, like extreme religious intolerance; racism and ethnic hatred in Bosnia, Yugoslavia, and Rwanda; and various forms of secular and religious terrorism and other forms of state-sponsored violence.[21] Mark Juergensmeyer has persuasively analyzed the global rise of fundamentalist violence, at home and abroad, in terms of a highly gendered armoring of humiliated men in a cosmic war. What triggers such violence are perceived threats to manhood:

> Nothing is more intimate than sexuality, and no greater humiliation can be experienced than failure over what one perceives to be one's sexual role. Such failures are often the basis of domestic violence; and when these failures are linked with the social roles of masculinity and femininity, they can lead to public violence. Terrorist acts, then, can be forms of symbolic empowerment for men whose traditional sexual roles – their very manhood – is perceived to be at stake.[22]

The terrorism of Islamic fundamentalism is a good example of the toxic combination of technological know-how with deplorable ethical and political values, rooted, inter alia, in extreme religious intolerance (most obviously anti-Semitism). Most believers in Islam condemn such terrorism, but there is a larger problem of political culture here, which makes such fundamentalism possible and must be addressed. The political culture of most Islamic nations is problematic on two scores: its lack of separation of church and state and its sexism.[23] These are certainly interdependent problems, as it is the elaboration of the argument for toleration (underlying separation of church and state) that makes possible the protest of forms of structural injustice, including sexism. Any religion can, I believe, be corrupted to unjust ends when political leaders corruptly use religion to entrench and legitimate their own power. Islam is only the most notable contemporary example of a phenomenon that has, at earlier historical points, afflicted other

[21] See, on these points, Chris Hedges, *War Is a Force that Gives Us Meaning* (New York: Public Affairs, 2002); Michael Ignatieff, *The Warrior's Honor: Ethnic War and the Modern Conscience* (New York: Henry Holt, 1997); Amin Maalouf, *In the Name of Identity: Violence and the Need to Belong*, trans. Barbara Bray (New York: Penguin, 2003); Daniel Pipes, *Militant Islam Reaches America* (New York: W.W. Norton, 2002); Kanan Makiya, *Cruelty and Silence: War, Tyranny, Uprising, and the Arab World* (New York: W.W. Norton, 1993); Avishai Margalit, "The Suicide Bombers," *New York Review of Books*, Jan. 16, 2003, pp. 36–9; Bernard Lewis, *What Went Wrong? Western Impact and Middle Eastern Response* (Oxford: Oxford University Press, 2002).

[22] Mark Juergensmeyer, *Terror in the Mind of God: The Global Rise of Religious Violence* (Berkeley: University of California Press, 2000), p. 195.

[23] See, on these points, Lewis, *What Went Wrong?*

religions, notably the various forms of Christianity before constitutional developments in dominantly Christian nations called for a separation of church and state as much in the interest of a just politics as of an authentic Christianity based on the historical Jesus of Nazareth. It would, of course, be a great mistake to suppose that these nations are still not afflicted by sectarian religious, ethnic, and gender intolerance, and that such intolerance sometimes motors ethnocentric forms of unjust imperialism. And there is no reason to think that believers in Islam cannot reasonably free themselves of the corrupt politicians who afflict them, and there is reason to think one place to start would be taking seriously antipatriarchal voices of Islamic women usually not attended to.[24]

In contrast, we can see the sources of the violence of Islamic fundamentalism in what motivated one of its founding martyrs Sayyid Qutb, who warred both on the separation of church and state and on the sexual freedom of women. Qutb had turned his back on marriage in Egypt because "he had been unable to find a suitable bride from the 'dishonorable' women who allowed themselves to be seen in public."[25] If the problem in Egypt was that women were not traditionally patriarchal enough, what threatened Qutb in his 1948 visit to the United States was, above all, the freer sexuality and sexual voices of American women,[26] an American sexual permissiveness that he took to be established by the Kinsey Report (including the high incidence reported there of homosexual relations among American men).[27] Qutb advocated the Islamic fundamentalism he did as an expression of patriarchal violence at the freer sexual voices and lives of women in Egypt and the United States. Out of this swamp emerged the ideology and terror of al-Qaeda, expressing the same impulses.

It confirms the explanatory power of my approach to these matters that when Ian Buruma sensitively studies the roots of the violent murder of the Dutch movie maker Theo van Gogh by an Islamic fundamentalist, Mohammed Bouyeri, a Dutch citizen and son of Moroccan immigrants, he plausibly traces the violence to a patriarchal sense of rage at the freer sexuality of Moroccan women immigrants, including Bouyeri's own sister,[28] including the resisting voice of the Dutch politician Ayaan Hirsi Ali who made a movie with van Gogh subjecting to criticism the way Islam treated women. Ali had come fundamentally to question her own Islamic heritage as a Somali immigrant to Holland and a woman. "What," Buruma asks, "turned Mohammed into a character from Conrad [or

[24] See, e.g., Leila Ahmed, *A Border Passage: From Cairo to America – A Woman's Journey* (New York: Farrar, Straus and Giroux, 1999); Fatema Mernissi, *Islam and Democracy: Fear of the Modern World*, trans. Mary Jo Lakeland (Cambridge, Mass.: Perseus, 1992); *The Veil and the Male Elite: A Feminist Interpretation of Women's Rights in Islam* (Cambridge, Mass.: Perseus, 1991).

[25] Lawrence Wright, *The Looming Tower: Al-Qaeda and the Road to 9/11* (New York: Alfred A. Knopf, 2006), p. 9.

[26] See *id.*, pp. 15, 20.

[27] *Id.*, p. 12.

[28] See, on this point, Ian Buruma, *Murder in Amsterdam: The Death of Theo van Gogh and the Limits of Tolerance* (New York: Penguin, 2006).

Dostoyevsky]?"[29] What is incendiary to a patriarchal man, like Bouyeri, is, above all, the freer sexual voice and lives of the women from his tradition who question its patriarchal traditions. Such violence against sexual voice is, we have argued, as ancient as Rome and is now as contemporary as van Gogh's murder. My argument, while rooted in history, could not be more urgently contemporary. What is at the heart of contemporary fundamentalism is repressive rage precisely at the free sexual voice that reasonably challenges its reactionary patriarchal demands, which rest on a long-standing tradition of the unjust repression of voice.

The great historical lesson of the totalitarianisms of the twentieth century, which almost brought civilization as we know it to cataclysmic destruction on several occasions, is the terrifying price we pay when our technology is so much in advance of our ethics and politics. But we know that the political violence of fascism, for example, with its genocidal murder of 6 million innocent Jews, was motored fundamentally by an aggressively political anti-Semitism, and that it fed on and cultivated a sense of manhood based on codes of honor at least as old as *The Iliad*. Unjust gender stereotypes were quite central to a Nazi manhood hardened even to genocidal murder of millions.[30] And the bloody totalitarianism of Stalin's communism (including the starvation of at least 5 million peasants[31]) was crucially motored by an indoctrination into an ideal of the soldier constantly on duty,[32] which, as with Hitler's fascism, bizarrely justified state-imposed mass killing as self-defense.[33] It is no accident that there are close links in totalitarian political method between fascism and Soviet communism,[34] based, as they are, on conceptions of a hardened manhood rooted in violence against any dissent to or doubt about the terms of state-enforced structural injustice.[35] It is when humiliated patriarchal manhood most powerfully actuates politics (as it did after Germany's defeat in World War I) that its rage turns on a feminized scapegoat (the Jews) and, in light of modern technologies of violence, achieves appalling levels of genocidal murder and mayhem.

I agree with Elisabeth Young-Bruehl that aspects of Hannah Arendt's analysis of the role of terroristic violence in totalitarianism illuminate our contemporary situation in which violence increasingly wars on the very possibility of the kind of responsible exercise of voice that Arendt regarded as central to the values of

[29] See *id.*, p. 195.

[30] See, for a general study of this gender issue in German fascism, Claudia Koonz, *The Nazi Conscience*; see also Koonz, *Mothers in the Fatherland: Women, the Family, and Nazi Politics* (New York: St. Martin's Press, 1987).

[31] See Robert Conquest, *Stalin: Breaker of Nations* (New York: Penguin, 1991), pp. 163–5.

[32] See Walter Laqueur, *The Dream That Failed: Reflections on the Soviet Union* (New York: Oxford University Press, 1994), p. 13.

[33] See, on all these points, Francois Furet, *The Passing of an Illusion: The Idea of Communism in the Twentieth Century*, trans. Deborah Furet (Chicago: University of Chicago Press, 1999).

[34] See *id.*, pp. 174–5, 178, 189–90.

[35] See, on these points, Arthur Koestler, *Darkness at Noon*, trans. Daphne Hardy (New York: Bantam Books, 1968) (originally published in 1941), at pp. 124–9, 134–7, 153, 182–5, 189–90, 205.

democratic politics.[36] What Arendt painfully learned from her analysis of the roots of totalitarianism in a German high culture she loved was that it expressed strands of a nihilist romanticism (in her erstwhile lover and teacher Heidegger, among others) that, having no ethical core, could be enlisted in abject worship of an autocratic leader's immoral aims, including genocidal murder of 6 million Jews. Such political romanticism, a kind of narcissistic idealism,[37] is made psychologically possible by the crushing of the human faculties that express themselves in a human voice that understands and resists injustice. Arendt identifies totalitarian politics as systematic modes of terror that crush such voice, a voice that for Arendt is at the heart of the defensible human values of democratic politics. What marks such politics is the priority it accords the constitutional protection of free and equal voice, a voice preserved from any threat of violence or intimidation, as the necessary condition for the legitimacy of a properly democratic politics in which political disagreements are resolved through democratic dialogue and debate and regular elections shaped by such debate. It is a profound misunderstanding of the role of free conscience and speech in constitutional democracies to limit the scope of constitutional protection only to convictions that offend no one, which effectively censors from public discussion precisely the convictions most worthy of reasonable discussion and debate among free people, including, of course, religious convictions. Such censorship, now quite widespread even in constitutional democracies in Europe (including Britain), compromises precisely the value of free and equal voice that legitimates democracy, and certainly cannot reasonably be justified on the ground that it lessens the popularity of evils like anti-Semitism, racism, sexism, and homophobia when, in fact, it immunizes them from the reasonable challenge by free people they richly deserve.[38]

What made totalitarianism so distinctive in the modern period was both its techniques of terror and its insistence on a violence directed at quashing democratic voice, making possible the moral enormities of Hitler's Germany and Stalin's Russia, as well as Mao's China and Pol Pot's Cambodia. My analysis more deeply explains why this problem is still so much with us, as the forms of terror not only are state supported (as in the case of Hitler's Germany and Stalin's Russia) but also mobilize networks of fundamentalists operating largely outside the state system. The root of the problem is the degree to which patriarchal patterns still uncritically persist not only abroad but at home, expressed in forms of violence directed at the free sexual voice of women and men, only recently emancipated by the resistance movements we have discussed. What we need critically to understand is why such free and equal sexual voice is so incendiary, rationalizing forms of violence, including terror, that seek, as Arendt clearly saw,

[36] See Elisabeth Young-Bruehl, *Why Arendt Matters* (New Haven, Conn.: Yale University Press, 2006).

[37] See, on this point, Buruma, *Murder in Amsterdam*, p. 220.

[38] See, for an elaboration of this argument, David A. J. Richards, *Free Speech and the Politics of Identity* (Oxford: Oxford University Press, 1999).

to crush human faculties, making possible an abject devotion to a patriarchally imagined leader.

The pattern is as ancient as Roman patriarchy,[39] a pattern that crucially depended both on the repression of sexually loving voice and on violence directed at such a free sexual voice. Robert O. Paxton observed trenchantly in *The Anatomy of Fascism* that fascism was empty of any coherent political theory.[40] Instead, fascism was marked by its "legitimation of violence against a demonized internal enemy.[41] . . . 'The fist,' asserted a Fascist militant in 1920, 'is the synthesis of our theory.'"[42] When the appeal of a political movement is so empty of ideas, we must turn to political psychology, in this case, the way Mussolini, later followed by Hitler, self-consciously appealed so successfully to reviving the psychology of Roman patriarchal manhood, the psychology of humiliated men, traumatized by defeat in World War I, a psychology that expressed itself in violence against imagined enemies, including, in Hitler's case, 6 million European Jews.[43]

Christopher Hedges has argued in his *American Fascists* that religious fundamentalists in America express this psychology.[44] It is a harsh criticism that does not do justice to the distinctively democratic features of American religion, the ways in which, because of our constitutional arrangements (free exercise and anti-establishment), religion in America often depends on the support of the people, leading to the high levels of religious belief and feeling in the United States in contrast to the nations of Western Europe with religious establishments.[45] Such widespread American religious feeling has often, in turn, actively supported the constitutional arrangements that made it possible, including the separation of church and state. And while American religions have sometimes supported evils like slavery, racism, anti-Semitism, sexism, and homophobia, others have questioned such evils. In contrast, it was the hostility to religion as such that led Mussolini and Hitler, under the influence of Nietzsche, genocidally to abandon any ethical constraints on anti-Semitism in a way in which Christian anti-Semitism had not.[46] Religious fundamentalism in the United States also has risen

39 See, on this point, Carol Gilligan and David Richards, *The Deepening Darkness: Patriarchy, Resistance, and Democracy's Future* (Cambridge: Cambridge University Press, 2009).

40 See, on this point, Robert O. Paxton, *The Anatomy of Fascism* (New York: Vintage Books, 2004), pp. 3–23.

41 See *id.*, p. 84. Benito Mussolini himself defined fascism not positively but solely in terms of its enemies. See, on this point, Mussolini, "The Political and Social Doctrine of Fascism," in *My Autobiography with "The Political and Social Doctrine of Fascism,"* trans. Jane Soames (Mineola, N.Y.: Dover Publications, 2006), pp. 227–40.

42 Paxton, *Anatomy of Fascism*, p. 17.

43 For further defense of this claim, see Gilligan and Richards, *Deepening Darkness*, chap. 9.

44 See Chris Hedges, *American Fascists: The Christian Right and the War on America* (New York: Free Press, 2006).

45 See, on this point, Andrew J. Cherlin, *The Marriage-Go-Round: The State of Marriage and the Family in America Today* (New York: Alfred A. Knopf, 2009), pp. 72, 103–15. See, in general, John Micklethwait and Adrian Wooldridge, *God Is Back: How the Global Revival of Faith Is Changing the World* (New York: Penguin Press, 2009).

46 See, on these points, Gilligan and Richards, *The Deepening Darkness*, pp. 232–8.

from its democratic appeal, and its apologists sometimes claim they have a secular basis, which at least pays homage to the values of our constitutionalism, including separation of church and state. American fundamentalism in such circumstances has at least sometimes democratized religion (American Catholicism, for example, takes a quite different form than Catholicism elsewhere). And if we measured democracy by political participation, then fundamentalist religion has democratized believers because it has mobilized them from passivity into quite aggressive political activism.[47]

However, political participation does not measure the legitimacy of democracy, as fascism in Italy and Germany famously vaunted its democracy (over British or American constitutional democracy) by its allegedly higher levels of political participation. What political fascism shows us, as Hedges clearly sees, is that political participation of a certain sort is hostile to democracy, in particular, when it mindlessly appeals to aggressive forms of political activism against outsiders (in Germany, Jews; in Italy, liberals and socialists) to enforce a fascist ideal of nationhood of unquestionable authority, based on patriarchal manhood and womanhood.[48] What Mussolini and Hitler condemned in liberal democracy was precisely its constitutional limits on state power (protecting basic human rights) and its deliberative politics, supported by free speech, representative government, several parties, and regular elections. But fundamentalist politics is mindlessly populist in some of these ways (expressing itself in initiatives that abridge basic rights), and fundamentalism in law, as we have seen, seeks to limit the scope of constitutionally protected rights, including the separation of church and state that is one of our most precious heritages from the founders. And fundamentalism's war on the rights of other citizens sometimes expresses this aggression in violence precisely at the exercise of their constitutionally guaranteed human rights (the murder of abortion doctors, or homophobic violence against, including murder of, uncloseted homosexuals, including gay youths who are particularly vulnerable to such violence).

It also does not follow from the claim of fundamentalists that their arguments are reasonable on secular grounds that they are reasonable on such grounds. There are esoteric and exoteric forms of fundamentalism: the esoteric forms are put in terms appealing only to sectarian believers; the exoteric forms disingenuously mask their sectarian basis and claim to rest on claims of secular reason. We cannot, however, take these latter claims at face value, in particular, when they claim to justify the power of the state to deny the basic constitutional rights of fellow Americans. As I have argued at some length, we can see the religious fundamentalism of some views (e.g., new natural law; see Chapter 4) only after critical examination, on reasonable internal and external grounds, of their arguments.

47 See, for defense of this and related claims, Jon A. Shields, *The Democratic Virtues of the Christian Right* (Princeton, N.J.: Princeton University Press, 2009). I criticize these claims in the text that follows.

48 See, for further analysis, Gilligan and Richards, *Deepening Darkness*, pp. 232–8.

Fundamentalists sometimes believe and certainly in the United States sometimes publicly argue as if they had secular grounds for their views, and sometimes they even claim that they are as much a movement for human rights as any other. But their views have no reasonable appeal to the many people, women and men, who do not share their sectarian conception of God's patriarchal will in matters of sexuality and gender. On examination, it is such a sectarian basis that leads them aggressively to seek to use the power of the state to forbid or discourage the actions of others who reject their sectarian conception. To take their claims of a secular basis at face value is not to take seriously the demands of public reason at the heart of American constitutionalism.

No one denies that fundamentalist views are held as matters of conviction, but it does not follow that political advocacy of such views can reasonably be regarded as on par with the movements for basic human rights that arose and have had such appeal since the 1960, let alone earlier abolitionist struggles against slavery and American racism and sexism. What marks these latter movements is that traditionally dehumanized groups freed their moral voices in protesting the injustices inflicted on them, grounding their views not in sectarian religion but in often radically heterodox forms of religion that challenged the role patriarchy had played in supporting such injustices.[49] In contrast, fundamentalists aggressively entered American politics in reaction to such claims for human rights, seeking to reimpose the patriarchal constraints on voice that had given rise to such injustices.

But it is at a deeper level of political psychology that Hedges is right about the appeal of European fascists and American fundamentalists. In both cases, the appeal is not to any coherently developed reasonable argument, for there is none. The question, rather, is one of psychology, asking how and why women and men of sometimes-diverse demographic backgrounds resonate to fundamentalist arguments. The seemingly democratic appeal of fundamentalist religions conceals, indeed masks, like fascism, the role of antidemocratic patriarchal structures of authority in these religions that remain quite powerful and entrenched, and are now perceived to be at threat. We know that the roots of fascism in Mussolini's Italy and Hitler's Germany lay in a sense of humiliated patriarchal manhood after the perceived defeats of both nations in World War I, inventing scapegoats on whom violence was unleashed. The scapegoats tended to be precisely those people who defended humane values like liberalism or socialism, values that sometimes questioned dominant patriarchal arrangements.[50] It is, on examination, the same reactionary patriarchal psychology that motivates the aggressive attacks of American fundamentalists in religion and law on those who most conspicuously challenge patriarchal values and practices, women (straight and gay) who seek

49 See, on this point, Richards, *Women, Gays, and the Constitution: The Grounds for Feminism and Gay Rights in Culture and Law* (Chicago: University of Chicago Press, 1998).

50 See, for further analysis, Gilligan and Richards, *Deepening Darkness*, pp. 232–8.

reproductive autonomy and men and women (straight and gay) who seek equality in love. Patriarchal men and women find a common basis for political action in stereotypes that dehumanize, failing to take seriously the women who responsibly have abortions or the gay men and lesbians who love one another deeply and humanely; and, in a culture in which patriarchy remains powerful, fundamentalist views have more appeal than they should. What makes such dehumanization psychologically possible are uncritical stereotypes that erase persons as living and caring individuals. These stereotypes express themselves in objectification, for example, graphic images of aborted fetuses, a kind of visual pornography whose force depends on silencing the ethical voice of real people who come responsibly to resist patriarchal constraints.[51] Fundamentalists cannot hear because they cannot see such real people. Only this can explain how innocent people of goodwill, who are in fact the unjust victims of their patriarchal rage, are transformed by them into aggressors.

Patriarchy hides, as it were, in democracy, masking as democratic what subverts the basic values of democratic constitutionalism, respect for human rights under the rule of law. This has expressed itself in the American debates in an attack on the judiciary, as antidemocratic, precisely when the judiciary is performing its indispensable normative value in our constitutionalism, extending human rights to despised minorities whom democratic majorities love to hate (e.g., when courts have recognized same-sex marriage as a constitutionally guaranteed right under state constitutional law). There may be good reasons, in general, that support forms of democratic constitutionalism (like Great Britain), which traditionally lacked American-style judicial review.[52] But there is something cynical and worse in supporting American-style judicial review (including protection of basic rights) everywhere but where it is most justified.

So, the appeal of fundamentalist religions, although real and sometimes quite populist, is not democratic or, if democratic, is democratic in the way Hitler's appeal to the German people was real and populist. After the Holocaust, we see such a "democracy" for what it is, not a democracy, certainly not a constitutional democracy but a populist, fascist state drawing its appeal from a mindless political anti-Semitism that was to prove monstrously genocidal. We need, as Americans, to ask ourselves hard questions about the roots and consequences of the similar kind of populist support that fundamentalist religions have both fomented and enjoyed in the United States, a support that brings no credit to either them or to us.

[51] See, on this point, Jon A. Shields, *The Democratic Virtues of the Christian Right* (Princeton, N.J.: Princeton University Press, 2009), pp. 102–7. Shields does not see, let alone take seriously, this psychology.

[52] See, on this point, Jeremy Waldron, *Law and Disagreement* (Oxford: Oxford University Press, 1999); Richard Bellamy, *Political Constitutionalism: A Republican Defence of the Constitutionality of Democracy* (Cambridge: Cambridge University Press, 2007); Mark Tushnet, *Taking the Constitution Away from the Courts* (Princeton, N.J.: Princeton University Press, 1999).

Think of the populist rage, easily fomented and politically mobilized and acquiesced in by politicians, at gay marriage, What motivates such rage appears to be the ways in which gay and lesbian loving relationships (otherwise indistinguishable from many heterosexual marriages) challenge the gender binary, as if sexual love is defined in terms of masculine traits that only men can have and feminine traits that only women can have, and as if marriage required a gender hierarchy defined by the gender binary required by nature. It is common knowledge that the gender binary is false: men often are caring and tender just as women are; and women often are competitive and aggressive as men are; and love often flourishes between equals. What we have here are, at bottom, culturally entrenched essentialist stereotypes of masculinity and femininity and a further culturally entrenched assumption that the stereotypes must be arranged hierarchically with one over the other. So, why are Americans psychologically vulnerable to feel rage at gay marriage? They feel that something is at stake, and indeed it is, namely their uncritical investment in patriarchy in intimate life, maintaining a gender binary in marriage that is so clearly both factually and ethically indefensible, willfully, brutally blind to the role both experience and equality play in both love and democracy.

The psychological power of patriarchy has always critically been focused on the patriarchal love laws, which have forbidden intimate relations across the barriers of religion or race and ethnicity or gender. It is such traumatic breaks in intimate relationships that make psychologically possible the forms of extreme prejudice (e.g., anti-Semitism and racism) that dehumanize whole classes of persons. If one can kill any possibility of love across such barriers, one extinguishes the intimate relationships through which we come to value another person as a beloved individual. It is this psychological trauma that expresses itself in the forms of patriarchal violence unleashed on any person who challenges these barriers, thus supporting larger patterns of irrational prejudice in other domains. We have now come to a point in our constitutional development at which we reject, as unconstitutional, the barriers of religion or ethnicity or race in intimate life that enforced the irrational prejudices of anti-Semitism and racism. We now face that constitutional barrier of gender that prohibitions on same-sex marriage continue to enforce. As the Supreme Court in *Lawrence v. Texas* only recently held unconstitutional the criminalization of same-sex relationships, it is not surprising that the psychology of trauma that underlies the application of the patriarchal love laws to gay and lesbian relationships remains very much intact. It is this reactionary psychology that will not and cannot see, indeed wars on, the happiness of individual same-sex couples who passionately love and care for each other in relationships that are indistinguishable from heterosexual marriages. It is a feature of the continuing power of American patriarchal religion that it thus frames the terms of intimate life for many Americans, masking the lack of a secular basis for their views, in the same way that, in democratic India, some states forbid the killing of cows on the ground of a sectarian Hindu view, itself very much in doubt as a Hindu view, that cows are sacred.[53] It is through such masking that patriarchy hides in democracy, as if majority support for sectarian patriarchal rage at gay marriage could and should nullify constitutional guarantees of human rights under the rule of law. That is not democracy but fascism, and American patriarchy is the worm in the bud that makes this psychologically possible.

What gay marriage challenges is the uncritical way patriarchy insists on maintaining the gender binary in marriage, which gays and lesbian challenge in their love lives in the same way many heterosexual men and women challenge them in theirs. There is a repressive psychology at work here of fear and anger, but there is also a conspicuous lack of any good argument. When movements are so mindlessly empty of ideas, and yet so easy to believe, we can find in patriarchal political psychology, as I have argued at length in this book, their appeal. Their appeal is reactionary, based on a sense of manhood humiliated by a reasonable threat to its legitimacy from the free voices of women and men who challenge the justice of patriarchal demands. Why exactly is the love of equals unmanly, indeed taken as an insult or an attack? The humiliation expresses itself in repressive violence against patriarchally imagined enemies: unregulated women, religious and ethnic others, and men who challenge dominant norms. As I observed earlier, Lincoln's criticism of Stephen Douglas for indulging racism applies to politicians who indulge sexism and homophobia today: "[H]e is blowing out the moral lights around us.... [H]e is, in my judgment, penetrating the human soul and eradicating the light of reason and the love of liberty in this American people."[54] We are thus divided from our common humanity by something as unreal as the Jewish threat was in Hitler's Germany, mobilized by politicians into an unjust cultural and political war on unreal enemies. The psychological power of patriarchy remains all too real even for Americans who live with such pride under their democratic constitutionalism. The psychologically driven paradox is that it is our Constitution that they are betraying.

There is reason to believe that there may be hope to recover our constitutional sanity when persons, including persons of fundamentalist faith, suspend these divisive patriarchal barriers and come into reasonable dialogue with others. Through such honest dialogue, Evangelicals come to doubt that gay/lesbian sexuality is a matter of choice or is subject to change, and even come to see the harm done by insistence on fruitless and harmful sexual reorientation programs aimed at Evangelical gays and lesbians. Such dialogue may indeed lead to a reasonable consensus that "the world would be a happier and healthier place if, for *all* people, love, sex, and, yes, marriage went together."[55]

53 See, on this point, Wendy Doniger, *The Hindus: An Alternative History* (New York: Penguin Press, 2009), pp. 657–9.

54 Quoted in Richards, *Conscience and the Constitution*, p. 55.

55 David G. Myers, "Bridging the Gay-Evangelical Divide," *The Wall Street Journal*, August 28, 2009, at W11.

As a general matter, however, patriarchal repression and violence mark our contemporary situation at home and abroad. What we need is to understand such fundamentalist violence for what it is – at war with the role of free and equal voice in democratic politics. We cannot be the democrats we believe we are until the persistence of patriarchy becomes central to what our democratic voices resist and, in the spirit of the resistance movements I have discussed, challenge as failures and corruptions of democracy.

It is in that spirit that I have addressed this book not to the fundamentalisms abroad but to the antidemocratic fundamentalisms at home, which fester in our religion and in our law. It is much easier to identify and resist the fundamentalisms abroad, which are so hostile to the very idea of constitutional democracy, than it is to look critically at chauvinistic patriarchal astigmatism when it comes to our own institutions. Such violence from abroad, when successful, challenges our manhood, a manhood now self-consciously in transition between patriarchal and democratic manhood. The worry is that our response will be inconsistent with our considered values, values that include traditions of nonviolent dissent that we rightly honor.[56] Arundhati Roy recently put the worry in the following terms:

> Any government's condemnation of terrorism is only credible if it shows itself to be responsive to persistent, reasonable, closely argued, nonviolent dissent. And yet, what's happening is just the opposite. The world over, nonviolent resistance movements are being crushed and broken. If we do not respect and honor them, by default we privilege those who turn to violent means.[57]

We need now, more than ever, to remind ourselves of the traditions that Roy worries we may forget, traditions of nonviolence that, as in the American civil rights movement of the 1960s, were brilliantly successful at a cost in human life that, though deplorable, was small compared with "a single day of battle in the Civil War or World War II."[58] Nonviolence, in comparison to violence, may better advance and secure justice at less cost. We need now, more than ever, to keep such nonviolent alternatives clearly, lucidly in mind. In contrast, Roy points acidly to the rise of religious fascism in Gandhi's democratic India, as politicians manipulatively encourage and fail to punish pogroms that use political violence to sustain religious and ethnic intolerance.[59] What Roy sees in her native India (resort to violence rather than nonviolent protest), she claims to see in democratic America's comparable betrayal of the politics of Martin Luther King in its response to terrorism, both the war in Afghanistan and in Iraq: wounded manhood turning without compelling reason to violence.[60] Roy, a feminist, is

[56] See, on this point, David A. J. Richards, *Disarming Manhood: Roots of Ethical Resistance* (Athens: Ohio University/Swallow Press, 2005).

[57] Arundhati Roy, *War Talk* (Cambridge, Mass.: South End Press, 2003).

[58] See David L. Chappell, *A Stone of Hope: Prophetic Religion and the Death of Jim Crow* (Chapel Hill: University of North Carolina Press, 2004), p. 153.

[59] See Roy, *War Talk*, pp. 18–19, 34, 50, 105.

[60] See, in general, Roy, *War Talk*.

asking the right questions, as she does, for example, when she insists we face Churchill's contradictions[61] and our own. In particular, she sees in American wars in Afghanistan and Iraq a patriarchally grounded corruption of judgment about the aims and means of the just use of force, a corruption made possible by overwhelming feelings of shame and humiliation at the unjust use of violence against ourselves. A nation so patriarchally corrupted in its judgments confuses its justice and power with legitimacy in the use of force, resorting to violence unnecessarily and in ways that fuel violence, not voice and dialogue. Roy asks us: are we keeping faith with our best democratic traditions or are we allowing an enemy through insult to remake ourselves in his violently repressive patriarchal image (undertaking preemptive wars, unsupported by imminent and proportional threat, and conducting such wars in ways that contradict the values of democratic equal dignity we claim to uphold)? We need to understand ourselves and our traditions, and to ask, as Roy does, the right questions, which interrogate our own psyches, including our vulnerabilities to shame and violence.

If I am right, patriarchy is an American problem, and one that exists and continues to exist in tension with our democratic constitutionalism. Gunnar Myrdal in 1944 argued that American racism and democracy posed, as he put is, "an American dilemma," because racism was so contradictory to our democratic principles and ideals.[62] In light of the progress we have made since Myrdal made his argument, and yet the continuing power of irrational prejudice in our public and private lives, the argument of this book may be regarded as a deepening of Myrdal's analysis: what held us back when Myrdal wrote and what, despite all our progress since Myrdal wrote, still holds us back is patriarchy in our democracy or hiding in our democracy, our twenty-first-century American dilemma. The unjust power of fundamentalism in American religion and law, the subject of this book, illustrates how alive this problem is in America today. And if I am right about India and other democracies, it is not only our dilemma: it is the dilemma of all democracies in the twenty-first century.

We in the United States may have come to a turning point in the election of Barack Obama to the presidency of the United States. As I earlier suggested (Chapter 8), Obama has opposed 'originalism' more courageously and intelligently than any other American politician, and his position on this and other issues may plausibly be regarded as the expression of the life and ideas of a man who resists patriarchy and has been brought to resistance to 'originalism' for this reason. If so, this book may be regarded as a way of understanding how important Obama's election may be to the future of American constitutional democracy. What Obama's election shows is that the rejection of 'originalism' is itself reasonably appealing to the American people, which suggests that the American people

61 See, on Churchill's rather racist way of dismissing the claims of the Palestinians, Roy, *War Talk*, p. 58.

62 See Gunner Myrdal, *An American Dilemma: The Negro Problem and Modern Democracy*, 2 vols. (1944; repr., New York: Pantheon Books, 1972).

today can be (as they have been) mobilized by resistance to patriarchy, in a way I would once have thought improbable, if not impossible. Obama has shown us the power in politics of something we know, as we know we are human: that resistance to patriarchy is rooted in our loving human natures, and the love of equals is the basis of democracy. The very democratic appeal Obama has enjoyed and continues to enjoy suggests that more and more Americans are being reasonably persuaded that resistance to patriarchy is crucial to the integrity of our democratic constitutionalism. They are right.

Liberal constitutionalists like myself have watched with dismay the appeal of 'originalism' and have spent much time thinking about how the judicial appointments process might better be reconfigured to limit such appeal.[63] I have argued in this book that the problem cannot be limited to the appointments process but must be understood more generally in terms of the alliance between religious and constitutional fundamentalists and the role they have played in the politics of the Republican Party and American politics generally. Thoughtful Republicans I have known in my life, including both my father and my mother, both Roman Catholics, were repelled by this alliance, and would not have recognized as their party the bigoted thing it has become.

We have come too far as a people not to face critically and honestly our own deepest problems, in particular, when those problems, like patriarchy, go to the integrity of our democratic constitutionalism. We need neither a religion nor a law that makes no reasonable sense of the humanity and justice of its founding, nor religious or political leaders who uncritically pander to and indeed foment our worst prejudices and fears. We need to take seriously what the demands of democratic reason are and ask why and when we find it so easy, all too easy to ignore, even to denigrate such demands. I have therefore made this book a work of critique and a work of diagnosis and a call to resistance, calling on the reason of a democratic people to resist fundamentalisms that war unjustly not only on fellow citizens but also, in sober truth, on democratic constitutionalism itself.

[63] See, for a notable example of this mode of argument, Christopher L. Eisgruber, *The Next Justice: Repairing the Supreme Court Appointments Process* (Princeton, N.J.: Princeton University Press, 2007).

BIBLIOGRAPHY

Abzug, Robert H. *Cosmos Crumbling: American Reform and the Religious Imagination* (New York: Oxford University Press, 1994).

Acton, J. E. E. D. (Lord). *The History of Freedom and Other Essays* (London: Macmillan, 1907).

Ahlstrom, Sydney E. *A Religious History of the American People*, 2nd ed. (New Haven, Conn.: Yale University Press, 2004).

Ahmed, Leila. *A Border Passage: From Cairo to America – A Woman's Journey* (New York: Farrar, Straus and Giroux, 1999).

Albright, W. E. and C. S. Mann. *The Anchor Bible: Matthew* (New York: Doubleday, 1971).

"All This We Will Do," *New York Times*, January 21, 2009, at 215.

Alter, Robert. *The Art of Biblical Narrative* (New York: Basic Books, 1981).

Amar, Akhil Reed. "Heller, HLR, and Holistic Legal Reasoning," 122 *Harv. L. Rev.* 145 (2008).

Anscombe, G. E. M. and P. T. Geach. *Three Philosophers* (Oxford: Basil Blackwell, 1961).

Aquinas, Thomas. *On the Truth of the Catholic Faith*, 5 vols. (Garden City, N.Y.: Image, 1955–7).

Aquinas, Thomas. *Summa Theologica*, vol. 1, trans. Fathers of the English Dominican Province (Allen, Tex.: Christian Classics, 1948).

Arendt, Hannah. *Eichmann in Jerusalem: A Report on the Banality of Evil* (New York: Penguin, 1992).

Arendt, Hannah. *The Origins of Totalitarianism* (New York: Harcourt Brace Jovanovich, 1973).

Aristotle. *Nicomachean Ethics*, trans. Martin Ostwald (New York: Library of Liberal Arts, 1962).

Aristotle. *Politics*, trans. Ernest Barker (New York: Oxford University Press, 1962).

Arkes, Hadley. *Natural Rights and the Right to Choose* (Cambridge: Cambridge University Press, 2002).

Ashcraft, Richard. *Locke's Two Treatises of Government* (London: Allen & Unwin, 1987).

Augustine. *City of God*, trans. Henry Bettenson (Harmondsworth, U.K.: Penguin, 1972).

Augustine. *Confessions*, trans. Henry Chadwick (Oxford: Oxford University Press, 1991).

Augustine. *The Trinity*, Vol. 8., *Augustine: Later Works*, trans. John Burnaby (Philadelphia: Westminster Press, 1955).

Bailey, Derrick S. *Homosexuality and the Western Christian Tradition* (New York: Longmans, Green, 1955).

Baker, Peter and Susan Saulny. "At Notre Dame, Obama Calls for Civil Tone in Abortion Debate," *New York Times*, May 18, 2009, A1 and A3.
Baldwin, James. *Early Novels and Stories*, ed. Toni Morrison (New York: Library of America, 1998).
Balint, Michael. *Primary Love and Psycho-Analytic Technique* (New York: Liveright, 1965).
Balter, Joni. "Gay Power Brokers – Money, Stature and Savvy Give Leaders More Clout," *Seattle Times*, August 1, 1993.
Bamforth, Nicholas and David A. J. Richards. *Patriarchal Religion, Sexuality, and Gender: A Critique of New Natural Law* (Cambridge: Cambridge University Press, 2008).
Banville, John. "A Century of Looking the Other Way," *New York Times*, May 23, 2009, at A21.
Barnes, Jonathan, ed. *The Complete Works of Aristotle*, vols. 1–2 (Princeton, N.J.: Princeton University Press, 1984).
Barnett, Walter. *Sexual Freedom and the Constitution* (Albuquerque: University of New Mexico Press, 1973).
Barringer Gordon, Sarah. *The Mormon Question: Polygamy and Constitutional Conflict in Nineteenth Century America* (Chapel Hill: University of North Carolina Press, 2002).
Bayle, Pierre. *Philosophique Commentaire sur ces paroles de Jesus Christ "Constrain-les d/entrée," Oevres Diverses de Mr. Pierre Bayle*, vol. 2 (The Hague: Chez P. Husson et al., 1727).
Becker, Jo and Adam Liptak. "Assertive Style Raises Questions on Demeanor," *New York Times*, May 29, 2009, at A14.
Beecher, Catharine E. *Woman Suffrage and Woman's Profession* (Hartford, Conn.: Brown and Gross, 1871).
Bell, Alan P. and Martin S. Weinberg. *Homosexualities* (New York: Simon and Schuster, 1978).
Bell, Alan P., Martin S. Weinberg, and Sue Kiefer Hammersmith. *Sexual Preference: Its Development in Men and Women* (Bloomington: Indiana University Press, 1981).
Bellamy, Richard. *Political Constitutionalism: A Republican Defence of the Constitutionality of Democracy* (Cambridge: Cambridge University Press, 2007).
Bendroth, Margaret Lamberts. *Fundamentalism and Gender: 1875 to the Present* (New Haven, Conn.: Yale University Press, 1993).
Benedict, Michael Les. *A Compromise of Principle: Congressional Republicans and Reconstruction, 1863–1869* (New York: W. W. Norton, 1974).
Berger, Raoul. *Death Penalties* (Cambridge, Mass.: Harvard University Press, 1982).
Berger, Raoul. *Government by Judiciary* (Cambridge, Mass.: Harvard University Press, 1977).
Beschle, Donald L. "Catechism or Imagination: Is Justice Scalia's Judicial Style Typically Catholic?" 37 *Villanova L. Rev.* 1329 (1992).
Biale, David. *Eros and the Jews: From Biblical Israel to Contemporary America* (New York: Basic Books, 1992).
Biggar, Nigel and Rufus Black, eds. *The Revival of Natural Law: Philosophical, theological and ethical responses to the Finnis-Grisez School* (Aldershot, U.K.: Ashgate, 2000).
Blackstone, William. *Commentaries on the Laws of England*, vol. 4 (Chicago: University of Chicago Press, 1979).
Bloom, Harold. *The American Religion: The Emergence of the Post-Christian Nation* (New York: Touchstone, 1992).
Blow, Charles M. "Rogues, Robes and Racists," *New York Times*, May 30, 2009, at A19.
Blumenberg, Hans. *The Legitimacy of the Modern Age*, trans. Robert M. Wallace (Cambridge: Massachusetts Institute of Technology Press, 1983).

Blumstein, Philip and Pepper Schwartz. *American Couples: Money Work Sex* (New York: William Morrow, 1983).
Bonhoeffer, Dietrich. *Letters and Papers from Prison*, ed. Eberhard Bethge (New York: Touchstone Books, 1971).
Bork, Robert H. "Neutral Principles and Some First Amendment Problems," 47 *Ind. L.J.* 9 (1971).
Bork, Robert H. *Tradition and Morality in Constitutional Law* (Washington, D.C.: American Enterprise Institute, 1984).
Borresen, Kari Elisabeth. *Subordination and Equivalence: The Nature and Role of Woman in Augustine and Thomas Aquinas*, trans. Charles H. Talbot (Washington, D.C.: University Press of America, 1981).
Boswell, John. *Same-Sex Unions in Premodern Europe* (New York: Villard Books, 1994).
Bouyer, Louis. "Erasmus in Relation to the Medieval Biblical Tradition," in *The Cambridge History of the Bible*, vol. 2, ed. G. W. H. Lampe (Cambridge: Cambridge University Press, 1969).
Boyarin, Daniel. *Unheroic Conduct: The Rise of Heterosexuality and the Invention of the Jewish Man* (Berkeley: University of California Press, 1997).
Boyarin, Daniel. *A Radical Jew: Paul and the Politics of Identity* (Berkeley: University of California Press, 1994).
Boyarin, Daniel. *Carnal Israel: Reading Sex in Talmudic Culture* (Berkeley: University of California Press, 1993).
Boyer, Peter J. "Annals of Religion: A Hard Faith – How the New Pope and His Predecessor Redefined Vatican II," *New Yorker*, May 16, 2005, p. 54.
Bradley, Denis J. M. "John Finnis on Aquinas 'The Philosopher,'" 41 *Heythrop J.* 1 (2000).
Bransford, Stephen. *Gay Politics vs. Colorado and America: The Inside Story of Amendment 2* (Cascade, Colo.: Sardis Press, 1994).
Brasher, Brenda E. *Godly Women: Fundamentalism and Female Power* (New Brunswick, N.J.: Rutgers University Press, 1998).
Bravin, Jess. "Rethinking Original Intent," *Wall Street Journal*, March 14–15, 2009.
Bravin, Jess. "Legal Realism Informs Judge's Views," *Wall Street Journal*, May 28, 2009, at A3.
Bravin, Jess. "John McCain: Looking to the Framers," *Wall Street Journal*, October 7, 2008.
Brecher, Edward M. *The Sex Researchers* (London: Andre Deutsch, 1970).
Bringhurst, Newell G., ed. *Reconsidering No Man Knows My History: Fawn M. Brodie and Joseph Smith in Retrospect* (Logan: Utah State University Press, 1996).
Brisbin, Richard A., Jr. *Justice Antonin Scalia and the Conservative Revival* (Baltimore: Johns Hopkins University Press, 1997).
Brodie, Fawn M. *No Man Knows My History: The Life of Joseph Smith* (New York: Vintage, 1995).
Brown, Peter. *Augustine of Hippo: A Biography* (Berkeley: University of California Press, 2000).
Brown, Peter. *The Body and Society: Men, Women, and Sexual Renunciation in Early Christianity* (New York: Columbia University Press, 1988).
Brown, Peter. *The Making of Late Antiquity* (Cambridge, Mass.: Harvard University Press, 1978).
Brown, Raymond E. *The Anchor Bible: The Gospel According to John I–XII* (New York: Doubleday, 1966).
Buber, Martin. *I and Thou*, trans. Walter Kaufmann (New York: Charles Scribner's Sons, 1970).

Bull, Chris and John Gallagher. *Perfect Enemies: The Religious Right, the Gay Movement, and the Politics of the 1990's* (New York: Crown Publishers, 1996).
Buruma, Ian. *Murder in Amsterdam: The Death of Theo van Gogh and the Limits of Tolerance* (New York: Penguin, 2006).
Bushman, Richard L. *Joseph Smith and the Beginnings of Mormonism* (Urbana: University of Illinois Press, 1984).
Bushman, Richard L. *Joseph Smith: Rough Stone Rolling* (New York: Alfred A. Knopf, 2005).
Bynum, Caroline Walker. *Jesus as Mother: Studies in the Spirituality of the High Middle Ages* (Berkeley: University of California Press, 1982).
Callahan, Daniel. *The Catholic Case for Contraception* (London: Arlington Books, 1969).
Canaday, Margot. *The Straight State: Sexuality and Citizenship in Twentieth-Century America* (Princeton, N.J.: Princeton University Press, 2009).
Carpenter, Joel A. *Revive Us Again: The Reawakening of American Fundamentalism* (New York: Oxford University Press, 1997).
Carroll, James. *Constantine's Sword: The Church and the Jews* (Boston: Houghton Mifflin, 2001).
Carroll, James. *An American Requiem: God, My Father, and the War that Came between Us* (Boston: Houghton Mifflin, 1996).
Carroll, Michael P. *The Cult of the Virgin Mary: Psychological Origins* (Princeton, N.J.: Princeton University Press, 1986).
Carroll, Robert and Stephen Prickett, eds. *The Bible: Authorized King James Version* (Oxford: Oxford University Press, 1998).
Cash, W. J. *The Mind of the South* (New York: Vintage Books, 1941).
Catechism of the Catholic Church (New York: Image, 1995).
Chappell, David L. *A Stone of Hope: Prophetic Religion and the Death of Jim Crow* (Chapel Hill: University of North Carolina Press, 2004).
Chemerinsky, Erwin. "It's Still the Kennedy Court," 11 *Green Bag* 2d 427, 429–31 (2008).
Cherlin, Andrew J. *The Marriage-Go-Round: The State of Marriage and the Family in America Today* (New York: Alfred A. Knopf, 2009).
Chesler, Ellen. *Woman of Valor: Margaret Sanger and the Birth Control Movement* (New York: Anchor, 1992).
Church, Forrest. *So Help Me God: The Founding Fathers and the First Great Battle over Church and State* (Orlando: Harcourt, 2007).
Cobb, Thomas R. R. *An Inquiry into the Law of Negro Slavery in the United States of America* (New York: Negro Universities Press, 1968).
Cochrane, Charles N. *Christianity and Classical Culture* (London: Oxford University Press, 1944).
Colby, Thomas B. and Peter J. Smith. " Living Originalism," available at http://papers.ssrn.com/sol3/papers.cfm?abstract_id=1090282.
Colman, John. *John Locke's Moral Philosophy* (Edinburgh: Edinburgh University Press, 1983).
Conquest, Robert. *Stalin: Breaker of Nations* (New York: Penguin, 1991).
"Constitutional Limits on Anti-Gay-Rights Initiatives," Note, 106 *Harv. L. Rev.* 1905 (1993).
Cooke, Jacobe E., ed. *The Federalist* (Middletown, Conn.: Wesleyan University Press, 1961).
Copleston, F. C. *Aquinas* (London: Penguin, 1991).
Cornell, Saul. *A Well Regulated Militia: The Founding Fathers and the Origins of Gun Control in America* (Oxford: Oxford University Press, 2006).

Cossman, Brenda and Ratna Kapur. *Secularism's Last Sigh? Hindutva and the (Mis)Rule of Law* (Oxford: Oxford University Press, 2001).
Crapanzano, Vincent. *Serving the Word: Literalism in America from the Pulpit to the Bench* (New York: New Press, 2000).
Curran, Charles and Richard McCormick, eds. *Dissent in Moral Theory* (New York: Paulist Press, 1988).
Curran, Charles E. and Richard A., McCormick S. J. *Readings in Moral Theology No. 7: Natural Law and Theology* (New York: Paulist Press, 1991).
Curry, Thomas J. *The First Freedoms: Church and State in America to the Passage of the First Amendment* (New York: Oxford University Press, 1986).
Daube, David. *The New Testament and Rabbinic Judaism* (Peabody, Mass.: Hendrickson, 1998).
Davies, Brian. *The Thought of Thomas Aquinas* (Oxford: Clarendon Press, 1992).
Davies, W. D. *The Setting of the Sermon on the Mount* (Cambridge: Cambridge University Press, 1964).
DeBerg, Betty A. *Ungodly Women: Gender the First Wave of American Fundamentalism* (Macon, Ga.: Mercer University Press, 2000).
D'Emilio, John. *Making Trouble* (New York: Routledge, 1992).
De Gruchy, John W., ed. *The Cambridge Companion to Dietrich Bonhoeffer* (Cambridge: Cambridge University Press, 2002).
Department of Health and Human Services. *Report of the Secretary's Task Force on Youth Suicide* (Washington, D.C.: Department of Health and Human Services, 1989).
"Developments in the Law – Sexual Orientation and the Law," 102 *Harv. L. Rev.* 1508 (1989).
Devlin, Patrick. *The Enforcement of Morals* (London: Oxford University Press, 1965).
"Did Bush Promise to Appoint a Justice Like Scalia," http://mediamatters.org/items/w005101300005.p. 202.
Dodds, E. R. *Pagan and Christian in an Age of Anxiety* (Cambridge: Cambridge University Press, 1965).
Dostoyevsky, Fyodor. *The Brothers Karamazov*, trans. David McDuff (London: Penguin, 1993).
Douglas, Ann. *The Feminization of American Culture* (New York: Alfred A. Knopf, 1977).
Douglas, Mary. *In the Wilderness: The Doctrine of Defilement in the Book of Numbers* (Sheffield: Sheffield Academic Press, 1993).
Douglas, Mary. *Leviticus as Literature* (Oxford: Oxford University Press, 1999).
Dowd, Maureen. "The Long, Lame Goodbye," *New York Times*, January 18, 2009.
Dunn, John. *The Political Thought of John Locke* (Cambridge: Cambridge University Press, 1969).
Duster, Alfreda M., ed. *Crusade for Justice: The Autobiography of Ida B. Wells* (Chicago: University of Chicago Press, 1970).
Dworkin, Ronald. *Freedom's Law: The Moral Reading of the American Constitution* (Cambridge, Mass.: Harvard University Press, 1996).
Dworkin, Ronald. *Is Democracy Possible Here? Principles for a New Political Debate* (Princeton, N.J.: Princeton University Press, 2006).
Dworkin, Ronald. *Justice in Robes* (Cambridge, Mass.: Belknap Press, Harvard University Press, 2006).
Dworkin, Ronald. *Life's Dominion: An Argument about Abortion, Euthanasia, and Individual Freedom* (New York: Knopf, 1993).
Dworkin, Ronald. "Sex, Drugs, and the Court," *New York Review of Books*, August 8, 1996.

Dworkin, Ronald. *The Supreme Court Phalanx: The Court's New Right-Wing Bloc* (New York: New York Review Books, 2008).
Dyson, R. W., ed. *Aquinas: Political Writings* (Cambridge: Cambridge University Press, 2002).
Eckenrode, H. J. *Separation of Church and State in Virginia* (New York: De Capo Press, 1971).
Eisenstein, Elizabeth. *The Printing Press as an Agent of Change*, 2 vols. (Cambridge: Cambridge University Press, 1979).
Eisgruber, Christopher L. *The Next Justice: Repairing the Supreme Court Appointments Process* (Princeton, N.J.: Princeton University Press, 2007).
Eisgruber, Christopher L. and Lawrence G. Sager. *Religious Freedom and the Constitution* (Cambridge, Mass.: Harvard University Press, 2007).
Elliot, Jonathan. *The Debates in the Several State Conventions on the Adoption of the Federal Constitution*, vols. 2–3 (Washington, D.C.: Printed for the editor, 1836).
Elon, Amos. *Herzl* (New York: Hold, Rinehart and Winston, 1975).
Elon, Amos. *The Pity of It All: A Portrait of the German-Jewish Epoch 1743–1933* (New York: Picador, 2002).
Epstein, Richard A. "Live and Let Live," *Wall Street Journal*, July 13, 2004, at A14.
Erikson, Erik H. "The Galilean Sayings and the Sense of 'I,'" 70 *Yale Rev.* 321 (1981).
Erikson, Erik H. *Gandhi's Truth: On the Origins of Militant Nonviolence* (New York: W. W. Norton, 1993).
Erikson, Erik H. *Young Man Luther: A Study in Psychoanalysis and History* (New York: W. W. Norton, 1962).
Eskridge, William N., Jr. *The Case for Same-Sex Marriage: From Sexual Liberty to Civilized Commitment* (New York: Free Press, 1996).
Eskridge, William N., Jr., and Darren R. Spediale. *Gay Marriage: For Better or for Worse?* (New York: Oxford University Press, 2006).
Estlund, David M. and Martha C. Nussbaum, eds. *Sex, Preference, and Family: Essays on Law and Nature* (New York: Oxford University Press, 1997).
Evans, Sara. *Personal Politics: The Roots of Women's Liberation in the Civil Rights Movement and the New Left* (New York: Vintage Books, 1980).
Faust, Drew Gilpin, ed. *The Ideology of Slavery: Proslavery Thought in the Antebellum South, 1830–1860* (Baton Rouge: Louisiana State University Press, 1981).
Fehrenbacher, Don E. *The Dred Scott Cases: Its Significance in American Law and Politics* (New York: Oxford University Press, 1978).
Feldman, Noah. *Divided by God: America's Church-State Problem – and What We Should Do about It* (New York: Farrar, Straus and Giroux, 2005).
Festinger, Leon. *A Theory of Cognitive Dissonance* (Stanford, Calif.: Stanford University Press, 1957).
Festinger, Leon, Henry W. Riecken, and Stanley Schachter. *When Prophecy Fails: A Social and Psychological Study of a Modern Group that Predicted the Destruction of the World* (New York: Harper Torchbooks, 1964).
Fetner, Tina. *How the Religious Right Shaped Lesbian and Gay Activism* (Minneapolis: University of Minnesota Press, 2008).
Finnis, John. *Aquinas: Moral, Political, and Legal Theory* (Oxford: Oxford University Press, 1998).
Finnis, John. "The Good of Marriage and the Morality of Sexual Relations: Some Philosophical and Historical Observations," 42 *Am. J. Juris.* 97 (1997).
Finnis, John. "Law, Morality, and 'Sexual Orientation,'" 9 *Notre Dame J. Law, Ethics, and Public Policy* 11 (1995).

Finnis, John. "Law, Morality, and 'Sexual Orientation,'" 69 *Notre Dame L. Rev.* 1049, (1994).
Finnis, John. *Moral Absolutes: Tradition, Revision, and Truth* (Washington, D.C.: Catholic University of America Press, 1991).
Finnis, John. *Natural Law and Natural Rights* (Oxford: Clarendon Press, 1980).
Finnis, John and Germain Grisez. "The Basic Principles of Natural Law: A Reply to Ralph McInerny," 26 *Am. J. Juris.* 21 (1981).
Fiorenza Schussler, Elisabeth. *In Memory of Her: A Feminist Theological Reconstruction of Christian Origins* (New York: Crossroad, 2002).
Fiorenza Schussler, Elisabeth. *Jesus: Miriam's Child, Sophia's Prophet* (New York: Continuum, 1994).
Fiorenza Schussler, Elisabeth, ed. *Searching Scriptures*, 2 vols. (New York: Crossroad, 1993–4).
Fitzhugh, George. *Cannibals All! or, Slaves without Masters*, ed. C. Vann Woodward (Cambridge, Mass.: Belknap Press, Harvard University Press, 1960).
Flusser, David. *Jesus* (Jerusalem: Magnes Press, Hebrew University, 2001).
Flusser, David. *Judaism and the Origins of Christianity* (Jerusalem: Magnes Press, Hebrew University, 1988).
Foner, Eric. *Reconstruction: America's Unfinished Revolution 1863–1877* (New York: Harper & Row, 1988).
Ford, Clellan S. and Frank A. Beach. *Patterns of Sexual Behavior* (New York: Harper Colophon Books, 1951).
Fox, Robin Lane. *The Unauthorized Version: Truth and Fiction in the Bible* (New York: Alfred A. Knopf, 1992).
Foxhall, Lin and John Salmon, eds. *When Men Were Men: Masculinity, Power and Identity in Classical Antiquity* (London: Routledge, 1998).
Frankfort, Henri. *Kingship and the Gods: A Study of Ancient Near Eastern Religion as the Integration of Society and Nature* (Chicago: University of Chicago Press, 1948).
Frankfort, Henri, H. A. Frankfort, John A. Wilson, and Thorkild Jacobsen. *Before Philosophy: The Intellectual Adventure of Ancient Man* (Baltimore: Penguin, 1961).
Fredrickson, George M. *The Black Image in the White Mind: The Debate on Afro-American Character and Destiny, 1817–1914* (Middleton, Conn.: Wesleyan University Press, 1981).
Fredriksen, Paula. *Augustine and the Jews: A Christian Defense of Jews and Judaism* (New York: Doubleday, 2008).
Fredriksen, Paula. *From Jesus to Christ* (New Haven, Conn.: Yale University Press, 2000).
Fredriksen, Paula. *Jesus of Nazareth, King of the Jews: A Jewish Life and the Emergence of Christianity* (New York: Alfred A. Knopf, 2000).
Freud, Anna. *The Ego and the Mechanisms of Defense*, rev. ed. (Madison, Wis.: International Universities Press, 2000).
Fried, Charles. *Modern Liberty and the Limits of Government* (New York: W. W. Norton, 2007).
Furet, Francois. *The Passing of an Illusion: The Idea of Communism in the Twentieth Century*, trans. Deborah Furet (Chicago: University of Chicago Press, 1999).
Gaca, Kathy L. *The Making of Fornication: Eros, Ethics, and Political Reform in Greek Philosophy and Early Christianity* (Berkeley: University of California Press, 2003).
Gager, John A. *The Origins of Anti-Semitism: Attitudes toward Judaism in Pagan and Christian Antiquity* (New York: Oxford University Press, 1983).
Gay Stolberg, Sheryl. "Gay Issues in View, Obama Is Pressed to Engage," *New York Times*, May 7, 2009.

Gebhard, Paul H., John H. Gagnon, Wardell B. Pomeroy, and Cornelia V. Christenson. *Sex Offenders* (New York: Bantam, 1967).

Genovese, Eugene D. *Roll, Jordan, Roll: The World the Slaves Made* (New York: Vintage Books, 1974).

George, Robert. *In Defense of Natural Law* (Oxford: Clarendon Press, 1999).

George, Robert, ed. *Natural Law and Moral Inquiry: Ethics, Metaphysics, and Politics in the Work of German Grisez* (Washington, D.C.: Georgetown University Press, 1998).

George, Robert P. *Natural Law, Liberalism, and Morality* (Oxford: Oxford University Press, 2002).

George, Robert P. and Christopher Wolfe, eds. *Natural Law and Public Reason* (Washington, D.C.: Georgetown University Press, 2000).

Gerber, Scott Douglas. *First Principles: The Jurisprudence of Clarence Thomas* (New York: New York University Press, 1999).

Gerstmann, Evan. *Same-Sex Marriage and the Constitution* (Cambridge: Cambridge University Press, 2004).

Giddings, Paula. *When and Where I Enter: The Impact of Black Women on Race and Sex in America* (New York: William Morrow, 1984).

Gilligan, Carol. *The Birth of Pleasure* (New York: Knopf, 2002).

Gilligan, Carol. *The Birth of Pleasure: A New Map of Love* (New York: Vintage Books, 2003).

Gilligan, Carol. *In a Different Voice: Psychological Theory and Women's Development* (Cambridge, Mass.: Harvard University Press, 1982).

Gilligan, Carol and David A. J. Richards. *The Deepening Darkness: Patriarchy, Resistance, and Democracy's Future* (Cambridge: Cambridge University Press, 2009).

Gilmore, David D., ed. *Honour and Shame and the Unity of the Mediterranean* (Washington, D.C.: American Anthropological Association, 1987).

Gilson, Etienne. *God and Philosophy* (New Haven, Conn.: Yale University Press, 1941).

Goldhill, Simon. *Foucault's Virginity: Ancient Erotic Fiction and the History of Sexuality* (Cambridge: Cambridge University Press, 1995).

Goody, Jack. *The Domestication of the Savage Mind* (Cambridge: Cambridge University Press, 1977).

Gossett, Thomas F. *Race: The History of an Idea in America* (New York: Schocken Books, 1965).

Gould, Stephen Jay. *The Mismeasure of Man* (New York: W. W. Norton, 1981).

Greenawalt, Kent. "How Persuasive Is Natural Law Theory?" 75 *Notre Dame L. Rev.* 1647 (2000).

Greenawalt, Kent. *Private Consciences and Public Reasons* (New York: Oxford University Press, 1995).

Greenawalt, Kent. *Religion and the Constitution*, 2 vols. (Princeton, N.J.: Princeton University Press, 2006–8).

Greenawalt, Kent. *Religious Convictions and Political Choice* (New York: Oxford University Press, 1988).

Greenberg, David F. *The Construction of Homosexuality* (Chicago: University of Chicago Press, 1988).

Greenberg, Kenneth S. *Masters and Statesmen: The Political Culture of American Slavery* (Baltimore: Johns Hopkins University Press, 1985).

Greenberg, Steven (Rabbi). *Wrestling with God and Men: Homosexuality in the Jewish Tradition* (Madison: University of Wisconsin Press, 2004).

Greenslade, S. D., ed. *The Cambridge History of the Bible*, vol. 3 (Cambridge: Cambridge University Press, 1963).

Griffith, R. Marie. *God's Daughters: Evangelical Woman and the Power of Submission* (Berkeley: University of California Press, 1993).
Grisez, Germain. *Abortion: The Myths, the Realities, and the Arguments* (New York: Corpus Books, 1970).
Grisez, Germain. *Contraception and the Natural Law* (Milwaukee: Bruce, 1964).
Grisez, Germain. *The Way of the Lord Jesus*, 3 vols. (Quincy, Ill.: Franciscan Press, 1993–7).
Grisez, Germain, Joseph Boyle, and John Finnis. "Practical Principles, Moral Truth, and Ultimate Ends," 32 *Am. J. Juris.* 99 (1987).
Gutman, Herbert G. *The Black Family in Slavery and Freedom, 1750–1925* (New York: Vintage Books, 1976).
Hagendahl, Harald. *Augustine and the Latin Classics* (Göteborg: Elanders Boktrycheri Aktiebolag, 1967).
Halbertal, Moshe. *People of the Book: Canon, Meaning, and Authority* (Cambridge, Mass.: Harvard University Press, 1997).
Halbertal, Moshe and Avishai Margalit. *Idolatry*, trans. Naomi Goldblum (Cambridge, Mass.: Harvard University Press, 1992).
Halbertal, Tova Hartman. *Appropriately Subversive: Modern Mothers in Traditional Religions* (Cambridge, Mass.: Harvard University Press, 2002).
Haller, John S., Jr. *Outcasts from Evolution: Scientific Attitudes of Racial Inferiority, 1859–1900* (New York: McGraw-Hill, 1971).
Hallie, Philip P. *Let Innocent Blood Be Shed: The Story of the Village of Le Chambon and How Goodness Happened There* (New York: Harper & Row, 1979).
Hamilton, Edith and Huntington Cairns, eds. *The Collected Dialogues of Plato* (New York: Pantheon, 1961).
Harris, Trudier, ed. *Selected Works of Ida B. Wells-Barnett* (New York: Oxford University Press, 1991).
Hart, H. L. A. *Law, Liberty, and Morality* (Stanford, Calif.: Stanford University Press, 1963).
Hart, H. L. A. "Social Solidarity and the Enforcement of Morals," 35 *U. Chi. L. Rev.* 1 (1967).
Hasnas, John. "The 'Unseen' Deserve Empathy, Too," *Wall Street Journal*, May 29, 2009, at A15.
Hassey, Janette. *No Time for Silence: Evangelical Women in Public Ministry around the Turn of the Century* (Grand Rapids, Mich.: Academic Books, 1986).
Hawthorne, Nathaniel. *The Scarlet Letter* (New York: Penguin, 1983).
Heather, Peter. *The Fall of the Roman Empire: A New History of Rome and the Barbarians* (Oxford: Oxford University Press, 2006).
Hedges, Chris. *American Fascists: The Christian Right and the War on America* (New York: Free Press, 2006).
Hedges, Chris. *War Is a Force That Gives Us Meaning* (New York: Public Affairs, 2002).
Herman, Didi. *The Antigay Agenda: Orthodox Vision and the Christian Right* (Chicago: University of Chicago Press, 1997).
Hernandez, Raymond and David W. Chen. "Nominee's Links with Advocates Fuel Her Critics," *New York Times*, May 29, 2009, A1 and A14.
Herzog, Dagmar. *Sex in Crisis: The New Sexual Revolution and the Future of American Politics* (New York: Basic Books, 2008).
Heschel, Abraham. *The Prophets* (New York: Perennial Classics, 2001).
Higgins, Nathan, ed. *W. E. B. DuBois* (1896; New York: Library of America, 1986).
Hitler, Adolf. *Mein Kampf* (New York: Reynal & Hitchcock, 1940).

Hofstadter, Richard. *Anti-Intellectualism in American Life* (New York: Vintage Books, 1963).

Hogg, Michael A. and Joel Cooper, eds. *The Sage Handbook of Social Psychology: Concise Student Edition* (Los Angeles: Sage Publications, 2007).

Honoré, Tony. *Sex Law* (London: Duckworth, 1978).

Hont, Istvan and Michael Ignatieff, eds. *Wealth and Virtue: The Shaping of Political Economy in the Scottish Enlightenment* (Cambridge: Cambridge University Press, 1983).

Hope Franklin, John. *The Militant South, 1800–1861* (Cambridge, Mass.: Belknap Press, Harvard University Press, 1956).

Horsman, Reginald. *Race and Manifest Destiny: The Origins of American Racial Anglo-Saxonism* (Cambridge, Mass.: Harvard University Press, 1981).

Hrdy, Sarah Blaffer. *Mother Nature: Maternal Instincts and How They Shape the Human Species* (New York: Ballantin Books, 1999).

Hrdy, Sarah Blaffer. *Mothers and Others: The Evolutionary Origins of Mutual Understanding* (Cambridge, Mass.: The Belknap Press of Harvard University Press, 2009).

Hutcheson, Francis. *A System of Moral Philosophy*, 2 vols. in 1 (New York: Augustus M. Kelley, 1968).

Ignatieff, Michael. *The Warrior's Honor: Ethnic War and the Modern Conscience* (New York: Henry Holt, 1997).

Irving, Helen. *Gender and the Constitution: Equity and Agency in Comparative Constitutional Design* (Cambridge: Cambridge University Press, 2008).

Jackowski, Karol. *The Silence We Keep: A Nun's View of the Catholic Priest Scandal* (New York: Harmony Books, 2004).

Jackson, Emily. *Regulating Reproduction: Law, Technology and Autonomy* (Oxford, U.K.: Hart Publishing, 2001).

Jacobson, Dan. *The Story of the Stories: The Chosen People and Its God* (New York: Harper & Row, 1982).

Jeremias, Joachim. *The Sermon on the Mount* (London: Athlone Press, 1961).

Johnson, Paul E. and Sean Wilentz. *The Kingdom of Matthias: A Story of Sex and Salvation in 19th-Century America* (New York: Oxford University Press, 1994).

Jones, James H. *Alfred C. Kinsey* (New York: W. W. Norton, 1997).

Jordan, Mark D. *The Invention of Sodomy in Christian Theology* (Chicago: University of Chicago Press, 1997).

Juergensmeyer, Mark. *Terror in the Mind of God: The Global Rise of Religious Violence* (Berkeley: University of California Press, 2000).

Kadish, Sanford H, Stephen J. Schulhofer, and Carol S. Steiker. *Criminal Law and Its Processes*, 8th ed. (New York: Aspen, 2007).

Kahan, Dan M. and Donald Braman. "More Statistics, Less Persuasion: A Cultural Theory of Gun-Risk Perceptions," 151 *U. Pa. L. Rev.* 1291 (2003).

Kahan, Dan M., David A. Hoddman, and Donald Braman. "Whose Eyes Are You Going to Believe: *Scott v. Harris* and the Perils of Cognitive Illiberalism," 122 *Harv. L. Rev.* 838 (2009).

Kalven, Harry, Jr.. *The Negro and the First Amendment* (Chicago: University of Chicago Press, 1965).

Kannar, George. "The Constitutional Catechism of Antonin Scalia," 99 *Yale L.J.* 1297 (1990).

Kant, Immanuel. *Foundations of the Metaphysics of Morals*, trans. Lewis W. Beck (New York: Liberal Arts Press, 1959).

Kant, Immanuel. *Kant's Political Writings*, ed. Hans Reiss, trans. H. B. Nisbet (Cambridge: Cambridge University Press).

Kapur, Ratna. *Erotic Justice: Law and the New Politics of Postcolonialism* (London: Glasshouse Press, 2005).
Kaufmann, Walter. *Critique of Religion and Philosophy* (Princeton, N.J.: Princeton University Press, 1958).
Kaufmann, Walter. *The Portable Nietzsche* (New York: Viking Press, 1954).
Kell, Carl L. and L. Raymond Camp. *In the Name of the Father: The Rhetoric of the New Southern Baptist Convention* (Carbondale: Southern Illinois University Press, 1999).
Kennedy, Eugene. *The Unhealed Wound: The Church and Human Sexuality* (New York: St. Martin's Press, 2001).
Kenny, Anthony. *Aquinas* (Oxford: Oxford University Press, 1980).
Kenny, Anthony. *Aquinas on Mind* (London: Routledge, 1993).
Kenny, Anthony. *The Five Ways: St. Thomas Aquinas's Proofs of God's Existence* (New York: Schocken Books, 1969).
Kershaw, Ian. *Hitler: 1963–1945: Nemesis* (New York: W. W. Norton, 2000).
Kertzer, David I. *Sacrifices for Honor: Italian Infant Abandonment and the Politics of Reproductive Control* (Boston: Beacon Press, 1993).
Kertzer, David I. and Richard P. Saller, eds. *The Family in Italy from Antiquity to the Present* (New Haven, Conn.: Yale University Press, 1991).
Kinsey, Alfred C., Wardell B. Pomeroy, and Clyde E. Martin. *Sexual Behavior in the Human Male* (Philadelphia: W. B. Saunders, 1948).
Kinsey, Alfred C., Wardell B. Pomeroy, Clyde E. Martin, and Paul H. Gebhard. *Sexual Behavior in the Human Female* (New York: Pocket Books, 1970).
Kirkpatrick, David D. "A Judge's Focus on Race Issues May Be Hurdle," *New York Times*, May 30, 2009, at A1 and A8.
Koestler, Arthur. *Darkness at Noon*, trans. Daphne Hardy (New York: Bantam Books, 1968).
Koonz, Claudia. *Mothers in the Fatherland: Women, the Family, and Nazi Politics* (New York: St. Martin's Press, 1987).
Koonz, Claudia. *The Nazi Conscience* (Cambridge, Mass.: Belknap Press, Harvard University Press, 2003).
Koppelman, Andrew, with Tobias Barrington Wolff. *A Right to Discriminate? How the Case of Boy Scouts of America v. James Dale Warped the Law of Free Association* (New Haven, Conn.: Yale University Press, 2009).
Koppelman, Andrew. "Is Marriage Inherently Heterosexual?" 42 *Am. J. Juris.* 51 (1997).
Korn, James H. *Illusions of Reality: A History of Deception in Social Psychology* (Albany: State University of New York Press, 1997).
Krakauer, Jon. *Under the Banner of Heaven A Story of Violent Faith* (New York: Anchor Books, 2004).
Kretzmann, Norman. *The Metaphysics of Theism: Aquinas's Natural Theory in Summa Contra Gentiles I* (Oxford, U.K.: Clarendon Press, 2001).
Krugman, Paul. "Reagan Did It," *New York Times*, June 1, 2009, at A21.
Lambert, Frank. *The Founding Fathers and the Place of Religion in America* (Princeton, N.J.: Princeton University Press, 2003).
Lambert, Frank. *Religion in American Politics: A Short History* (Princeton, N.J.: Princeton University Press, 2008).
Langmuir, Gavin I. *History, Religion, and Antisemitism* (Berkeley: University of California Press, 1990).
Langmuir, Gavin I. *Toward a Definition of Antisemitism* (Berkeley: University of California Press, 1990).

Laqueur, Walter. *The Dream That Failed: Reflections on the Soviet Union* (New York: Oxford University Press, 1994).

Laumann, Edward O., John H. Gagnon, Robert T. Michael, and Stuart Michaels. *The Social Organization of Sexuality: Sexual Practices in the United States* (Chicago: University of Chicago Press, 1994).

Laycock, Douglas. "Towards a General Theory of the Religion Clauses: The Case of Church Labor Relations and the Right to Church Autonomy," 81 *Columbia L. Rev.* 1371 (1981).

Leonhardt, David. "After the Great Recession: An Interview with President Obama," *New York Times Magazine*, May 3, 2009.

Levenson, Jon D. *Resurrection and the Restoration of Israel: The Ultimate Victory of the God of Life* (New Haven, Conn.: Yale University Press, 2006).

Levinson, Sanford. "Guns and the Constitution: A Complex Relationship," *Reviews in American History*, March 2008, pp. 1–14.

Levinson, Sanford. "What Follows Putting Reason in Its Place? 'Now Vee May Perhaps to Begin, Yes?'" 151 *U. Pa. L. Rev.* 1371 (2003).

Levy, Leonard W. *Blasphemy: Verbal Offense Against the Sacred from Moses to Salman Rushdie* (New York: Knopf, 1993).

Levy, Leonard W. *The Establishment Clause: Religion and the First Amendment* (New York: Macmillan, 1986).

Lewis, Bernard. *What Went Wrong? Western Impact and Middle Eastern Response* (Oxford: Oxford University Press, 2002).

Linker, Damon. *The Theocons: Secular America under Siege* (New York: Doubleday, 2006).

Liptak, Adam. "On the Bench and Off, the Eminently Quotable Justice Scalia," *New York Times*, May 12, 2009.

Livingood, J. M., ed. *National Institute of Mental Health Task Force on Homosexuality* (Washington, D.C.: U.S. Government Printing Office, 1972).

Lobdell, William. *Losing My Religion: How I Lost My Faith Reporting on Religion in America – and Found Unexpected Peace* (New York: HarperCollins, 2009).

Locke, John. *The Reasonableness of Christianity*, ed. I. T. Ramsey (Stanford, Calif.: Stanford University Press, 1958).

Locke, John. *Two Treatises of Government*, ed. Peter Laslett (Cambridge: Cambridge University Press, 1960).

Locke, John. *Works of John Locke, vol. 6, A Letter Concerning Toleration; A Second Letter Concerning Toleration; A Third Letter Concerning Toleration; A Fourth Letter for Toleration* (London: Thomas Davison, 1823).

Lofgren, Charles A. *The Plessy Case: A Legal Historical Interpretation* (New York: Oxford University Press, 1987).

Lovejoy, Arthur O. *The Great Chain of Being* (Cambridge, Mass.: Harvard University Press, 1936).

Lupu, Ira C. "*Employment Division v. Smith* and the Decline of Supreme-Court Centrism," 1993 *B.Y.U. L. Rev.* 259, 260 (1993).

Lupu, Ira C. "Free Exercise Exemptions and Religious Institutions," 67 *Boston U. L. Rev.* 391, 435–8 (1987).

Luther, Martin. *Luther's Works*, 56 vols. (Philadelphia: Fortress Press, 1963–6).

Lyall, Sarah. "Blaming Church, Ireland Details Scourge of Abuse," *New York Times*, May 21, 2009, at A1 and A4.

Lystra, Karen. *Searching the Heart: Woman, Men, and Romantic Love in Nineteenth-Century America* (New York: Oxford University Press, 1989).

Maalouf, Amin. *In the Name of Identity: Violence and the Need to Belong*, trans. Barbara Bray (New York: Penguin, 2003).
MacMullen, Ramsay. *Christianizing the Roman Empire A.D. 100–400* (New Haven, Conn.: Yale University Press, 1984).
Makiya, Kanan. *Cruelty and Silence: War, Tyranny, Uprising, and the Arab World* (New York: W. W. Norton, 1993).
Manning, Christel. *God Gave Us the Right: Conservative Catholic, Evangelical Protestant, and Orthodox Jewish Women Grapple with Feminism* (New Brunswick, N.J.: Rutgers University Press, 1999).
Margalit, Avishai. "The Suicide Bombers," *New York Review of Books*, January 16, 2003, p. 36.
Marsden, George M. *Fundamentalism and American Culture* Second Edition (New York: Oxford University Press, 2006) (originally published as *Fundamentalism and American Culture: The Shaping of Twentieth Century Evangelicalism 1870–1925* [New York: Oxford University Press, 1980]).
Masters, William H. *Human Sexual Response* (Boston: Little, Brown, 1966).
Masters, William H. and Virginia E. Johnson. *Homosexuality in Perspective* (Boston: Little, Brown, 1979).
Masters, William H. and Virginia E. Johnson. *Human Sexual Inadequacy* (Boston: Little, Brown, 1970).
Masters, William H., Virginia E. Johnson, and Robert C. Kolodny. *Heterosexuality* (New York: HarperCollins, 1994).
Matthews, Gareth B. *Thought's Ego in Augustine and Descartes* (Ithaca, N.Y.: Cornell University Press, 1992).
Matthews, Gareth B. *Augustine* (Malden, Mass.: Blackwell, 2005).
May, Elaine Tyler. *Barren in the Promised Land: Childless Americans and the Pursuit of Happiness* (New York: Basic Books, 1995).
Mayer, Jane and Jill Abramson. *Strange Justice: The Selling of Clarence Thomas* (Boston: Houghton Mifflin, 1994).
McBrien, Richard P. *Catholicism: New Study Edition* (New York: Harper Collins, 1994).
McCord, Louisa. "Enfranchisement of Woman," 21 *Southern Q. Rev.* 233–341 (1852).
[McCord, Louisa]. "Uncle Tom's Cabin," 7 *Southern Q. Rev.* 81–120 (n.s., 1853).
McGrade, A. S. "What Aquinas Should Have Said? Finnis's Reconstruction of Social and Political Thomism," 44 *Am. J. Juris.* 125 (1999).
McGreevy, John T. *Catholicism and American Freedom* (New York: W. W. Norton, 2003).
McKinley, Jesse and Kirk Johnson. "Mormons Tipped Scale in Ban on Gay Marriage," *New York Times*, November 15, 2008.
McKinnon, John D. "Businesses Encouraged by Nominee for Regulatory Czar," *Wall Street Journal*, May 13, 2009.
McLean, George P., ed. *Normative Ethics and Objective Reason* (Washington, D.C.: Paideia Publishers, 1998).
McLynn, Neil B. *Ambrose of Milan: Church and Court in a Christian Capital* (Berkeley: University of California Press, 1994).
McPherson, James M. *The Struggle for Equality: Abolitionists and the Negro in the Civil War and Reconstruction* (Princeton, N.J.: Princeton University Press, 1964).
Meier, John P. A *Marginal Jew: Rethinking the Historical Jesus*, 3 vols. (New York: Doubleday, 1991–2001).
Menn, Stephen. *Descartes and Augustine* (Cambridge: Cambridge University Press, 2002).
Mernissi, Fatema. *Islam and Democracy: Fear of the Modern World*, trans. Mary Jo Lakeland (Cambridge, Mass.: Perseus, 1992).

Mernissi, Fatema. *The Veil and the Male Elite: A Feminist Interpretation of Women's Rights in Islam* (Cambridge, Mass.: Perseus, 1991).

Michael, Robert T., John H. Gagnon, Edward O. Laumann, and Gina Kolata. *Sex in America: A Definitive Survey* (Boston: Little, Brown, 1994).

Micklethwait, John and Adrian Wooldridge. *God Is Back: How the Global Revival of Faith Is Changing the World* (New York: Penguin Press, 2009).

Milgrom, Jacob. *Leviticus 17–22: The Anchor Bible* (New York: Doubleday, 2000).

Miller, Perry. *The New England Mind: The Seventeenth Century* (Cambridge, Mass.: Belknap Press, Harvard University Press, 1939).

Miller, William Lee. *The First Liberty: Religion and the American Republic* (New York: Knopf, 1987).

Moore, G. E. *Principia Ethica* (Cambridge: Cambridge University Press, 1960).

Moore, Gareth. *A Question of Truth: Christianity and Homosexuality* (London: Continuum, 2003).

Moore, R. Laurence. *Religious Outsiders and the Making of Americans* (New York: Oxford University Press, 1986).

Morris, Charles R. *American Catholic: The Saints and Sinners Who Built America's Most Powerful Church* (New York: Vintage, 1997).

Mussolini, Benito. *My Autobiography with "The Political and Social Doctrine of Fascism,"* trans. Jane Soames (Mineola, N.Y.: Dover Publications, 2006).

Myers, David G. "Bridging the Gay-Evangelical Divide," *The Wall Street Journal*, August 28, 2009, at W11.

Myrdal, Gunner. *An American Dilemma: The Negro Problem and Modern Democracy*, 2 vols. (New York: Pantheon Books, 1972).

Needham, Anuradha Dingwaney and Rajeswari Sunder Rajan, eds. *The Crisis of Secularism in India* (Durham, N.C.: Duke University Press, 2007).

Nelson, William E. *The Fourteenth Amendment: From Political Principle to Judicial Doctrine* (Cambridge, Mass.: Harvard University Press, 1988).

Nichol, Gene R. "Justice Scalia and the *Printz* Case: The Trials of an Occasional Originalist," 70 *U. Colo. L. Rev.* 953 (1999).

Nietzsche, Friedrich. *Beyond Good and Evil: Prelude to a Philosophy of the Future*, trans. Helen Zimmern (Edinburgh: T. N. Foulis, 1907).

Nietzsche, Friedrich. *On the Genealogy of Morals*, trans. Douglas Smith (Oxford: Oxford University Press, 1996).

Noll, Mark A. *The Scandal of the Evangelical Mind* (Grand Rapids, Mich.: William B. Eerdmans, 1994).

Noonan, John T., Jr. *A Church That Can and Cannot Change* (Notre Dame, Ind.: University of Notre Dame Press, 2005).

Noonan, John T., Jr. *Narrowing the Nation's Power* (Berkeley: University of California Press, 2002).

Northcott, Michael S. *The Environment and Christian Ethics* (Cambridge: Cambridge University Press, 1996).

Numbers, Ronald L. *The Creationist: From Scientific Creationism to Intelligent Design* Expanded Edition (Cambridge, Mass.: Harvard University Press, 2006).

Nussbaum, Martha C. *The Clash Within: Democracy, Religious Violence, and India's Future* (Cambridge, Mass.: Belknap Press, Harvard University Press, 2007).

Nussbaum, Martha C. *Liberty of Conscience: In Defense of America's Tradition of Religious Equality* (New York: Basic Books, 2008).

Nussbaum, Martha C. "Platonic Love and Colorado Law," 80 *U. Va. L. Rev.* 1515 (1994).

O'Brien, Tim. *The Things They Carried* (New York: Broadway Books, 1990).

O'Donnell, James J. *Augustine: A New Biography* (New York: HarperCollins, 2005).
Obama, Barack. *The Audacity of Hope* (New York: Three Rivers Press, 2006).
Obama, Barack. *Dreams from My Father: A Story of Race and Inheritance* (New York: Three Rivers Press, 2004).
Obama, Barack. "Why Obama Voted against Roberts," *Wall Street Journal*, June 2, 2009, at A21.
Okin, Susan Moller. *Justice, Gender, and the Family* (New York: Basic Books, 1989).
Okin, Susan Moller. *Women in Western Political Thought* (Princeton, N.J.: Princeton University Press, 1979).
Olyan, Saul M. and Martha C. Nussbaum, eds. *Sexual Orientation and Human Rights in American Religious Discourse* (New York: Oxford University Press, 1998).
Ong, Walter J. *Orality and Literacy* (London: Methuen, 1982).
Pagels, Elaine. *Adam, Eve, and the Serpent* (New York: Random House, 1988).
Pagels, Elaine. *The Origin of Satan* (New York: Random House, 1996).
Paxton, Robert O. *The Anatomy of Fascism* (New York: Vintage Books, 2004).
Peristiany, J. G., ed. *Honour and Shame: The Values of Mediterranean Society* (Chicago: University of Chicago Press, 1966).
Persily, Nathaniel, Jack Citrin, and Patrick J. Egan. *Public Opinion and Constitutional Controversy* (New York: Oxford University Press, 2008).
Peyton Thomas, Andrew. *Clarence Thomas: A Biography* (San Francisco: Encounter Books, 2001).
Phillips, Kevin. *American Theocracy: The Peril and Politics of Radical Religion, Oil, and Borrowed Money in the 21st Century* (New York: Viking, 2006).
Pipes, Daniel. *Militant Islam Reaches America* (New York: W. W. Norton, 2002).
Plotinus. *The Enneads*, trans. Stephen MacKenna (London: Penguin, 1991).
Plumb, J. H. *The Death of the Past* (Boston: Houghton Mifflin, 1971).
Poliakov, Leon. *The History of Anti-Semitism*, 4 vols. (New York: Vanguard Press, 1965–85).
Popkin, Richard H. *The History of Scepticism from Erasmus to Spinoza* (Berkeley: University of California Press, 1979).
Porphyry. *The Life of Plotinus*, trans. Stephen McKenna (Edmonds, Wash.: Holmes Publishing, 2001).
Putney, Clifford. *Muscular Christianity: Manhood and Sports in Protestant America, 1889–1920* (Cambridge, Mass.: Harvard University Press, 2001).
Quinn, D. Michael. *Early Mormonism and the Magic World View*, rev. ed. (Salt Lake City: Signature Books, 1998).
Quinn, D. Michael. *Same-Sex Dynamics among Nineteenth-Century Americans: A Mormon Example* (Urbana: University of Illinois Press, 1996).
Ranke-Heinemann, Uta. *Eunuchs for the Kingdom of Heaven: The Catholic Church and Sexuality*, trans. John Brownjohn (London: Andre Deutsch, 1990).
Rasmussen, Larry. *Dietrich Bonhoeffer – His Significance for North Americans* (Minneapolis: Fortress Press, 1990).
Rawls, John. *A Theory of Justice* (Cambridge, Mass.: Harvard University Press, 1971).
Rawls, John. *Collected Papers*, ed. Samuel Freeman (Cambridge, Mass.: Harvard University Press).
Regan, Richard, S. J. *Conflict and Consensus: Religious Freedom and the Second Vatican Council* (New York: Macmillan, 1967).
Renehan, Edward J., Jr. *The Lion's Pride: Theodore Roosevelt and His Family in Peace and War* (New York: Oxford University Press, 1998).
Rex, Walter. *Essays on Pierre Bayle and Religious Controversy* (The Hague: Martinus Nijhoff, 1965).

Rich, Adrienne. *Of Woman Born: Motherhood as Experience and Institution*, 10th anniversary ed. (New York: W. W. Norton, 1986).
Richards, David A. J. *The Case for Gay Rights: From Bowers to Lawrence and Beyond* (Lawrence: University Press of Kansas, 2005).
Richards, David A. J. *Conscience and the Constitution: History, Theory, and Law of the Reconstruction Amendments* (Princeton, N.J.: Princeton University Press, 1993).
Richards, David A. J. *Disarming Manhood: Roots of Ethical Resistance* (Athens: Ohio University/Swallow Press, 2005).
Richards, David A. J. *Foundations of American Constitutionalism* (New York: Oxford University Press, 1989).
Richards, David A. J. *Free Speech and the Politics of Identity* (Oxford: Oxford University Press, 1999).
Richards, David A. J. *Identity and the Case for Gay Rights: Race, Gender, Religion as Analogies* (Chicago: University of Chicago Press, 1999).
Richards, David A. J. *Italian American: The Racializing of an Ethnic Identity* (New York: New York University Press, 1999).
Richards, David A. J. *Sex, Drugs, Death, and the Law: An Essay on Human Rights and Overcriminalization* (Totowa, N.J.: Rowman and Littlefield, 1982).
Richards, David A. J. *The Sodomy Cases: Bowers v. Hardwick and Lawrence v. Texas* (Lawrence: University Press of Kansas, 2009).
Richards, David A. J. *A Theory of Reasons for Action* (Oxford: Clarendon Press, 1971).
Richards, David A. J. *Toleration and the Constitution* (New York: Oxford University Press, 1986).
Richards, David A. J. *Tragic Manhood and Democracy: Verdi's Voice and the Powers of Musical Art* (Brighton, U.K.: Sussex Academic Press, 2004).
Richards, David A. J. *Women, Gays, and the Constitution: The Grounds for Feminism and Gay Rights in Culture and Law* (Chicago: University of Chicago Press, 1998).
Rist, John M. *Augustine: Ancient Thought Baptized* (Cambridge: Cambridge University Press, 1997).
Robinson, Paul. *The Modernization of Sex: Havelock Ellis, Alfred Kinsey, William Masters and Virginia Johnson* (New York: Harper & Row, 1976).
Rodrigues, Arnoldo and Robert V. Levine. *Reflections on 100 Years of Experimental Social Psychology* (New York: Basic Books, 1999).
Rousseau, Jean-Jacques. "The Social Contract," in *The Social Contract and Discourses*, trans. G. D. H. Cole (New York: Dutton, 1950).
Rove, Karl. "Republicans and Obama's Court Nominees," *Wall Street Journal*, May 7, 2009.
Roy, Arundhati. *The God of Small Things* (New York: HarperPerennial, 1998).
Roy, Arundhati. *War Talk* (Cambridge, Mass.: South End Press, 2003).
Ruddick, Sara. *Maternal Thinking: Toward a Politics of Peace* (Boston: Beacon Press, 1989).
Ruether, Rosemary Radford. *Sexism and God-Talk: Toward a Feminist Theology* (Boston: Beacon Press, 1993).
Sandeen, Ernest R. *The Roots of Fundamentalism: British and American Millenarianism 1800–1930* (Chicago: University of Chicago Press, 1970).
Sanders, E. P. *The Historical Figure of Jesus* (London: Allen Lane, 1993).
Sanders, E. P. *Jesus and Judaism* (Philadelphia: Fortress Press, 1985).
Sandmel, Samuel. *The Genius of Paul: A Study in History* (Philadelphia: Fortress Press, 1979).

Santayana, George. *The Life of Reason*, vol. 3, *Reason in Religion* (New York: Dover, 1982).

Savage, Charlie. "Conservatives Map Strategies on Court Fight," *New York Times*, May 17, 2009, at 1 and 20.

Savage, Charlie. "Scouring Obama's Past for Clues on Judiciary," *New York Times*, May 10, 2009.

Scalia, Antonin. "God's Justice and Ours," 123 *First Things* 17 (2002).

Scalia, Antonin. *A Matter of Interpretation: Federal Courts and the Law* (Princeton, N.J.: Princeton University Press, 1997).

Scanlon, T. M. *What We Owe to Each Other* (Cambridge, Mass.: Harvard University Press, 1998).

Schaefer, David Lewis. "When It Comes to Judges, 'Pragmatic' Means Unprincipled," *Wall Street Journal*, May 9–10, 2009.

Schiavone, Aldo. *The End of the Past: Ancient Rome and the Modern West*, trans. Margery J. Schneider (Cambridge, Mass.: Harvard University Press, 2000).

Schneidau, Henry N. *Sacred Discontent: The Bible and Western Tradition* (Baton Rouge: Louisiana State University Press, 1976).

Schoofs, Mark. "Mormons Boost Antigay Marriage Effort," *Wall Street Journal*, September 20–21, 2008.

Segal, Alan F. *Paul the Convert: The Apostolate and Apostasy of Saul the Pharisee* (New Haven, Conn.: Yale University Press, 1990).

Segall, Eric J. "A Century Lost: The End of the Originalism Debate," 15 *Const. Comment.* 411 (1998).

Shapiro, Barbara J. *Probability and Certainty in Seventeenth-Century England* (Princeton, N.J.: Princeton University Press, 1983).

Shaw, Brent D. "A Groom of One's Own?" *New Republic*, July 18 and 25, 1994.

Shields, Jon A. *The Democratic Virtues of the Christian Right* (Princeton, N.J.: Princeton University Press, 2009).

Siegel, Reva B. "Dead or Alive: Originalism as Popular Constitutionalism in *Heller*," 122 *Harv. L. Rev.* 191 (2008).

Simon, Stephanie. "Legal Fights Strain Polygamist Sect," *Wall Street Journal*, May 11, 2009.

Slater, Lauren. *Opening Skinner's Box: Great Psychological Experiments of the Twentieth Century* (New York: W. W. Norton, 2004).

Smith, Joseph. *The Book of Mormon, Doctrine and Covenants, The Pearl of Great Price*, (Salt Lake City: Church of Jesus Christ of Latter-Day Saints, 1973).

Sollors, Werner. *Beyond Ethnicity: Consent and Descent in American Culture* (New York: Oxford University Press, 1986).

Sreekumar, Sandeep. "An Argument about the Right to Life of the Foetus in Critical Morality," Ph.D. thesis, Corpus Christi College, Oxford University, 2005.

Stampp, Kenneth M. *The Peculiar Institution* (New York: Vintage, 1956).

Stark, Rodney. *The Rise of Christianity: A Sociologist Reconsiders History* (Princeton, N.J.: Princeton University Press, 1996).

Stein, Edward, ed. *Forms of Desire: Sexual Orientation and the Social Constructionist Controversy* (New York: Routledge, 1990).

Stein, Edward. *The Mismeasure of Desire: The Science, Theory, and Ethics of Sexual Orientation* (New York: Oxford University Press, 1999).

Steinfels, Peter. *A People Adrift: The Crisis of the Roman Catholic Church in America* (New York: Simon & Schuster, 2003).

Stocking, George W., Jr. A *Franz Boas Reader: The Shaping of American Anthropology, 1833–1911* (Chicago: University of Chicago Press, 1974).
Strachey, James, ed. and trans. *Standard Edition of the Complete Psychological Works of Sigmund Freud*, 24 vols. (London: Hogarth Press, 1906–64).
Stump, Eleanor and Michael J. Murray, eds. *Philosophy of Religion: The Big Questions* (Oxford: Blackwell Publishers, 1999).
Sunstein, Cass R. *A Constitution of Many Minds: Why the Founding Document Doesn't Mean What It Meant Before* (Princeton, N.J.: Princeton University Press, 2009).
Sunstein, Cass R. *One Case at a Time: Judicial Minimalism on the Supreme Court* (Cambridge, Mass.: Harvard University Press, 1999).
Sunstein, Cass R. *Radicals in Robes: Why Extreme Right-Wing Courts Are Wrong for America* (New York: Basic Books, 2005).
Sunstein, Cass R. "Second Amendment Minimalism: *Heller* as *Griswold*," 122 *Harv. L. Rev.* 246 (2008).
Taubes, Jacob. *The Political Theology of Paul*, trans. Dana Hollander (Stanford, Calif.: Stanford University Press, 2004).
Taylor, Charles. *A Secular Age* (Cambridge, Mass.: Belknap Press, Harvard University Press, 2007).
TeSelle, Eugene. *Augustine the Theologian* (Eugene, Ore.: Wipf and Stock, 2002).
Thayer, James B. "The Origin and Scope of the American Doctrine of Constitutional Law," 7 *Harv. L. Rev.* 129 (1893).
The New Oxford Annotated Bible (New York: Oxford University Press, 1991).
Thomas, Clarence. "How to Read the Constitution," *Wall Street Journal*, October 20, 2008.
Thomas, Clarence. *My Grandfather's Son: A Memoir* (New York: HarperCollins, 2007).
Tilly, Charles. *Contention and Democracy in Europe, 1650–2000* (Cambridge: Cambridge University Press, 2004).
Tilly, Charles. *Democracy* (Cambridge: Cambridge University Press, 2007).
Tilly, Charles. *Trust and Rule* (Cambridge: Cambridge University Press, 2005).
Toobin, Jeffrey. "No More Mr. Nice Guy: The Supreme Court's Stealth Hard-Liner," *New Yorker*, May 25, 2009, at 42–51.
Townsend, Kim. *Manhood at Harvard: William James and Others* (Cambridge, Mass.: Harvard University Press, 1996).
Tushnet, Mark V. *Out of Range: Why the Constitution Can't End the Battle over Guns* (Oxford: Oxford University Press, 2007).
Tushnet, Mark V. "Sex, Drugs and Rock 'n' Roll: Some Conservative Reflections on Liberal Jurisprudence," 82 *Columbia L. Rev.* 1531–43 (1982).
Tushnet, Mark. *Taking the Constitution Away from the Courts* (Princeton, N.J.: Princeton University Press, 1999).
Tussman, Joseph and Jacobus tenBroek. "The Equal Protection of the Laws," 37 *Calif. L. Rev.* 341 (1949).
Usdansky, Margaret S. "Gay Couples, by the Numbers – Data Suggest They're Fewer Than Believed, but Affluent," *USA Today*, April 12, 1993.
Uviller, H. Richard and William G. Merkel. *The Militia and the Right to Arms; or, How the Second Amendment Fell Silent* (Durham, N.C.: Duke University Press, 2002).
Van Leeuwen, Henry G. *The Problem of Certainty in English Thought, 1630–1690* (The Hague: Martinus Nijhoff, 1970).
Vermes, Geza. *The Changing Faces of Jesus* (New York: Viking Compass, 2001).
Vermes, Geza. *Jesus and the World of Judaism* (London: SCM Press, 1983).

Vermes, Geza. *Jesus the Jew: A Historian's Reading of the Gospels* (Philadelphia: Fortress Press, 1981).
Vermes, Geza. *The Religion of Jesus the Jew* (Minneapolis: Fortress Press, 1993).
Waldron, Jeremy. *Law and Disagreement* (Oxford: Oxford University Press, 1999).
Walters, Ronald G. *The Antislavery Appeal: American Abolitionism after 1830* (New York: W. W. Norton, 1978).
Weinberg, Martin S. and Colin J. Williams. *Male Homosexuals* (New York: Oxford University Press, 1974).
Weinberg, Martin S., Colin J. Williams, and Douglas W. Pryor. *Dual Attraction: Understanding Bisexuality* (New York: Oxford University Press, 1994).
Weisman, Jonathan and Naftali Bendavid. "Battle over Sotomayor Heats Up," *Wall Street Journal*, May 28, 2009, at A3.
Weisman, Jonathan and Jess Bravin. "Obama to Seek a Justice Attuned to 'Daily Realities,'" *Wall Street Journal*, May 2–3, 2009.
Weld, Theodore Dwight. *American Slavery as It Is* (New York: Arno Press and New York Times, 1968).
Wesley, Joya L. "With $394 Billion in Buying Power, Gays' Money Talks; and Corporate America Increasingly Is Listening," *Atlanta J. & Const.*, December 1, 1991.
Wheatcroft, Geoffrey. *The Controversy of Zion: Jewish Nationalism, the Jewish State, and the Unresolved Jewish Dilemma* (Reading, Mass.: Addison-Wesley, 1996).
Wildavsky, Aaron. *The Nursing Father: Moses as a Political Leader* (University: University of Alabama Press, 1984).
Wills, Garry. "The Bishops vs. the Bible," *New York Times*, June 27, 2004.
Wills, Garry. *Head and Heart: American Christianities* (New York: Penguin Press, 2007).
Wills, Garry. *Papal Sin* (New York: Doubleday, 2000).
Wills, Garry. *Saint Augustine* (New York: A Lipper/Viking Book, 1999).
Wills, Garry. *What Jesus Meant* (New York: Viking, 2006).
Wills, Garry. *What Paul Meant* (New York: Viking, 2006).
Wilson, A. N. *Jesus: A Life* (New York: Fawcett Columbine, 1992).
Witherington, Ben, III. *Women and the Genesis of Christianity* (Cambridge: Cambridge University Press, 1990).
Witherspoon, John. *Lectures of Moral Philosophy*, ed. Jack Scott (East Brunswick, N.J.: Associated University Presses, 1982).
Wolinsky, Marc and Kenneth Sherrill. *Gays and the Military: Joseph Steffan versus the United States* (Princeton, N.J.: Princeton University Press, 1993).
Woodward, C. Vann. *Reunion and Reaction: The Compromise of 1877 and the End of Reconstruction* (New York: Oxford University Press, 1966).
Woodward, C. Vann. *The Future of the Past* (New York: Oxford University Press, 1989).
Woolf, Virginia. *Women and Writing*, ed. Michele Barrett (Orlando, Fla.: Harvest Books, 1980).
Wright, Lawrence. *The Looming Tower: Al-Qaeda and the Road to 9/11* (New York: Alfred A. Knopf, 2006).
Wyatt-Brown, Bertram. *Honor and Violence in the Old South* (New York: Oxford University Press, 1986).
Yoo, John. "Partial-Birth Bigotry," *Wall Street Journal*, April 28–9, 2007.
Young-Bruehl, Elisabeth. *The Anatomy of Prejudices* (Cambridge, Mass.: Harvard University Press, 1996).
Young-Bruehl, Elisabeth. *Hannah Arendt: For Love of the World* (New Haven, Conn.: Yale University Press, 1982).

Young-Bruehl, Elisabeth. *Why Arendt Matters* (New Haven, Conn.: Yale University Press, 2006).

Zagorin, Perez. *How the Idea of Religious Toleration Came to the West* (Princeton, N.J.: Princeton University Press, 2003).

CASES

Baker v. State of Vermont, 744 A.2d 864 (Vt. 1999).

Bowers v. Hardwick, 478 U.S. 186 (1986).

Boy Scouts of America v. Dale, 530 U.S. 640 (2000).

Brown v. Board of Education, 347 U.S. 483 (1954).

Burstyn v. Wilson, 343 U.S. 495 (1952).

Carhart v. Gonzales, 550 U.S. 2007 (2007).

Church of the Lukumi Babalu Aye, Inc. v. City of Hialeah, 509 U.S. 520 (1993).

Craig v. Boren, 429 U.S. 190 (1976).

Cruzan v. Missouri Department of Health, 496 U.S. 261 (1990).

Davis v. Beason, 133 U.S. 333 (1890).

District of Columbia v. Heller, 128 S.Ct. 2783 (2008).

Dred Scott v. Sanford, 60 U.S. (19 How.) 393 (1857).

Eisenstadt v. Baird, 405 U.S. 438 (1972).

Elk Grove Unified School District v. Newdow, 542 U.S. 1 (2004).

Employment Division, Department of Human Resources of Oregon v. Smith, 494 U.S. 872 (1990).

Frontiero v. Richardson, 411 U.S. 677 (1973).

Goesaert v. Cleary, 335 U.S. 464 (1948).

Gonzales v. Carhart, 127 *S. Ct.* 1610 (2007).

Goodridge v. Department of Public Health, 798 N.E.2d 941 (Mass. 2003).

Griswold v. Connecticut, 381 U.S. 479 (1965).

Grutter v. Bollinger, 539 U.S. 306 (2003).

Harper v. Virginia Board of Elections, 383 U.S. 663 (1966).

Hoyt v. Florida, 368 U.S. 57 (1961).

Hurley v. Irish-American Gay, Lesbian and Bisexual Group of Boston (GLIB), 515 U.S. 557 (1995).

Lawrence v. Texas, 539 U.S. 558 (2003).

Loving v. Virginia, 388 U.S. 1 (1967).

Michael M. v. Superior Court, 450 U.S. 464 (1981).

Palmore v. Sidoti, 466 U.S. 429 (1984).

Planned Parenthood of Southeastern Pennsylvania v. Casey, 505 U.S. 833 (1992).

Plessy v. Ferguson, 163 U.S. 537 (1896).

Railway Express Agency v. New York, 336 U.S. 106 (1949).

Reed v. Reed, 404 U.S. 71 (1971).

Reynolds v. Sims, 377 U.S. 533 (1964).

Reynolds v. United States, 98 U.S. 145 (1878).

Roe v. Wade, 410 U.S. 113 (1973).

Romer v. Evans, 517 U.S. 620 (1996).

Rostker v. Goldberg, 453 U.S. 57 (1981).

Sherbert v. Verner, 374 U.S. 398 (1963).

Stanton v. Stanton, 421 U.S. 7 (1975).

Steffan v. Cheney, 780 F. Supp. 1 (Dist. D.C. 1991), *rev'd sub. nom., Steffan v. Aspin*, 8 F.3d 57 (D.C. Cir. 1993).

Sternberg v. Carhart, 530 U.S. 914 (2000).
Sweatt v. Painter, 339 U.S. 629 (1950).
Turner v. Safley, 482 U.S. 78 (1987).
United States v. Ballard, 322 U.S. 78 (1944).
United States v. Virginia, 518 U.S. 515 (1996).
Washington v. Glucksberg, 521 U.S. 702 (1997).
Wengler v. Druggists Mutual Insurance Co., 446 U.S. 142 (1980).
Williamson v. Lee Optical Co., 348 U.S. 483 (1955).
Zablocki v. Redhail, 434 U.S. 374 (1978).
Zelman v. Simmons-Harris, 536 U.S. 639 (2002).

INDEX